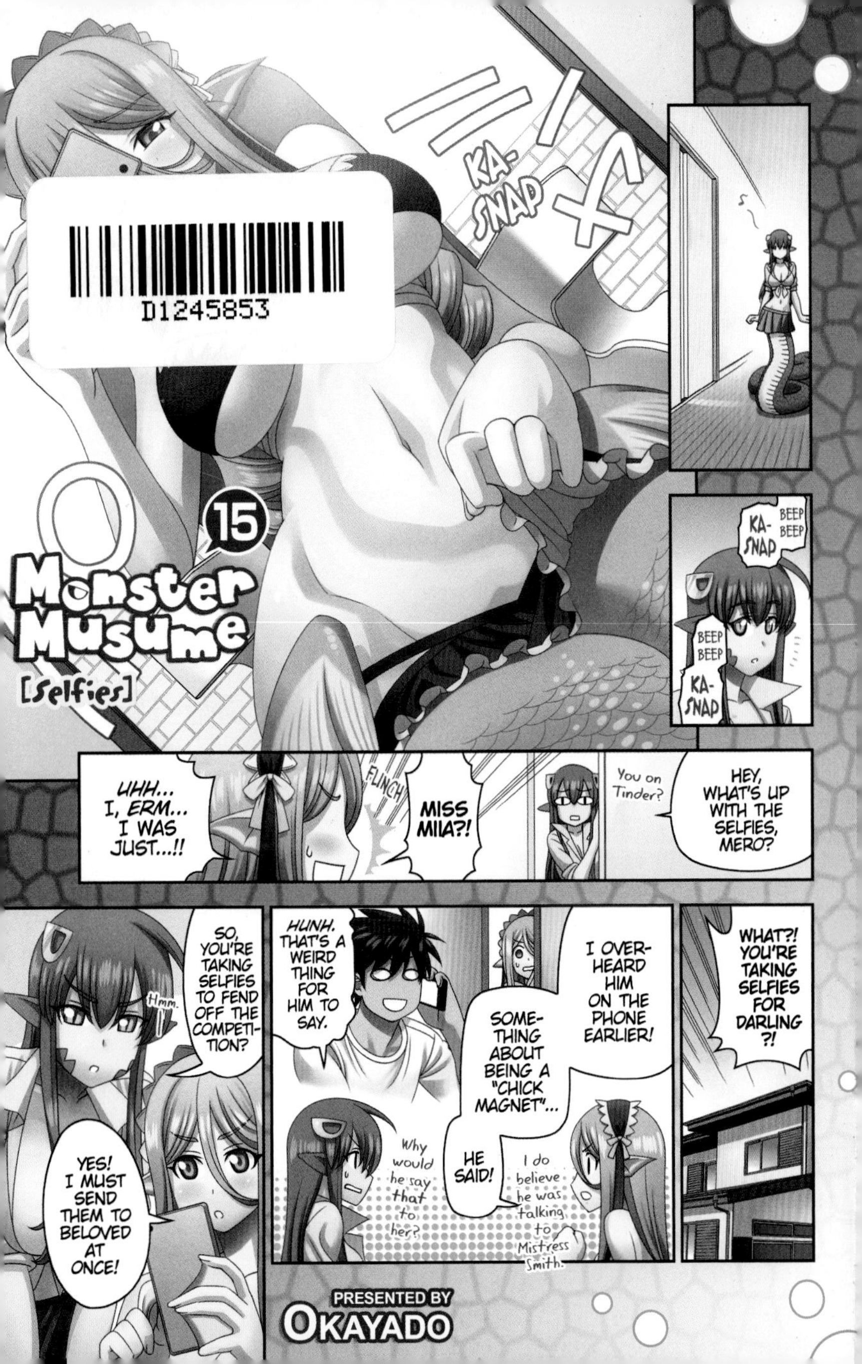
KA-SNAP
BEEP BEEP
BEEP BEEP
KA-SNAP
KA-SNAP
15
Monster Musume
[Selfies]
HEY, WHAT'S UP WITH THE SELFIES, MERO?
You on Tinder?
MISS MIIA?!
FLINCH
UHH... I, ERM... I WAS JUST...!!
WHAT?! YOU'RE TAKING SELFIES FOR DARLING ?!
I OVER-HEARD HIM ON THE PHONE EARLIER!
SOME-THING ABOUT BEING A "CHICK MAGNET"...
HE SAID!
HUNH. THAT'S A WEIRD THING FOR HIM TO SAY.
I do believe he was talking to Mistress Smith.
Why would he say that to her?
SO, YOU'RE TAKING SELFIES TO FEND OFF THE COMPETITION?
Hmm.
YES! I MUST SEND THEM TO BELOVED AT ONCE!
PRESENTED BY
OKAYADO

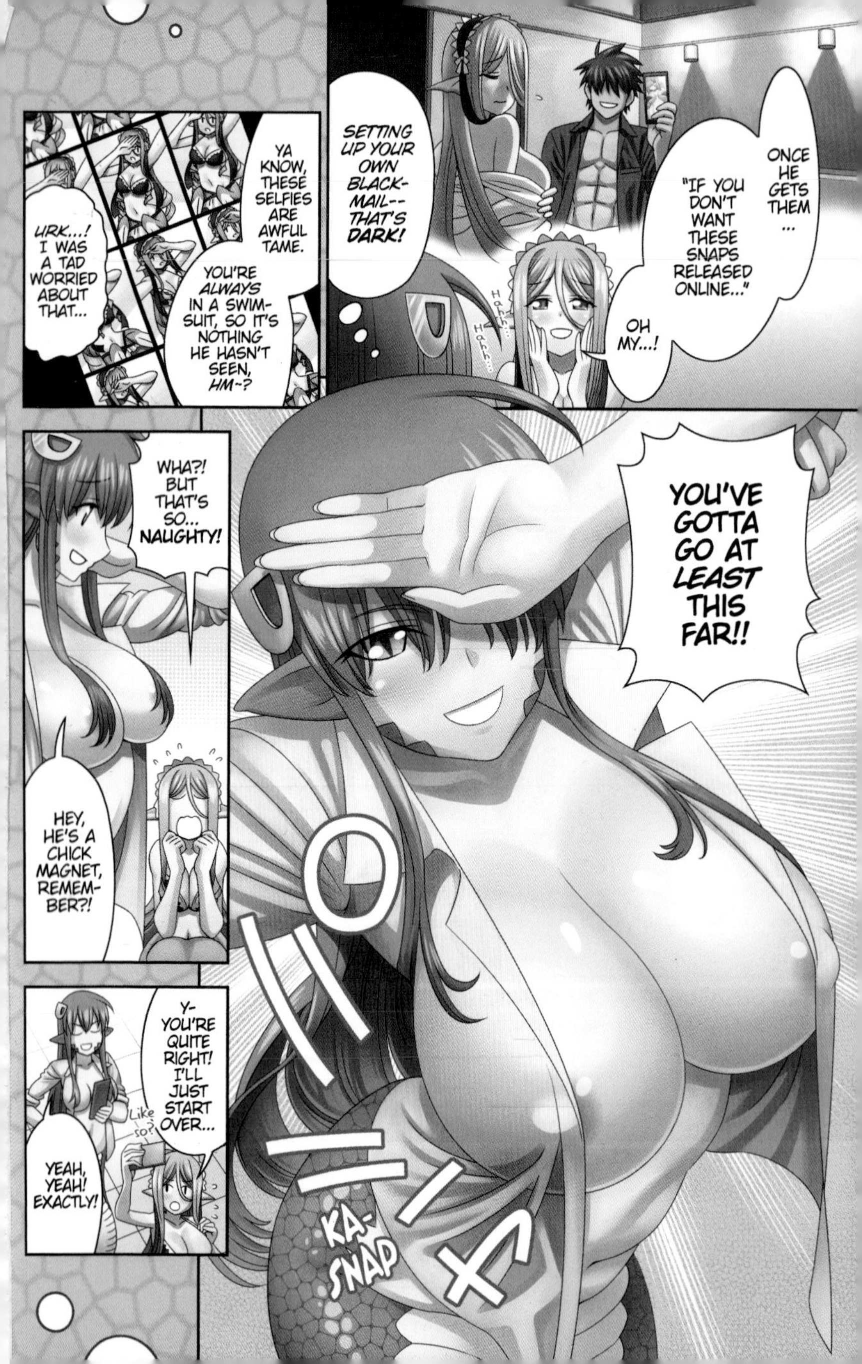
ONCE HE GETS THEM...
"IF YOU DON'T WANT THESE SNAPS RELEASED ONLINE..."
Hahh... Hahh...
OH MY...!
SETTING UP YOUR OWN BLACK-MAIL-- THAT'S DARK!
YA KNOW, THESE SELFIES ARE AWFUL TAME.
YOU'RE ALWAYS IN A SWIM-SUIT, SO IT'S NOTHING HE HASN'T SEEN, HM~?
URK...! I WAS A TAD WORRIED ABOUT THAT...
YOU'VE GOTTA GO AT LEAST THIS FAR!!
KA-SNAP
WHA?! BUT THAT'S SO... NAUGHTY!
HEY, HE'S A CHICK MAGNET, REMEMBER?!
Y-YOU'RE QUITE RIGHT! I'LL JUST START OVER...
Like so?
YEAH, YEAH! EXACTLY!

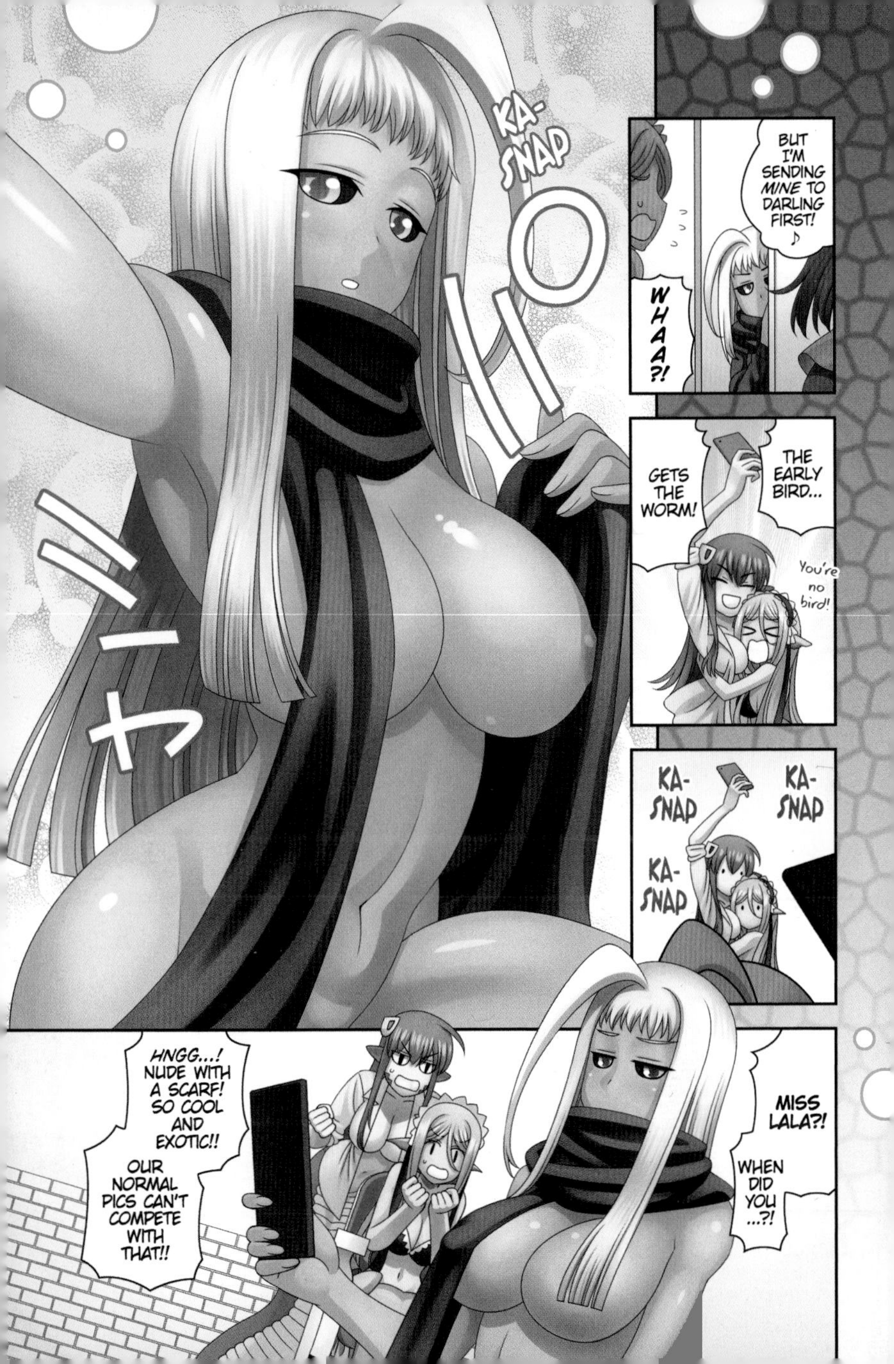
BUT I'M SENDING *MINE* TO DARLING FIRST! ♪
WHAAA?!
THE EARLY BIRD...
GETS THE WORM!
You're no bird!
KA-SNAP
KA-SNAP
KA-SNAP
KA-SNAP
MISS LALA?!
WHEN DID YOU ...?!
HNGG...! NUDE WITH A SCARF! SO COOL AND EXOTIC!!
OUR NORMAL PICS CAN'T COMPETE WITH THAT!!

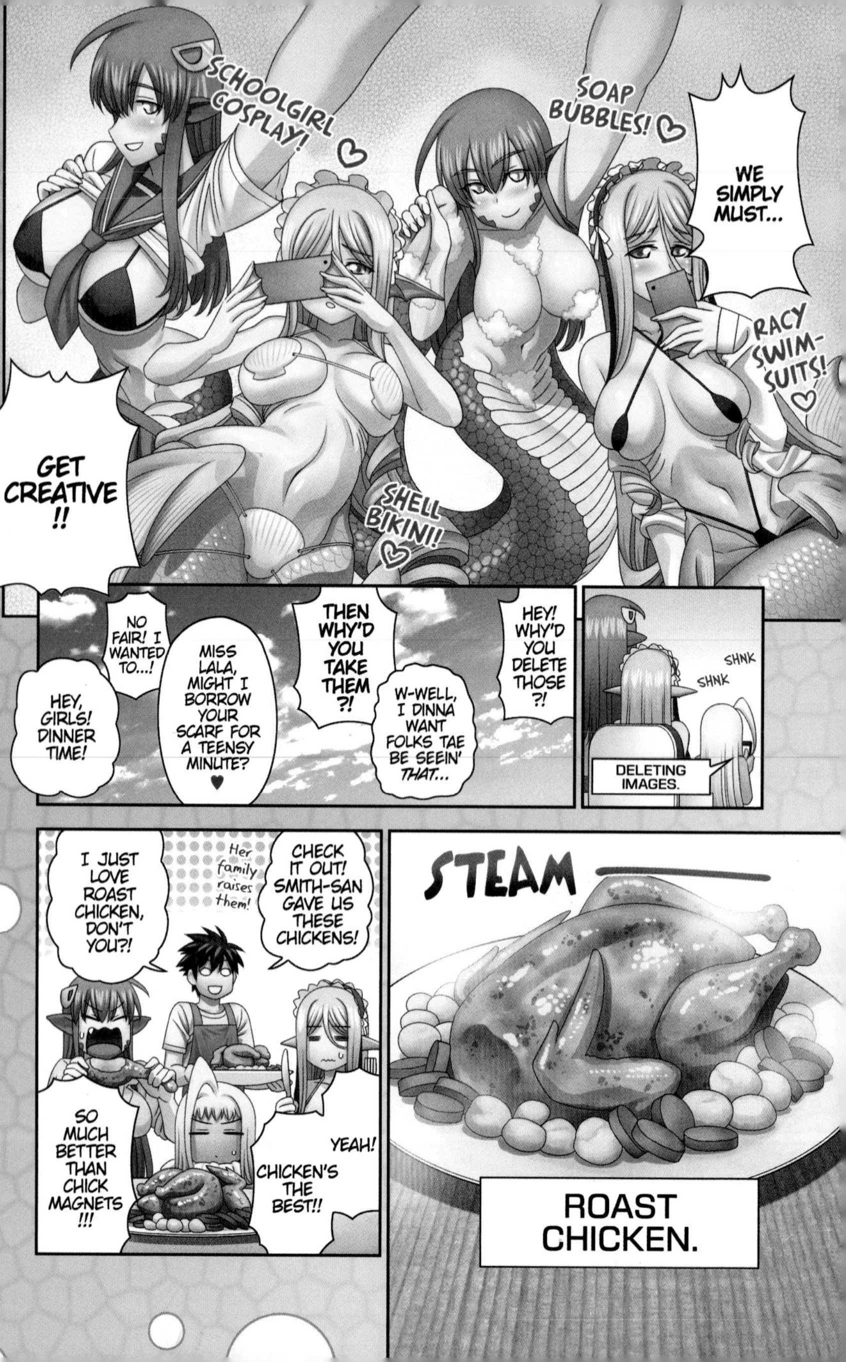
WE SIMPLY MUST...
SOAP BUBBLES! ♡
RACY SWIM-SUITS! ♡
SCHOOLGIRL COSPLAY! ♡
SHELL BIKINI! ♡
GET CREATIVE!!
SHNK
SHNK
DELETING IMAGES.
HEY! WHY'D YOU DELETE THOSE?!
W-WELL, I DINNA WANT FOLKS TAE BE SEEIN' *THAT*...
THEN WHY'D YOU TAKE THEM?!
MISS LALA, MIGHT I BORROW YOUR SCARF FOR A TEENSY MINUTE? ♥
NO FAIR! I WANTED TO...!
HEY, GIRLS! DINNER TIME!
STEAM
ROAST CHICKEN.
CHECK IT OUT! SMITH-SAN GAVE US THESE CHICKENS!
Her family raises them!
I JUST LOVE ROAST CHICKEN, DON'T YOU?!
YEAH!
CHICKEN'S THE BEST!!
SO MUCH BETTER THAN CHICK MAGNETS!!!

Chapter 60

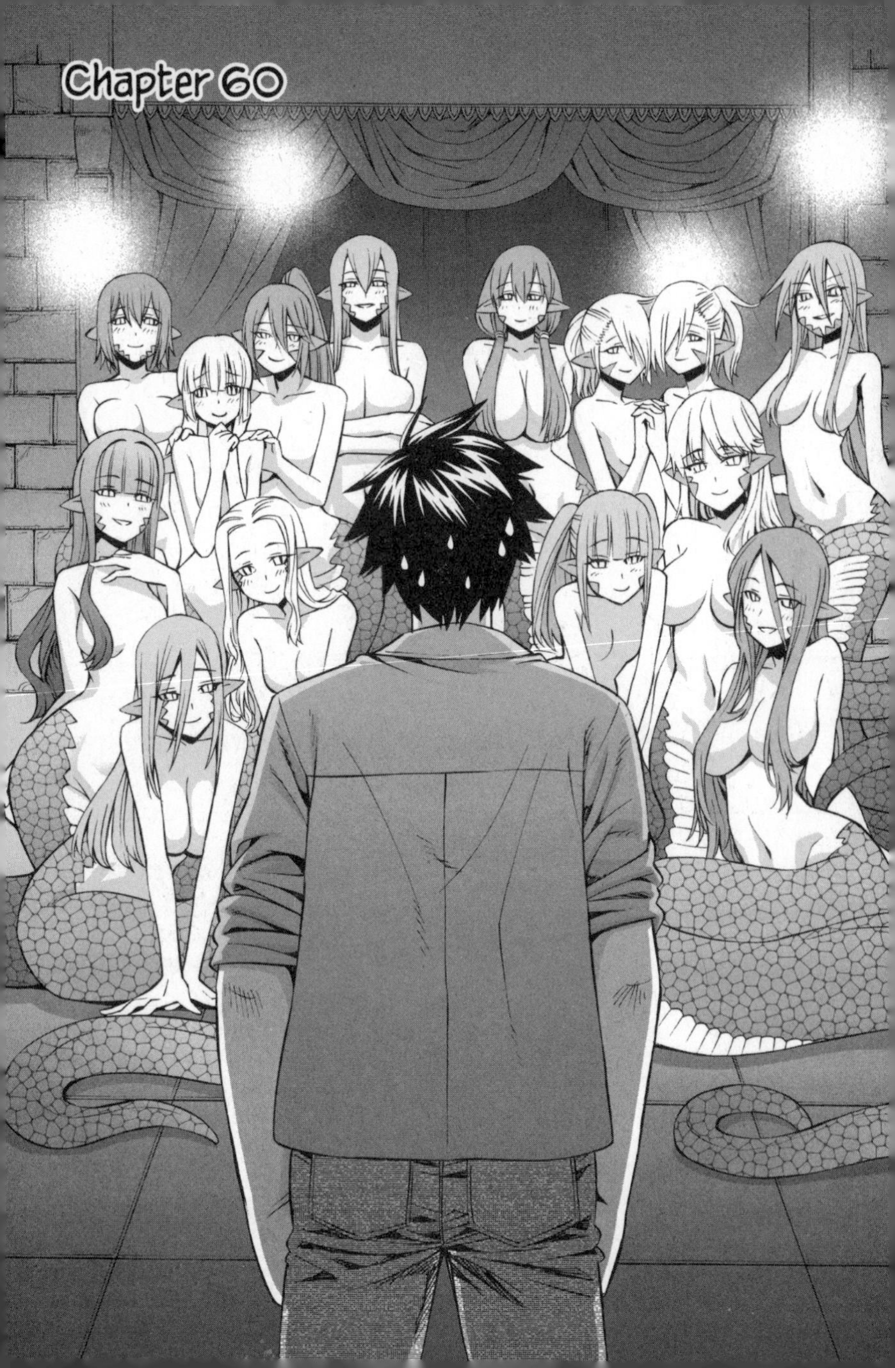

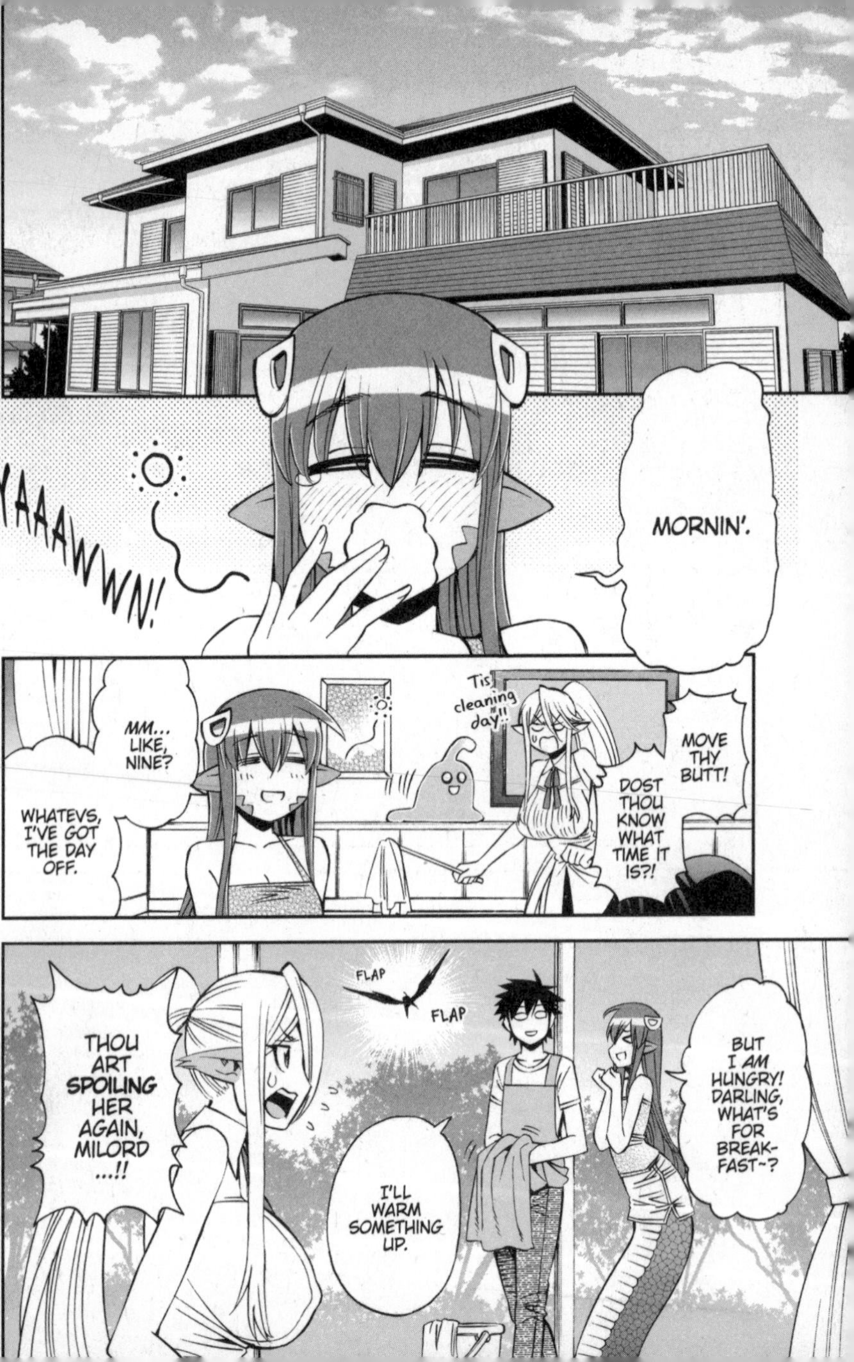
MORNIN'.
YAAAWWN!
MOVE THY BUTT!
DOST THOU KNOW WHAT TIME IT IS?!
Tis cleaning day!!
MM... LIKE, NINE?
WHATEVS, I'VE GOT THE DAY OFF.
BUT I AM HUNGRY! DARLING, WHAT'S FOR BREAK-FAST~?
I'LL WARM SOMETHING UP.
FLAP
FLAP
THOU ART SPOILING HER AGAIN, MILORD ...!!

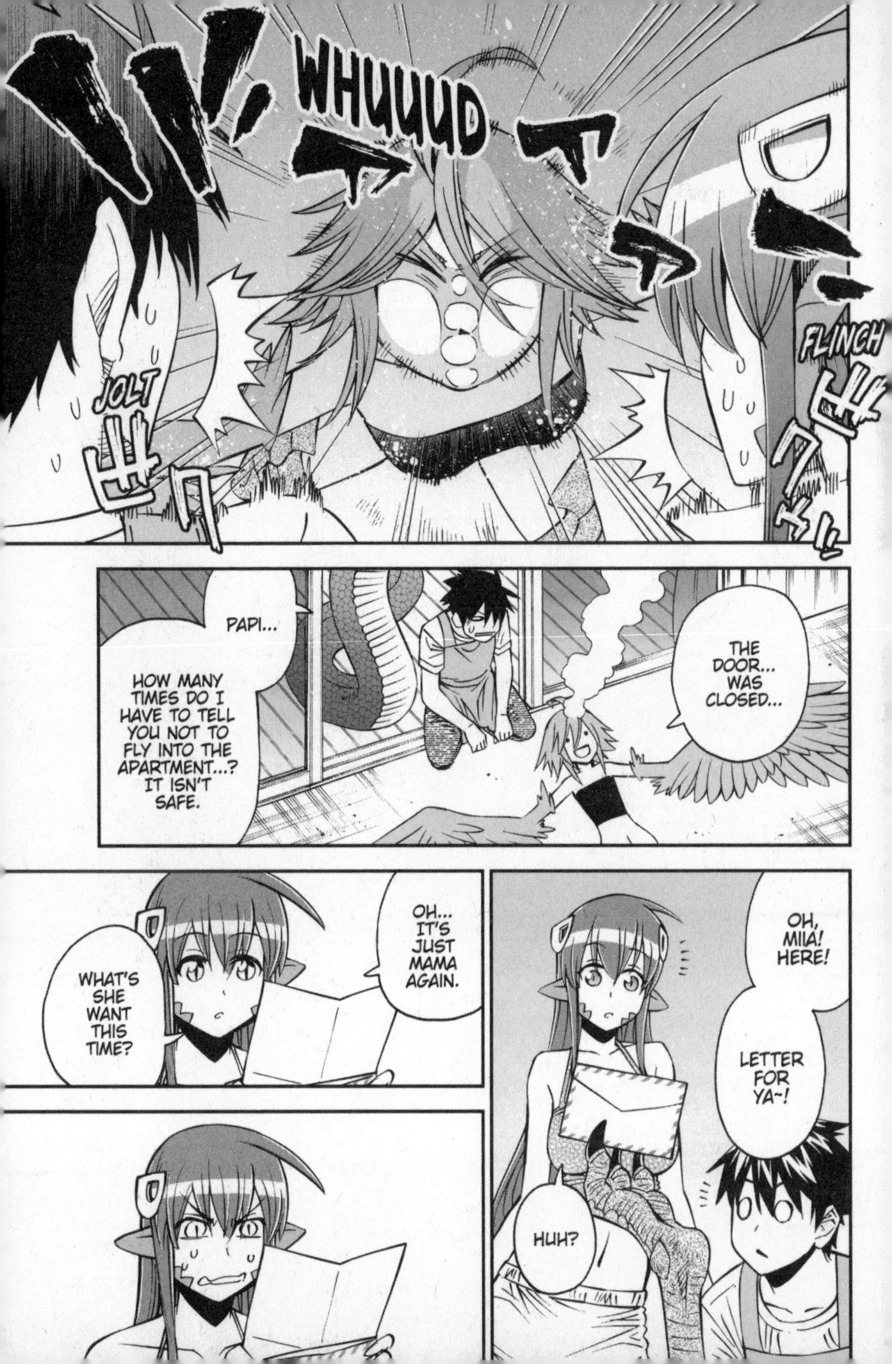
WHUUUD
FLINCH
JOLT
THE DOOR... WAS CLOSED...
PAPI...
HOW MANY TIMES DO I HAVE TO TELL YOU NOT TO FLY INTO THE APARTMENT...? IT ISN'T SAFE.
OH, MIIA! HERE!
LETTER FOR YA~!
HUH?
OH... IT'S JUST MAMA AGAIN.
WHAT'S SHE WANT THIS TIME?

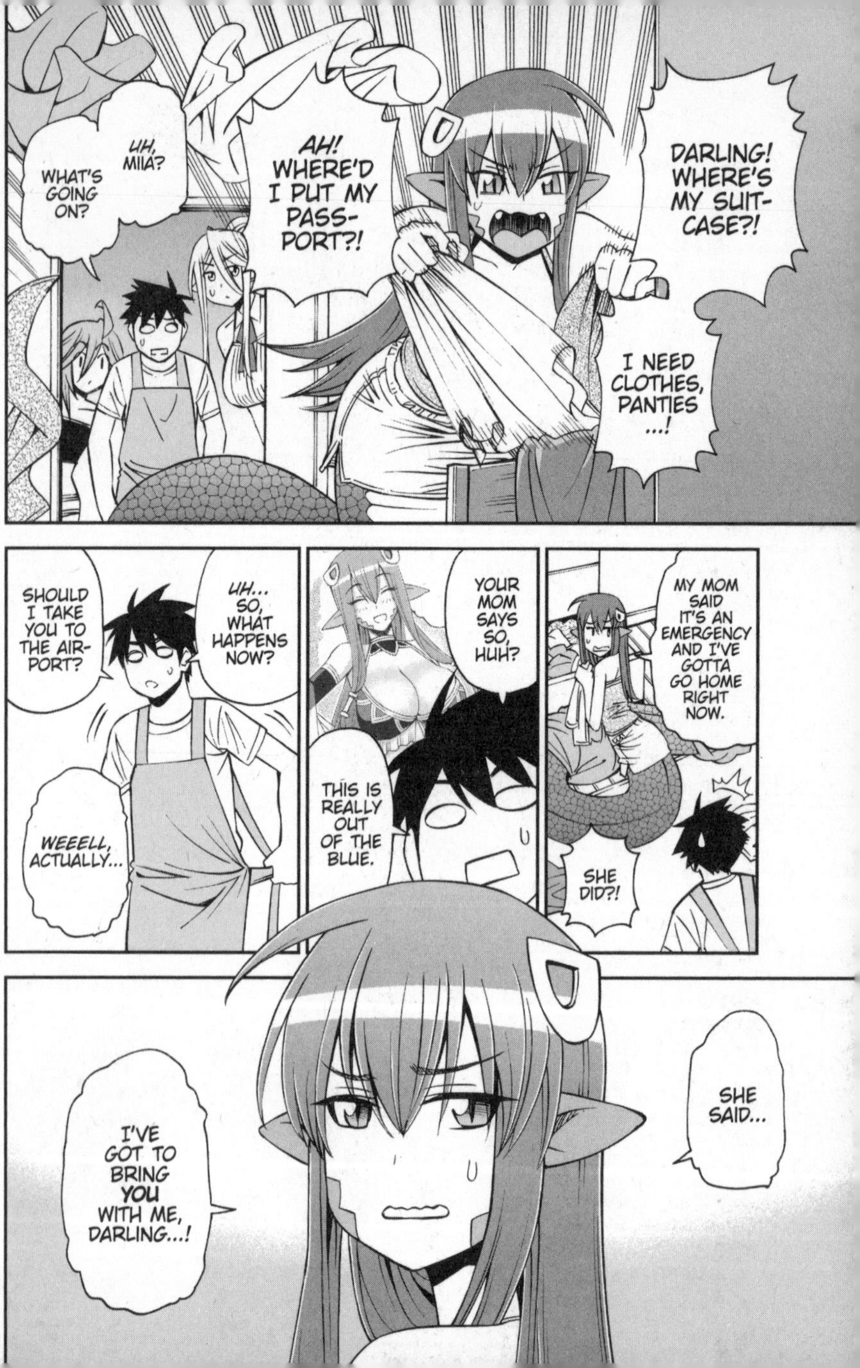
DARLING! WHERE'S MY SUIT-CASE?!
I NEED CLOTHES, PANTIES ...!
AH! WHERE'D I PUT MY PASS-PORT?!
UH, MIIA?
WHAT'S GOING ON?
MY MOM SAID IT'S AN EMERGENCY AND I'VE GOTTA GO HOME RIGHT NOW.
SHE DID?!
YOUR MOM SAYS SO, HUH?
THIS IS REALLY OUT OF THE BLUE.
UH... SO, WHAT HAPPENS NOW?
SHOULD I TAKE YOU TO THE AIR-PORT?
WEEELL, ACTUALLY...
SHE SAID...
I'VE GOT TO BRING YOU WITH ME, DARLING...!

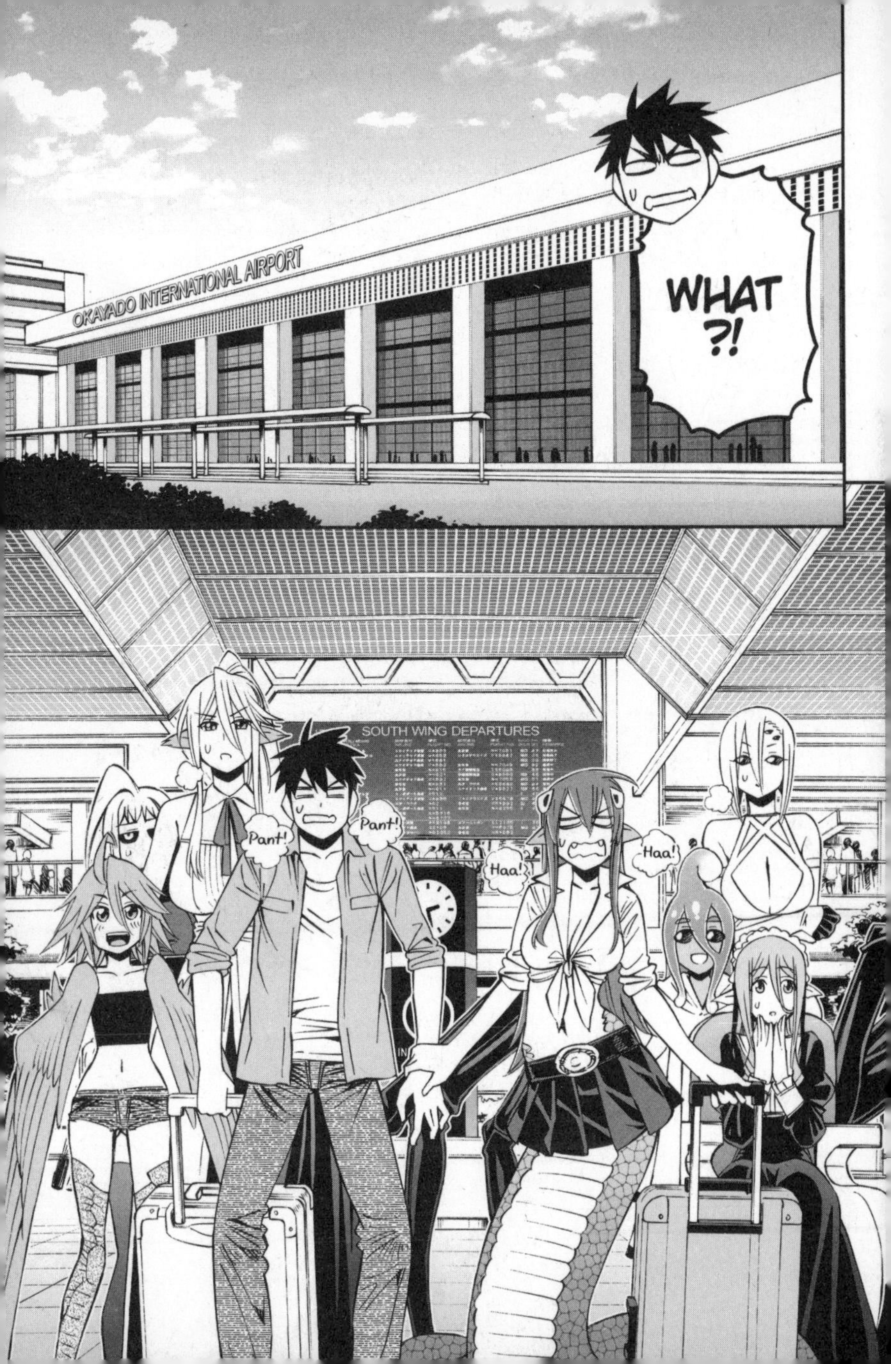
WHAT ?!
OKAYADO INTERNATIONAL AIRPORT
SOUTH WING DEPARTURES
Haa!
Haa!
Pant!
Pant!

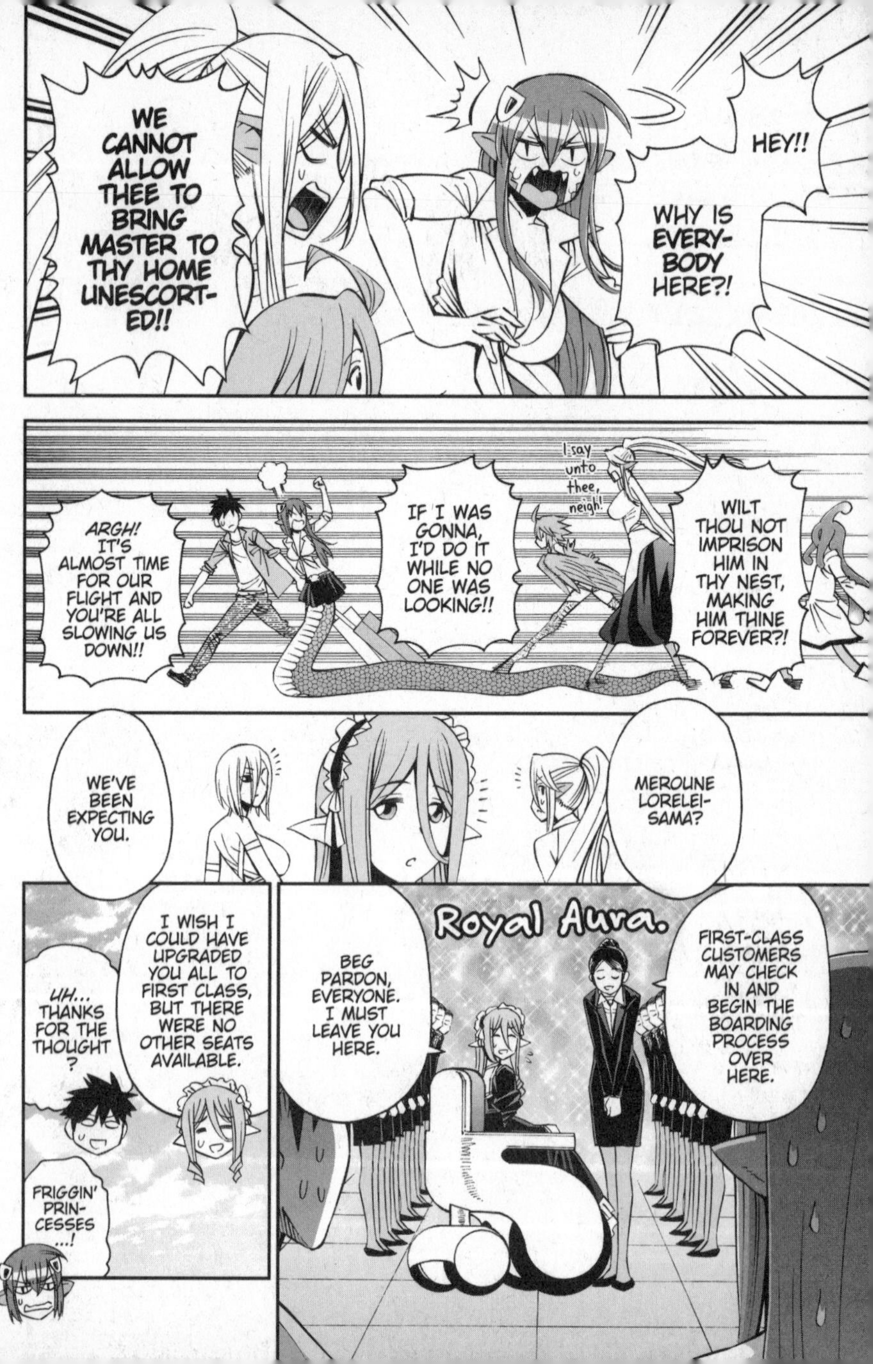
HEY!!
WHY IS EVERY-BODY HERE?!
WE CANNOT ALLOW THEE TO BRING MASTER TO THY HOME UNESCORT-ED!!
WILT THOU NOT IMPRISON HIM IN THY NEST, MAKING HIM THINE FOREVER?!
I say unto thee, neigh!
IF I WAS GONNA, I'D DO IT WHILE NO ONE WAS LOOKING!!
ARGH! IT'S ALMOST TIME FOR OUR FLIGHT AND YOU'RE ALL SLOWING US DOWN!!
MEROUNE LORELEI-SAMA?
WE'VE BEEN EXPECTING YOU.
FIRST-CLASS CUSTOMERS MAY CHECK IN AND BEGIN THE BOARDING PROCESS OVER HERE.
Royal Aura.
BEG PARDON, EVERYONE. I MUST LEAVE YOU HERE.
I WISH I COULD HAVE UPGRADED YOU ALL TO FIRST CLASS, BUT THERE WERE NO OTHER SEATS AVAILABLE.
UH... THANKS FOR THE THOUGHT?
FRIGGIN' PRIN-CESSES...!

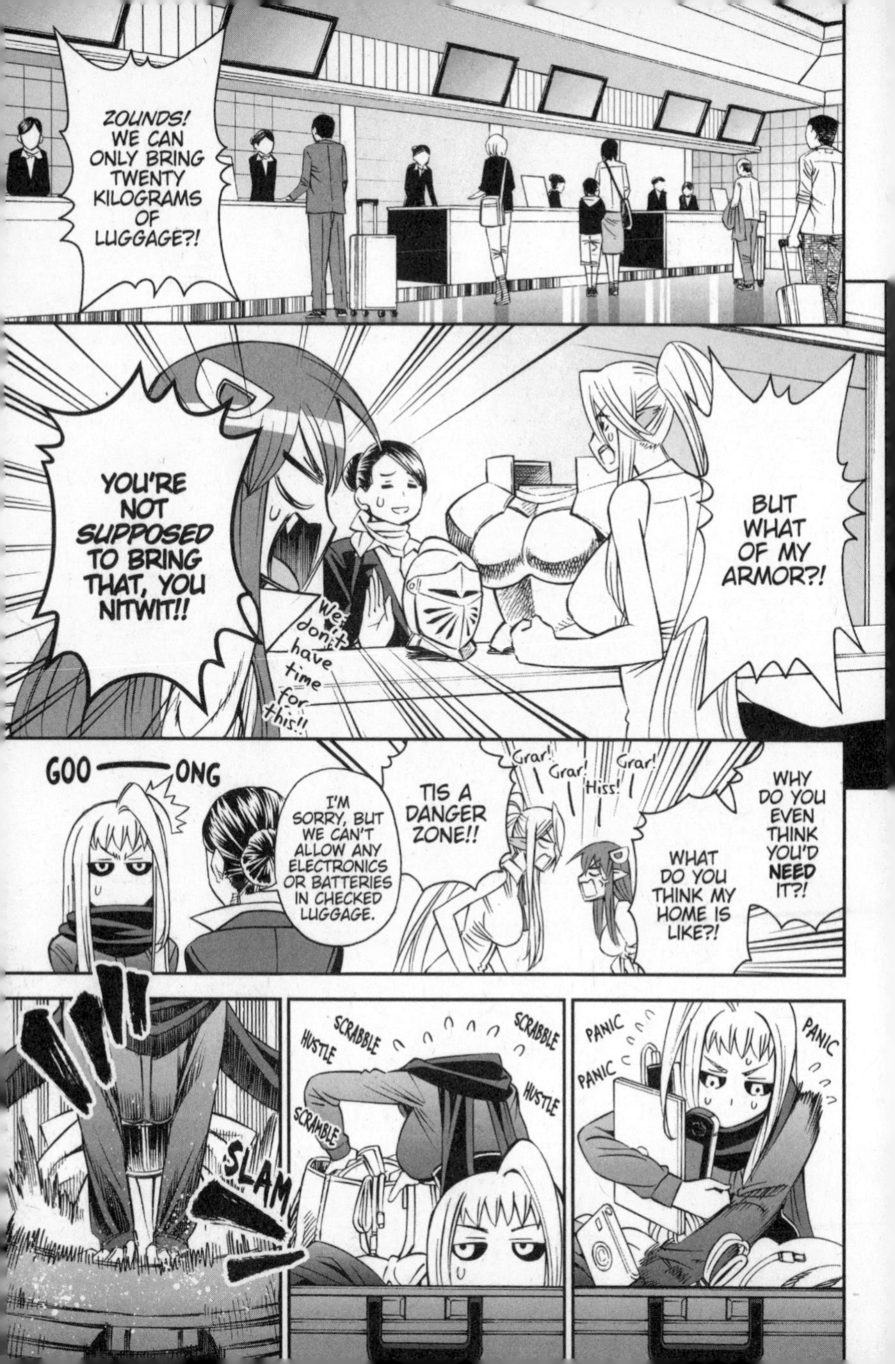
ZOUNDS! WE CAN ONLY BRING TWENTY KILOGRAMS OF LUGGAGE?!
BUT WHAT OF MY ARMOR?!
YOU'RE NOT SUPPOSED TO BRING THAT, YOU NITWIT!!
We don't have time for this!!
WHY DO YOU EVEN THINK YOU'D NEED IT?!
WHAT DO YOU THINK MY HOME IS LIKE?!
Grar! Grar! Hiss! Grar!
TIS A DANGER ZONE!!
I'M SORRY, BUT WE CAN'T ALLOW ANY ELECTRONICS OR BATTERIES IN CHECKED LUGGAGE.
GOO——ONG
PANIC
PANIC
PANIC
SCRABBLE
HUSTLE
SCRABBLE
HUSTLE
SCRABBLE
SLAM

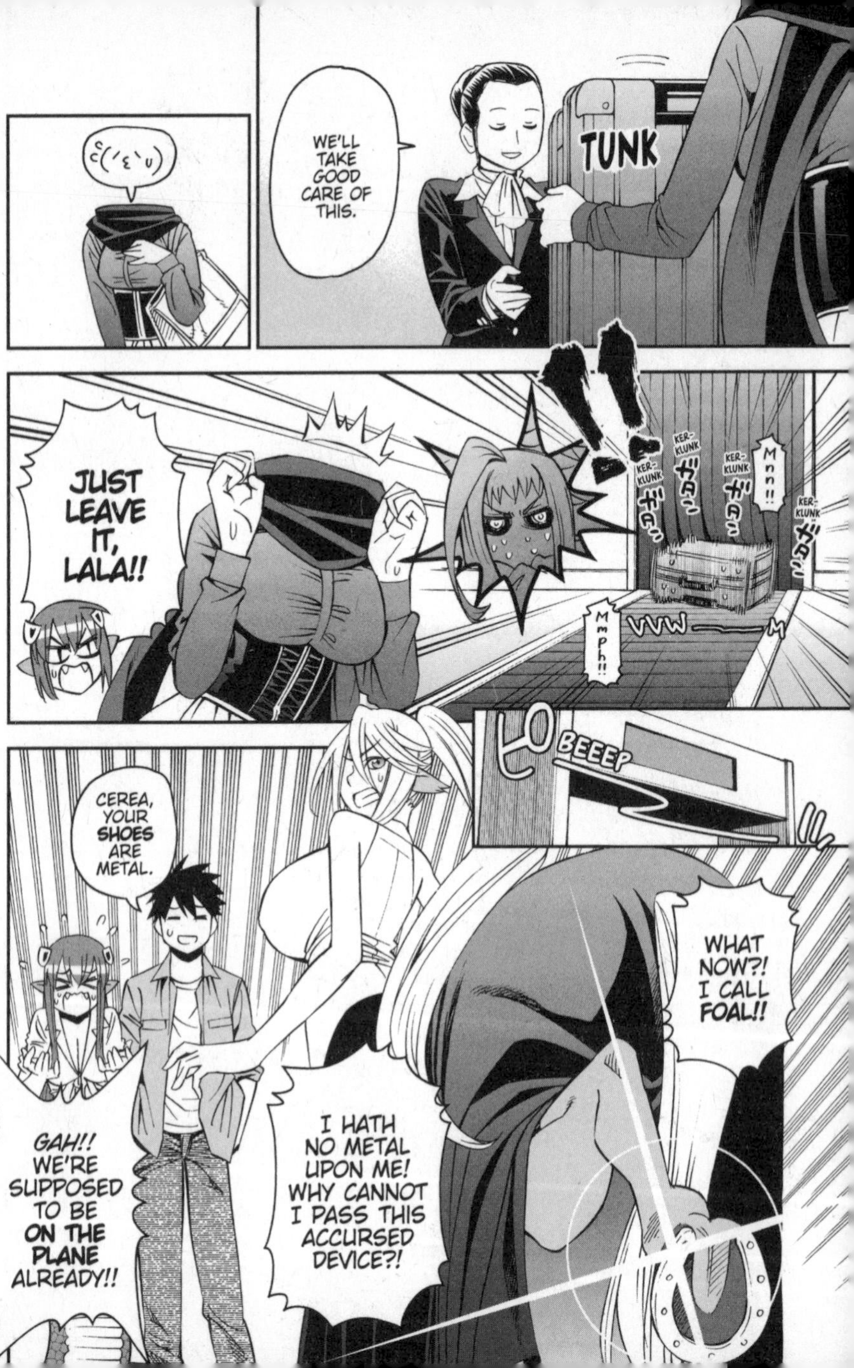

TUNK
WE'LL TAKE GOOD CARE OF THIS.
Mnn!!
KER-KLUNK
KER-KLUNK
KER-KLUNK
KER-KLUNK
VVW——M
Mmph!!
JUST LEAVE IT, LALA!!
BEEEP
WHAT NOW?! I CALL FOAL!!
I HATH NO METAL UPON ME! WHY CANNOT I PASS THIS ACCURSED DEVICE?!
CEREA, YOUR SHOES ARE METAL.
GAH!! WE'RE SUPPOSED TO BE ON THE PLANE ALREADY!!

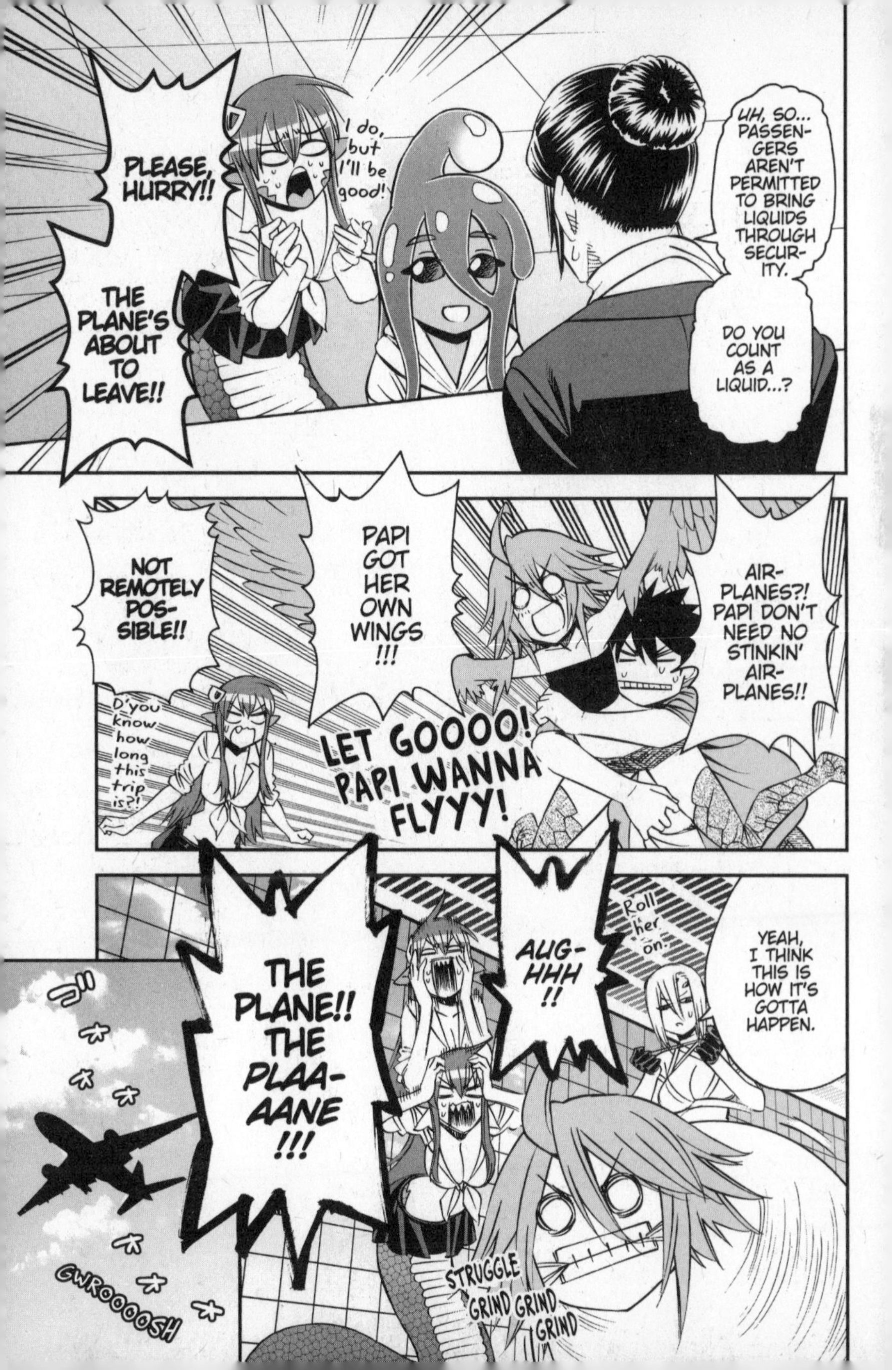
UH, SO... PASSENGERS AREN'T PERMITTED TO BRING LIQUIDS THROUGH SECURITY.
DO YOU COUNT AS A LIQUID...?
I do, but I'll be good!
PLEASE, HURRY!!
THE PLANE'S ABOUT TO LEAVE!!
AIRPLANES?! PAPI DON'T NEED NO STINKIN' AIRPLANES!!
PAPI GOT HER OWN WINGS!!!
NOT REMOTELY POSSIBLE!!
D'you know how long this trip is?!
LET GOOOO! PAPI WANNA FLYYY!
YEAH, I THINK THIS IS HOW IT'S GOTTA HAPPEN.
Roll her on.
AUGHHH!!
THE PLANE!! THE PLAAANE!!!
STRUGGLE
GRIND GRIND GRIND
ゴォォォォォ
GWROOOOOSH

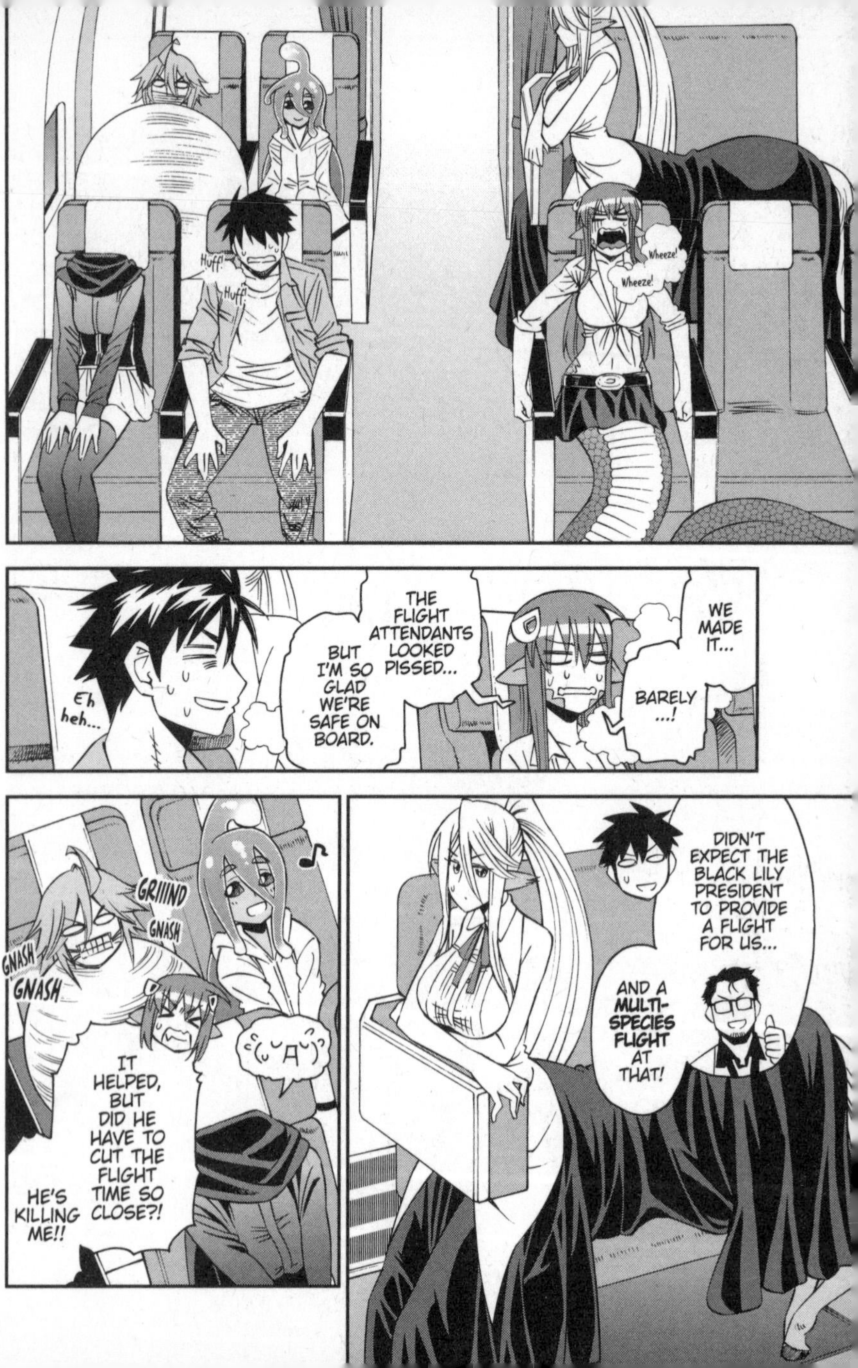
Wheeze!
Wheeze!
Huff!
Huff!
WE MADE IT... BARELY ...!
THE FLIGHT ATTENDANTS LOOKED PISSED... BUT I'M SO GLAD WE'RE SAFE ON BOARD.
Eh heh...
DIDN'T EXPECT THE BLACK LILY PRESIDENT TO PROVIDE A FLIGHT FOR US...
AND A MULTI-SPECIES FLIGHT AT THAT!
GRIIIND
GNASH
GNASH
GNASH
IT HELPED, BUT DID HE HAVE TO CUT THE FLIGHT TIME SO CLOSE?!
HE'S KILLING ME!!

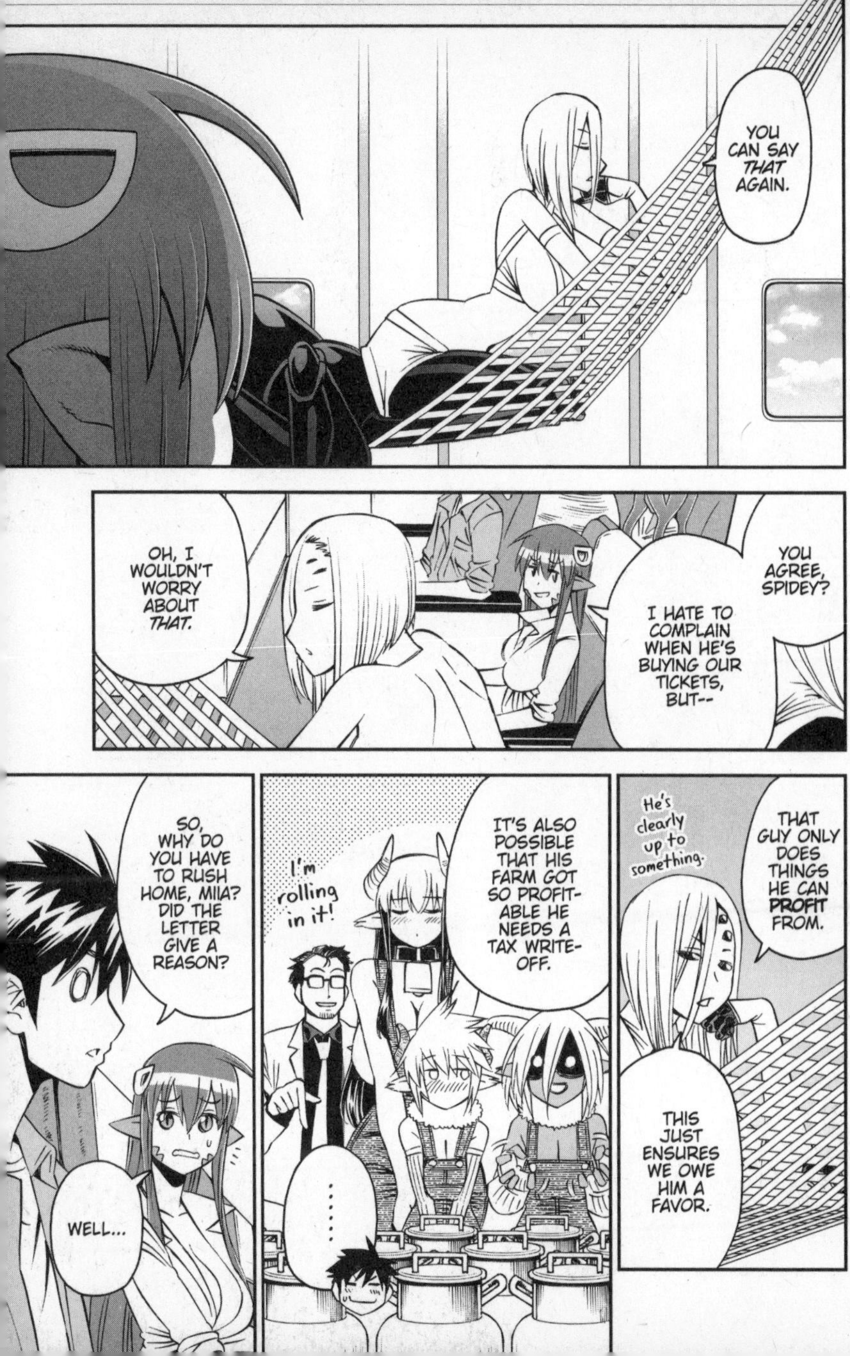
YOU CAN SAY *THAT* AGAIN.
YOU AGREE, SPIDEY?
I HATE TO COMPLAIN WHEN HE'S BUYING OUR TICKETS, BUT--
OH, I WOULDN'T WORRY ABOUT *THAT*.
THAT GUY ONLY DOES THINGS HE CAN **PROFIT** FROM.
He's clearly up to something.
THIS JUST ENSURES WE OWE HIM A FAVOR.
IT'S ALSO POSSIBLE THAT HIS FARM GOT SO PROFIT-ABLE HE NEEDS A TAX WRITE-OFF.
I'm rolling in it!
......
SO, WHY DO YOU HAVE TO RUSH HOME, MIIA? DID THE LETTER GIVE A REASON?
WELL...

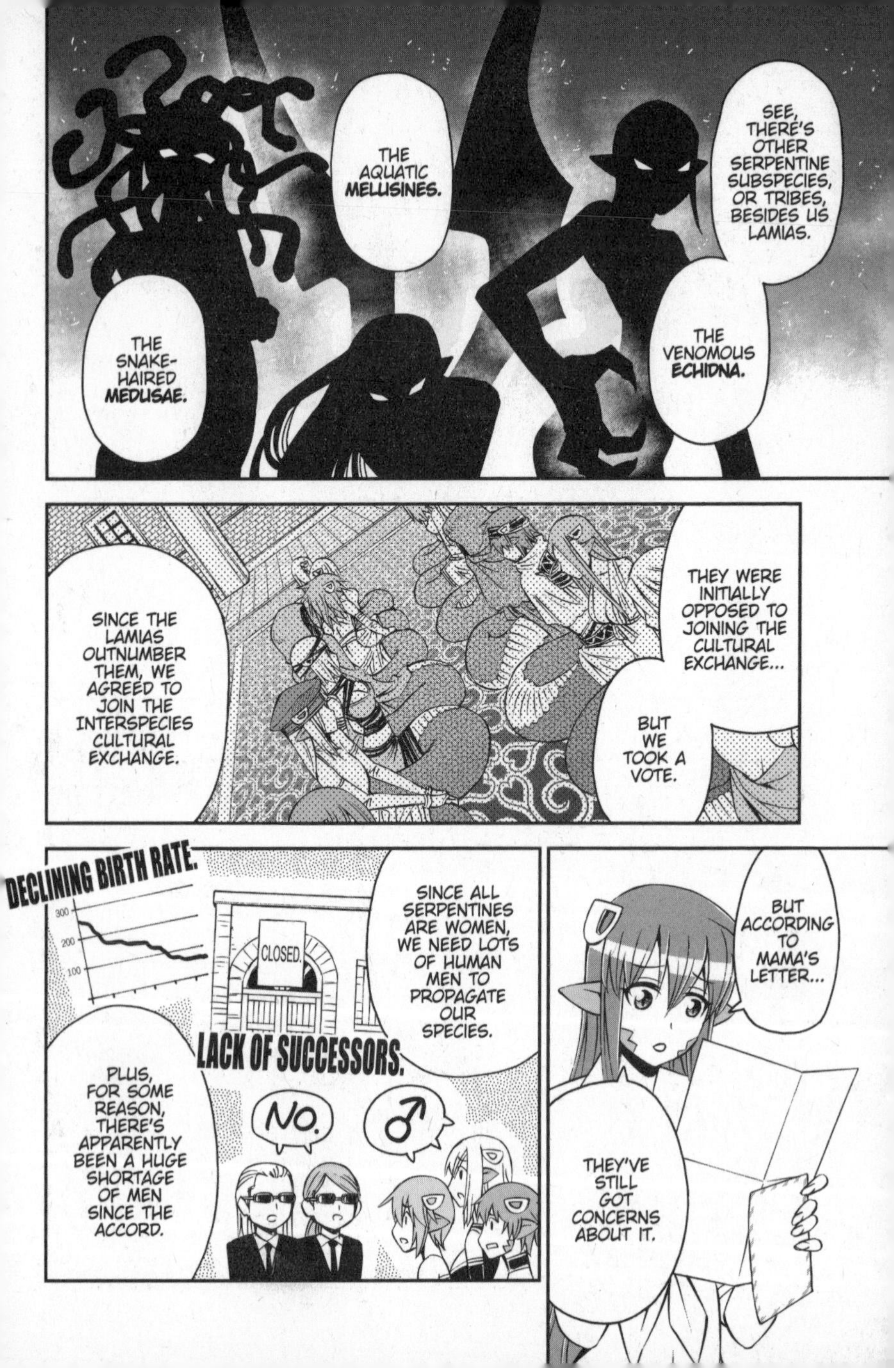

SEE, THERE'S OTHER SERPENTINE SUBSPECIES, OR TRIBES, BESIDES US LAMIAS.
THE AQUATIC MELUSINES.
THE VENOMOUS ECHIDNA.
THE SNAKE-HAIRED MEDUSAE.
THEY WERE INITIALLY OPPOSED TO JOINING THE CULTURAL EXCHANGE...
BUT WE TOOK A VOTE.
SINCE THE LAMIAS OUTNUMBER THEM, WE AGREED TO JOIN THE INTERSPECIES CULTURAL EXCHANGE.
BUT ACCORDING TO MAMA'S LETTER...
THEY'VE STILL GOT CONCERNS ABOUT IT.
SINCE ALL SERPENTINES ARE WOMEN, WE NEED LOTS OF HUMAN MEN TO PROPAGATE OUR SPECIES.
DECLINING BIRTH RATE.
300
200
100
CLOSED.
LACK OF SUCCESSORS.
PLUS, FOR SOME REASON, THERE'S APPARENTLY BEEN A HUGE SHORTAGE OF MEN SINCE THE ACCORD.
♂
NO.

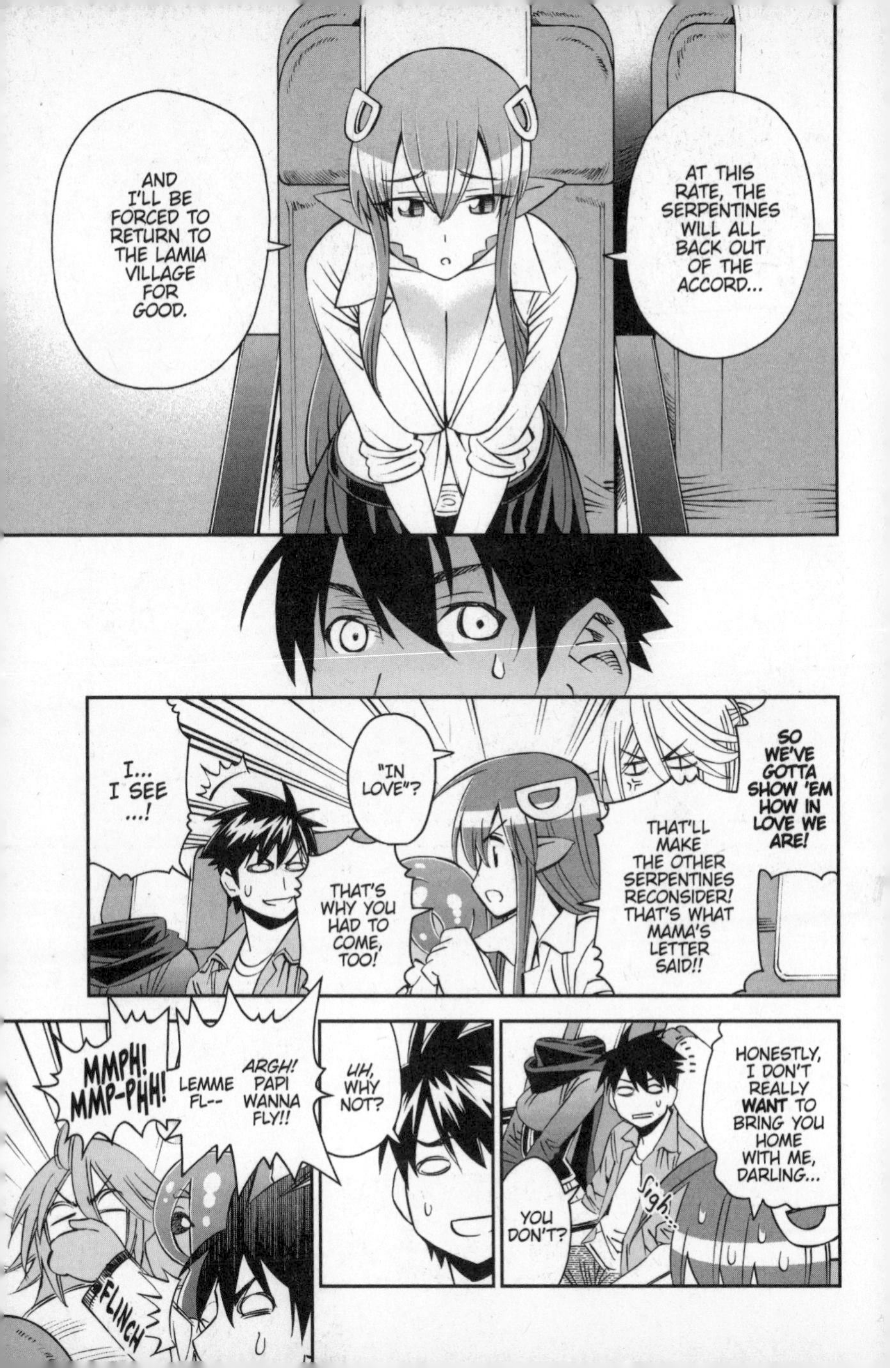
AT THIS RATE, THE SERPENTINES WILL ALL BACK OUT OF THE ACCORD...
AND I'LL BE FORCED TO RETURN TO THE LAMIA VILLAGE FOR GOOD.
SO WE'VE GOTTA SHOW 'EM HOW IN LOVE WE ARE!
THAT'LL MAKE THE OTHER SERPENTINES RECONSIDER! THAT'S WHAT MAMA'S LETTER SAID!!
"IN LOVE"?
THAT'S WHY YOU HAD TO COME, TOO!
I... I SEE ...!
HONESTLY, I DON'T REALLY WANT TO BRING YOU HOME WITH ME, DARLING...
Sigh...
YOU DON'T?
UH, WHY NOT?
ARGH! PAPI WANNA FLY!!
LEMME FL--
MMPH! MMP-PHH!
FLINCH

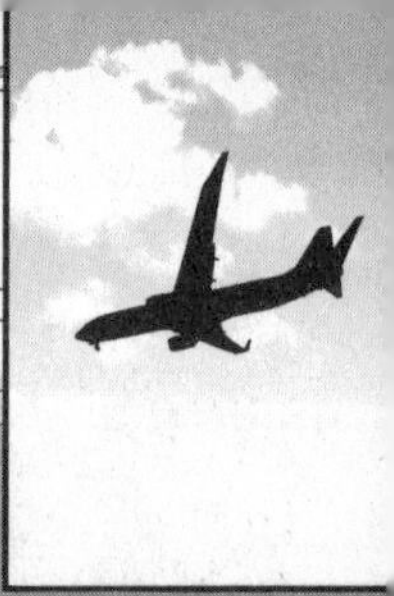
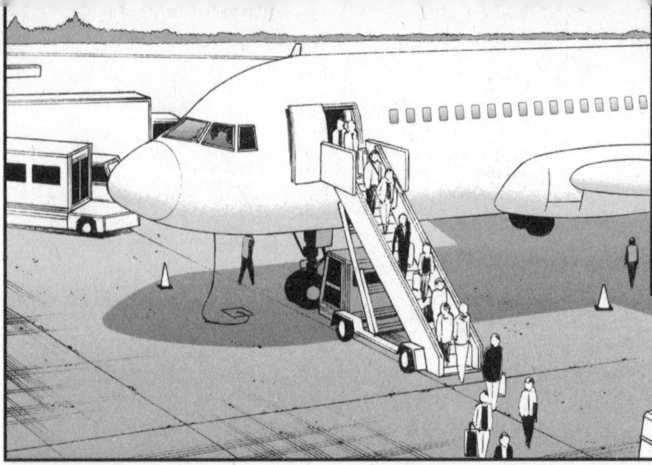
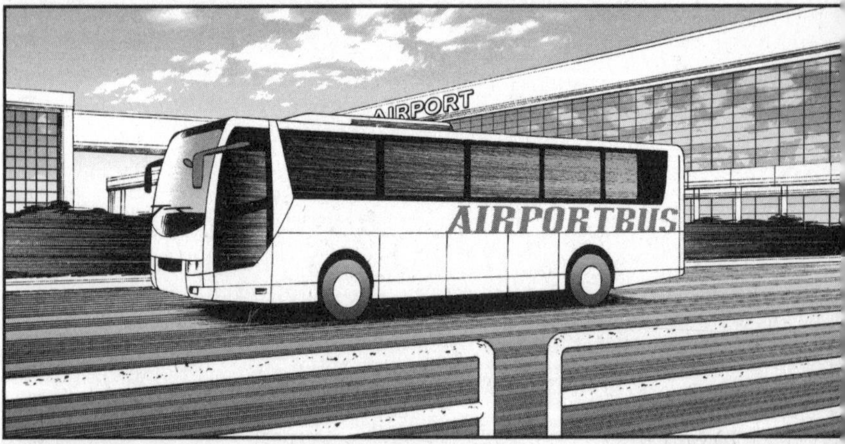
AIRPORT
AIRPORTBUS
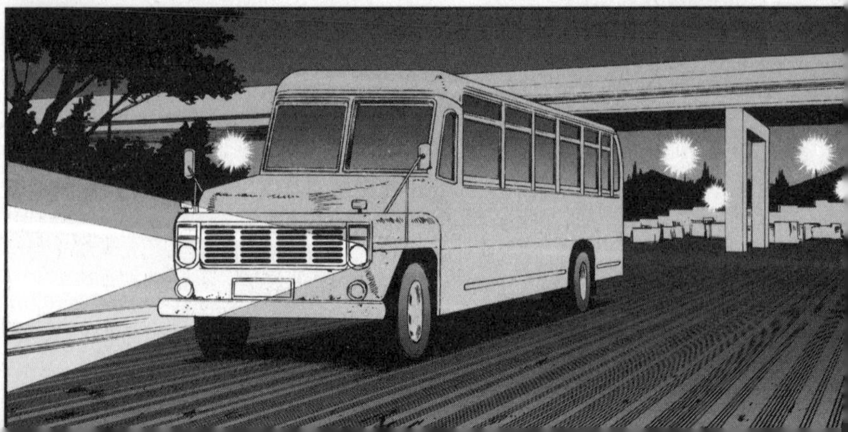

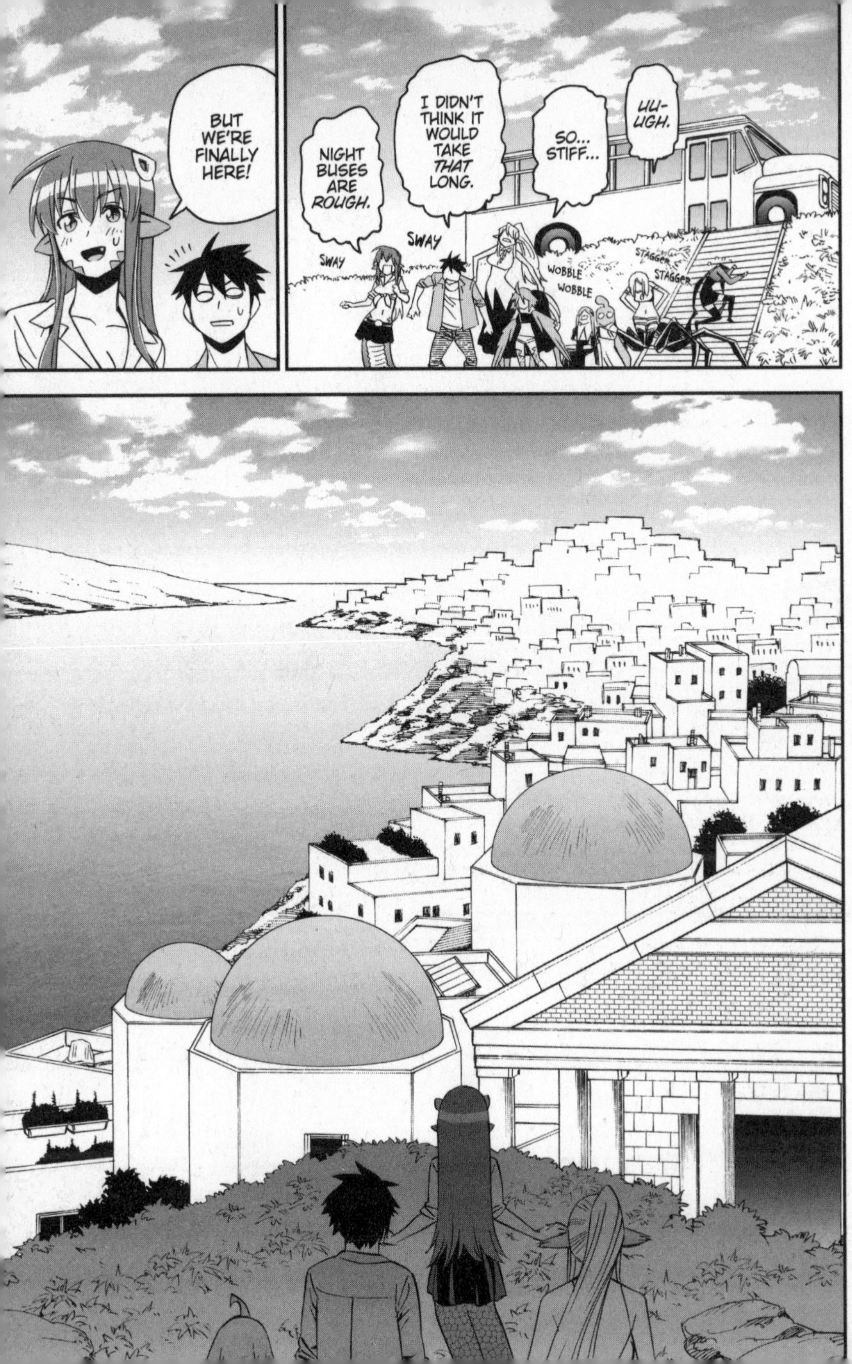
UU-UGH.
SO... STIFF...
I DIDN'T THINK IT WOULD TAKE *THAT* LONG.
NIGHT BUSES ARE *ROUGH.*
STAGGER
STAGGER
WOBBLE
WOBBLE
SWAY
SWAY
BUT WE'RE FINALLY HERE!

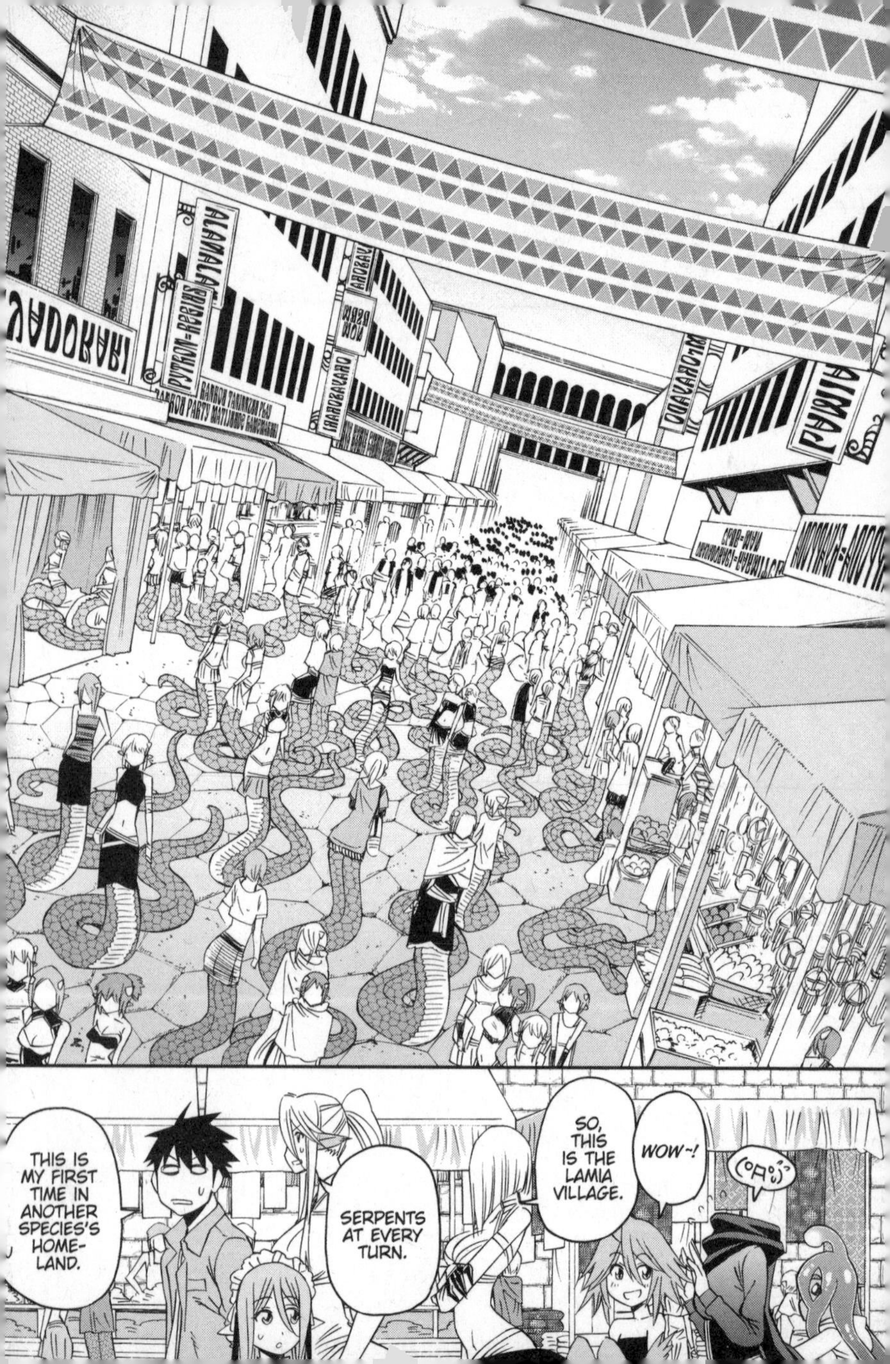
WOW~!
SO, THIS IS THE LAMIA VILLAGE.
SERPENTS AT EVERY TURN.
THIS IS MY FIRST TIME IN ANOTHER SPECIES'S HOME-LAND.

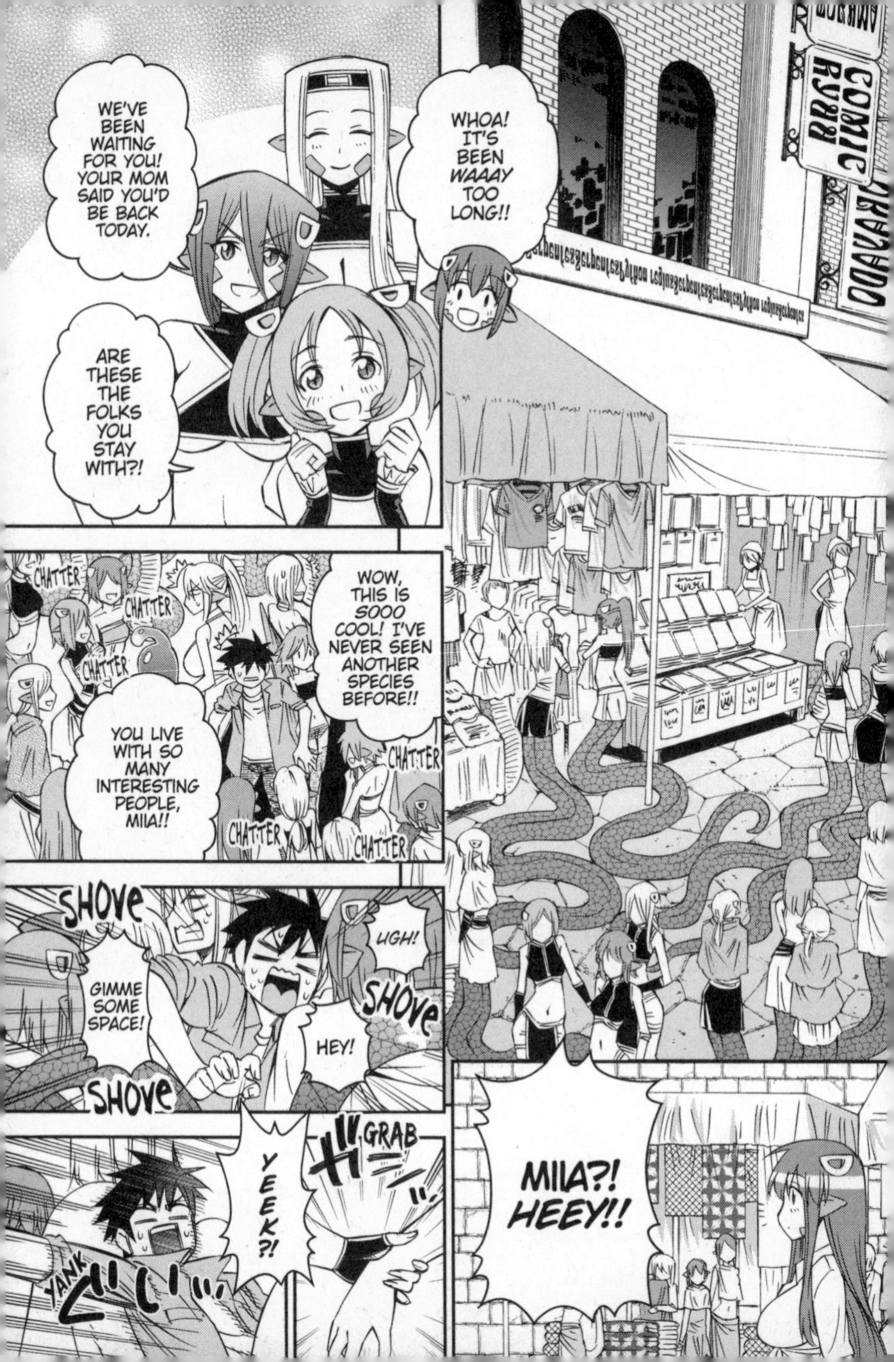

WHOA! IT'S BEEN *WAAAY* TOO LONG!!
WE'VE BEEN WAITING FOR YOU! YOUR MOM SAID YOU'D BE BACK TODAY.
ARE THESE THE FOLKS YOU STAY WITH?!
WOW, THIS IS *SOOO* COOL! I'VE NEVER SEEN ANOTHER SPECIES BEFORE!!
CHATTER
CHATTER
CHATTER
CHATTER
YOU LIVE WITH SO MANY INTERESTING PEOPLE, MIIA!!
CHATTER
CHATTER
UGH!
SHOVE
SHOVE
GIMME SOME SPACE!
HEY!
SHOVE
MIIA?! HEEY!!
GRAB
YEEK?!
YANK

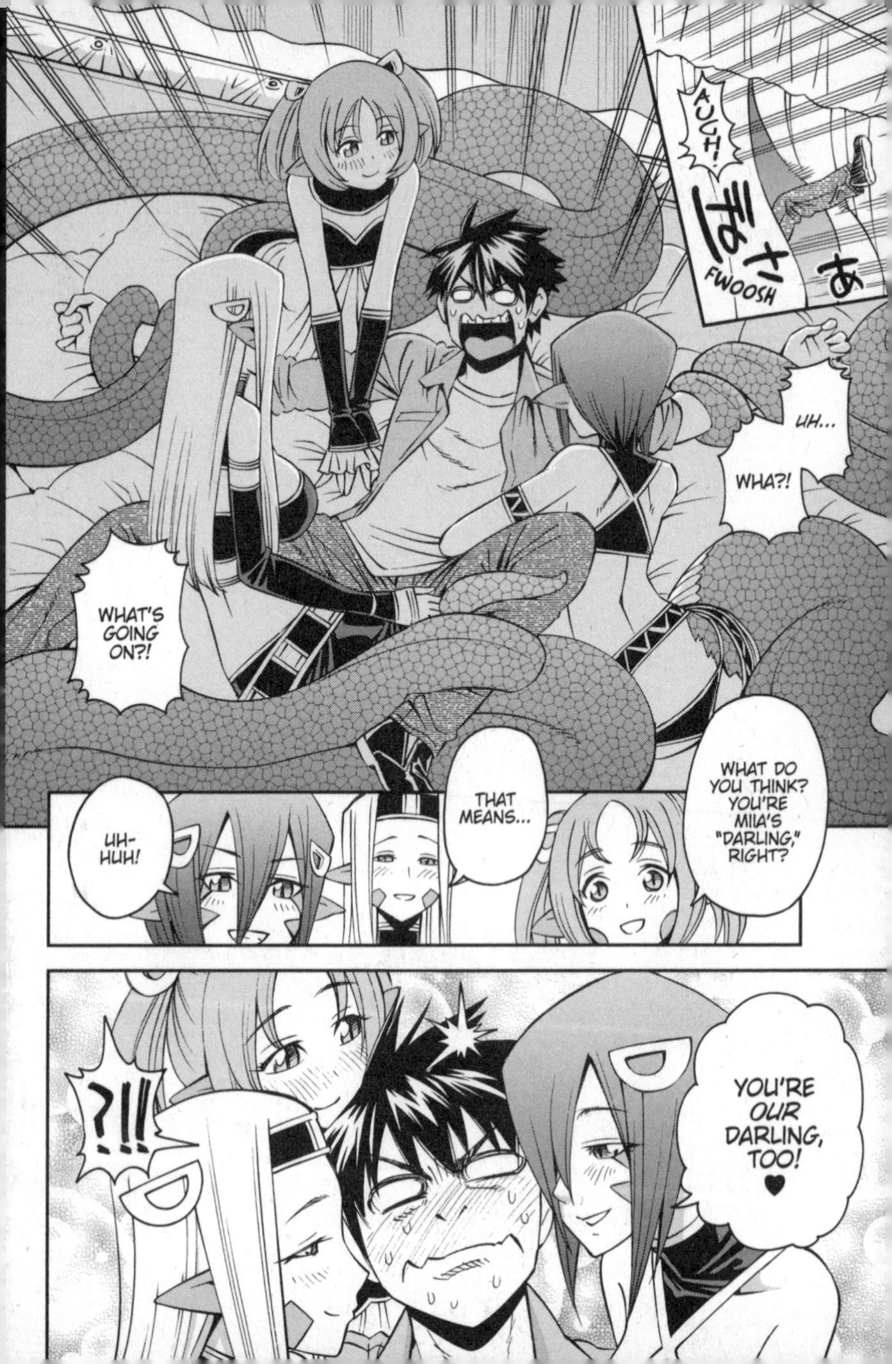

AUGH!
FWOOSH
UH...
WHA?!
WHAT'S GOING ON?!
WHAT DO YOU THINK? YOU'RE MIIA'S "DARLING," RIGHT?
THAT MEANS...
UH-HUH!
YOU'RE OUR DARLING, TOO! ♥
?!!

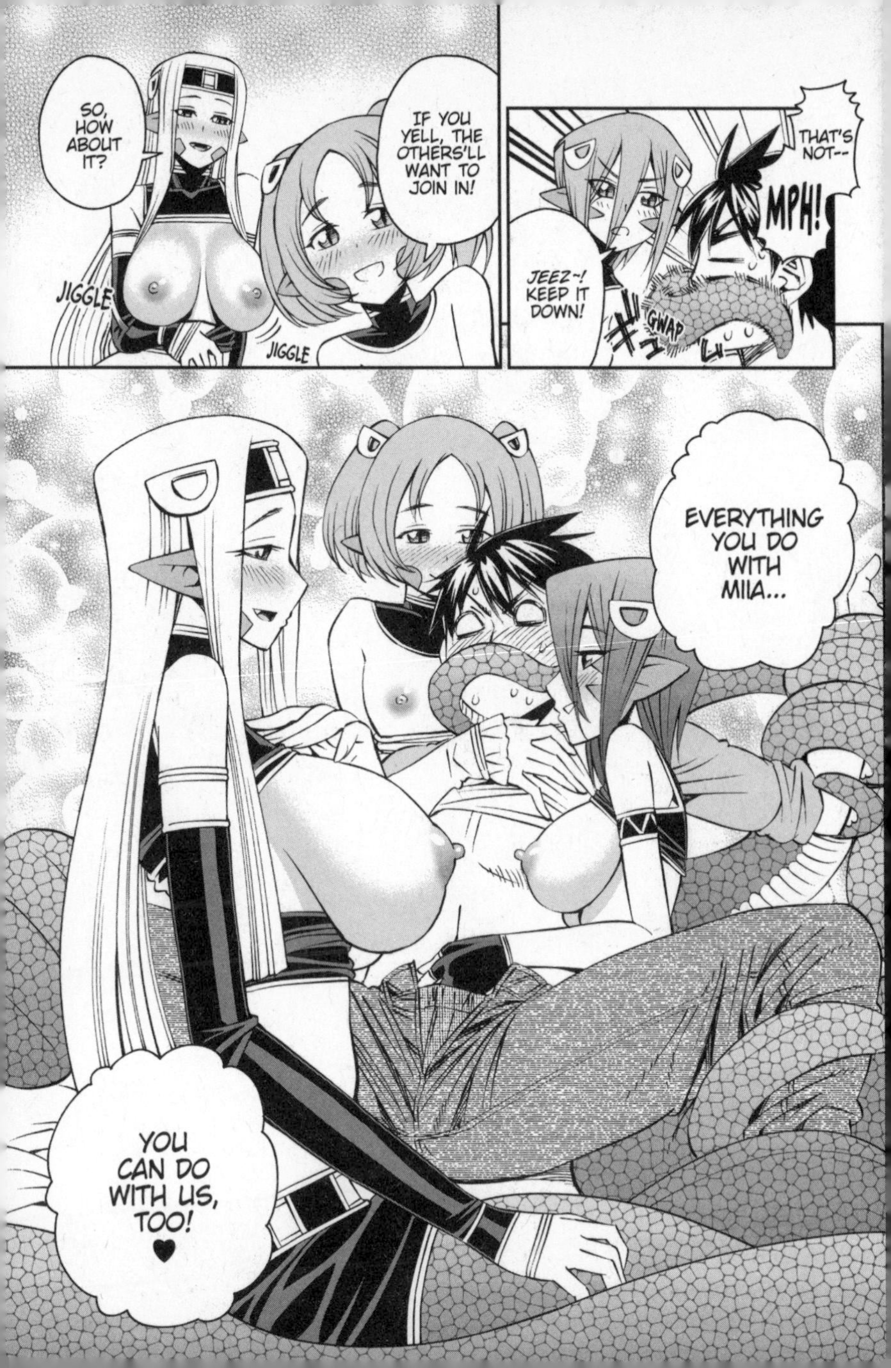
THAT'S NOT--
MPH!
JEEZ~! KEEP IT DOWN!
GWAP
IF YOU YELL, THE OTHERS'LL WANT TO JOIN IN!
SO, HOW ABOUT IT?
JIGGLE
JIGGLE
EVERYTHING YOU DO WITH MIIA...
YOU CAN DO WITH US, TOO! ♥

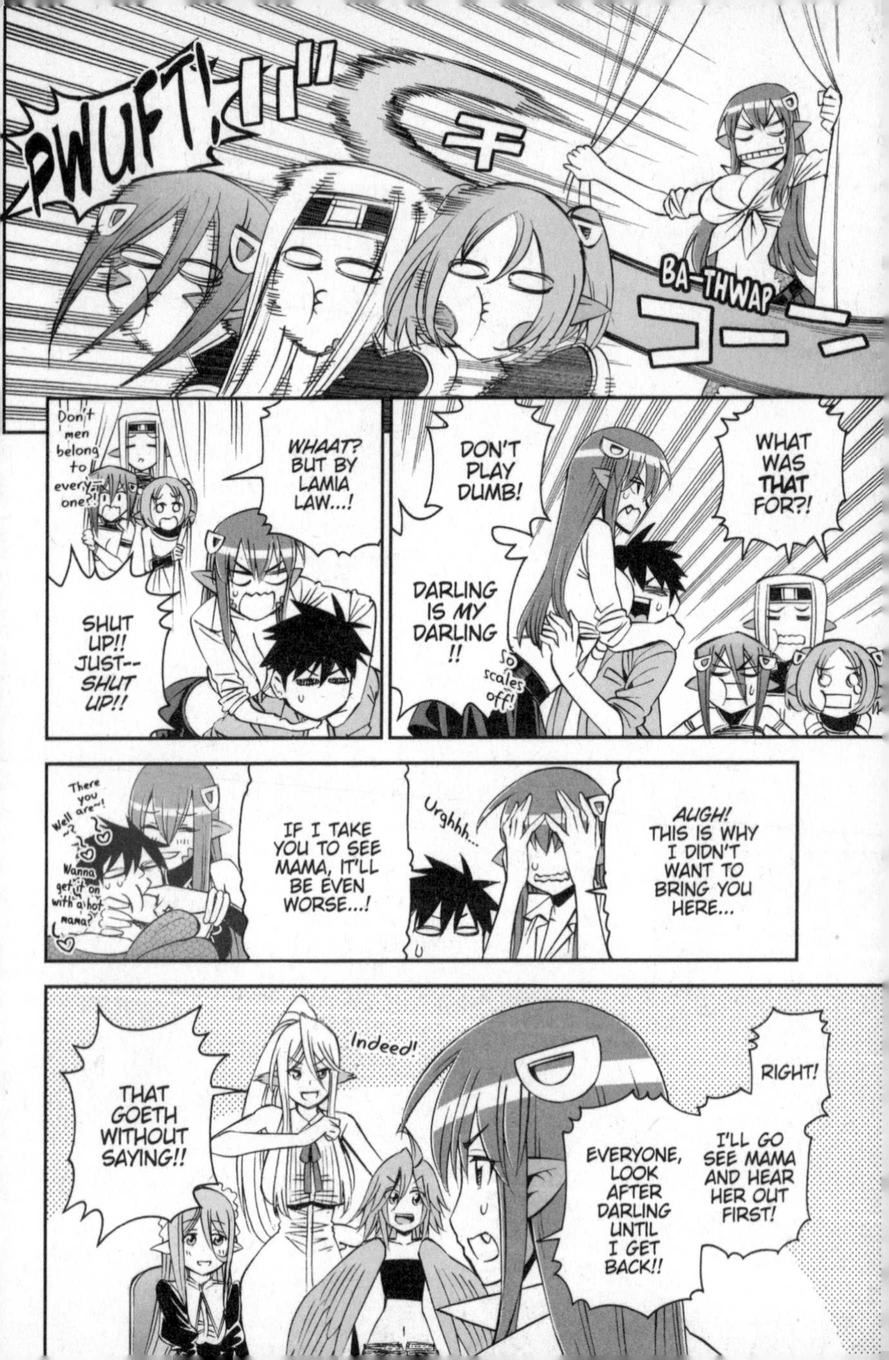
PWUFT!
BA-THWAP
WHAT WAS THAT FOR?!
DON'T PLAY DUMB!
DARLING IS MY DARLING!!
So scales off!
WHAAT? BUT BY LAMIA LAW...!
Don't men belong to every-one?!
SHUT UP!! JUST-- SHUT UP!!
AUGH! THIS IS WHY I DIDN'T WANT TO BRING YOU HERE...
Urghhh...
IF I TAKE YOU TO SEE MAMA, IT'LL BE EVEN WORSE...!
There you are~!
Well~?
Wanna get it on with a hot mama?
RIGHT!
I'LL GO SEE MAMA AND HEAR HER OUT FIRST!
EVERYONE, LOOK AFTER DARLING UNTIL I GET BACK!!
Indeed!
THAT GOETH WITHOUT SAYING!!

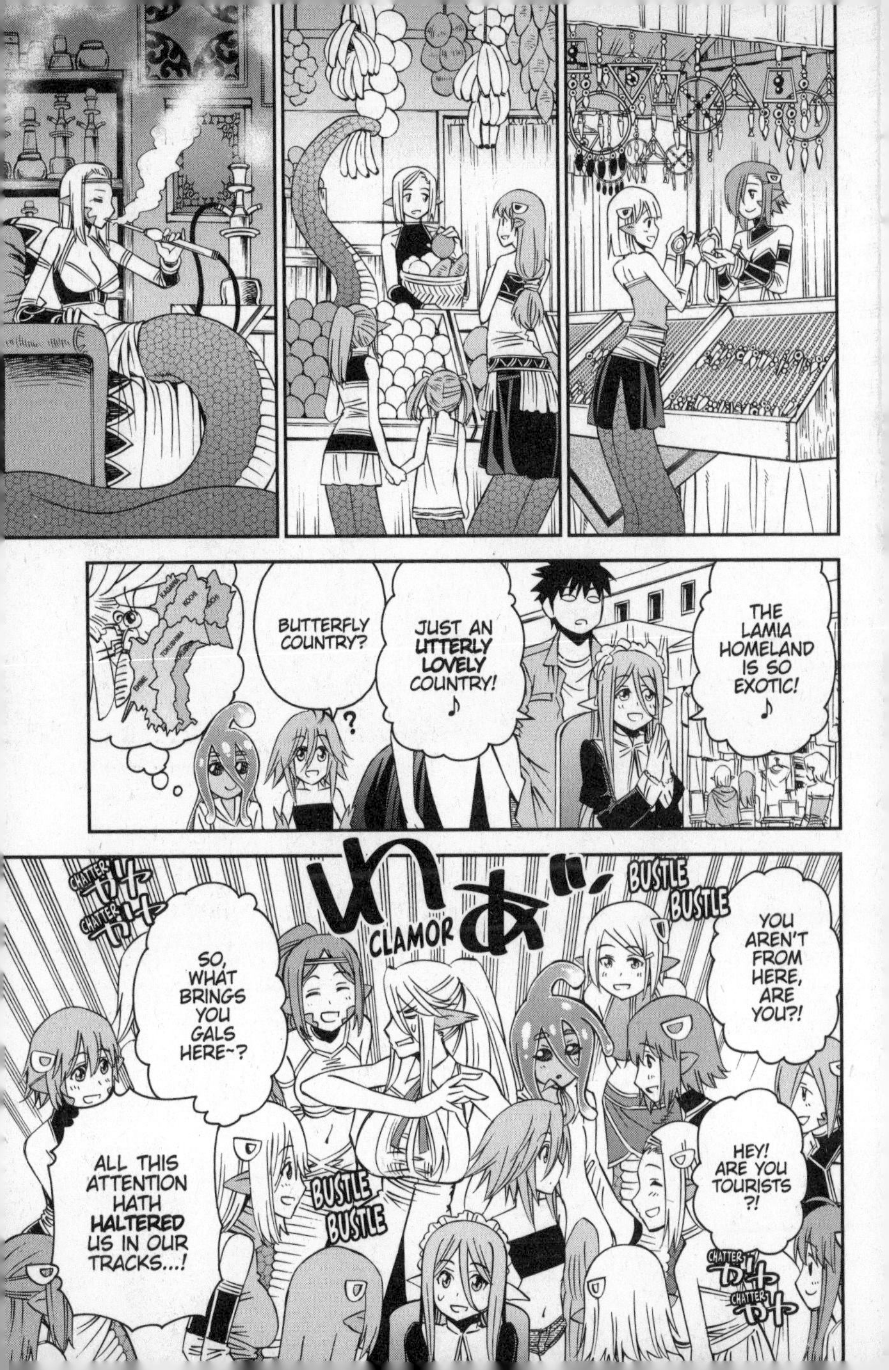
THE LAMIA HOMELAND IS SO EXOTIC! ♪
JUST AN UTTERLY LOVELY COUNTRY! ♪
BUTTERFLY COUNTRY?
?
BUSTLE BUSTLE
CLAMOR
YOU AREN'T FROM HERE, ARE YOU?!
SO, WHAT BRINGS YOU GALS HERE~?
CHATTER CHATTER
HEY! ARE YOU TOURISTS ?!
BUSTLE BUSTLE
ALL THIS ATTENTION HATH HALTERED US IN OUR TRACKS...!
CHATTER CHATTER

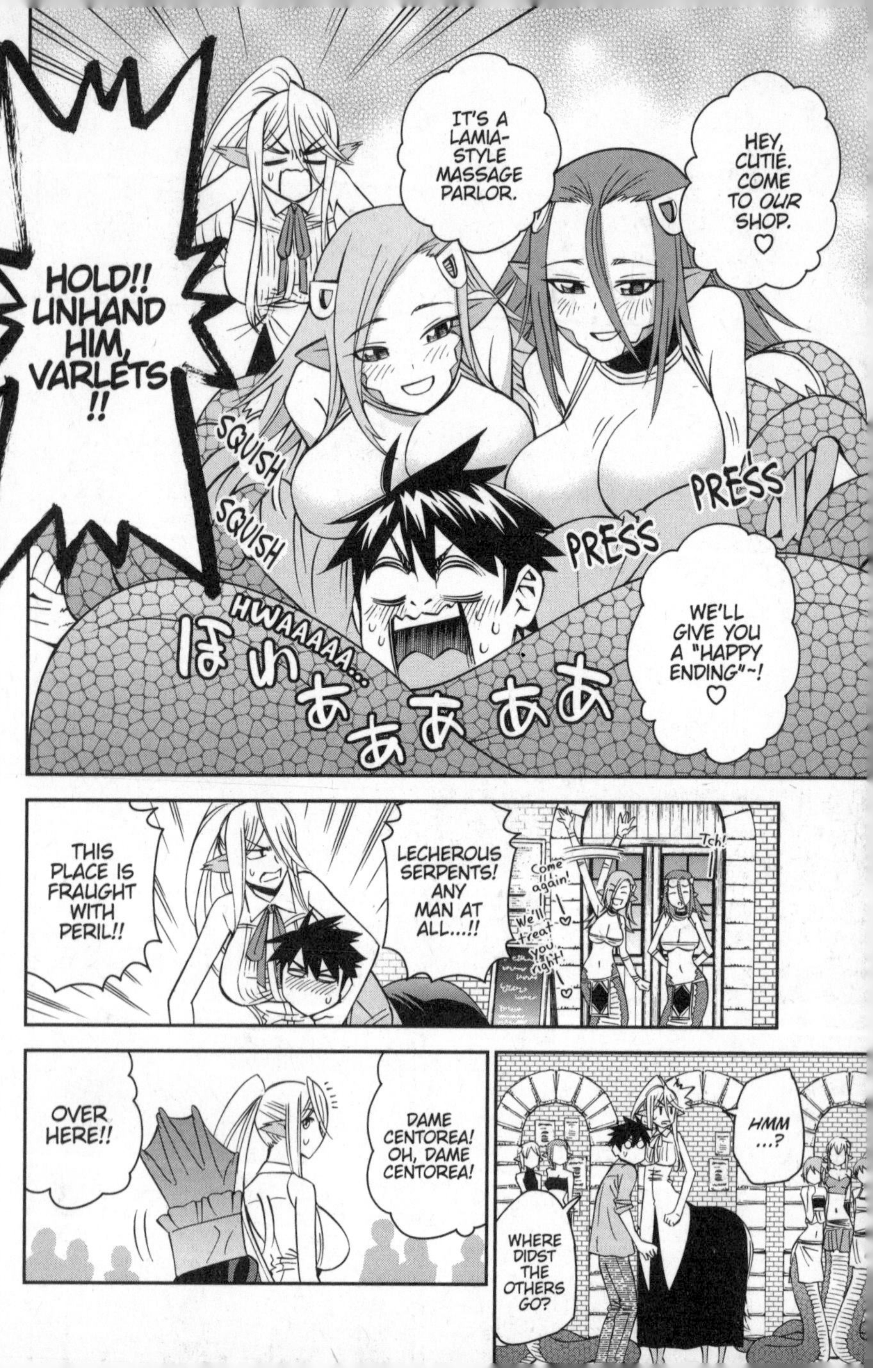
HEY, CUTIE. COME TO OUR SHOP. ♡
IT'S A LAMIA-STYLE MASSAGE PARLOR.
PRESS
PRESS
SQUISH
SQUISH
WE'LL GIVE YOU A "HAPPY ENDING"~! ♡
HWAAAAAA...
ほわああああ
HOLD!! UNHAND HIM, VARLETS!!
Tch!
Come again! We'll treat you right! ♡
LECHEROUS SERPENTS! ANY MAN AT ALL...!!
THIS PLACE IS FRAUGHT WITH PERIL!!
HMM...?
WHERE DIDST THE OTHERS GO?
DAME CENTOREA! OH, DAME CENTOREA!
OVER HERE!!

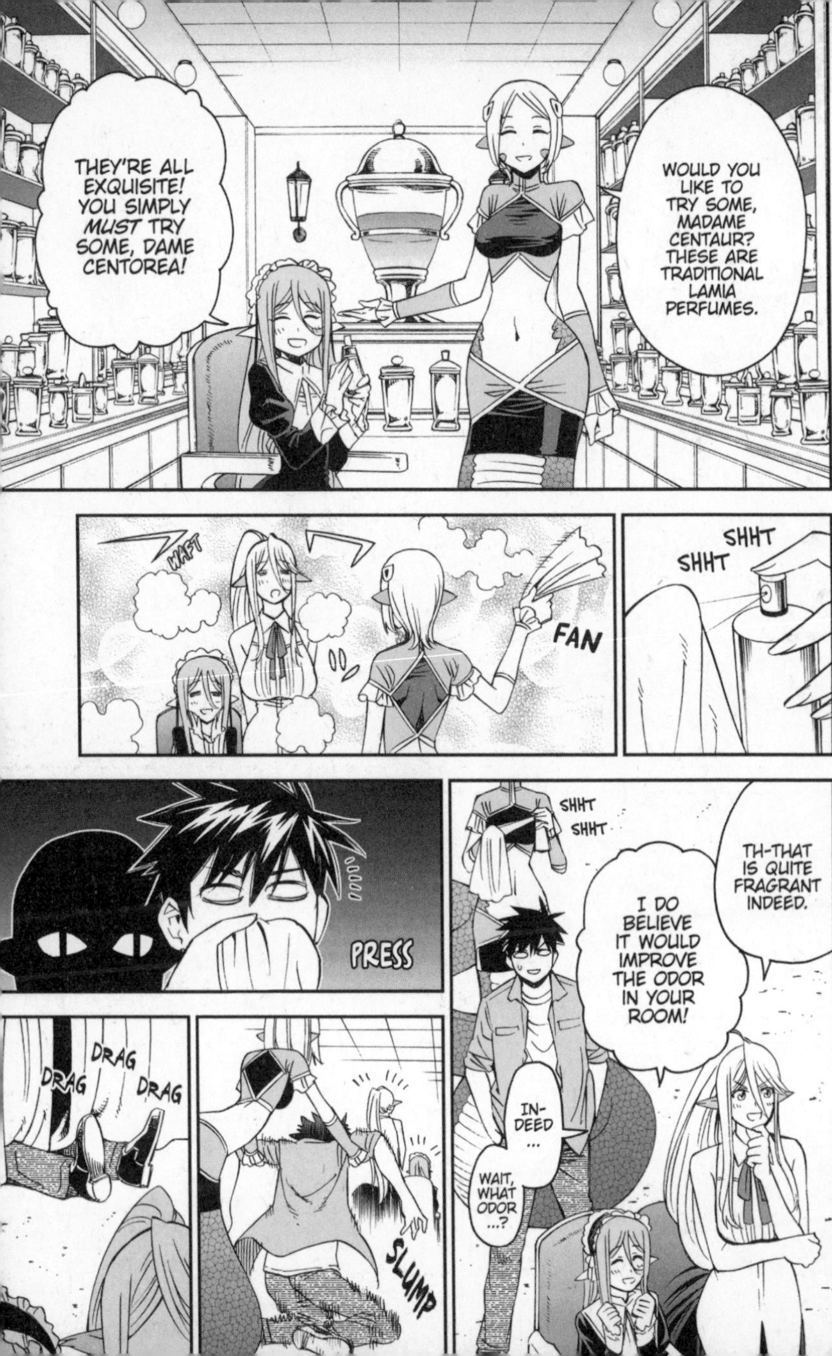
WOULD YOU LIKE TO TRY SOME, MADAME CENTAUR? THESE ARE TRADITIONAL LAMIA PERFUMES.
THEY'RE ALL EXQUISITE! YOU SIMPLY *MUST* TRY SOME, DAME CENTOREA!
SHHT
SHHT
WAFT
FAN
SHHT
SHHT
TH-THAT IS QUITE FRAGRANT INDEED.
I DO BELIEVE IT WOULD IMPROVE THE ODOR IN YOUR ROOM!
IN-DEED ...
WAIT, WHAT ODOR ...?
PRESS
SLUMP
DRAG
DRAG
DRAG

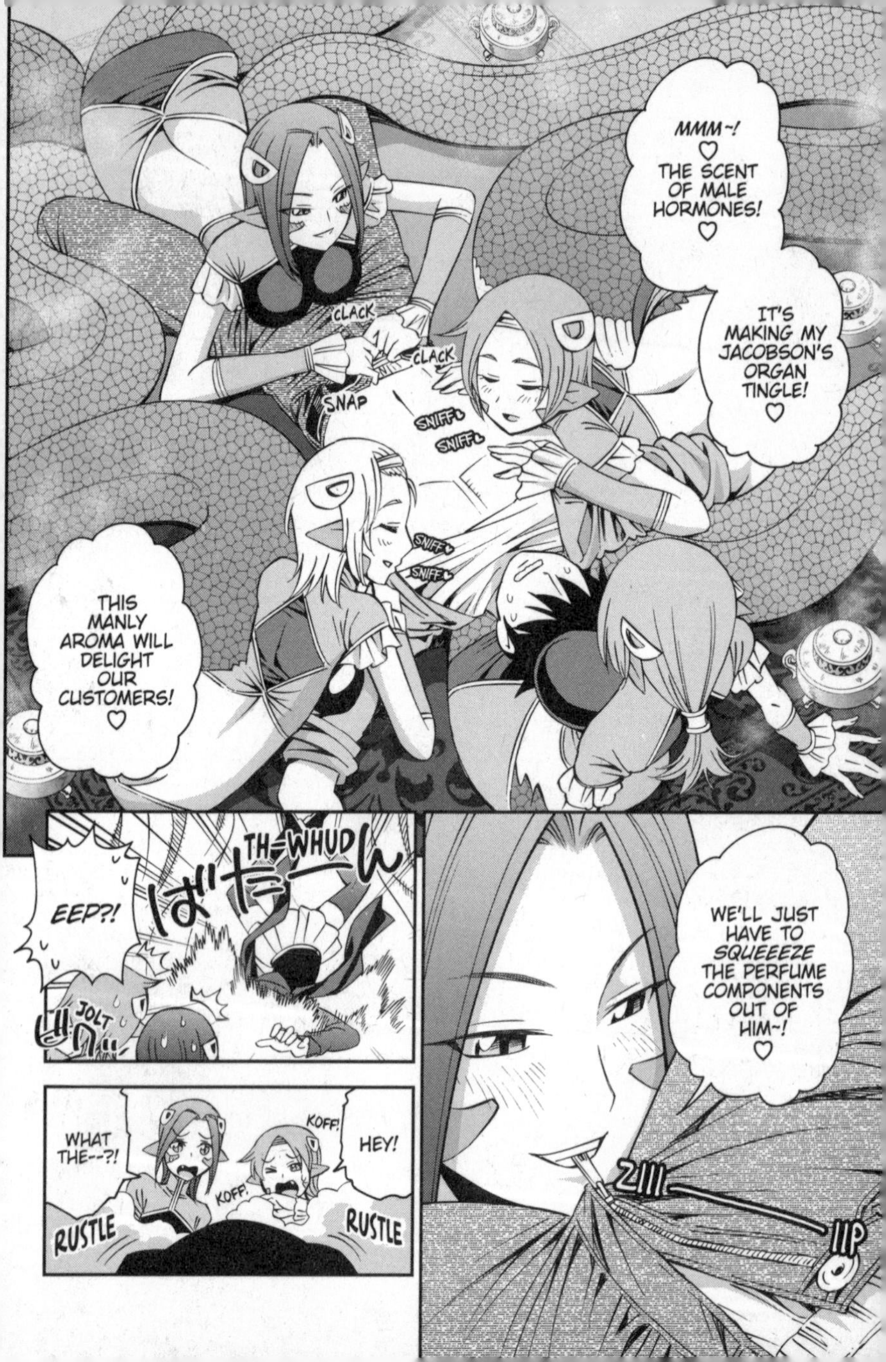
MMM~! ♡ THE SCENT OF MALE HORMONES! ♡
IT'S MAKING MY JACOBSON'S ORGAN TINGLE! ♡
CLACK
CLACK
SNAP
SNIFF
SNIFF
SNIFF
SNIFF
THIS MANLY AROMA WILL DELIGHT OUR CUSTOMERS! ♡
WE'LL JUST HAVE TO SQUEEEZE THE PERFUME COMPONENTS OUT OF HIM~! ♡
ZIII
IIP
TH-WHUD
ばたーん
EEP?!
JOLT
HEY!
KOFF!
WHAT THE--?!
KOFF!
RUSTLE
RUSTLE

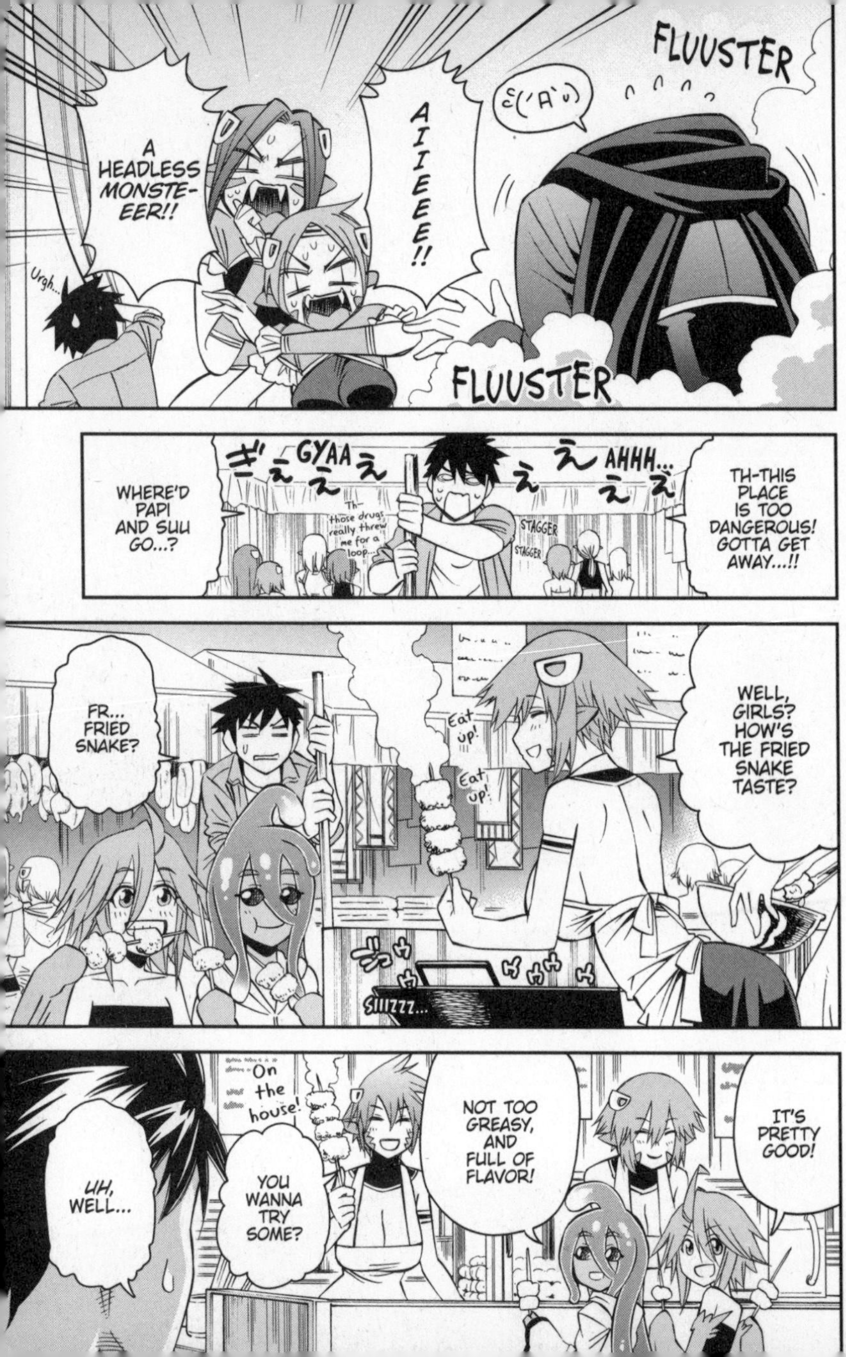
FLUUSTER
AIIEEEE!!
A HEADLESS MONSTEE-EER!!
Urgh...
FLUUSTER
TH-THIS PLACE IS TOO DANGEROUS! GOTTA GET AWAY...!!
AHHH...
GYAA
STAGGER
STAGGER
Th-those drugs really threw me for a loop...
WHERE'D PAPI AND SUU GO...?
WELL, GIRLS? HOW'S THE FRIED SNAKE TASTE?
Eat up!
Eat up!
FR... FRIED SNAKE?
SIIIZZZ...
IT'S PRETTY GOOD!
NOT TOO GREASY, AND FULL OF FLAVOR!
On the house!
YOU WANNA TRY SOME?
UH, WELL...

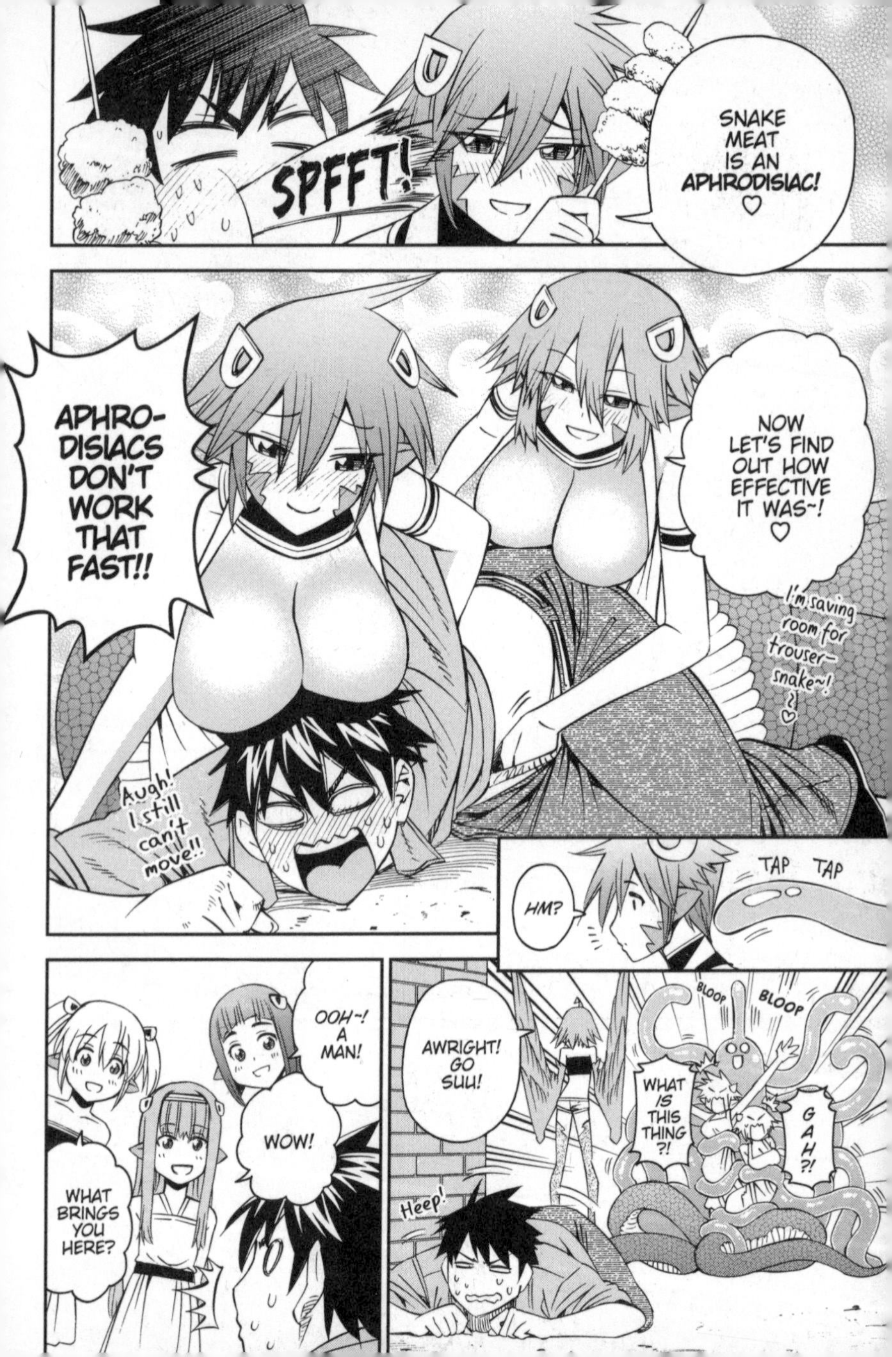
SPFFT!
SNAKE MEAT IS AN APHRODISIAC! ♡
NOW LET'S FIND OUT HOW EFFECTIVE IT WAS~! ♡
I'm saving room for trouser-snake~! ♡
APHRO-DISIACS DON'T WORK THAT FAST!!
Augh! I still can't move!!
TAP TAP
HM?
BLOOP BLOOP
GAH?!
WHAT IS THIS THING?!
AWRIGHT! GO SUU!
Heep!
OOH~! A MAN!
WOW!
WHAT BRINGS YOU HERE?

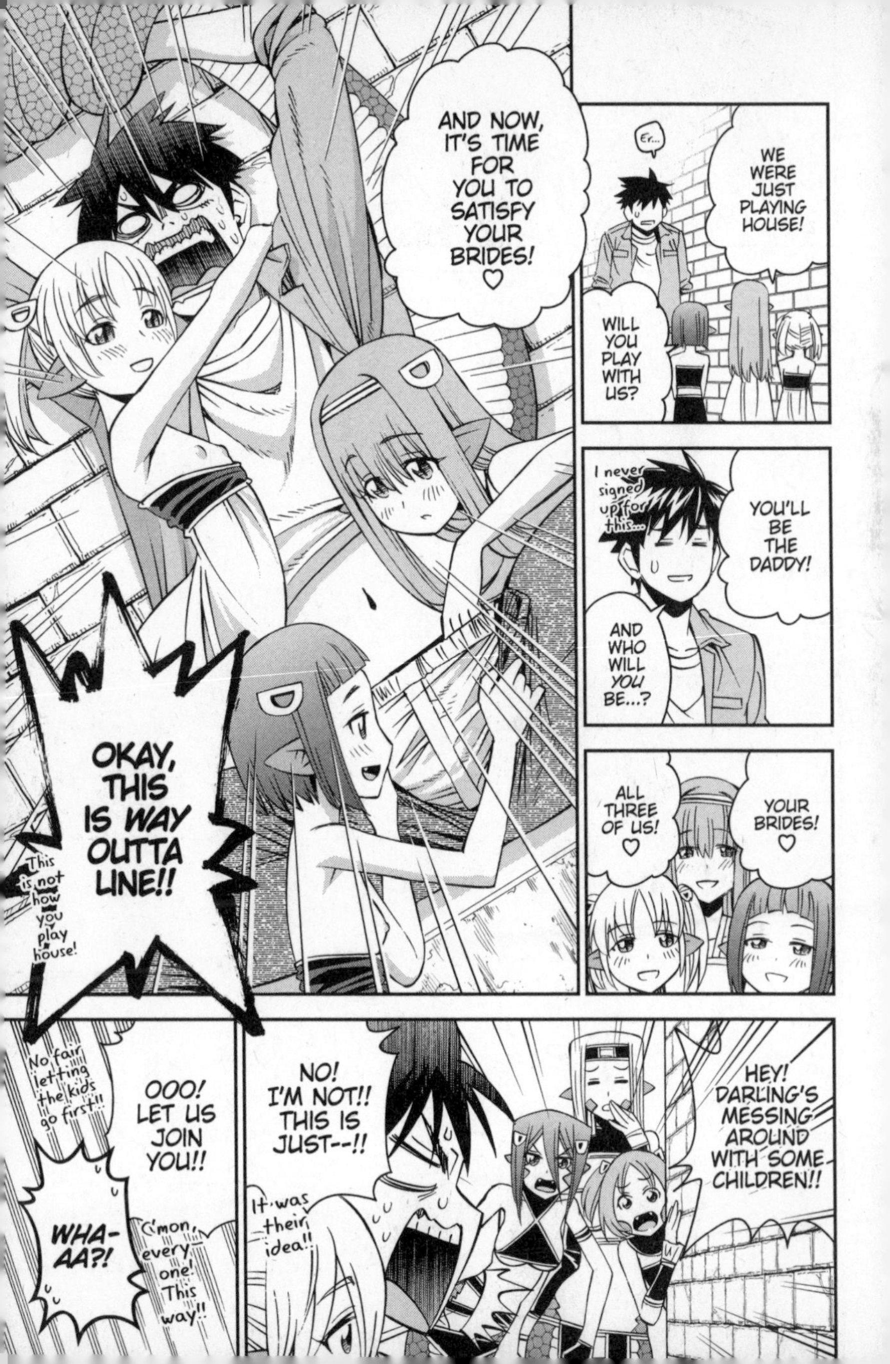
WE WERE JUST PLAYING HOUSE!
Er...
WILL YOU PLAY WITH US?
YOU'LL BE THE DADDY!
I never signed up for this...
AND WHO WILL YOU BE...?
YOUR BRIDES! ♡
ALL THREE OF US! ♡
AND NOW, IT'S TIME FOR YOU TO SATISFY YOUR BRIDES! ♡
OKAY, THIS IS WAY OUTTA LINE!!
This is not how you play house!
HEY! DARLING'S MESSING AROUND WITH SOME CHILDREN!!
NO! I'M NOT!! THIS IS JUST--!!
It was their idea!!
OOO! LET US JOIN YOU!!
No fair letting the kids go first!!
C'mon, every-one! This way!!
WHA-AA?!

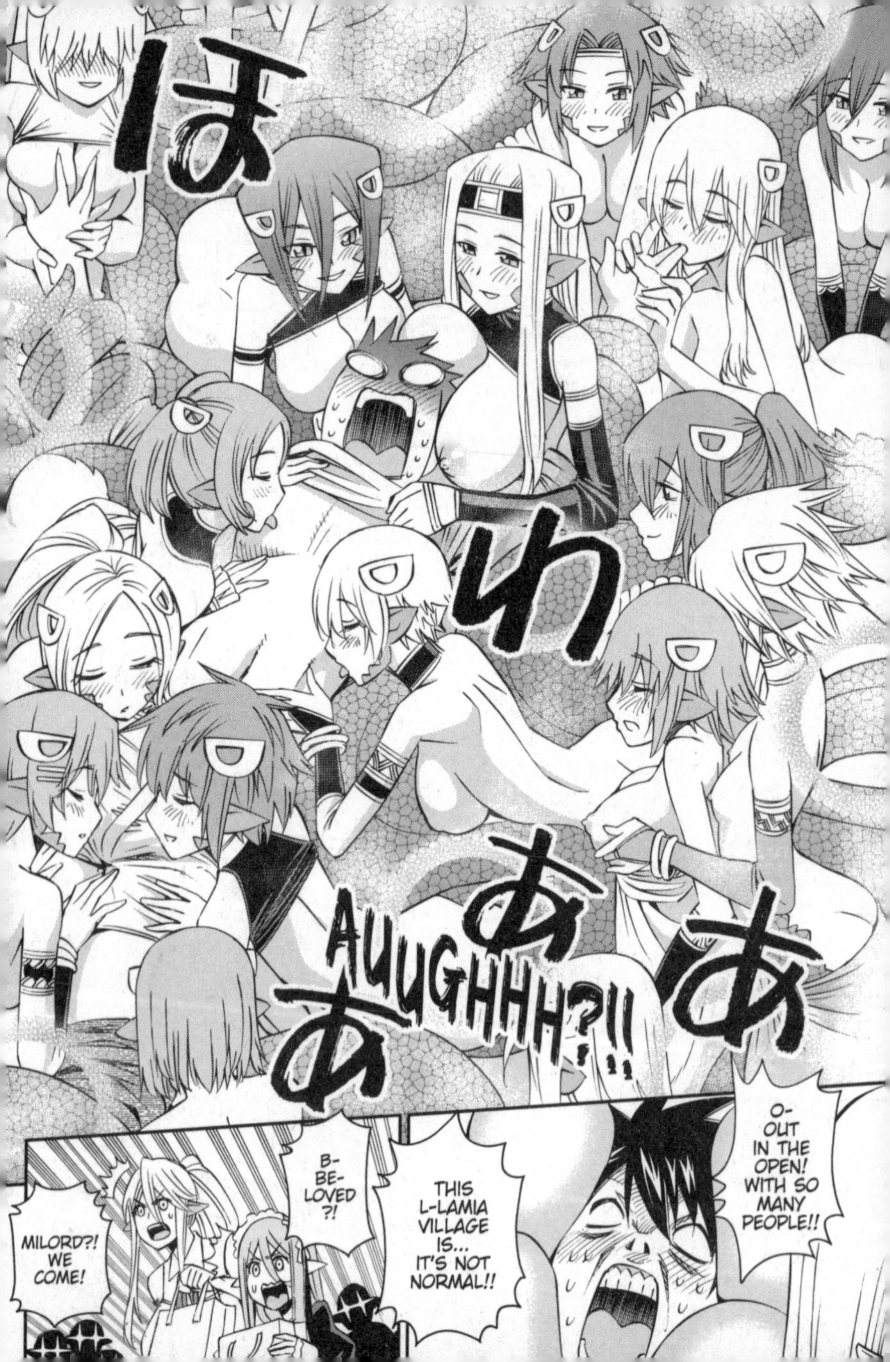
ほわあああ
AUUGHHH?!!
O- OUT IN THE OPEN! WITH SO MANY PEOPLE!!
THIS L-LAMIA VILLAGE IS... IT'S NOT NORMAL!!
B- BE- LOVED ?!
MILORD?! WE COME!

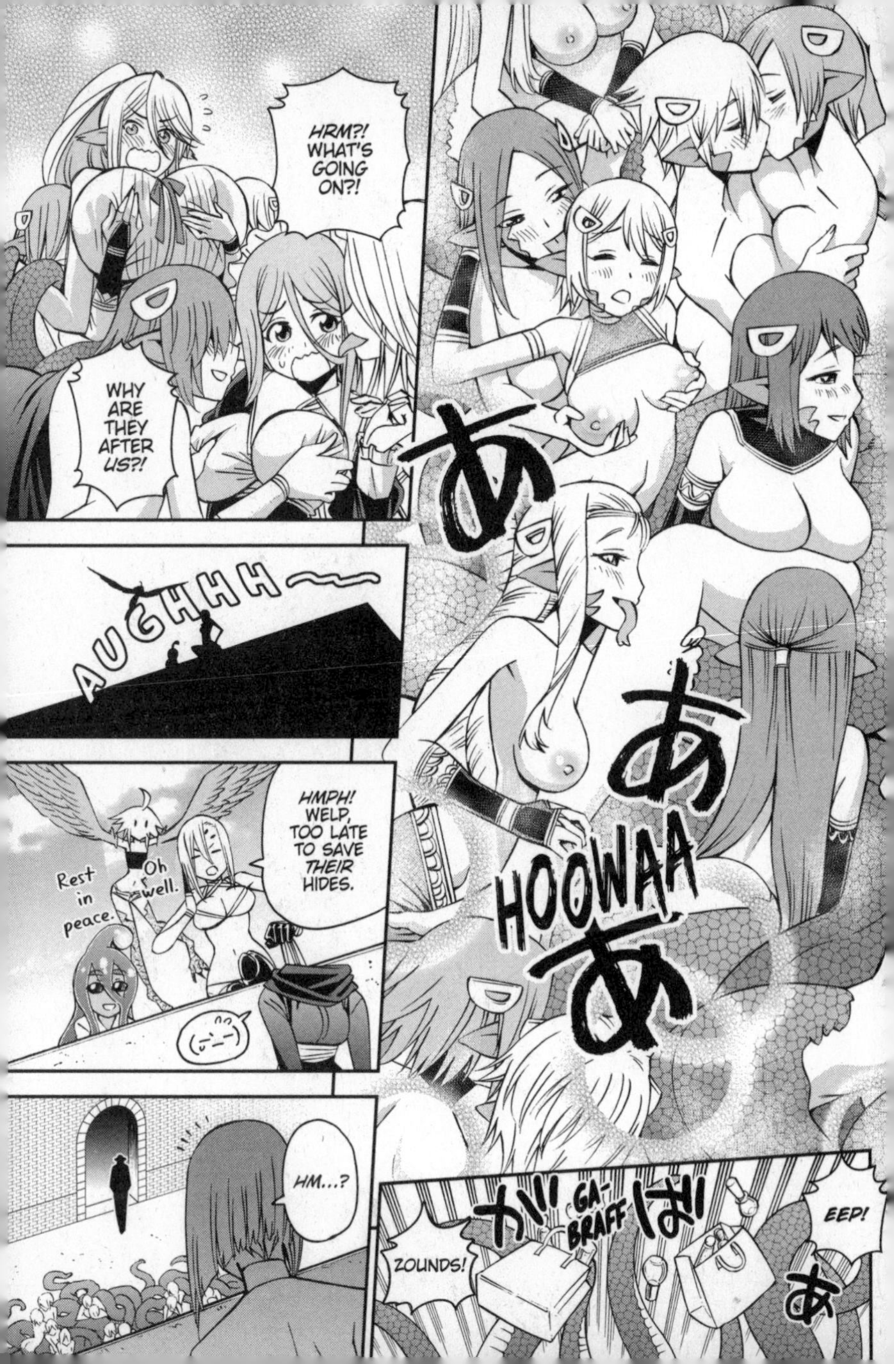
あ
あ
HOOWAA
あ
HRM?! WHAT'S GOING ON?!
WHY ARE THEY AFTER US?!
AUGHHH~~
HMPH! WELP, TOO LATE TO SAVE THEIR HIDES.
Oh well.
Rest in peace.
EEP!
が!!
GA-BRAFF
ば!!
ZOUNDS!
あ
HM...?

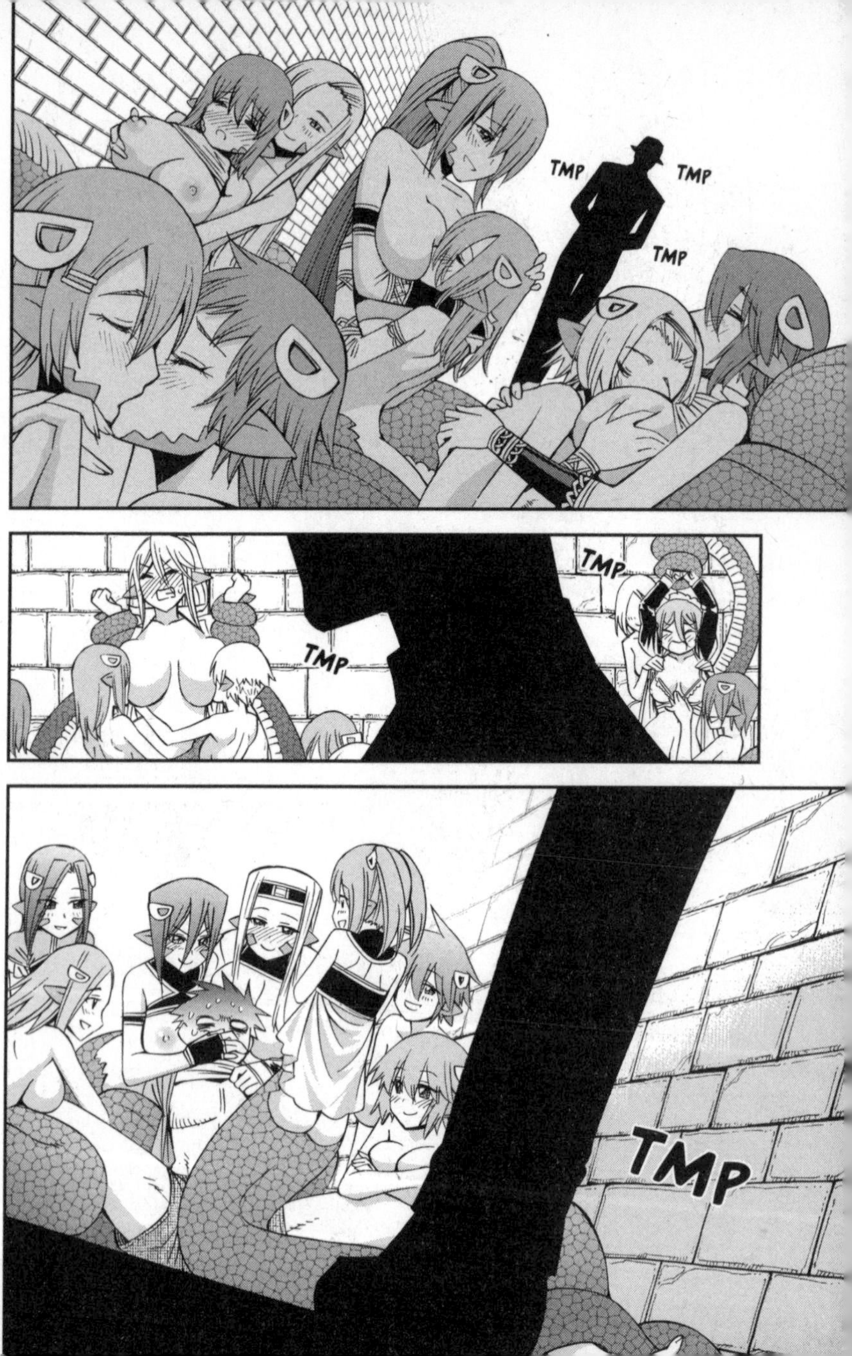
TMP
TMP
TMP
TMP
TMP
TMP

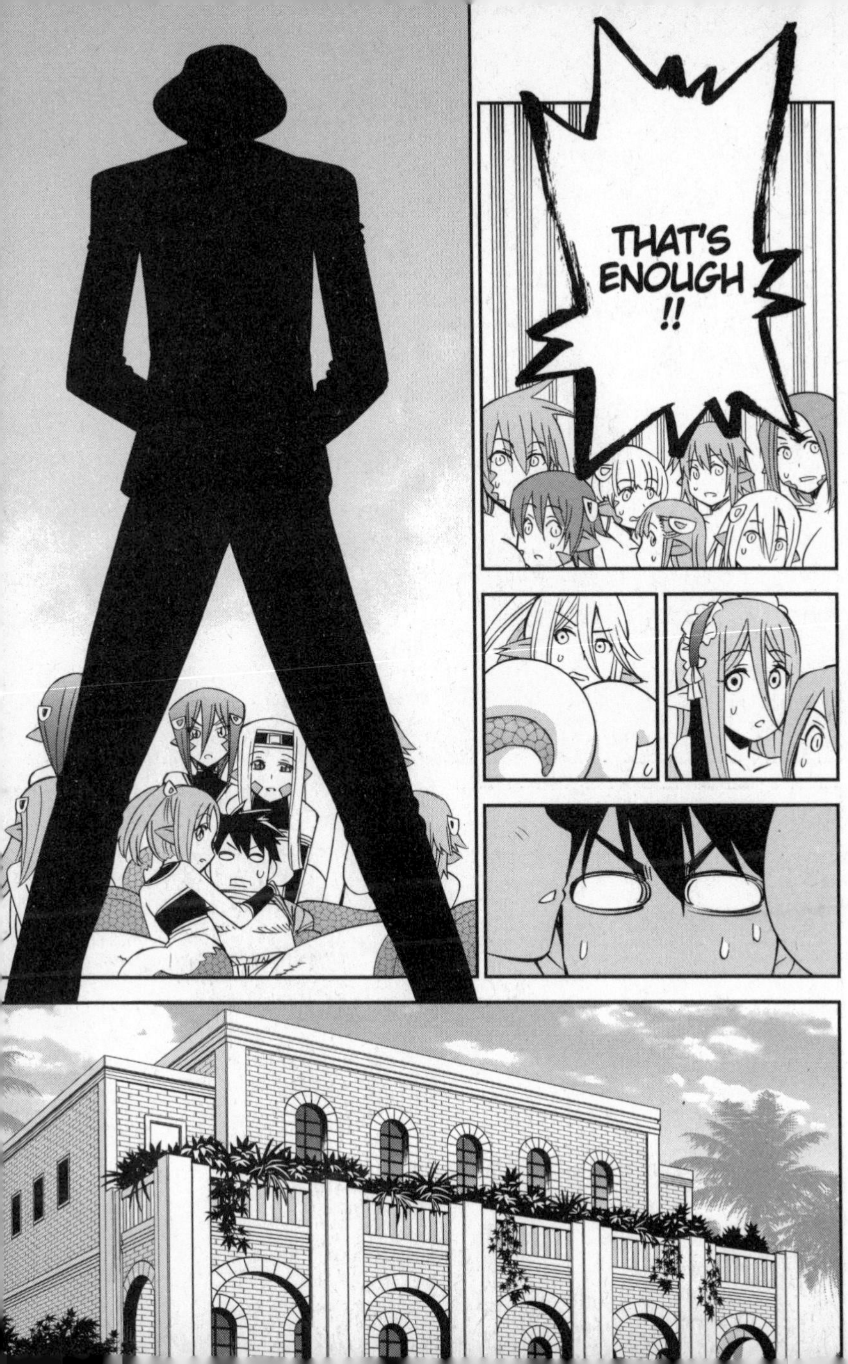
THAT'S ENOUGH !!

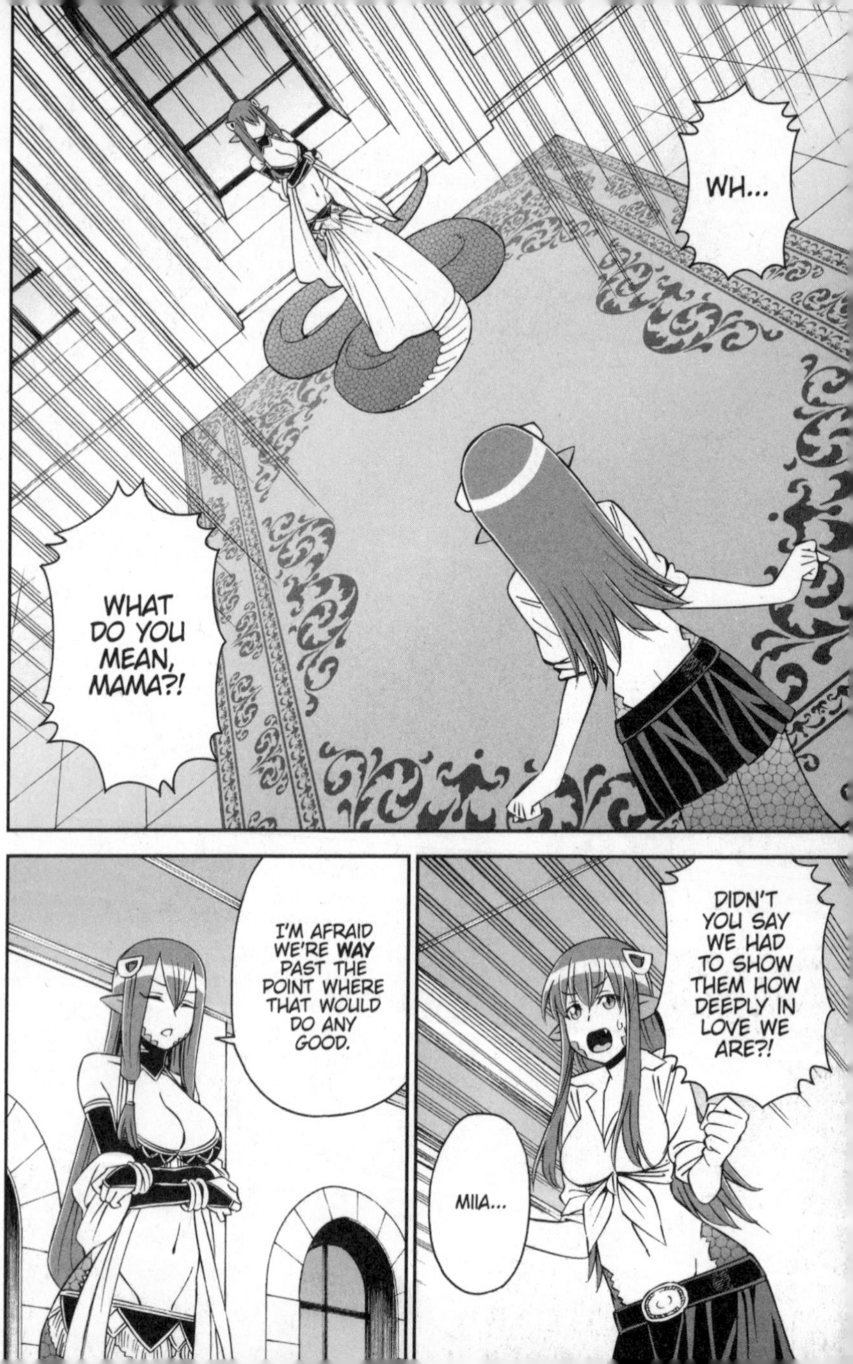
WH...
WHAT DO YOU MEAN, MAMA?!
DIDN'T YOU SAY WE HAD TO SHOW THEM HOW DEEPLY IN LOVE WE ARE?!
MIIA...
I'M AFRAID WE'RE **WAY** PAST THE POINT WHERE THAT WOULD DO ANY GOOD.

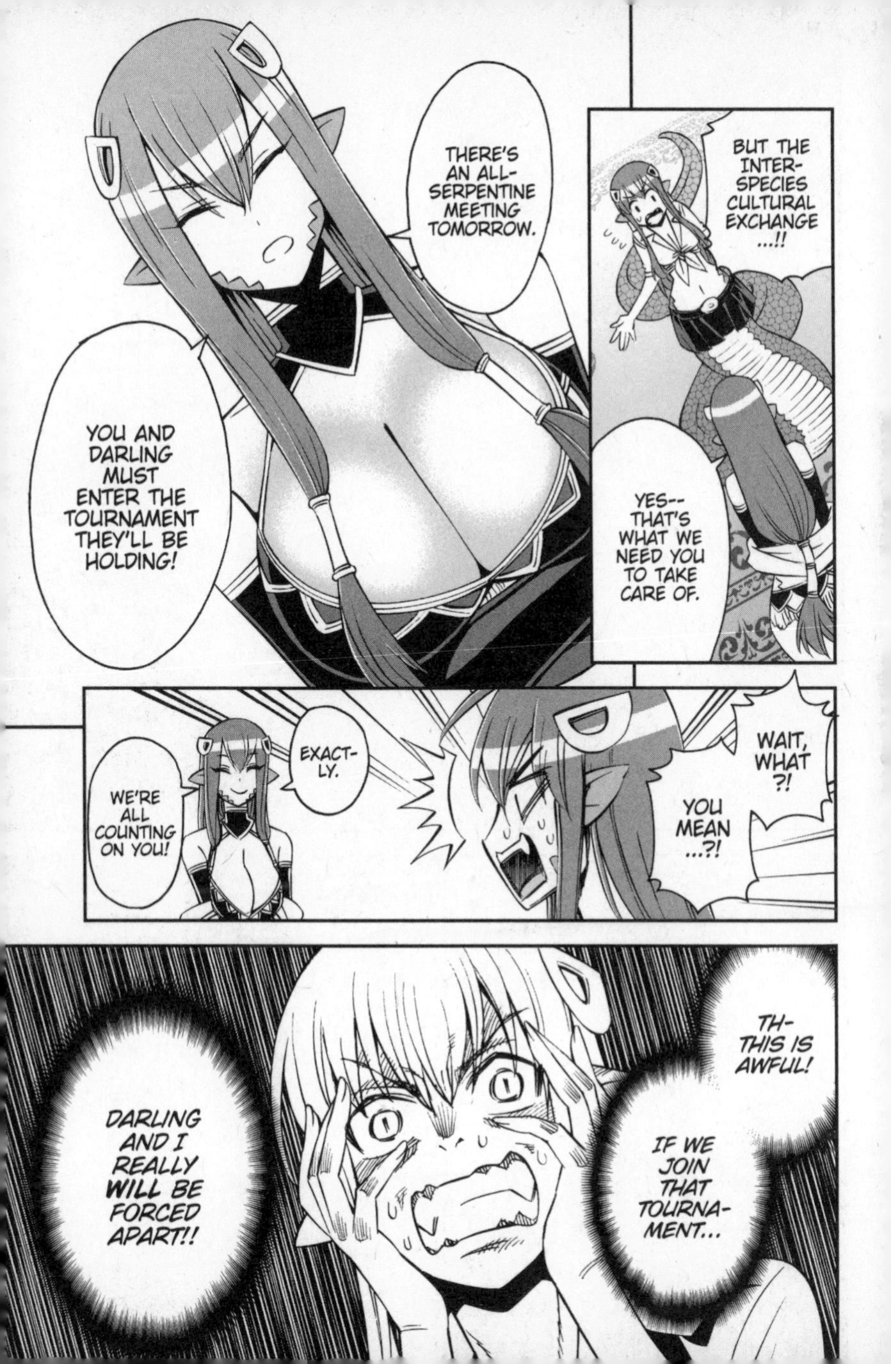
BUT THE INTER-SPECIES CULTURAL EXCHANGE ...!!
YES-- THAT'S WHAT WE NEED YOU TO TAKE CARE OF.
THERE'S AN ALL-SERPENTINE MEETING TOMORROW.
YOU AND DARLING MUST ENTER THE TOURNAMENT THEY'LL BE HOLDING!
WAIT, WHAT ?!
YOU MEAN ...?!
EXACT-LY.
WE'RE ALL COUNTING ON YOU!
TH-THIS IS AWFUL!
IF WE JOIN THAT TOURNA-MENT...
DARLING AND I REALLY **WILL** BE FORCED APART!!

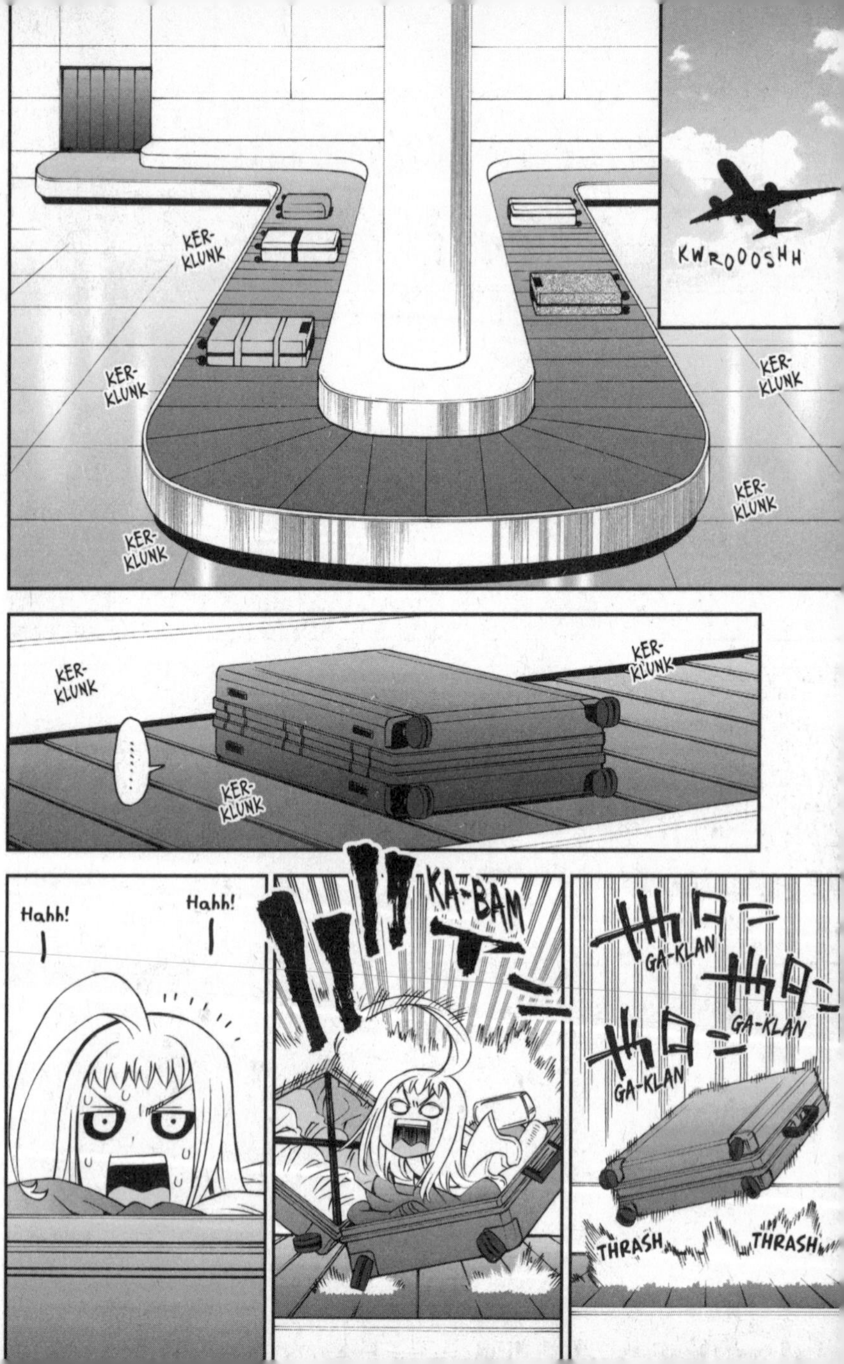
KWROOOSHH
KER-KLUNK
KER-KLUNK
KER-KLUNK
KER-KLUNK
KER-KLUNK
KER-KLUNK
KER-KLUNK
......
KER-KLUNK
GA-KLAN
GA-KLAN
GA-KLAN
THRASH
THRASH
KA-BAM
Hahh!
Hahh!

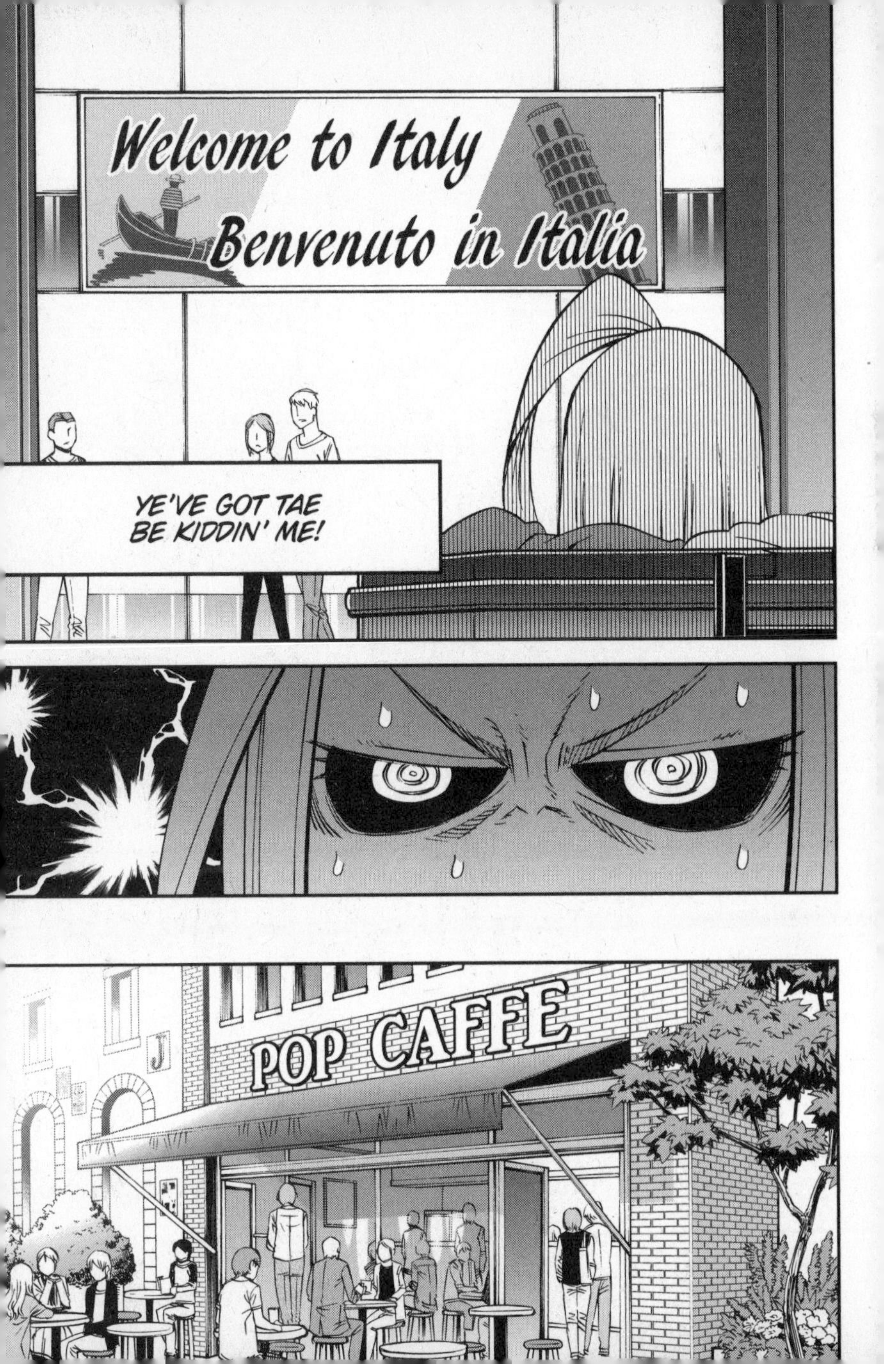
Welcome to Italy
Benvenuto in Italia
YE'VE GOT TAE BE KIDDIN' ME!
POP CAFFE

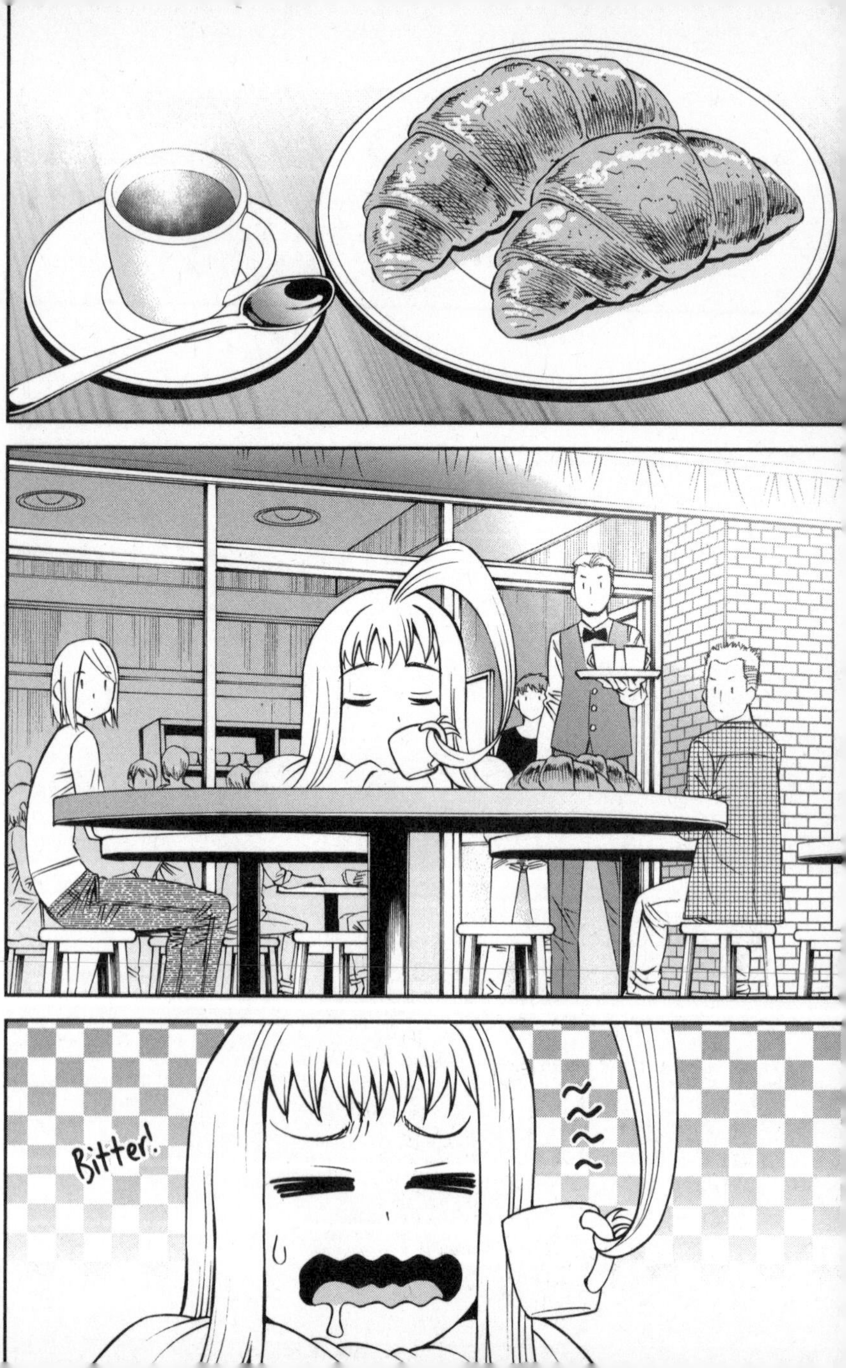
Bitter!

Monster Musume

Everyday Life with Monster Girls

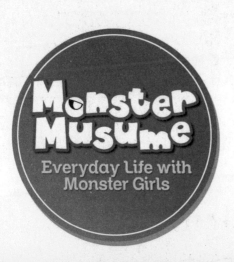

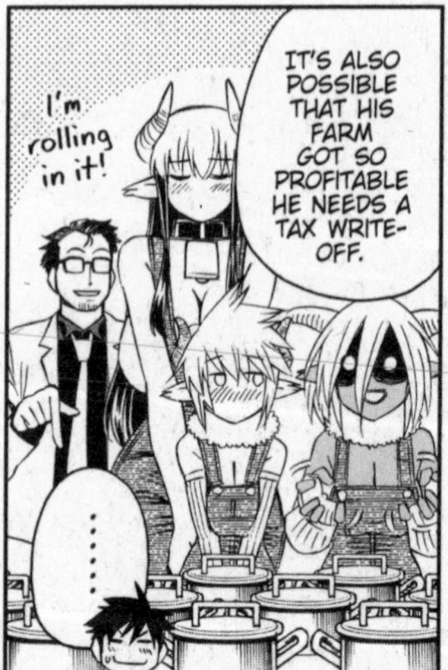
IT'S ALSO POSSIBLE THAT HIS FARM GOT SO PROFITABLE HE NEEDS A TAX WRITE-OFF.
I'm rolling in it!
......

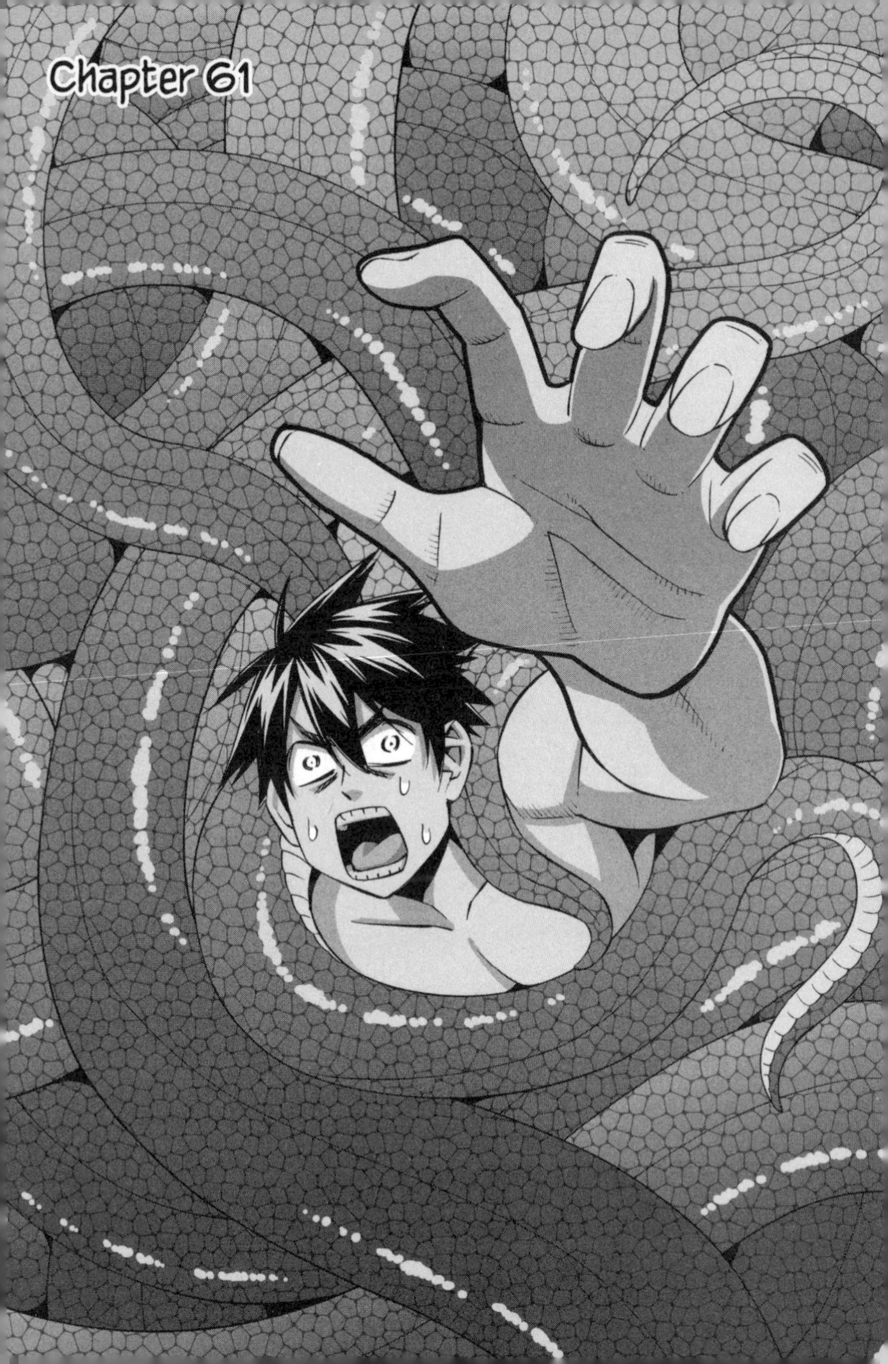
Chapter 61

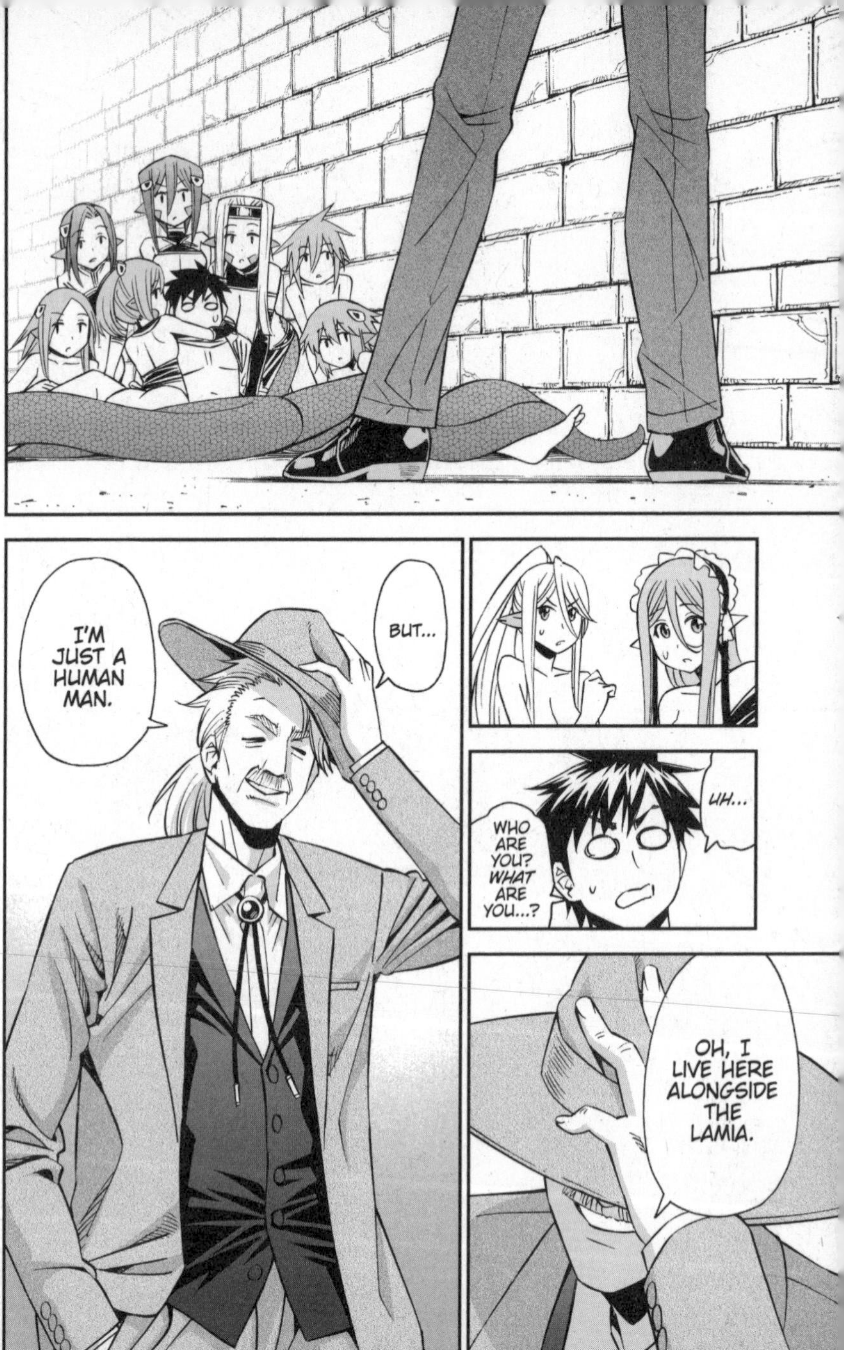
UH...
WHO ARE YOU? WHAT ARE YOU...?
OH, I LIVE HERE ALONGSIDE THE LAMIA.
BUT...
I'M JUST A HUMAN MAN.

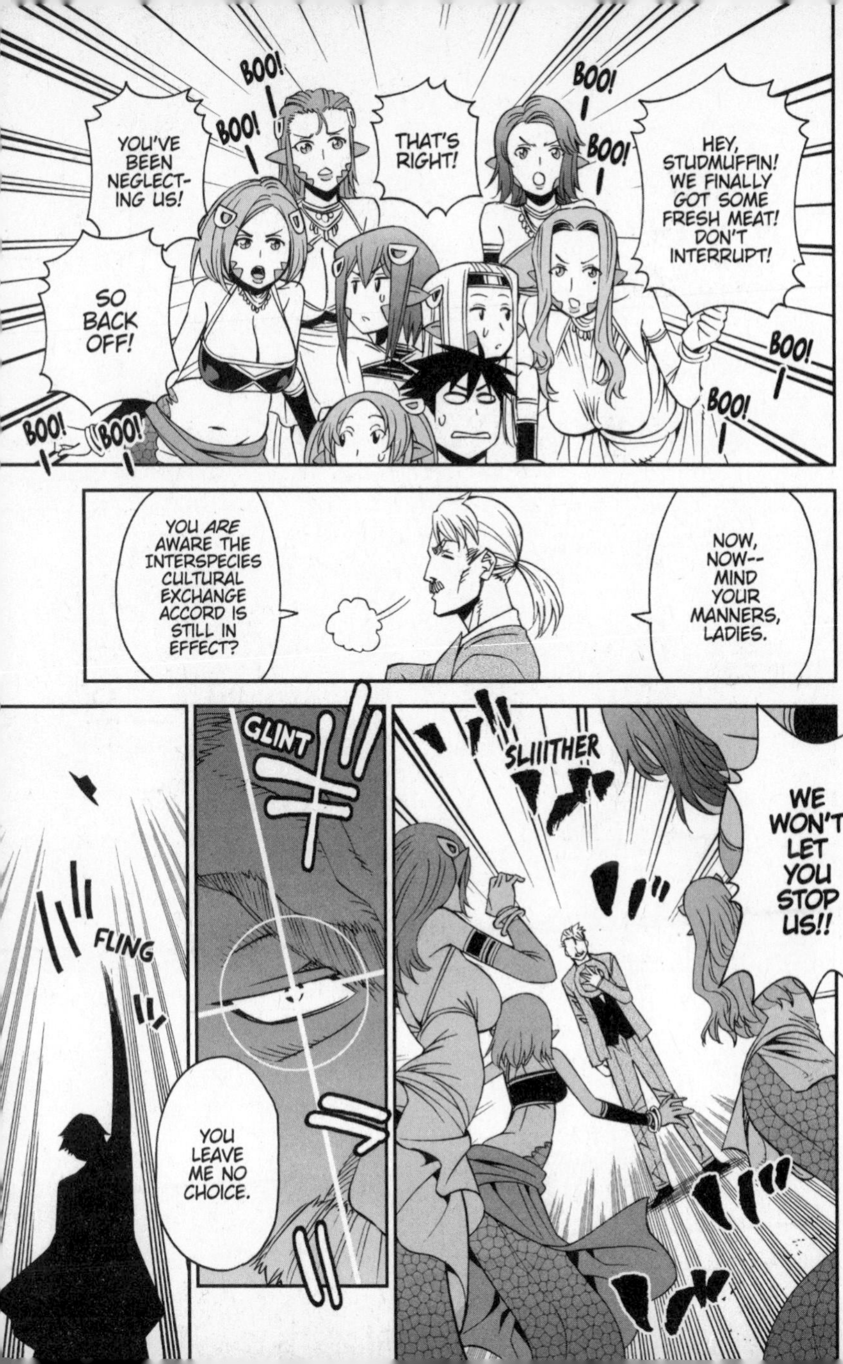
BOO!
BOO!
HEY, STUDMUFFIN! WE FINALLY GOT SOME FRESH MEAT! DON'T INTERRUPT!
BOO!
BOO!
BOO!
BOO!
THAT'S RIGHT!
BOO!
BOO!
YOU'VE BEEN NEGLECTING US!
SO BACK OFF!
BOO!
BOO!
NOW, NOW-- MIND YOUR MANNERS, LADIES.
YOU ARE AWARE THE INTERSPECIES CULTURAL EXCHANGE ACCORD IS STILL IN EFFECT?
SLIIITHER
WE WON'T LET YOU STOP US!!
GLINT
YOU LEAVE ME NO CHOICE.
FLING

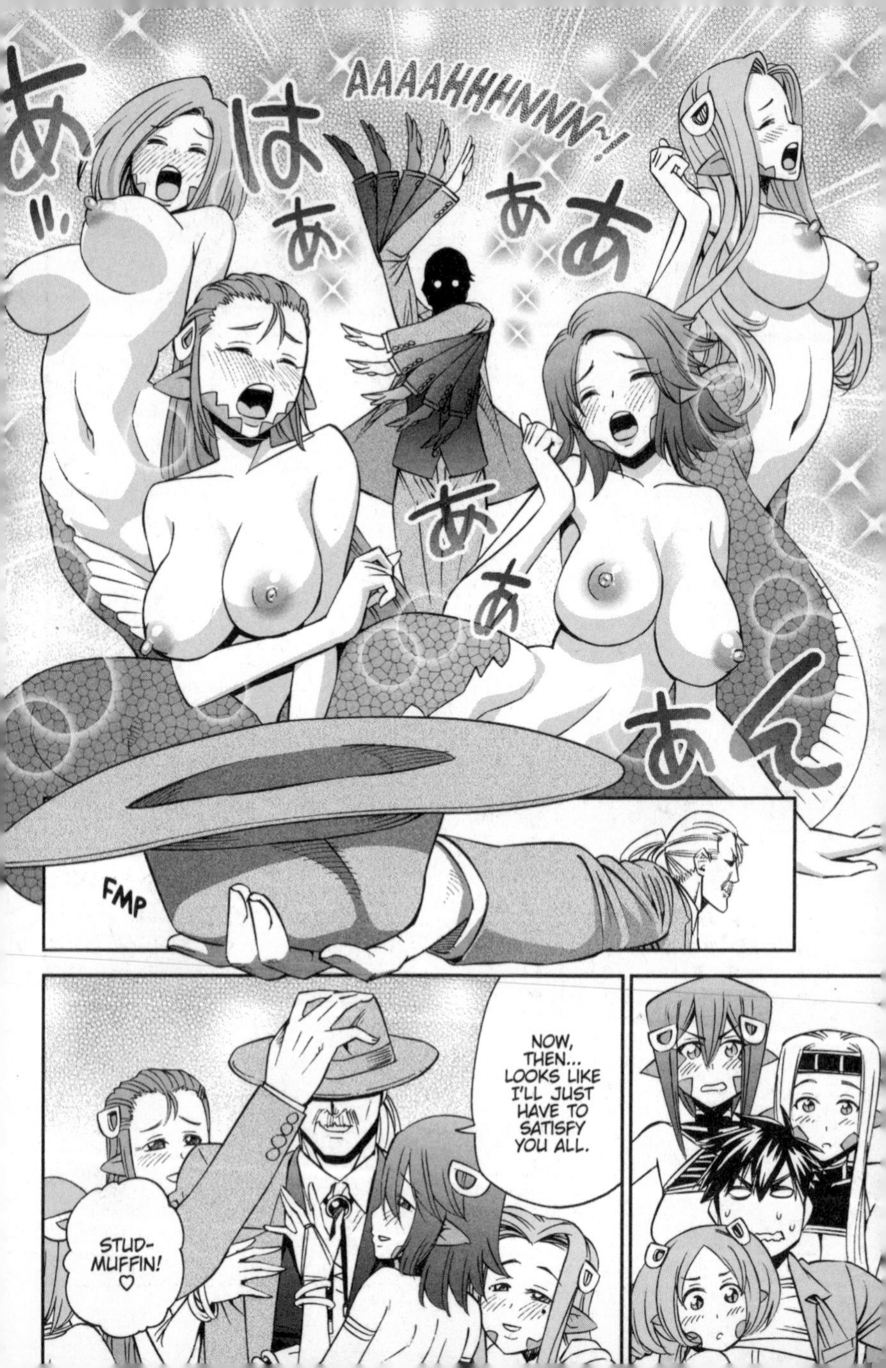
AAAAAHHHNNN~!
あ゛はぁぁああぁあん
FMP
NOW, THEN... LOOKS LIKE I'LL JUST HAVE TO SATISFY YOU ALL.
STUD-MUFFIN! ♡

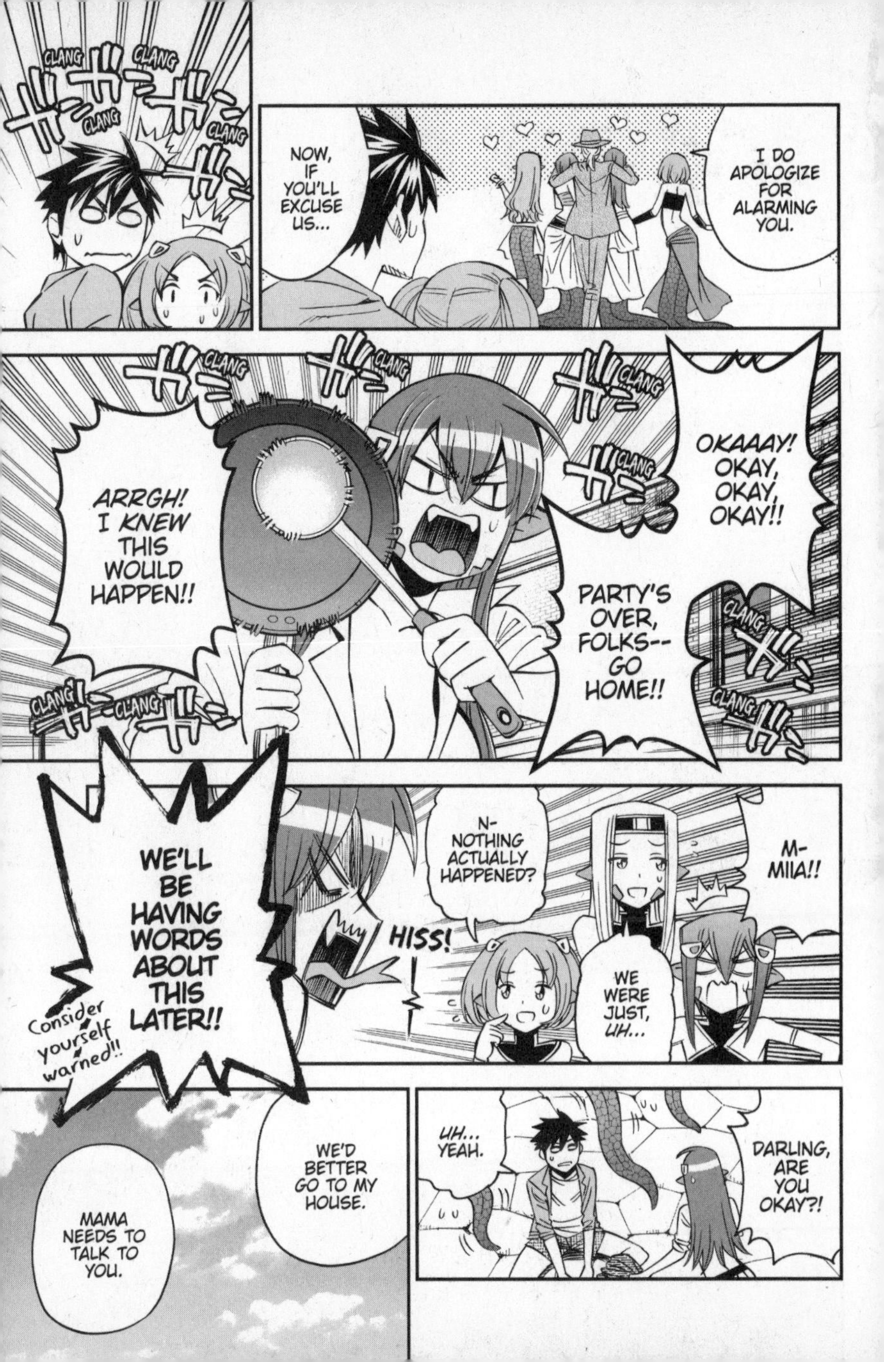
I DO APOLOGIZE FOR ALARMING YOU.
NOW, IF YOU'LL EXCUSE US...
CLANG
CLANG
CLANG
CLANG
OKAAAY! OKAY, OKAY, OKAY!!
PARTY'S OVER, FOLKS--GO HOME!!
CLANG
CLANG
CLANG
CLANG
CLANG
CLANG
ARRGH! I KNEW THIS WOULD HAPPEN!!
CLANG
CLANG
M-MIIA!!
N-NOTHING ACTUALLY HAPPENED?
WE WERE JUST, UH...
HISS!
WE'LL BE HAVING WORDS ABOUT THIS LATER!!
Consider yourself warned!!
DARLING, ARE YOU OKAY?!
UH... YEAH.
WE'D BETTER GO TO MY HOUSE.
MAMA NEEDS TO TALK TO YOU.

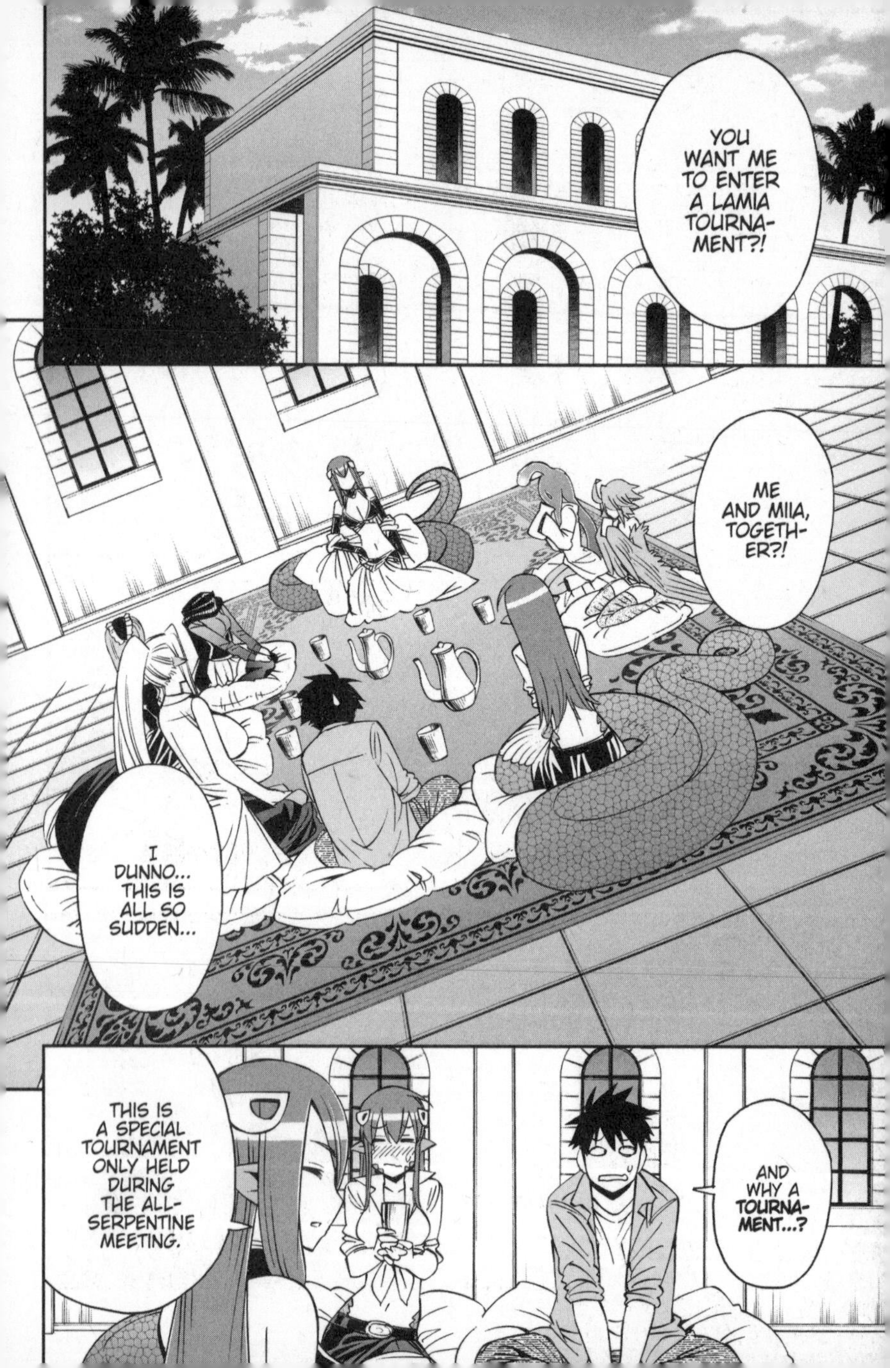
YOU WANT ME TO ENTER A LAMIA TOURNA-MENT?!
ME AND MIIA, TOGETH-ER?!
I DUNNO... THIS IS ALL SO SUDDEN...
AND WHY A TOURNA-MENT...?
THIS IS A SPECIAL TOURNAMENT ONLY HELD DURING THE ALL-SERPENTINE MEETING.

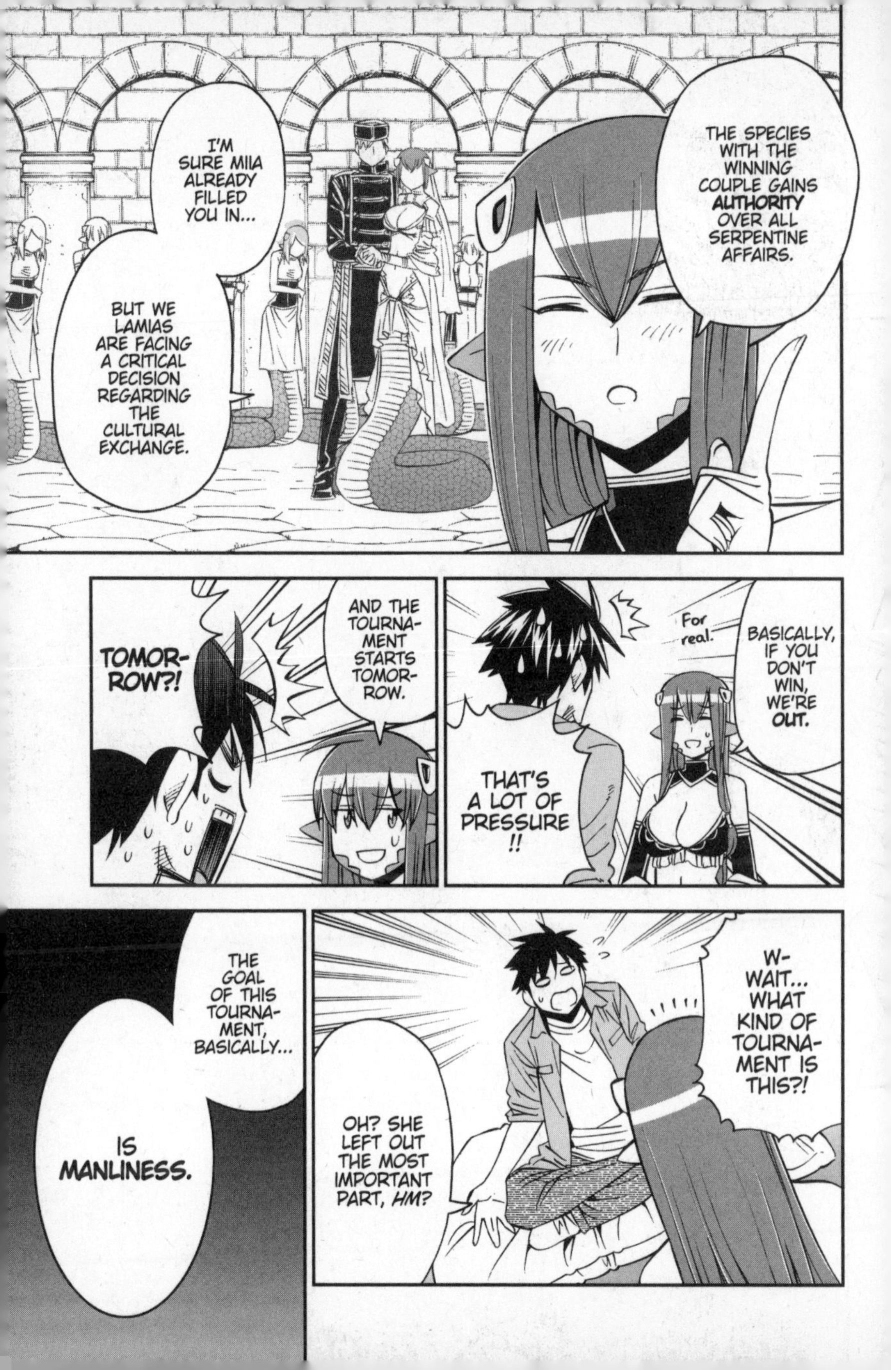
THE SPECIES WITH THE WINNING COUPLE GAINS AUTHORITY OVER ALL SERPENTINE AFFAIRS.
I'M SURE MIIA ALREADY FILLED YOU IN...
BUT WE LAMIAS ARE FACING A CRITICAL DECISION REGARDING THE CULTURAL EXCHANGE.
BASICALLY, IF YOU DON'T WIN, WE'RE OUT.
For real.
THAT'S A LOT OF PRESSURE!!
AND THE TOURNAMENT STARTS TOMORROW.
TOMORROW?!
W-WAIT... WHAT KIND OF TOURNAMENT IS THIS?!
OH? SHE LEFT OUT THE MOST IMPORTANT PART, HM?
THE GOAL OF THIS TOURNAMENT, BASICALLY...
IS MANLINESS.

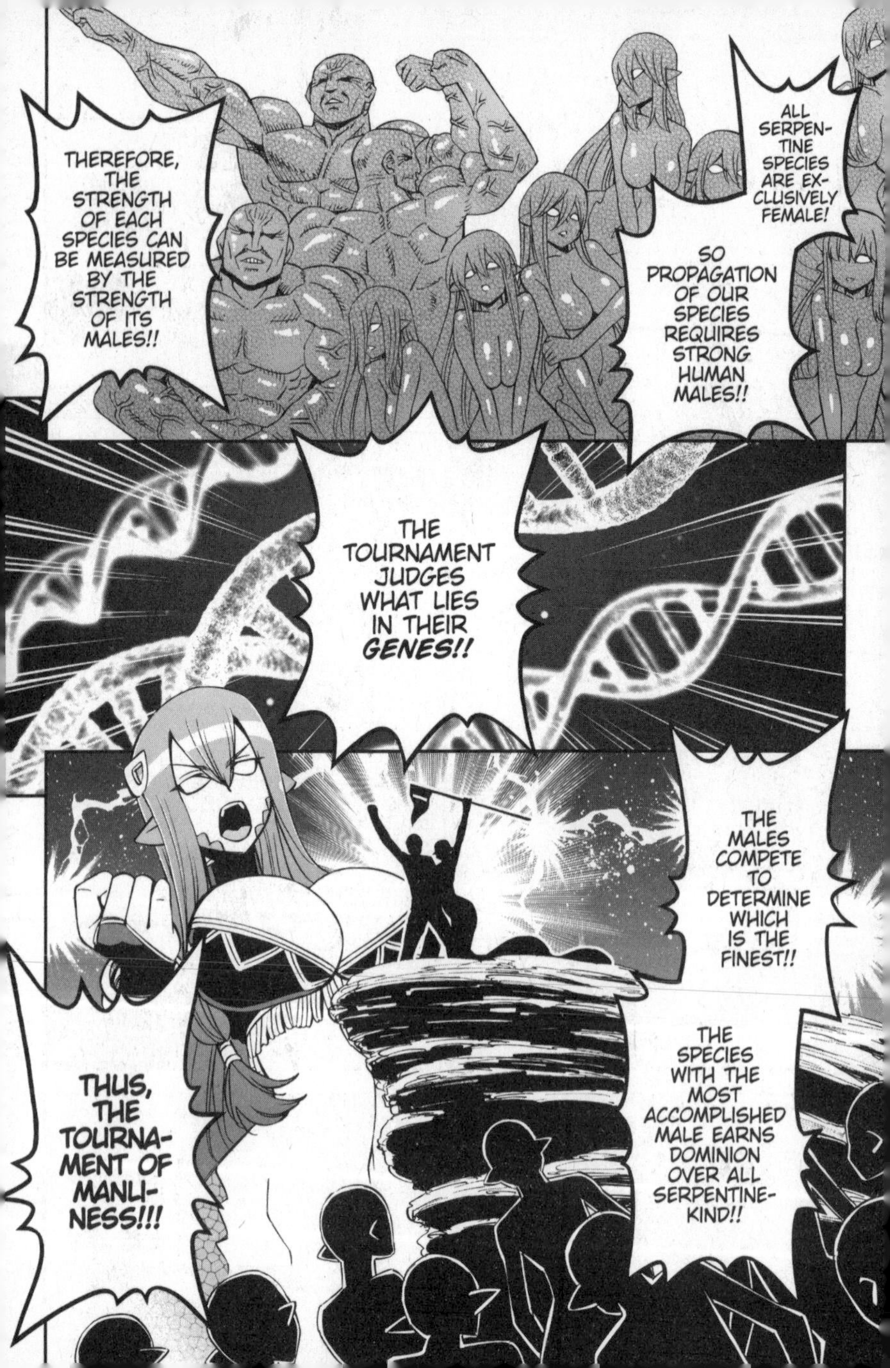

ALL SERPENTINE SPECIES ARE EXCLUSIVELY FEMALE!
SO PROPAGATION OF OUR SPECIES REQUIRES STRONG HUMAN MALES!!
THEREFORE, THE STRENGTH OF EACH SPECIES CAN BE MEASURED BY THE STRENGTH OF ITS MALES!!
THE TOURNAMENT JUDGES WHAT LIES IN THEIR *GENES!!*
THE MALES COMPETE TO DETERMINE WHICH IS THE FINEST!!
THE SPECIES WITH THE MOST ACCOMPLISHED MALE EARNS DOMINION OVER ALL SERPENTINE-KIND!!
THUS, THE TOURNAMENT OF MANLINESS!!!

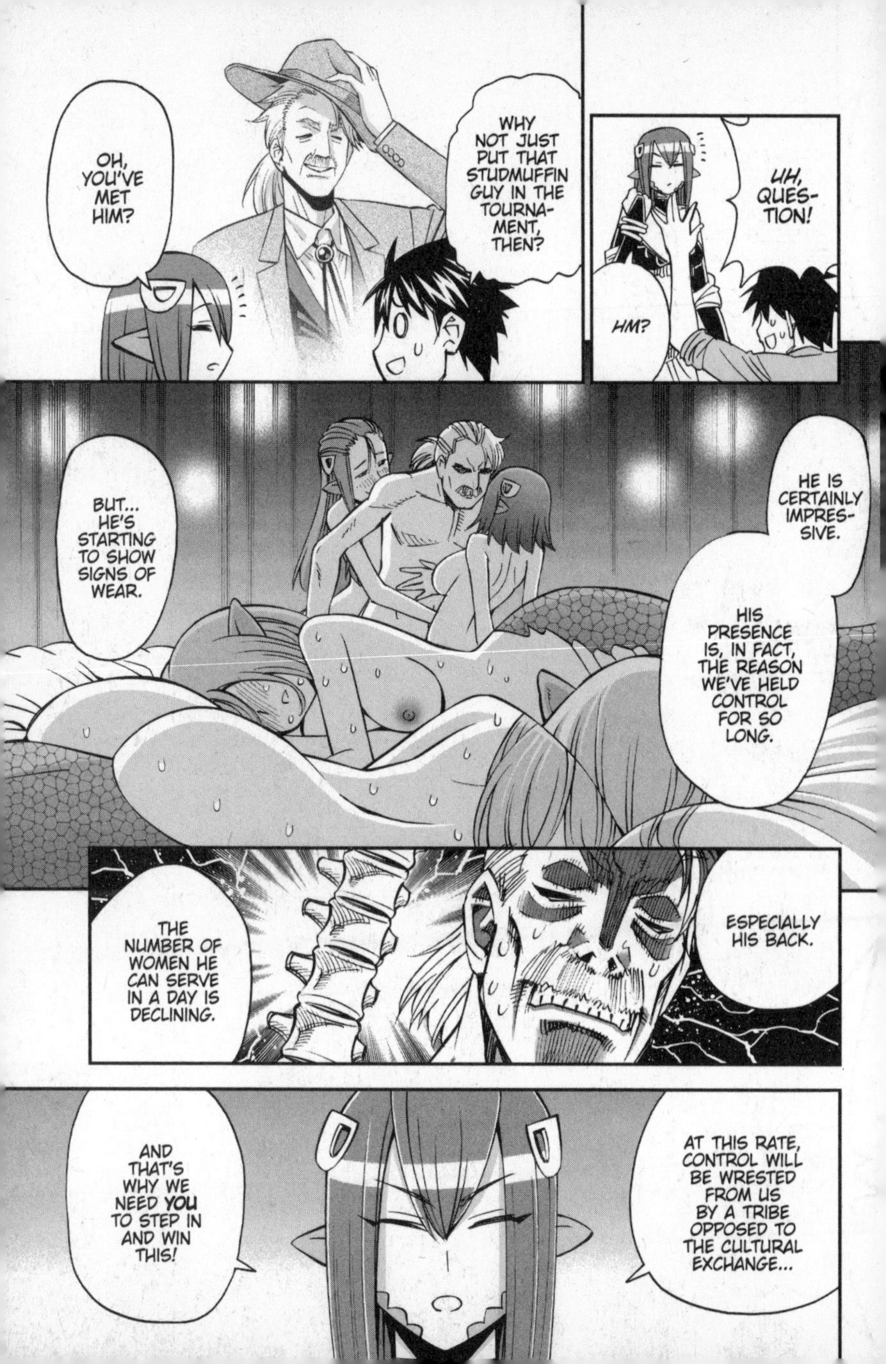
UH, QUESTION!
HM?
WHY NOT JUST PUT THAT STUDMUFFIN GUY IN THE TOURNAMENT, THEN?
OH, YOU'VE MET HIM?
HE IS CERTAINLY IMPRESSIVE.
HIS PRESENCE IS, IN FACT, THE REASON WE'VE HELD CONTROL FOR SO LONG.
BUT... HE'S STARTING TO SHOW SIGNS OF WEAR.
ESPECIALLY HIS BACK.
THE NUMBER OF WOMEN HE CAN SERVE IN A DAY IS DECLINING.
AT THIS RATE, CONTROL WILL BE WRESTED FROM US BY A TRIBE OPPOSED TO THE CULTURAL EXCHANGE...
AND THAT'S WHY WE NEED **YOU** TO STEP IN AND WIN THIS!

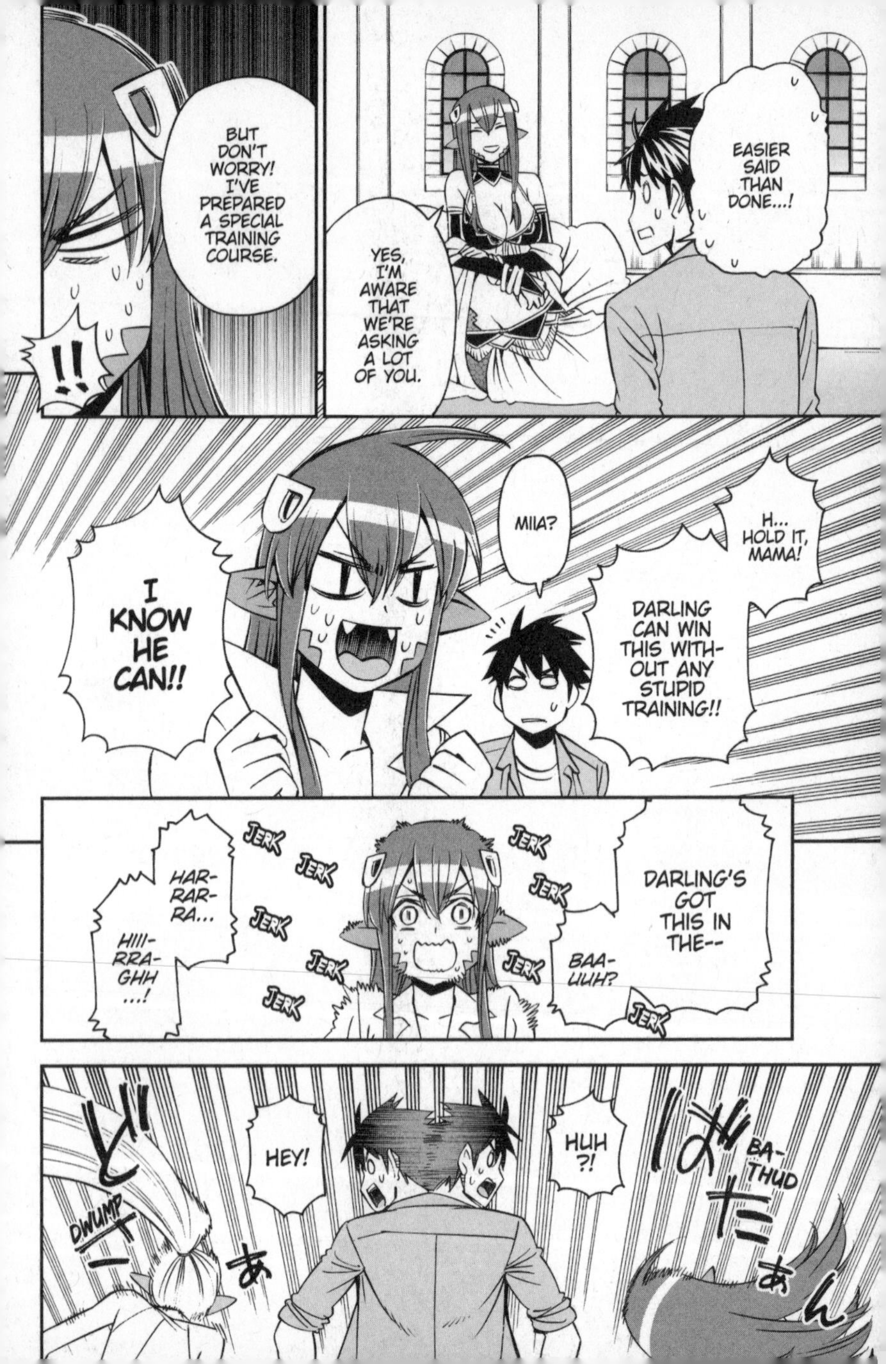
EASIER SAID THAN DONE...!
YES, I'M AWARE THAT WE'RE ASKING A LOT OF YOU.
BUT DON'T WORRY! I'VE PREPARED A SPECIAL TRAINING COURSE.
!!
H... HOLD IT, MAMA!
MIIA?
DARLING CAN WIN THIS WITH-OUT ANY STUPID TRAINING!!
I KNOW HE CAN!!
DARLING'S GOT THIS IN THE--
BAA-UUH?
JERK
JERK
JERK
JERK
JERK
JERK
JERK
JERK
JERK
HAR-RAR-RA...
HIII-RRA-GHH...!
BA-THUD
HUH ?!
HEY!
DWUMP

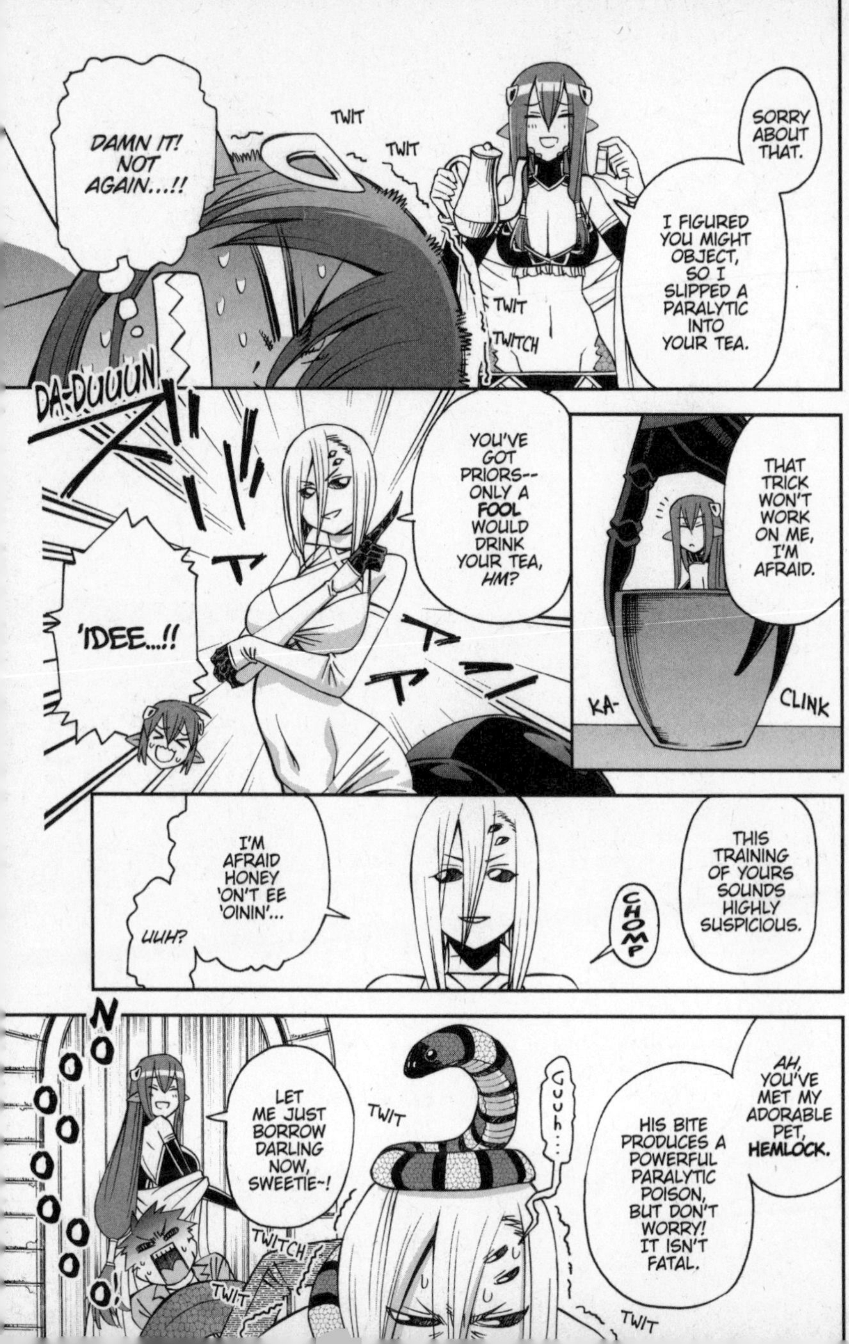
SORRY ABOUT THAT.
I FIGURED YOU MIGHT OBJECT, SO I SLIPPED A PARALYTIC INTO YOUR TEA.
TWIT
TWIT
TWIT
TWITCH
DAMN IT! NOT AGAIN...!!
THAT TRICK WON'T WORK ON ME, I'M AFRAID.
KA-
CLINK
DA-DUUUN
YOU'VE GOT PRIORS--ONLY A **FOOL** WOULD DRINK YOUR TEA, *HM?*
'IDEE...!!
THIS TRAINING OF YOURS SOUNDS HIGHLY SUSPICIOUS.
CHOMP
I'M AFRAID HONEY 'ON'T EE 'OININ'...
UUH?
AH, YOU'VE MET MY ADORABLE PET, **HEMLOCK.**
HIS BITE PRODUCES A POWERFUL PARALYTIC POISON, BUT DON'T WORRY! IT ISN'T FATAL.
Guuh...
TWIT
TWIT
LET ME JUST BORROW DARLING NOW, SWEETIE~!
TWITCH
TWIT
NOOOOOOOOOO!

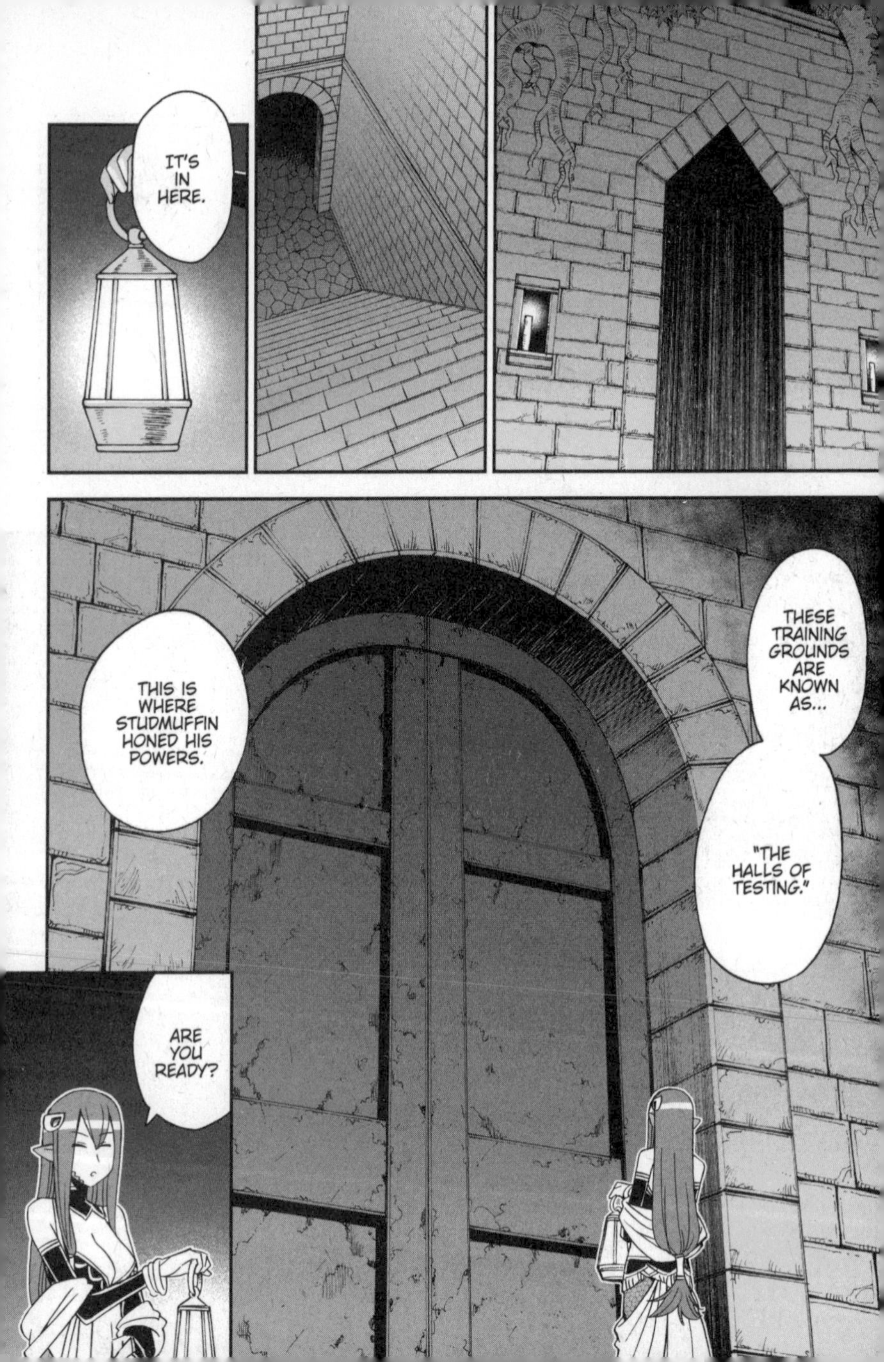
IT'S IN HERE.
THESE TRAINING GROUNDS ARE KNOWN AS...
"THE HALLS OF TESTING."
THIS IS WHERE STUDMUFFIN HONED HIS POWERS.
ARE YOU READY?

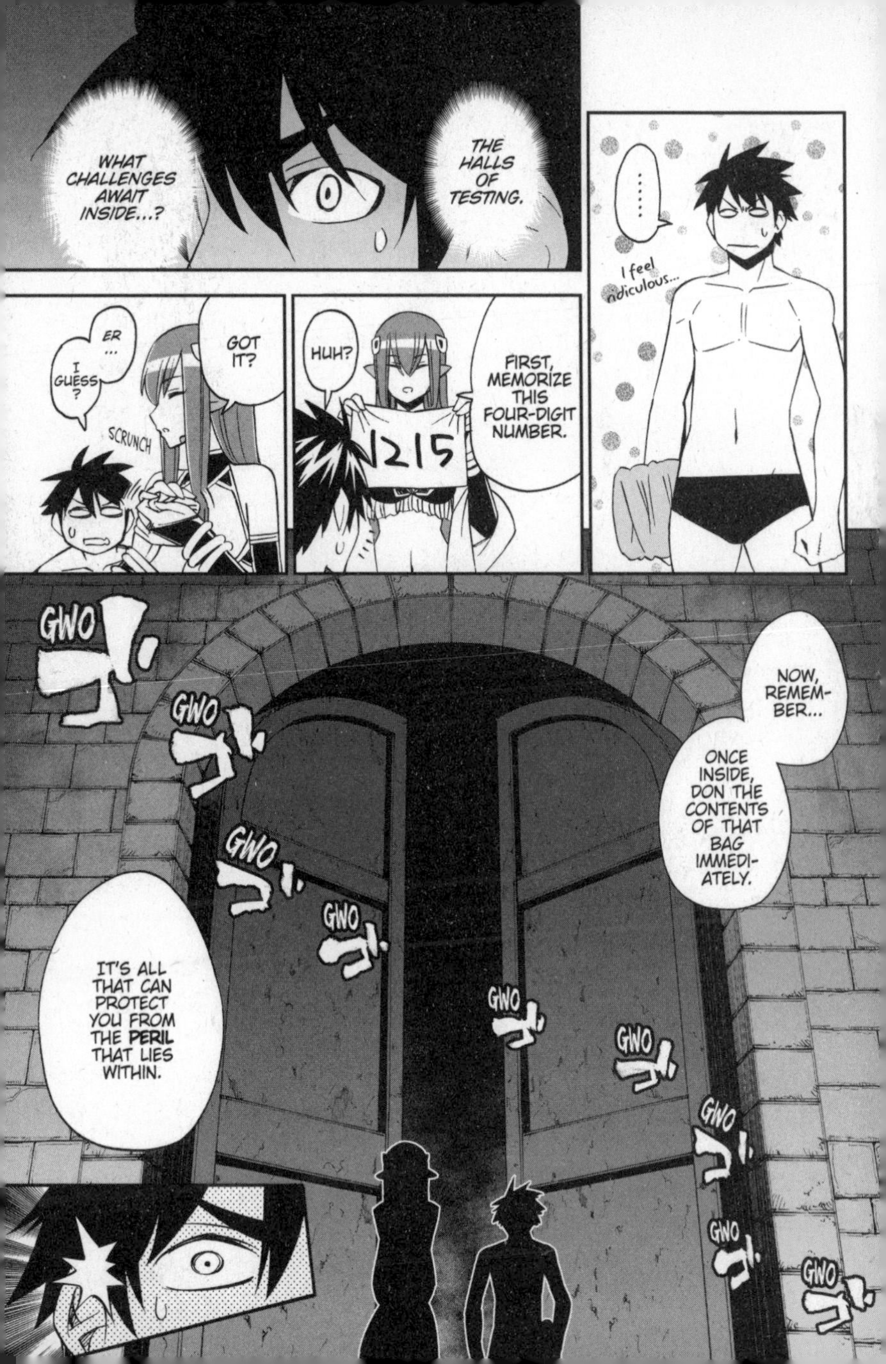

......
I feel ridiculous...
THE HALLS OF TESTING.
WHAT CHALLENGES AWAIT INSIDE...?
FIRST, MEMORIZE THIS FOUR-DIGIT NUMBER.
1215
HUH?
GOT IT?
ER... I GUESS?
SCRUNCH
NOW, REMEMBER...
ONCE INSIDE, DON THE CONTENTS OF THAT BAG IMMEDIATELY.
GWO
GWO
GWO
GWO
GWO
GWO
GWO
GWO
GWO
IT'S ALL THAT CAN PROTECT YOU FROM THE **PERIL** THAT LIES WITHIN.

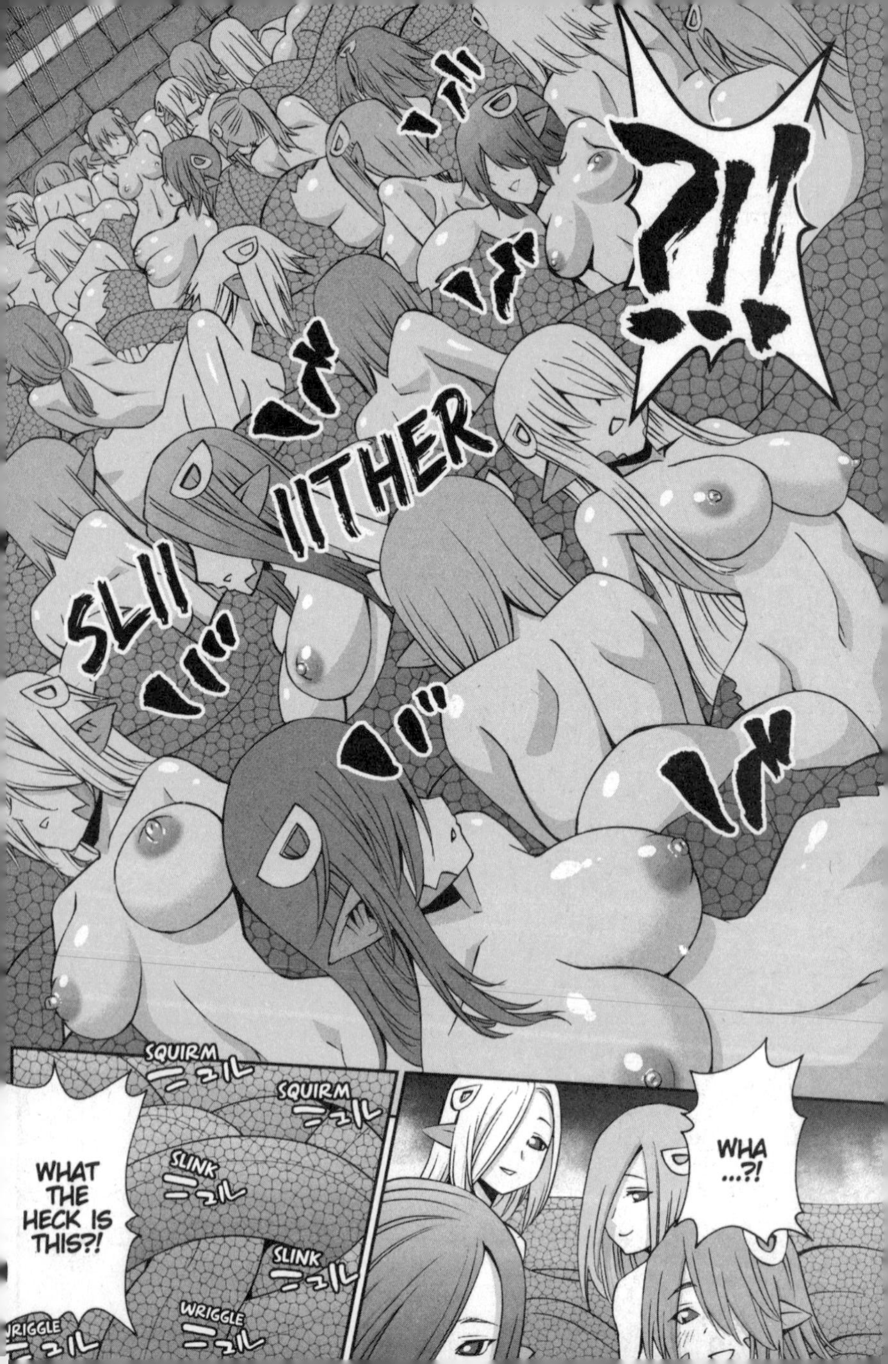

?!!
SLII
ITHER
WHA ...?!
SQUIRM
ニュル
SQUIRM
ニュル
WHAT THE HECK IS THIS?!
SLINK
ニュル
SLINK
ニュル
WRIGGLE
ニュル
RIGGLE
ニュル

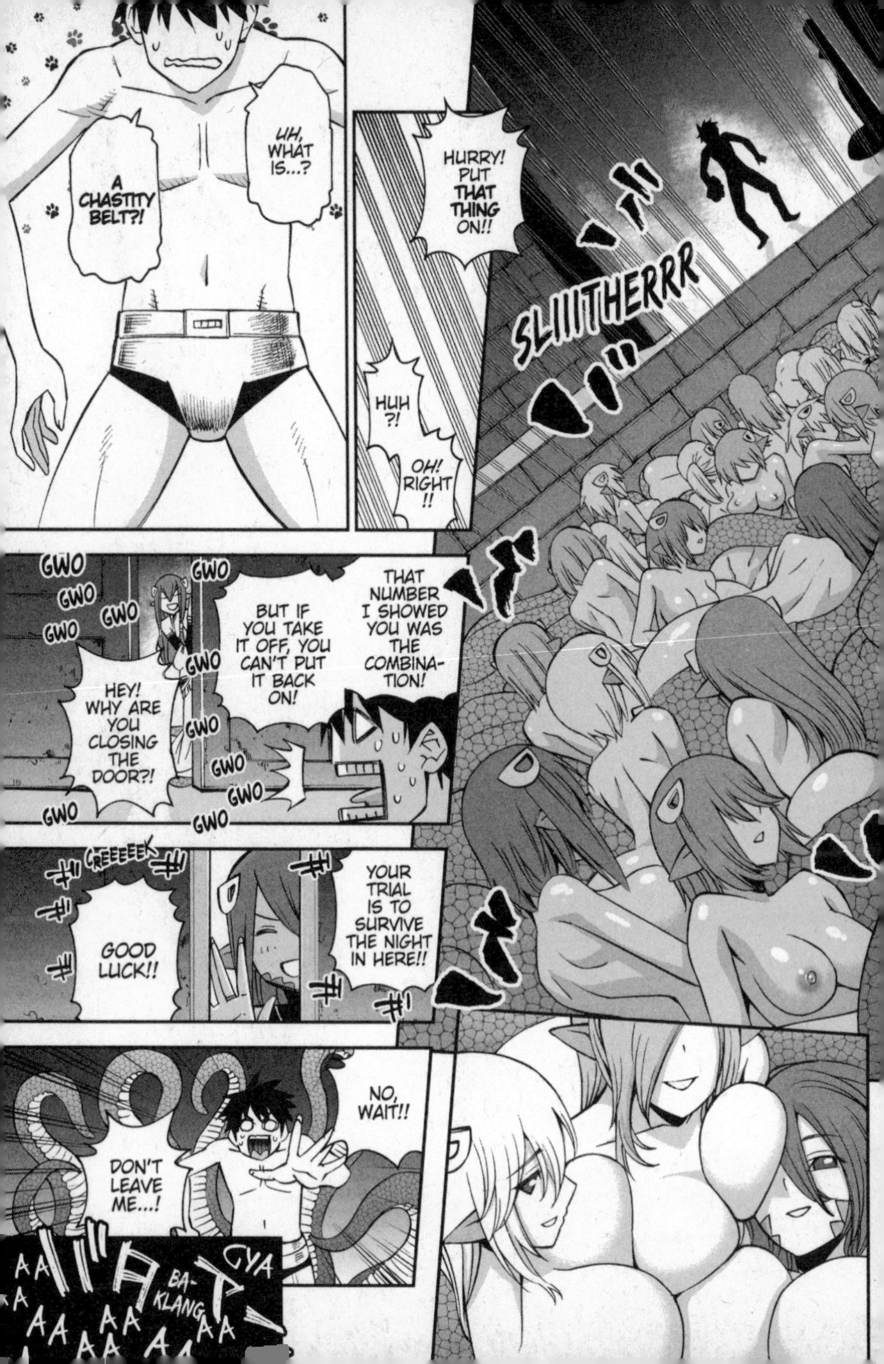
SLIIITHERRR
HURRY! PUT THAT THING ON!!
HUH?!
OH! RIGHT!!
UH, WHAT IS...?
A CHASTITY BELT?!
THAT NUMBER I SHOWED YOU WAS THE COMBINATION!
BUT IF YOU TAKE IT OFF, YOU CAN'T PUT IT BACK ON!
HEY! WHY ARE YOU CLOSING THE DOOR?!
GWO GWO GWO GWO GWO GWO GWO GWO GWO GWO GWO
YOUR TRIAL IS TO SURVIVE THE NIGHT IN HERE!!
GOOD LUCK!!
CREEEEEK
NO, WAIT!!
DON'T LEAVE ME...!
GYA
BA-KLANG
AAAAAAAAAAA

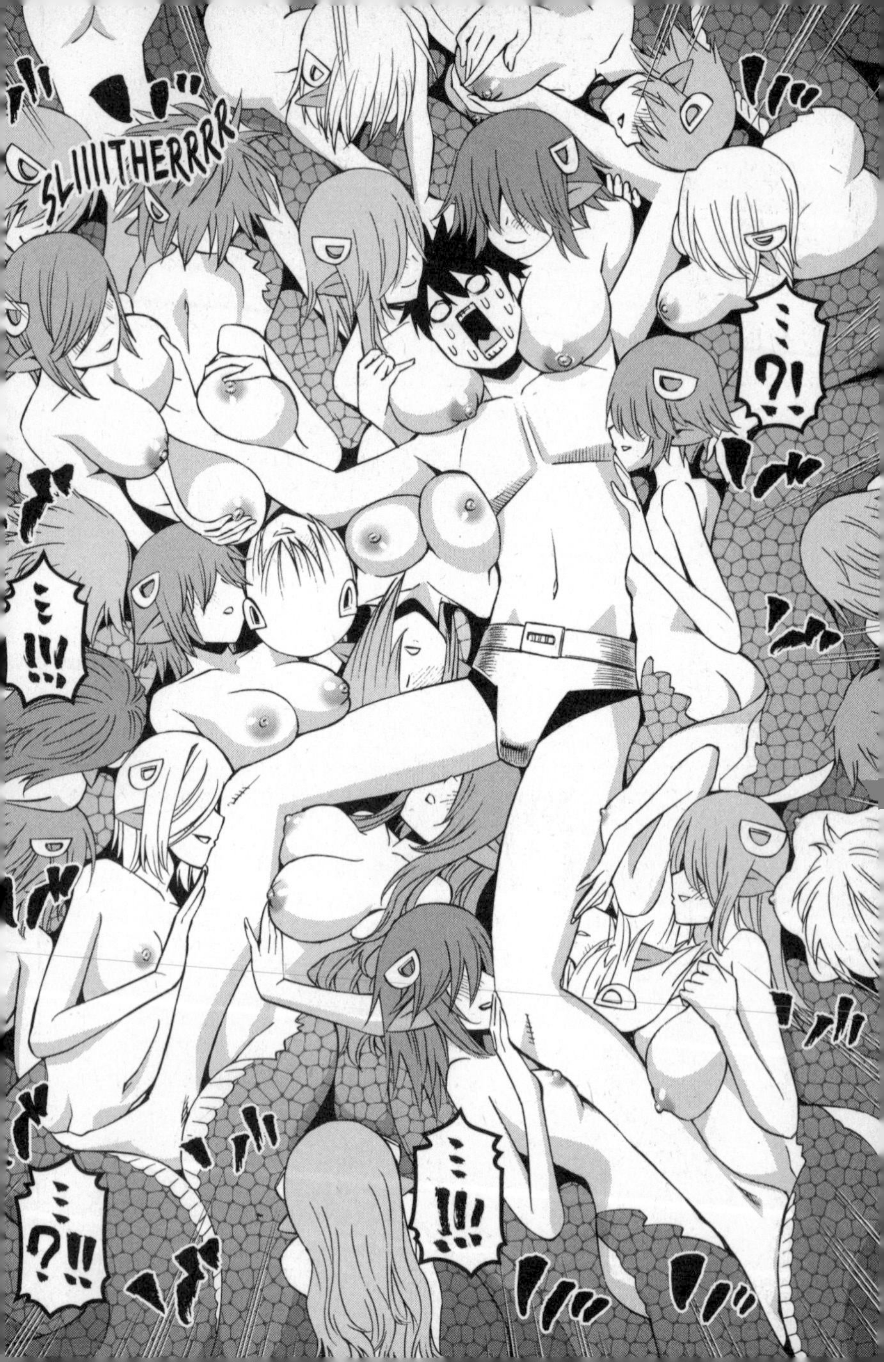
SLIIIITHERRRR
ミ?!
ミ!!!
ミ!!!
ミ?!!

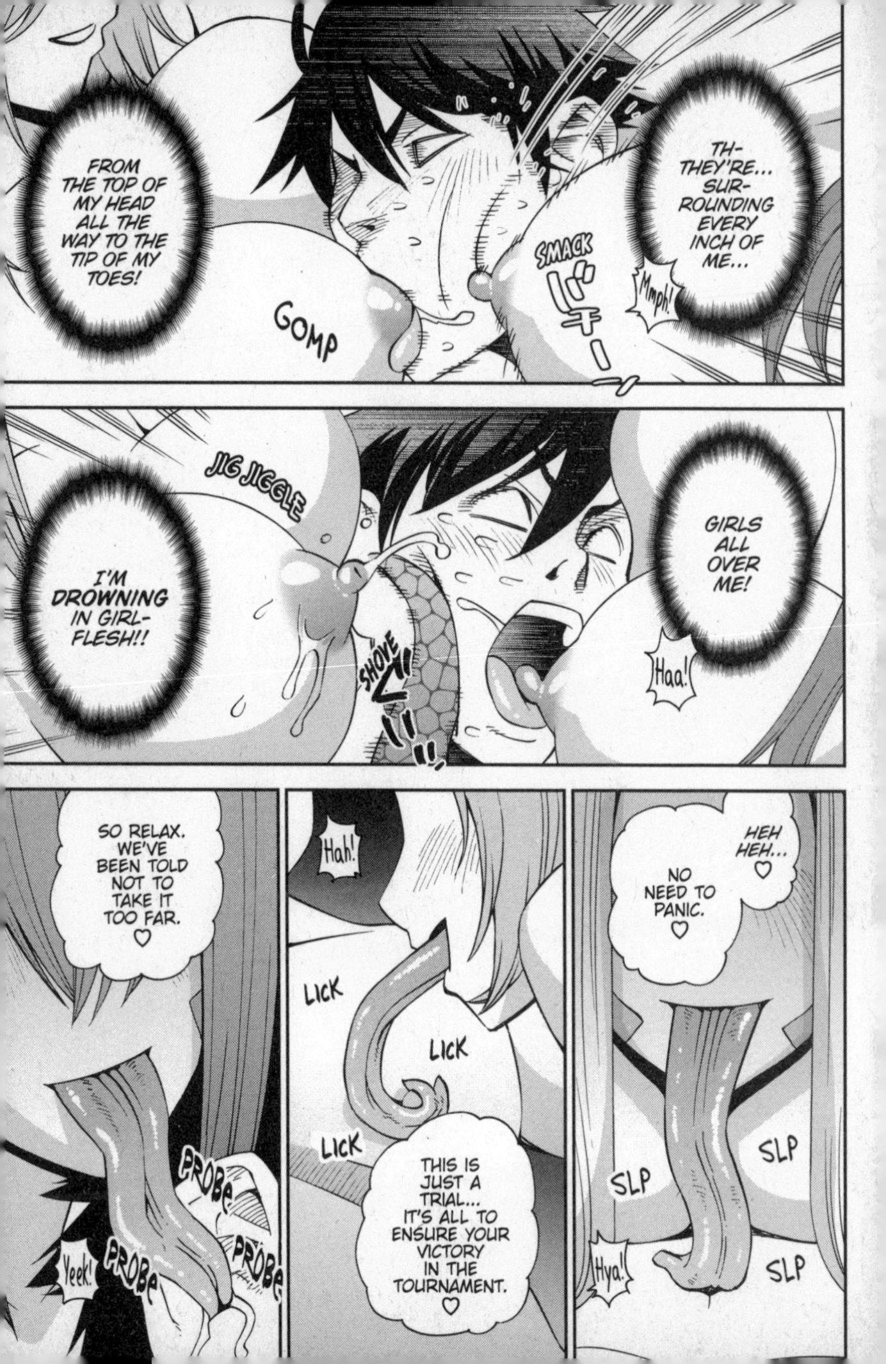
TH- THEY'RE... SUR-ROUNDING EVERY INCH OF ME...
SMACK
Mmph!
FROM THE TOP OF MY HEAD ALL THE WAY TO THE TIP OF MY TOES!
GOMP
GIRLS ALL OVER ME!
Haa!
JIG JIGGLE
I'M DROWNING IN GIRL-FLESH!!
SHOVE
HEH HEH... ♡
NO NEED TO PANIC. ♡
SLP
SLP
Hya!
SLP
Hah!
LICK
LICK
LICK
THIS IS JUST A TRIAL... IT'S ALL TO ENSURE YOUR VICTORY IN THE TOURNAMENT. ♡
SO RELAX. WE'VE BEEN TOLD NOT TO TAKE IT TOO FAR. ♡
PROBE
PROBE
Yeek!
PROBE

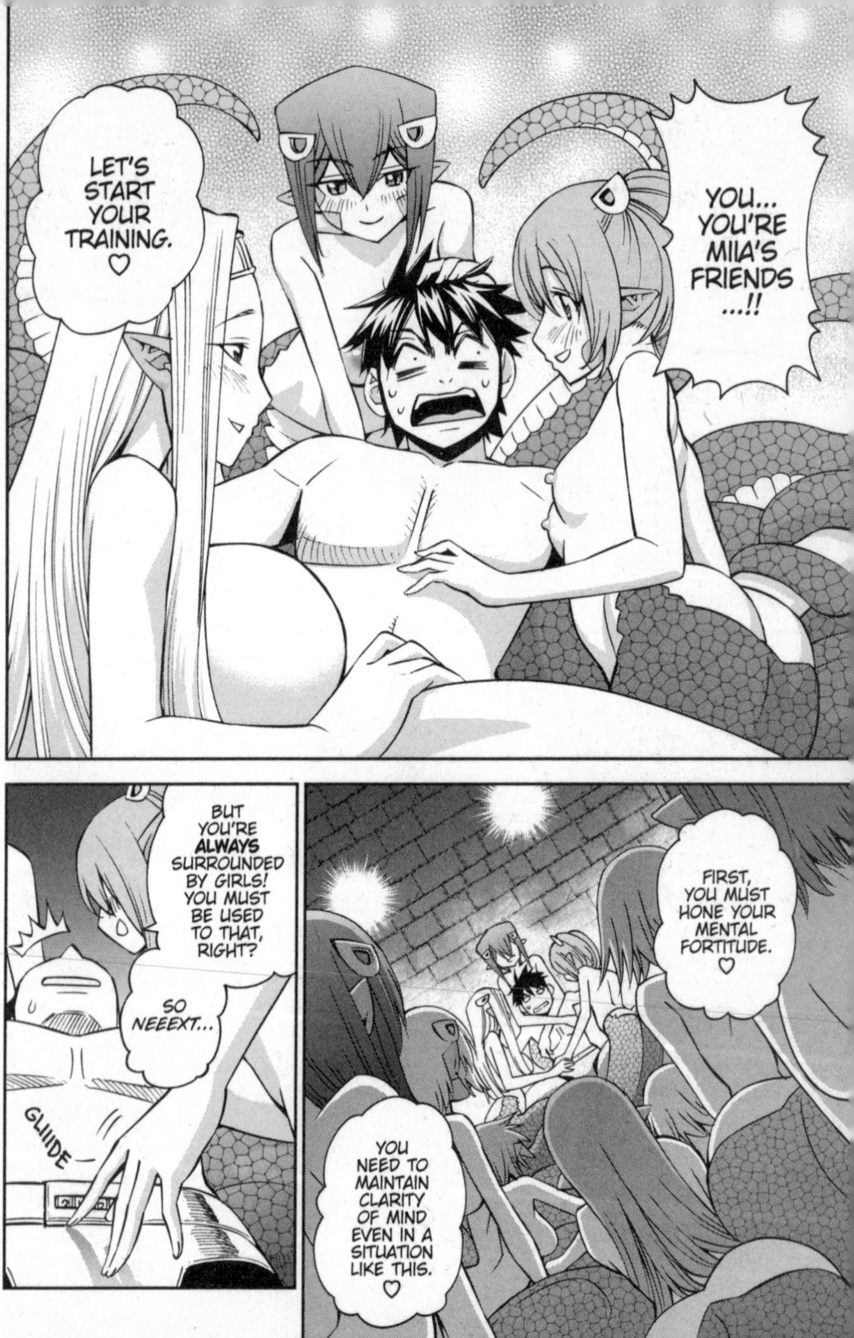
YOU... YOU'RE MIIA'S FRIENDS ...!!
LET'S START YOUR TRAINING. ♡
FIRST, YOU MUST HONE YOUR MENTAL FORTITUDE. ♡
YOU NEED TO MAINTAIN CLARITY OF MIND EVEN IN A SITUATION LIKE THIS. ♡
BUT YOU'RE **ALWAYS** SURROUNDED BY GIRLS! YOU MUST BE USED TO THAT, RIGHT?
SO NEEEXT...
GLIIIDE

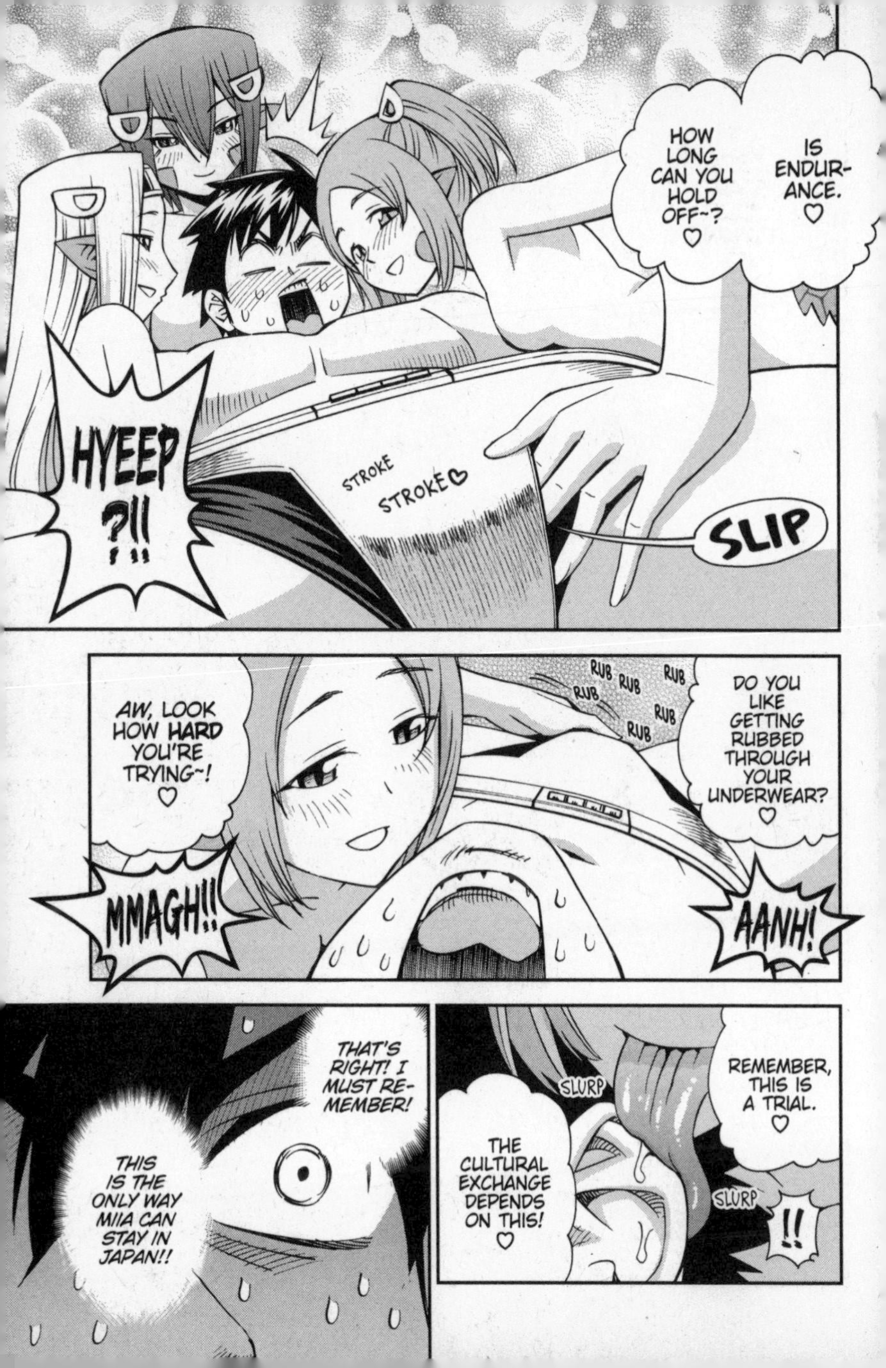
IS ENDURANCE. ♡
HOW LONG CAN YOU HOLD OFF~? ♡
SLIP
STROKE STROKE♡
HYEEP?!!
DO YOU LIKE GETTING RUBBED THROUGH YOUR UNDERWEAR? ♡
RUB RUB RUB RUB RUB RUB
AANH!
AW, LOOK HOW **HARD** YOU'RE TRYING~! ♡
MMAGH!!
REMEMBER, THIS IS A TRIAL. ♡
SLURP
SLURP
!!
THE CULTURAL EXCHANGE DEPENDS ON THIS! ♡
THAT'S RIGHT! I MUST REMEMBER!
THIS IS THE ONLY WAY MIIA CAN STAY IN JAPAN!!

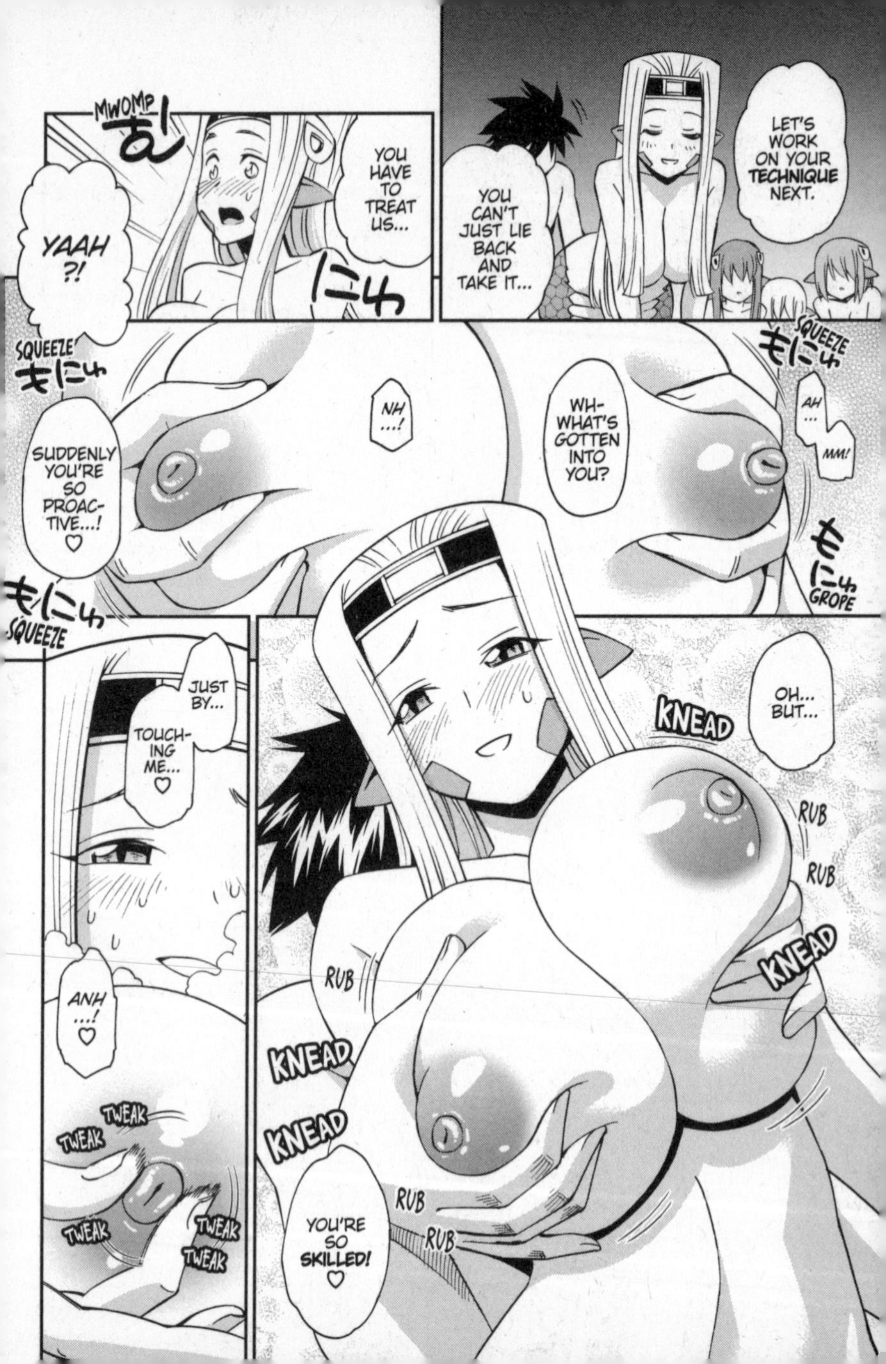
LET'S WORK ON YOUR TECHNIQUE NEXT.
YOU CAN'T JUST LIE BACK AND TAKE IT...
YOU HAVE TO TREAT US...
にゅ
MWOMP
YAAH?!
SQUEEZE もにゅ
AH... MM!
WH-WHAT'S GOTTEN INTO YOU?
NH...!
SUDDENLY YOU'RE SO PROACTIVE...! ♡
もにゅ GROPE
もにゅ SQUEEZE
OH... BUT...
KNEAD
RUB
RUB
KNEAD
RUB
KNEAD
KNEAD
RUB
RUB
YOU'RE SO SKILLED! ♡
JUST BY...
TOUCHING ME... ♡
ANH...! ♡
TWEAK
TWEAK
TWEAK
TWEAK
TWEAK

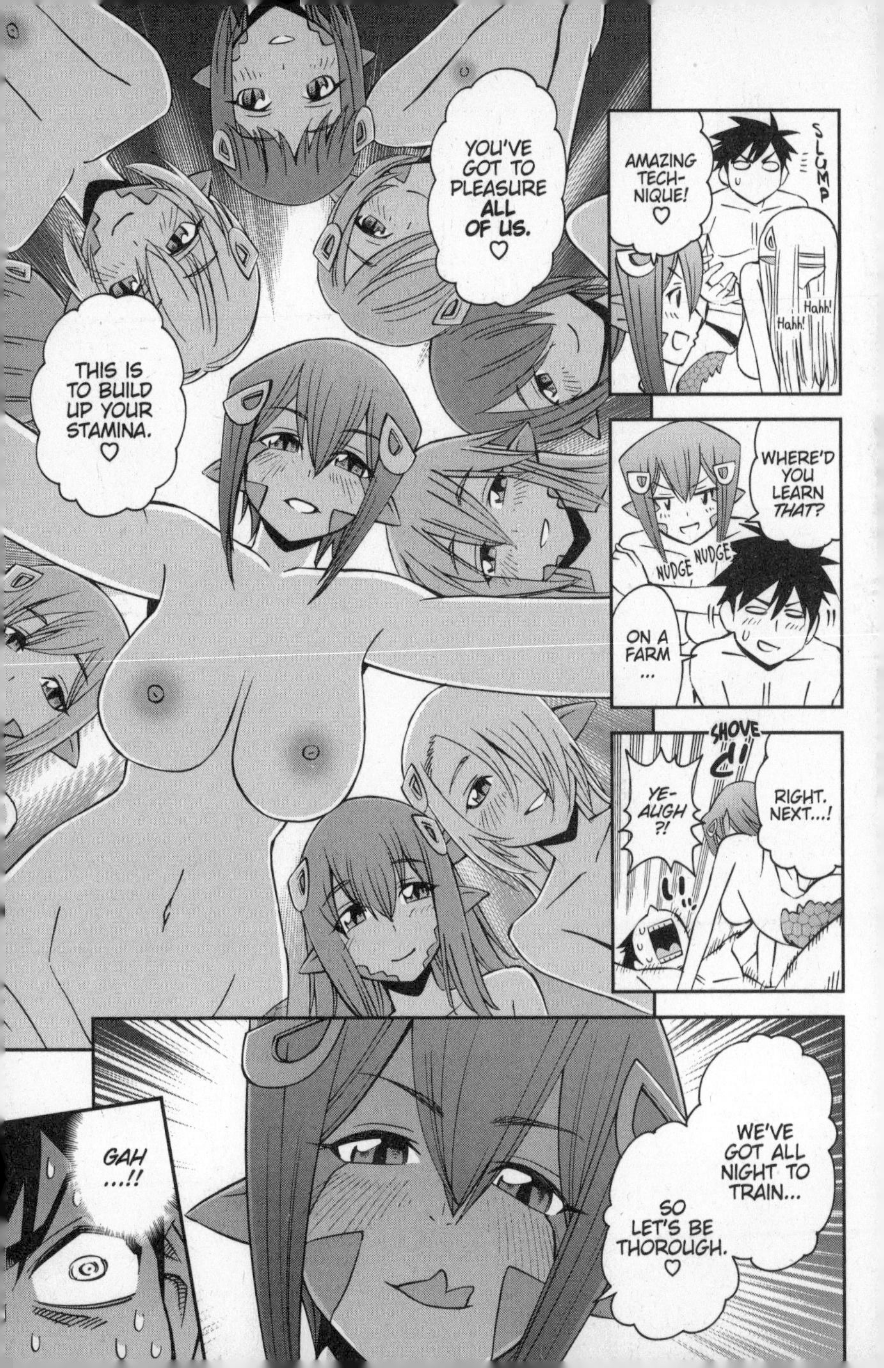
AMAZING TECH-NIQUE! ♡
SLUMP
Hahh!
Hahh!
WHERE'D YOU LEARN THAT?
NUDGE NUDGE
ON A FARM ...
RIGHT. NEXT...!
SHOVE
YE-AUGH ?!
YOU'VE GOT TO PLEASURE ALL OF US. ♡
THIS IS TO BUILD UP YOUR STAMINA. ♡
WE'VE GOT ALL NIGHT TO TRAIN...
SO LET'S BE THOROUGH. ♡
GAH ...!!

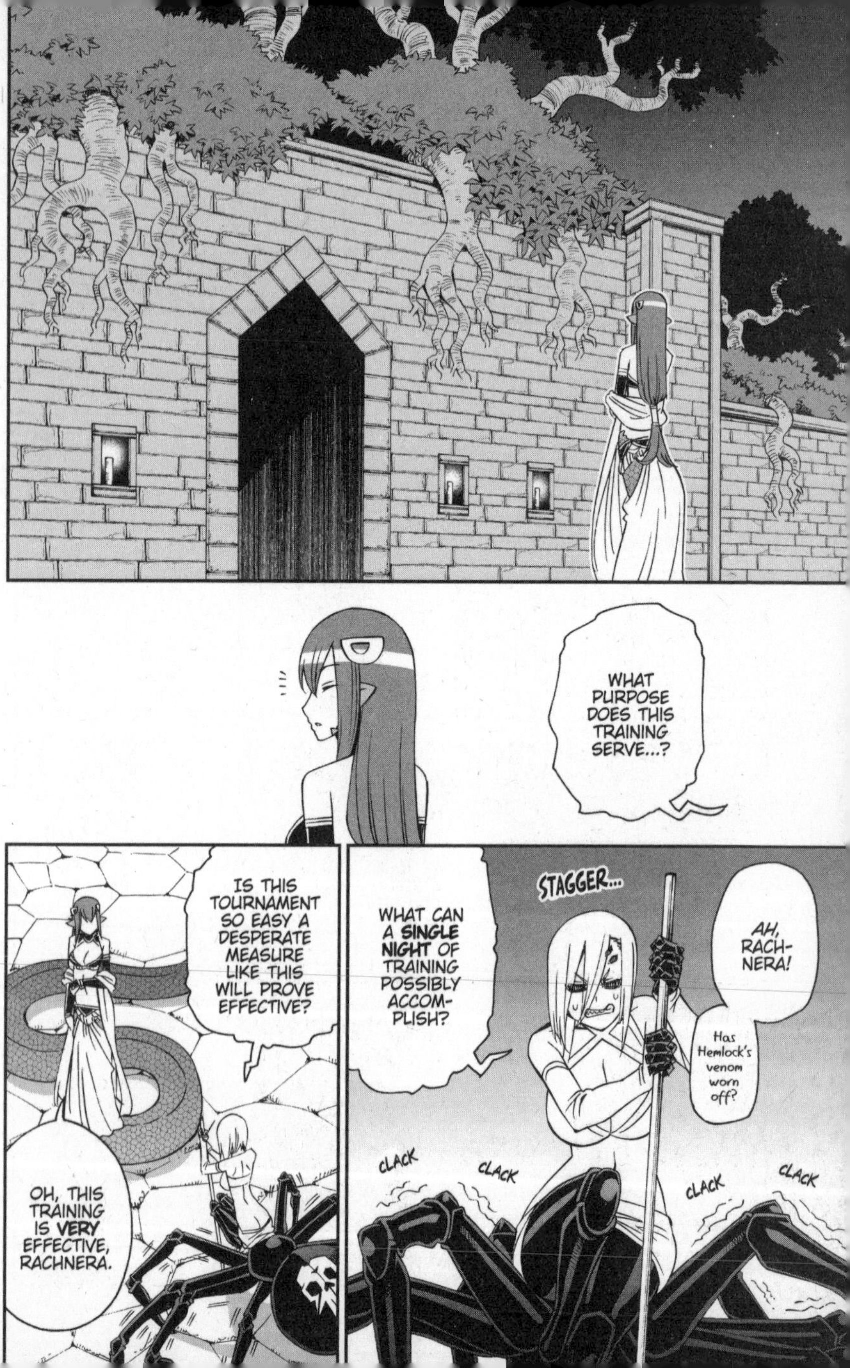
WHAT PURPOSE DOES THIS TRAINING SERVE...?
AH, RACHNERA!
Has Hemlock's venom worn off?
STAGGER...
WHAT CAN A SINGLE NIGHT OF TRAINING POSSIBLY ACCOMPLISH?
CLACK
CLACK
CLACK
CLACK
IS THIS TOURNAMENT SO EASY A DESPERATE MEASURE LIKE THIS WILL PROVE EFFECTIVE?
OH, THIS TRAINING IS VERY EFFECTIVE, RACHNERA.

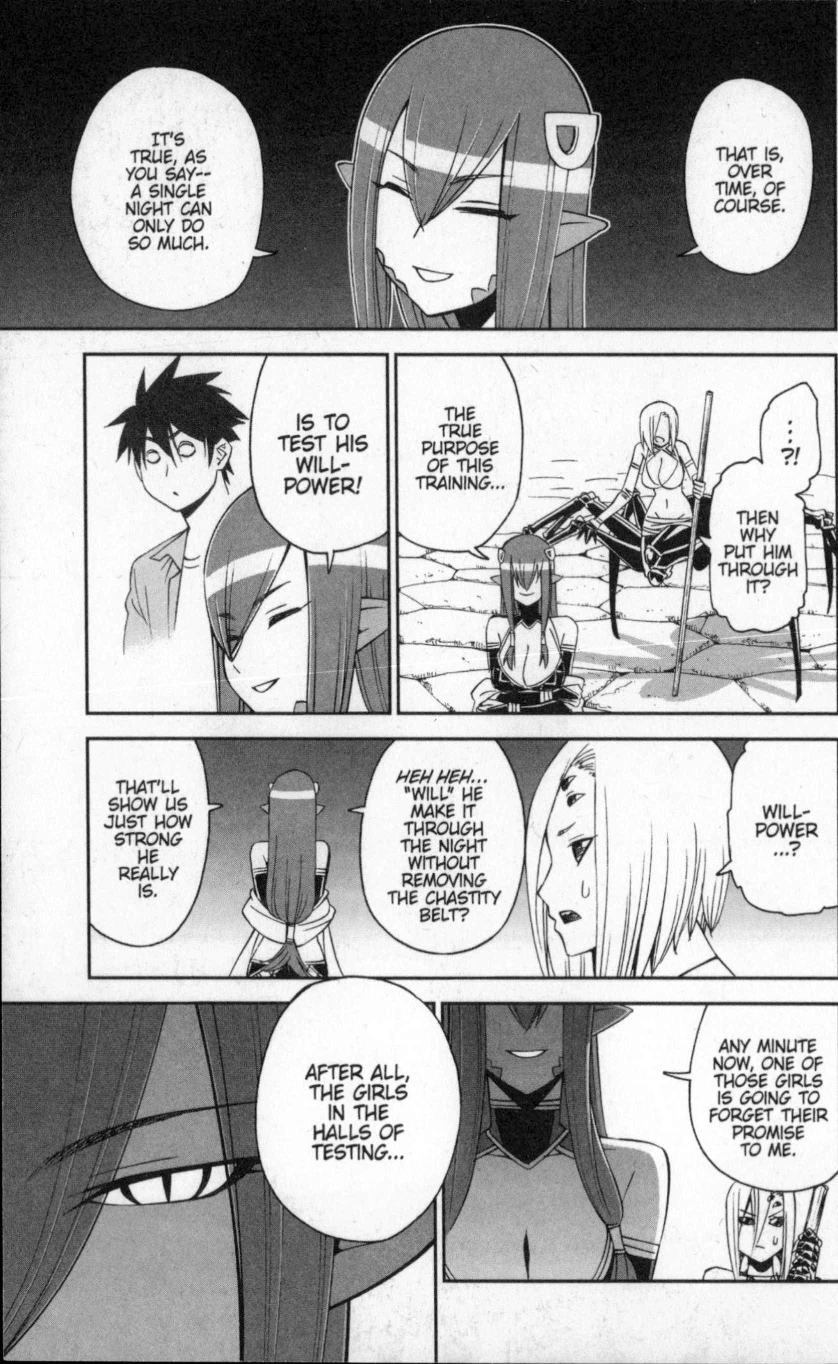
THAT IS, OVER TIME, OF COURSE.
IT'S TRUE, AS YOU SAY-- A SINGLE NIGHT CAN ONLY DO SO MUCH.
...?!
THEN WHY PUT HIM THROUGH IT?
THE TRUE PURPOSE OF THIS TRAINING...
IS TO TEST HIS WILL-POWER!
WILL-POWER ...?
HEH HEH... "WILL" HE MAKE IT THROUGH THE NIGHT WITHOUT REMOVING THE CHASTITY BELT?
THAT'LL SHOW US JUST HOW STRONG HE REALLY IS.
ANY MINUTE NOW, ONE OF THOSE GIRLS IS GOING TO FORGET THEIR PROMISE TO ME.
AFTER ALL, THE GIRLS IN THE HALLS OF TESTING...

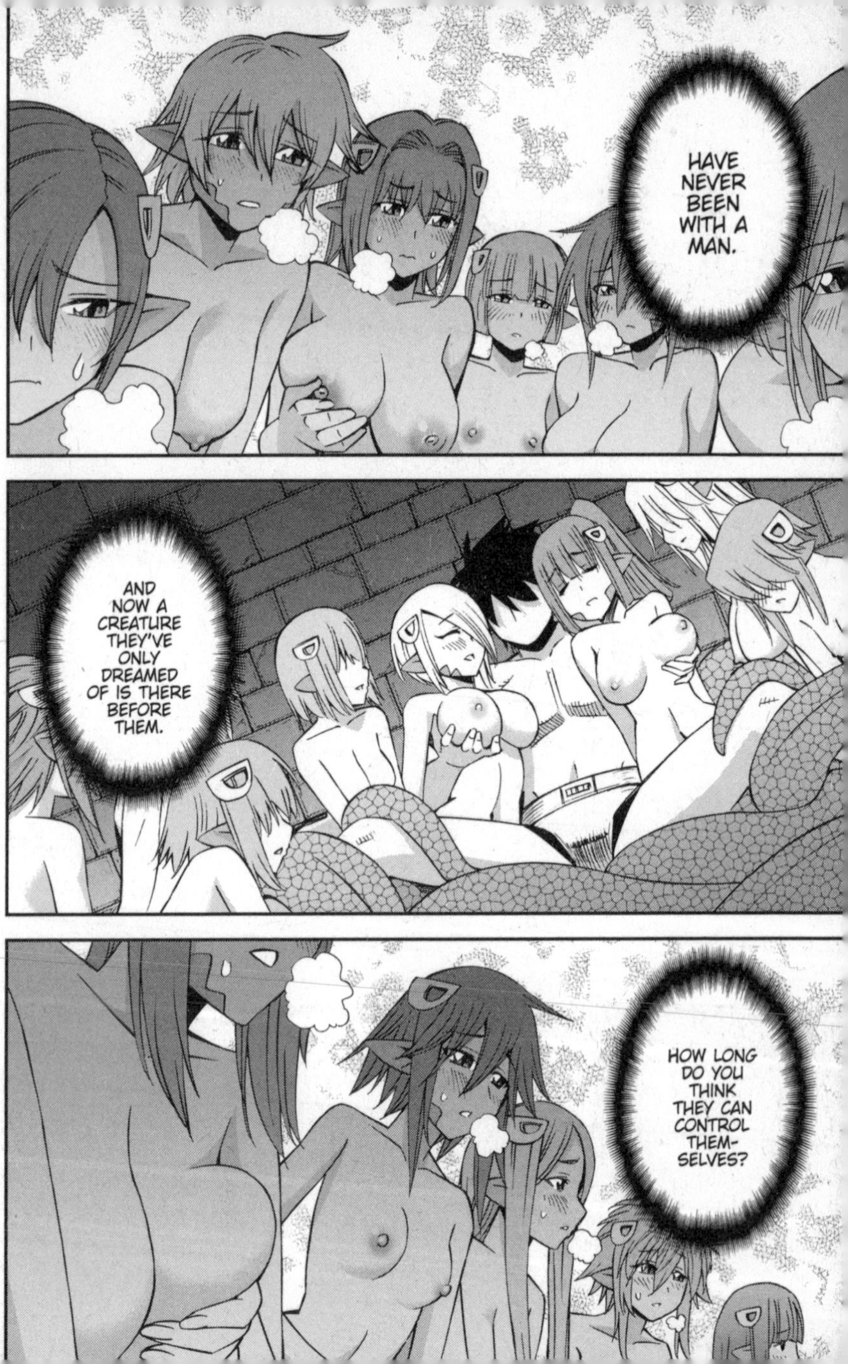
HAVE NEVER BEEN WITH A MAN.
AND NOW A CREATURE THEY'VE ONLY DREAMED OF IS THERE BEFORE THEM.
HOW LONG DO YOU THINK THEY CAN CONTROL THEM-SELVES?

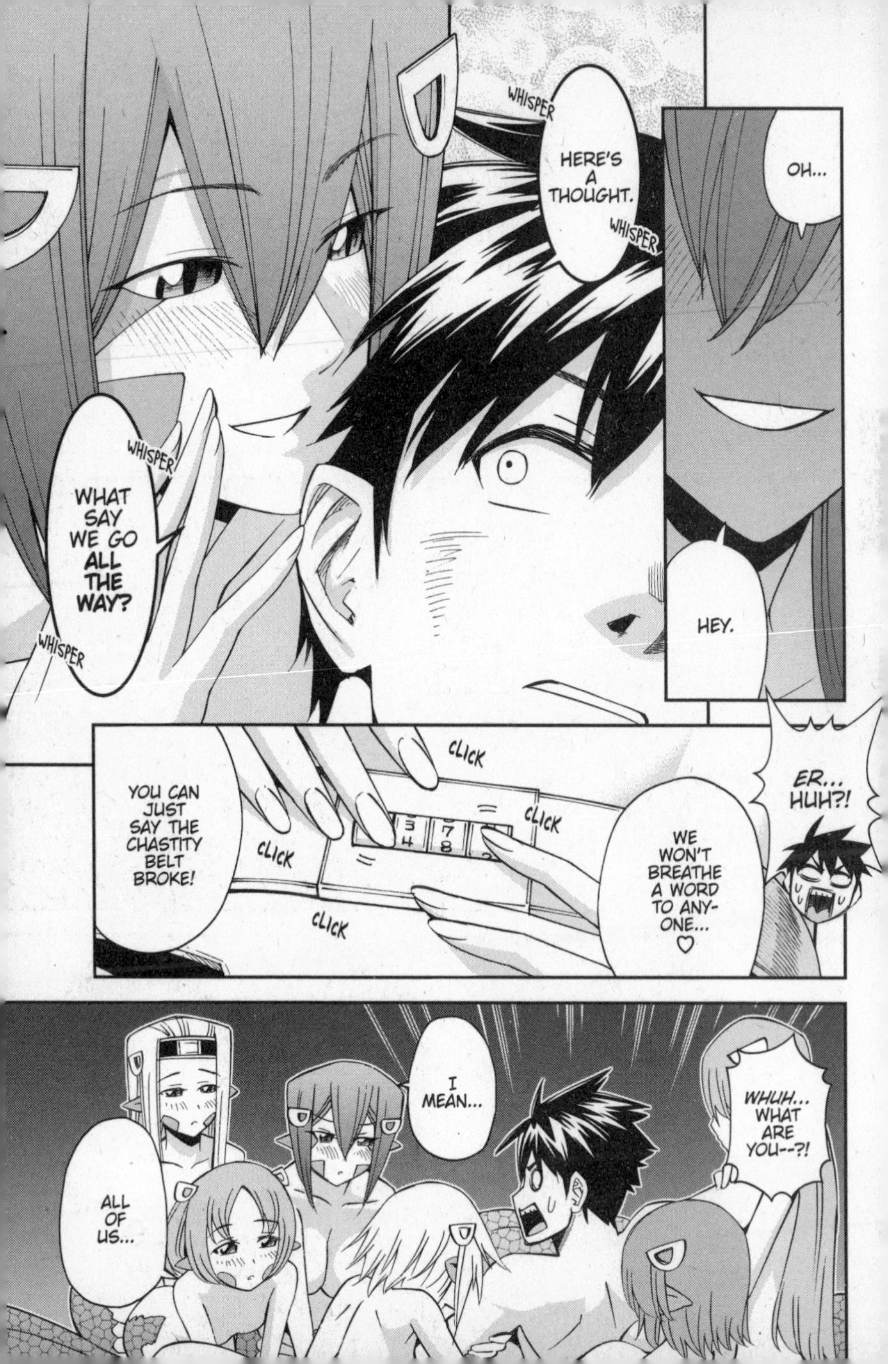
OH...
HEY.
WHISPER
HERE'S A THOUGHT.
WHISPER
WHISPER
WHAT SAY WE GO **ALL THE WAY?**
WHISPER
ER... HUH?!
WE WON'T BREATHE A WORD TO ANY-ONE... ♡
CLICK
CLICK
YOU CAN JUST SAY THE CHASTITY BELT BROKE!
CLICK
CLICK
WHUH... WHAT ARE YOU--?!
I MEAN...
ALL OF US...

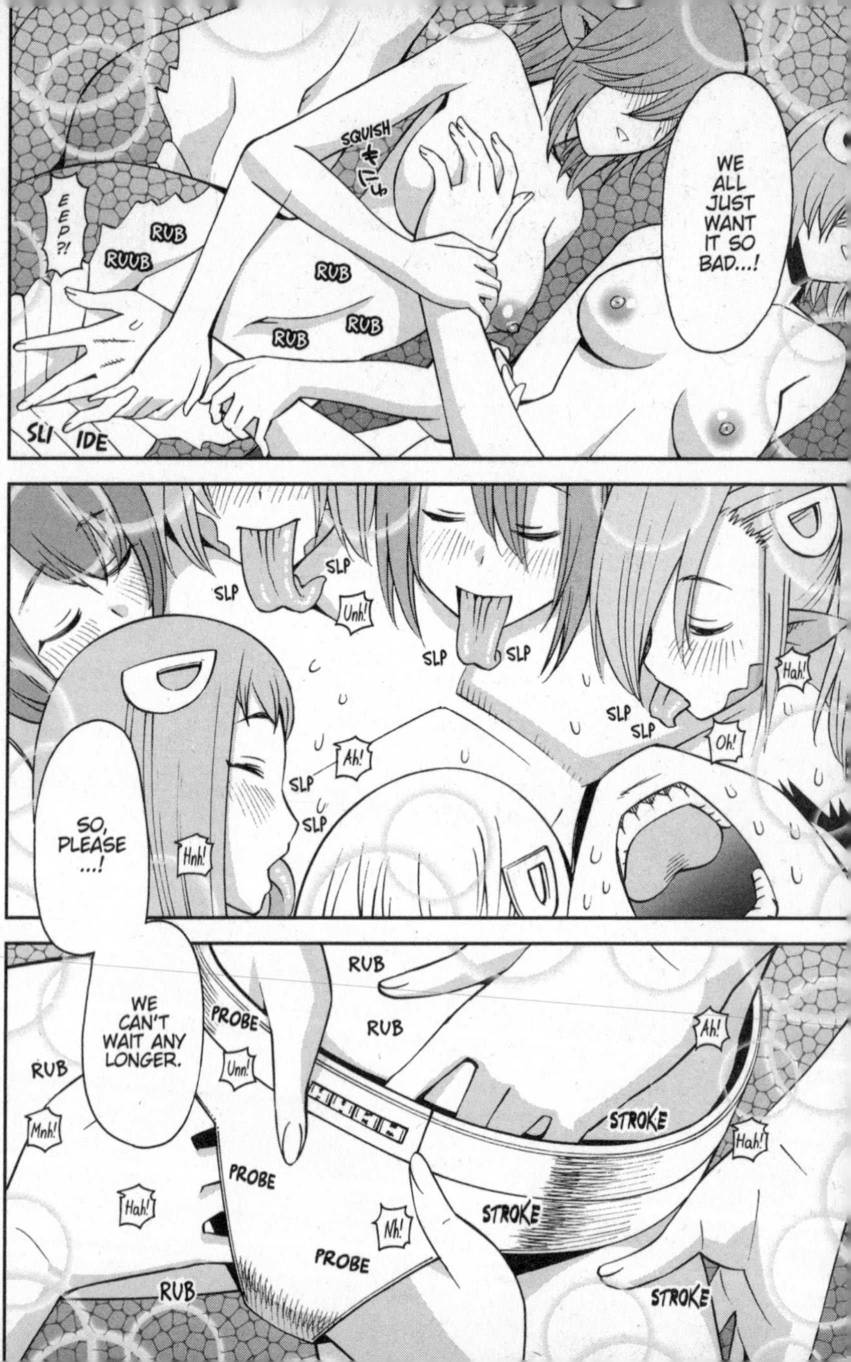
WE ALL JUST WANT IT SO BAD...!
SQUISH
RUB
EEP?!
RUUB
RUB
RUB
RUB
SLI IDE
Hah!
SLP
SLP
Unh!
SLP
SLP
SLP
SLP
Oh!
Ah!
SLP
SLP
Hnh!
SO, PLEASE ...!
Ah!
RUB
RUB
PROBE
WE CAN'T WAIT ANY LONGER.
Unn!
RUB
STROKE
Hah!
Mnh!
PROBE
STROKE
Nh!
Hah!
PROBE
STROKE
RUB

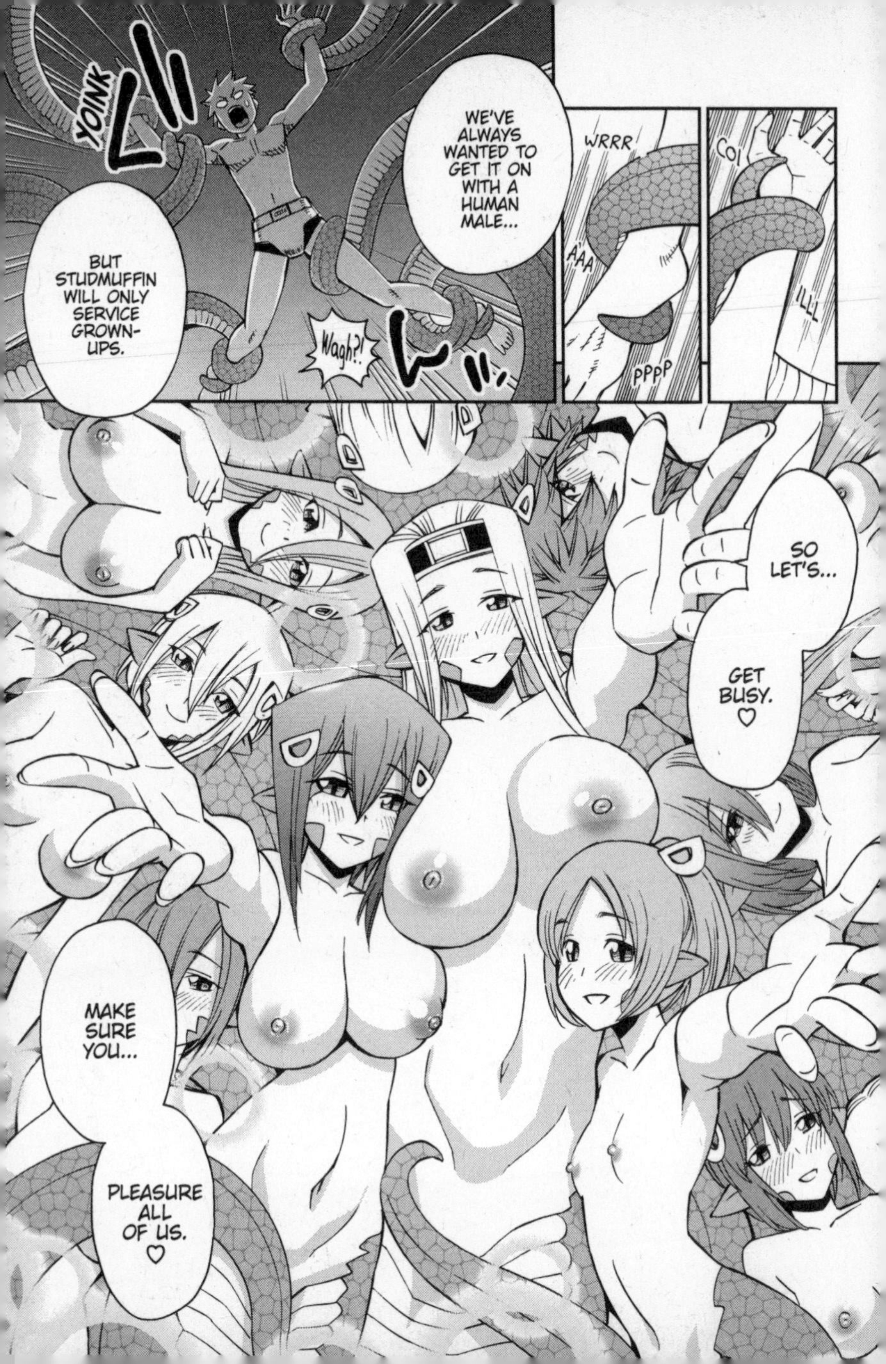
COI
ILLL
WRRR
AAA
PPPP
WE'VE ALWAYS WANTED TO GET IT ON WITH A HUMAN MALE...
YOINK
BUT STUDMUFFIN WILL ONLY SERVICE GROWN-UPS.
Wagh?!
SO LET'S...
GET BUSY. ♡
MAKE SURE YOU...
PLEASURE ALL OF US. ♡

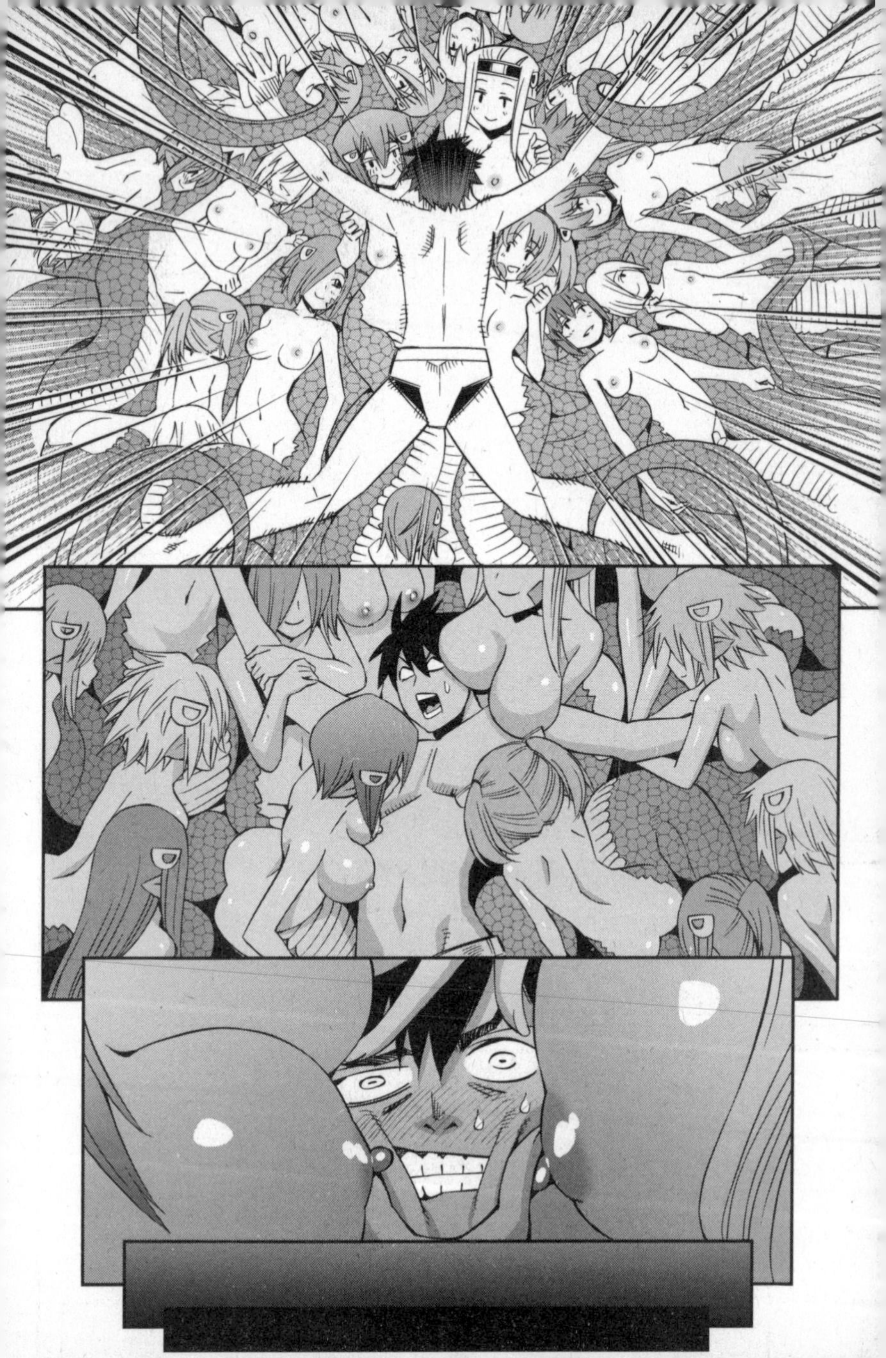

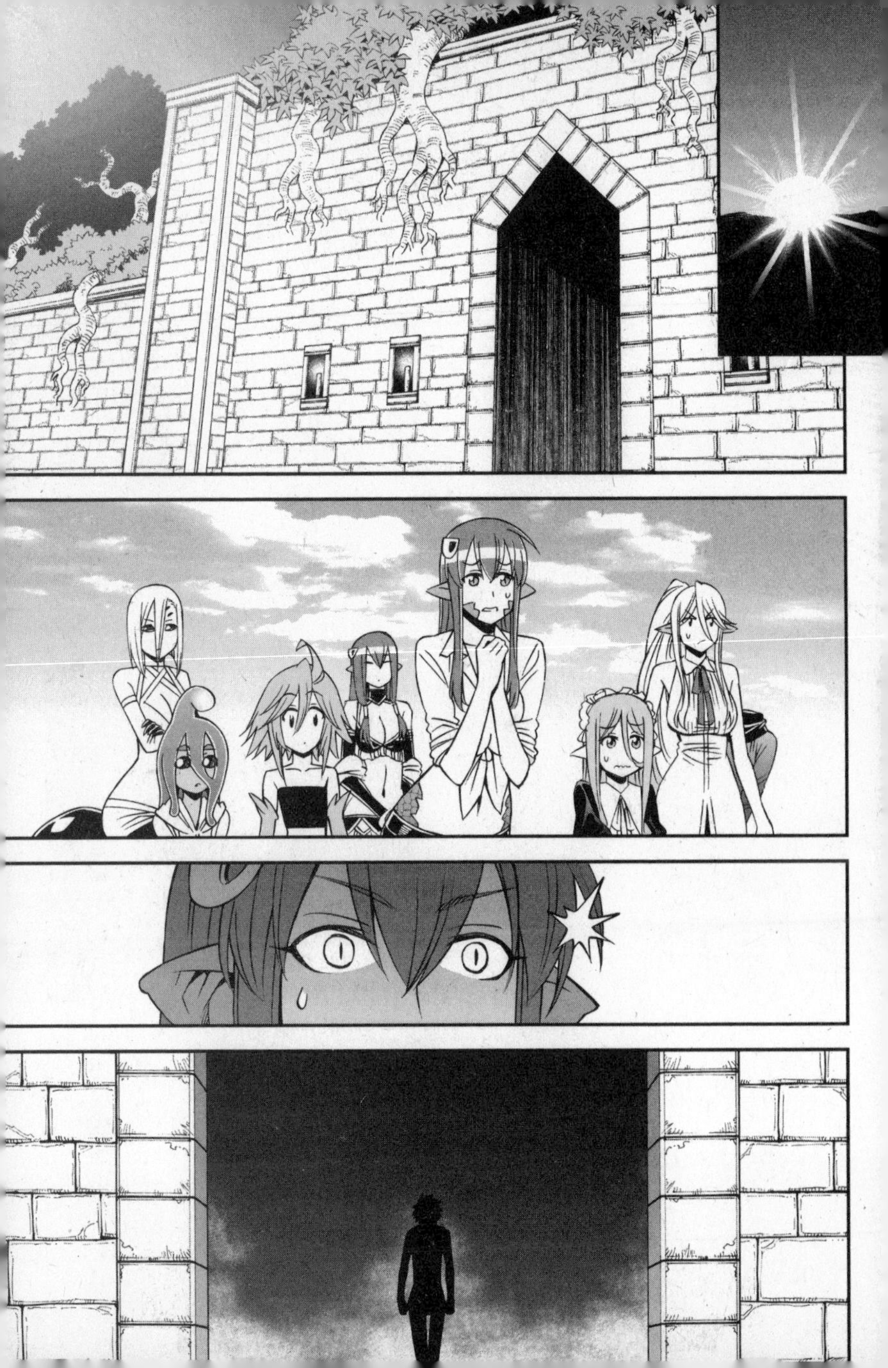

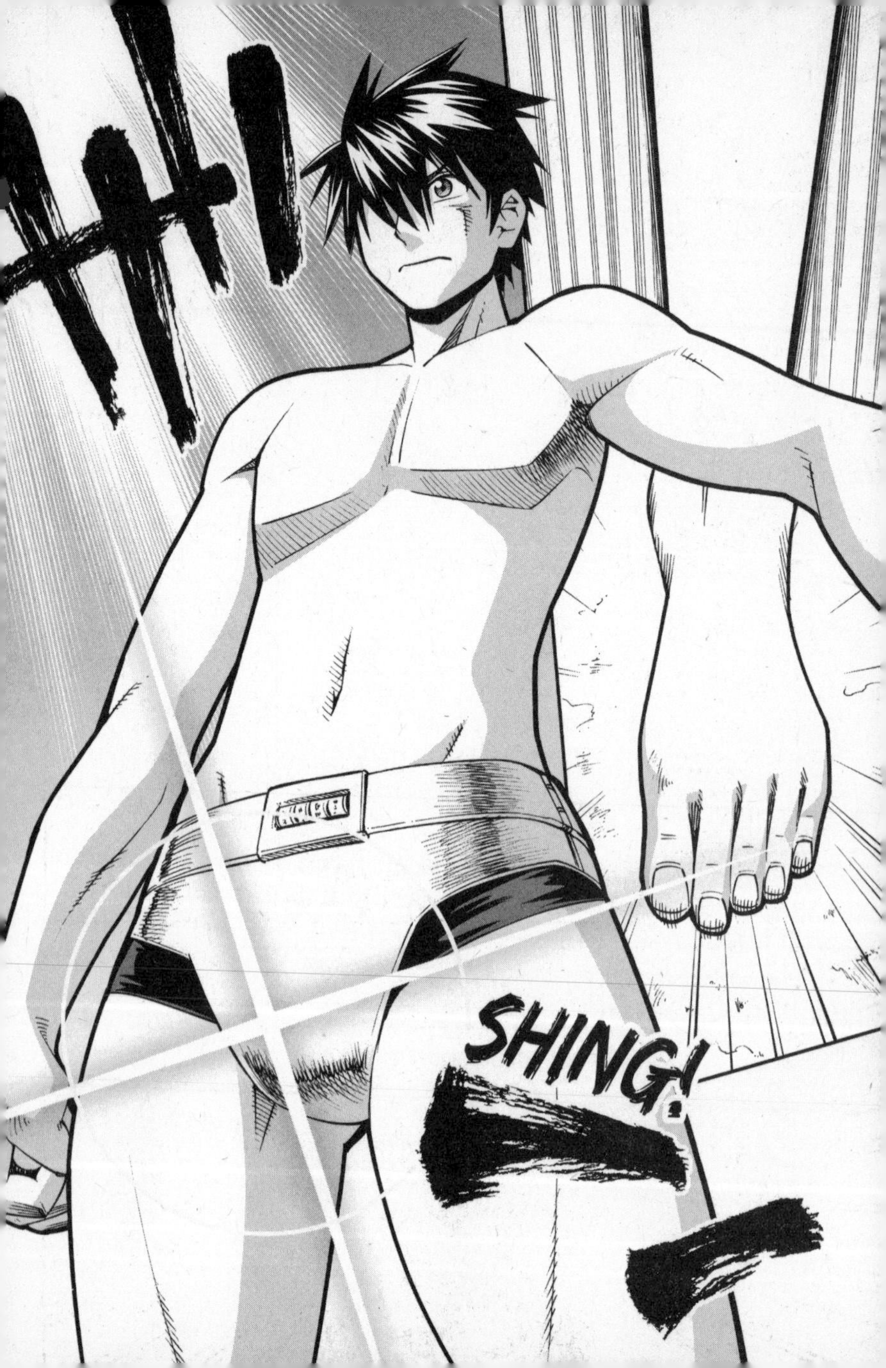
SHING!

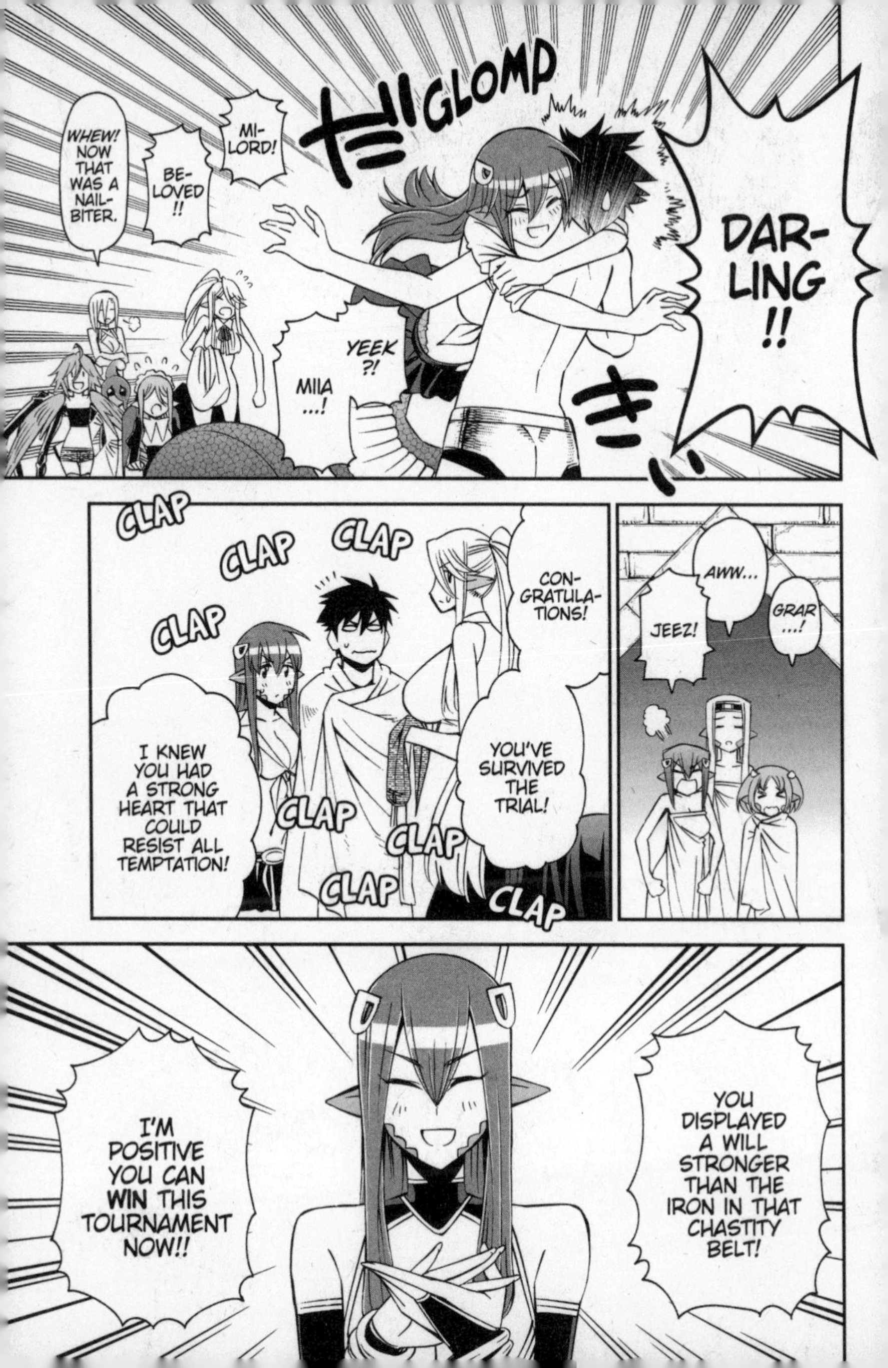
DARLING!!
GLOMP
YEEK?!
MIIA...!
MILORD!
BELOVED!!
WHEW! NOW THAT WAS A NAIL-BITER.
AWW...
GRAR...!
JEEZ!
CONGRATULATIONS!
CLAP
CLAP
CLAP
CLAP
YOU'VE SURVIVED THE TRIAL!
I KNEW YOU HAD A STRONG HEART THAT COULD RESIST ALL TEMPTATION!
CLAP
CLAP
CLAP
CLAP
YOU DISPLAYED A WILL STRONGER THAN THE IRON IN THAT CHASTITY BELT!
I'M POSITIVE YOU CAN WIN THIS TOURNAMENT NOW!!

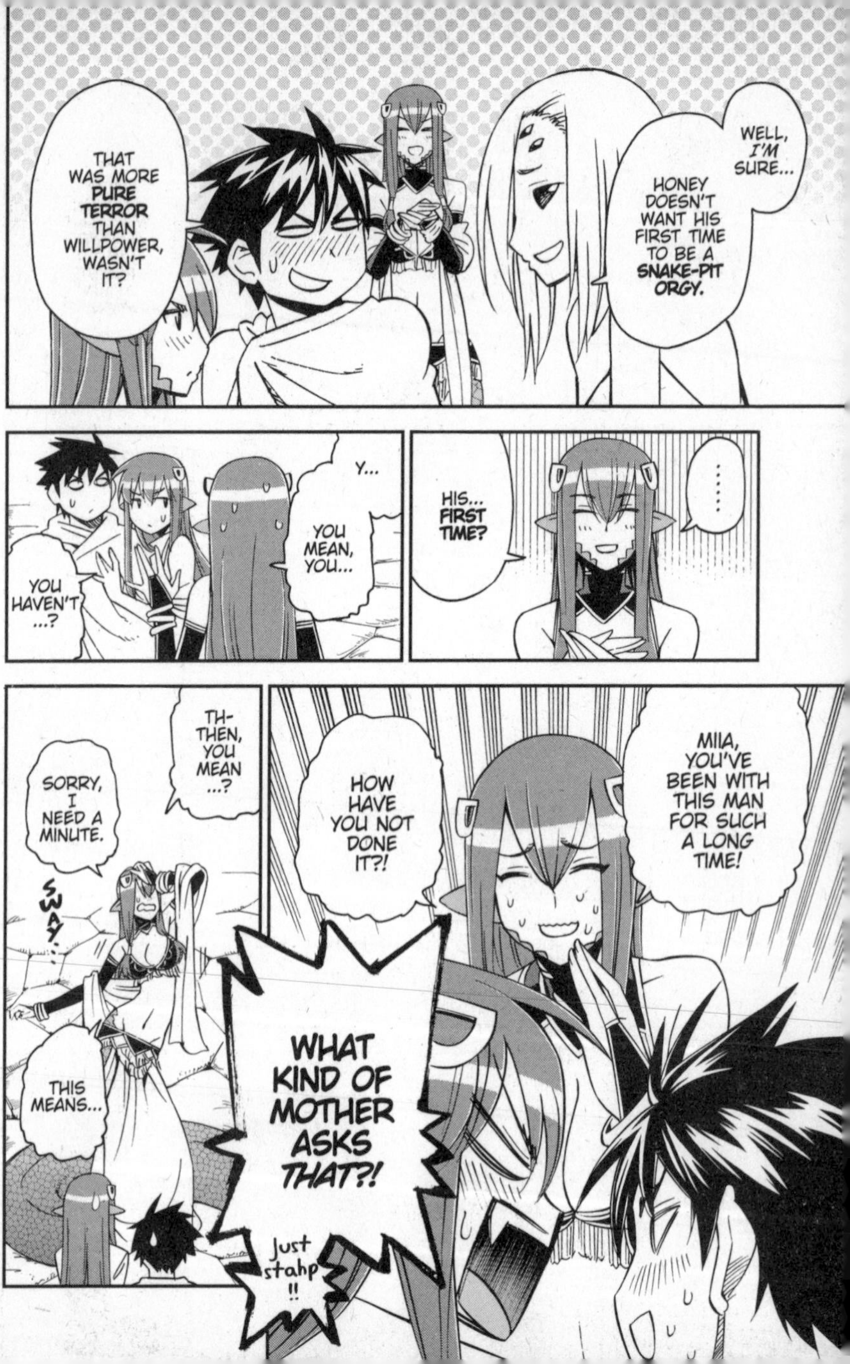
WELL, I'M SURE... HONEY DOESN'T WANT HIS FIRST TIME TO BE A SNAKE-PIT ORGY.
THAT WAS MORE PURE TERROR THAN WILLPOWER, WASN'T IT?
......
HIS... FIRST TIME?
Y...
YOU MEAN, YOU...
YOU HAVEN'T ...?
MIIA, YOU'VE BEEN WITH THIS MAN FOR SUCH A LONG TIME!
HOW HAVE YOU NOT DONE IT?!
WHAT KIND OF MOTHER ASKS THAT?!
Just stahp !!
TH-THEN, YOU MEAN ...?
SORRY, I NEED A MINUTE.
SWAY...
THIS MEANS...

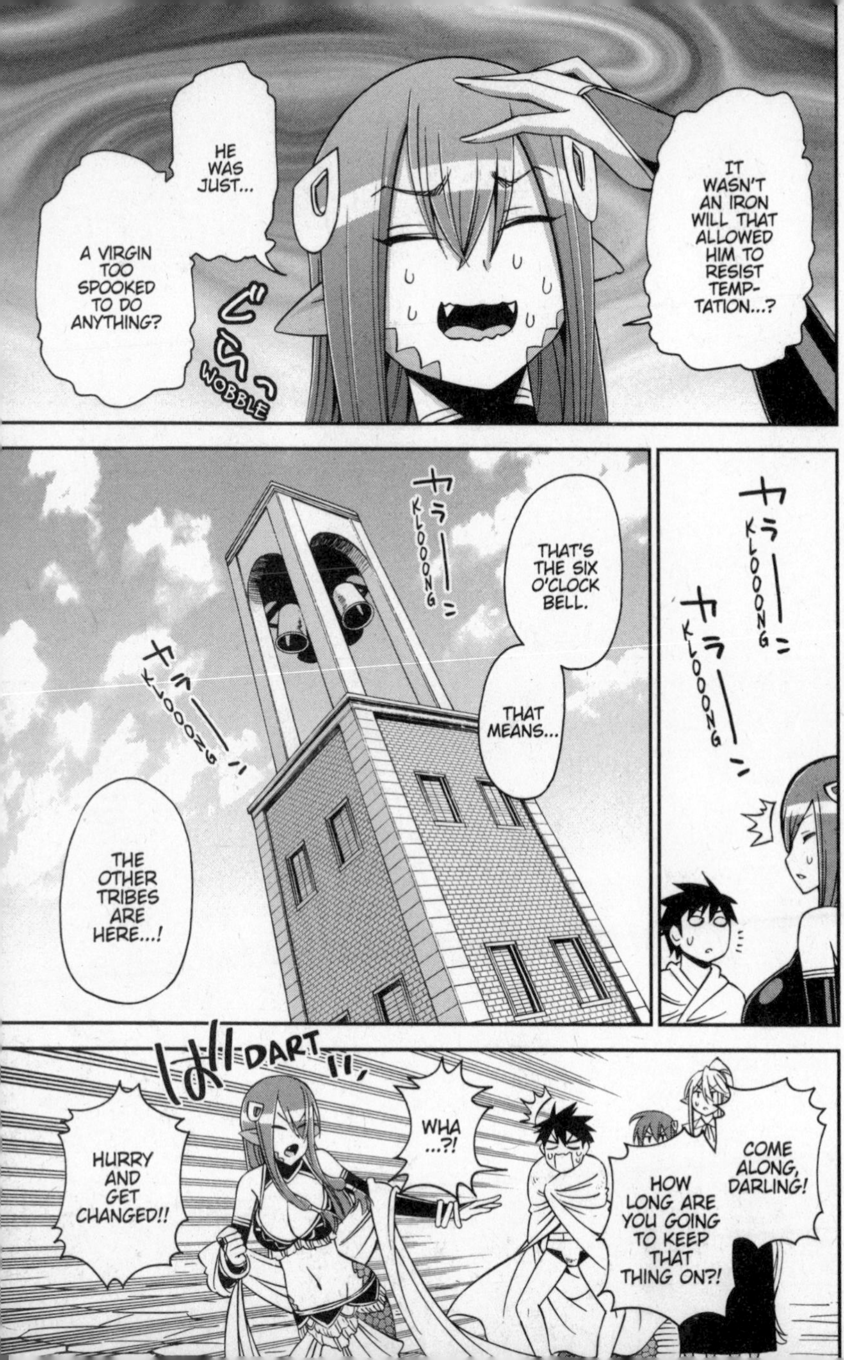
IT WASN'T AN IRON WILL THAT ALLOWED HIM TO RESIST TEMP-TATION...?
HE WAS JUST...
A VIRGIN TOO SPOOKED TO DO ANYTHING?
WOBBLE
KLOOOONG
KLOOOONG
KLOOOONG
THAT'S THE SIX O'CLOCK BELL.
THAT MEANS...
KLOOOONG
THE OTHER TRIBES ARE HERE...!
COME ALONG, DARLING!
HOW LONG ARE YOU GOING TO KEEP THAT THING ON?!
WHA...?!
DART
HURRY AND GET CHANGED!!

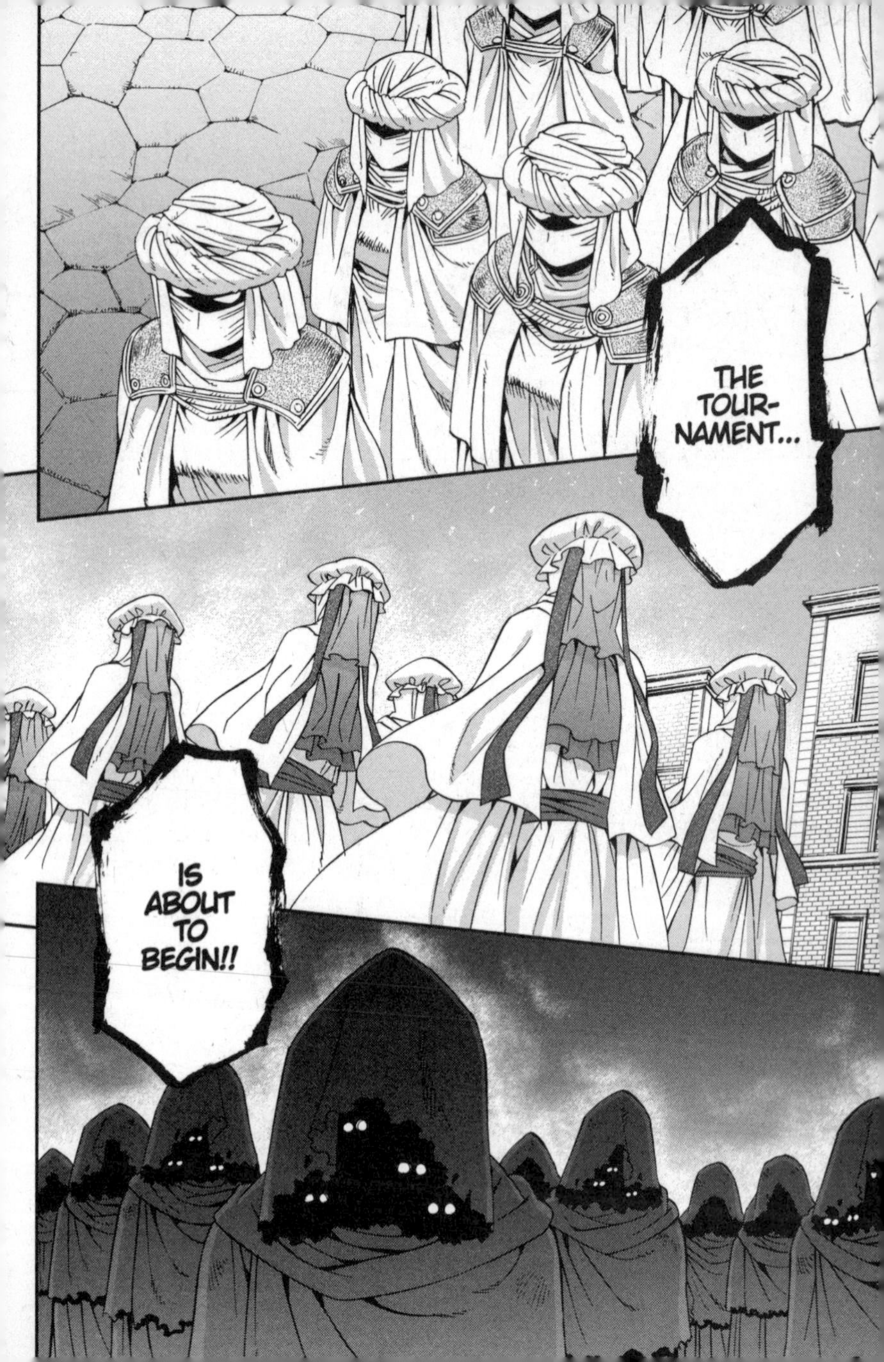
THE TOUR-NAMENT...
IS ABOUT TO BEGIN!!

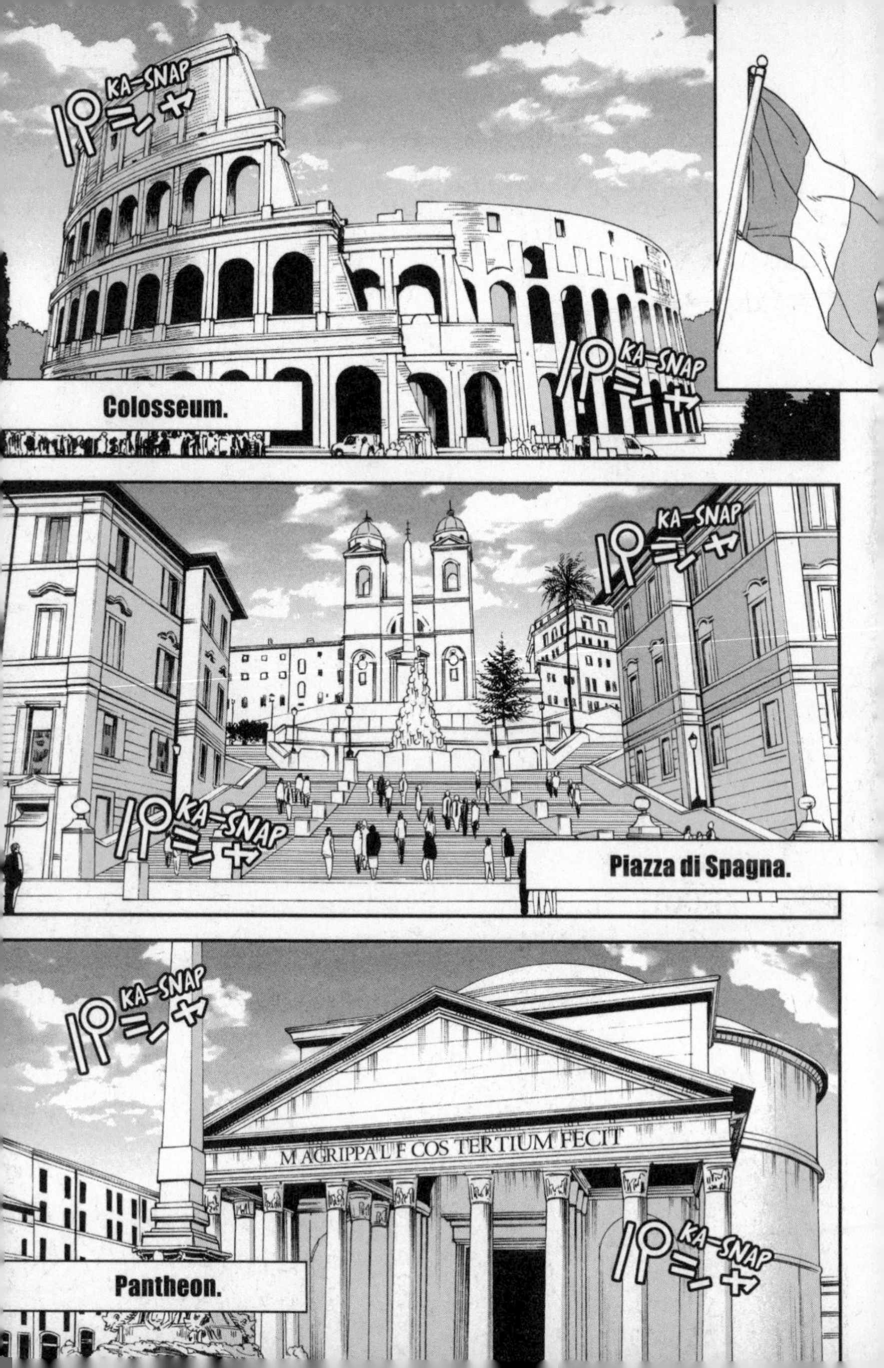
KA-SNAP
KA-SNAP
Colosseum.
KA-SNAP
KA-SNAP
Piazza di Spagna.
KA-SNAP
M AGRIPPA L F COS TERTIUM FECIT
KA-SNAP
Pantheon.

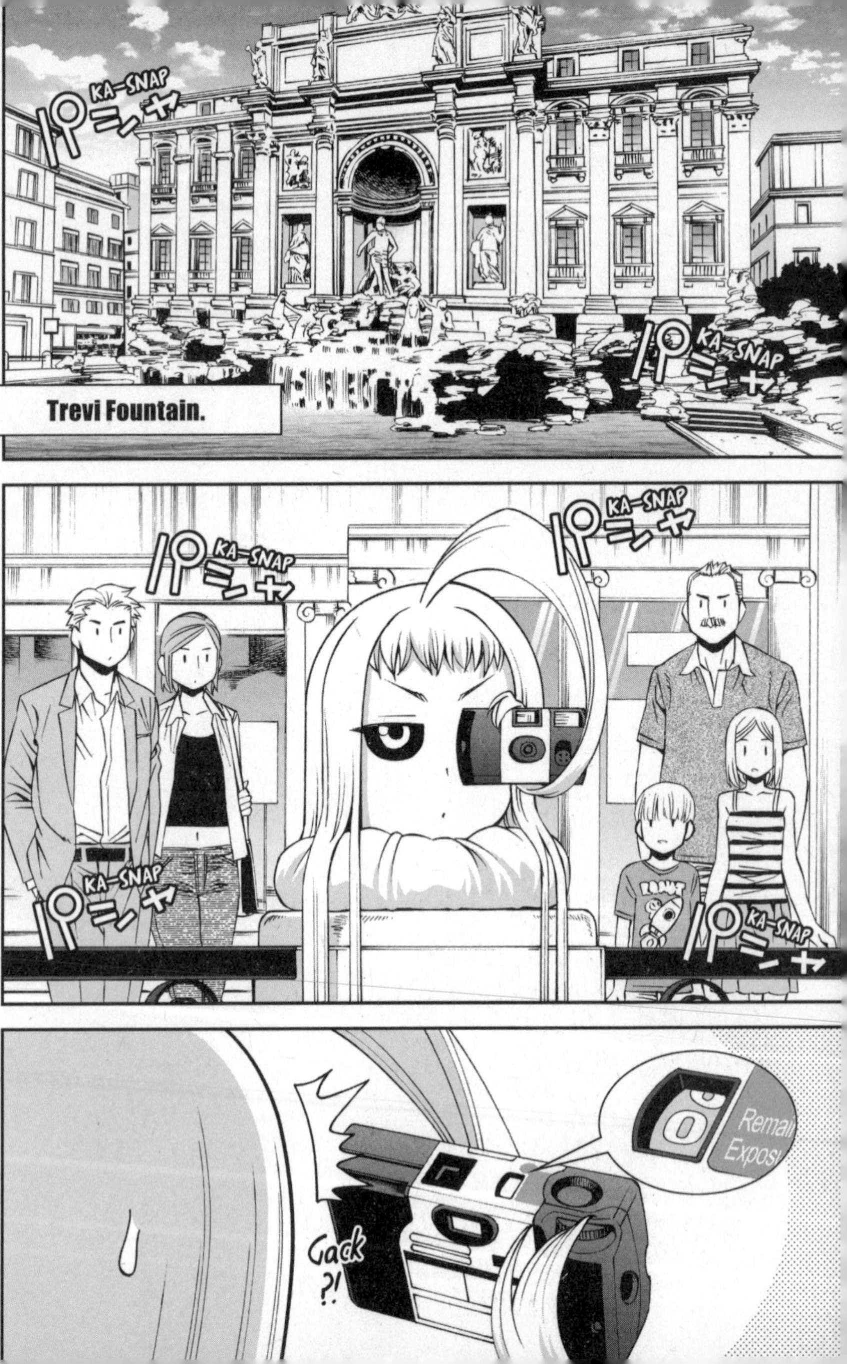
Trevi Fountain.
KA-SNAP
KA-SNAP
KA-SNAP
KA-SNAP
KA-SNAP
KA-SNAP
Remai
Expos
Gack ?!

Monster Musume

Everyday Life with Monster Girls

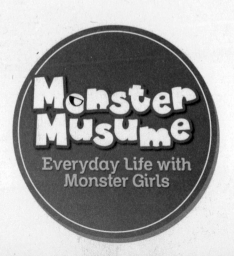

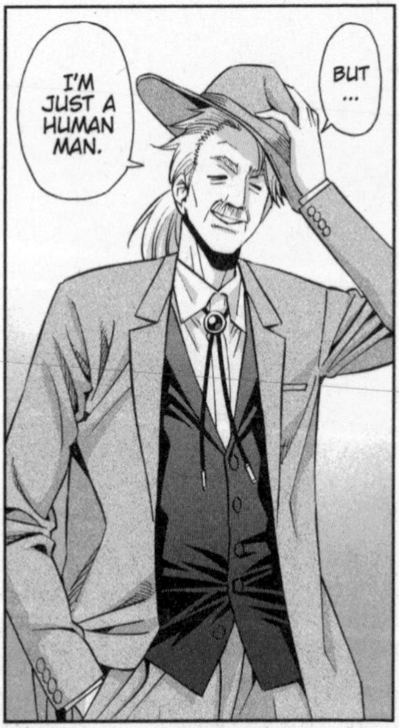
BUT ...
I'M JUST A HUMAN MAN.

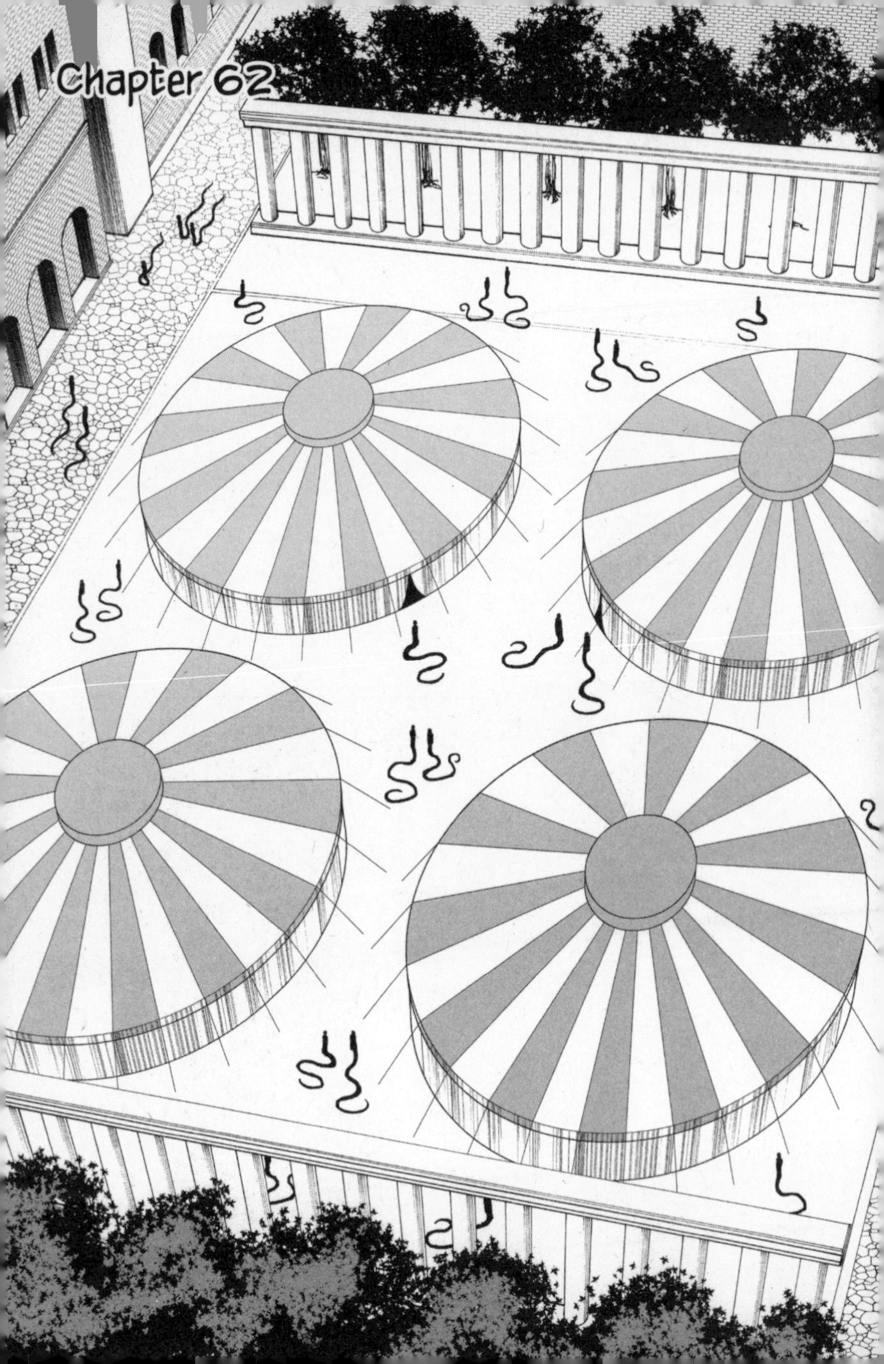
Chapter 62

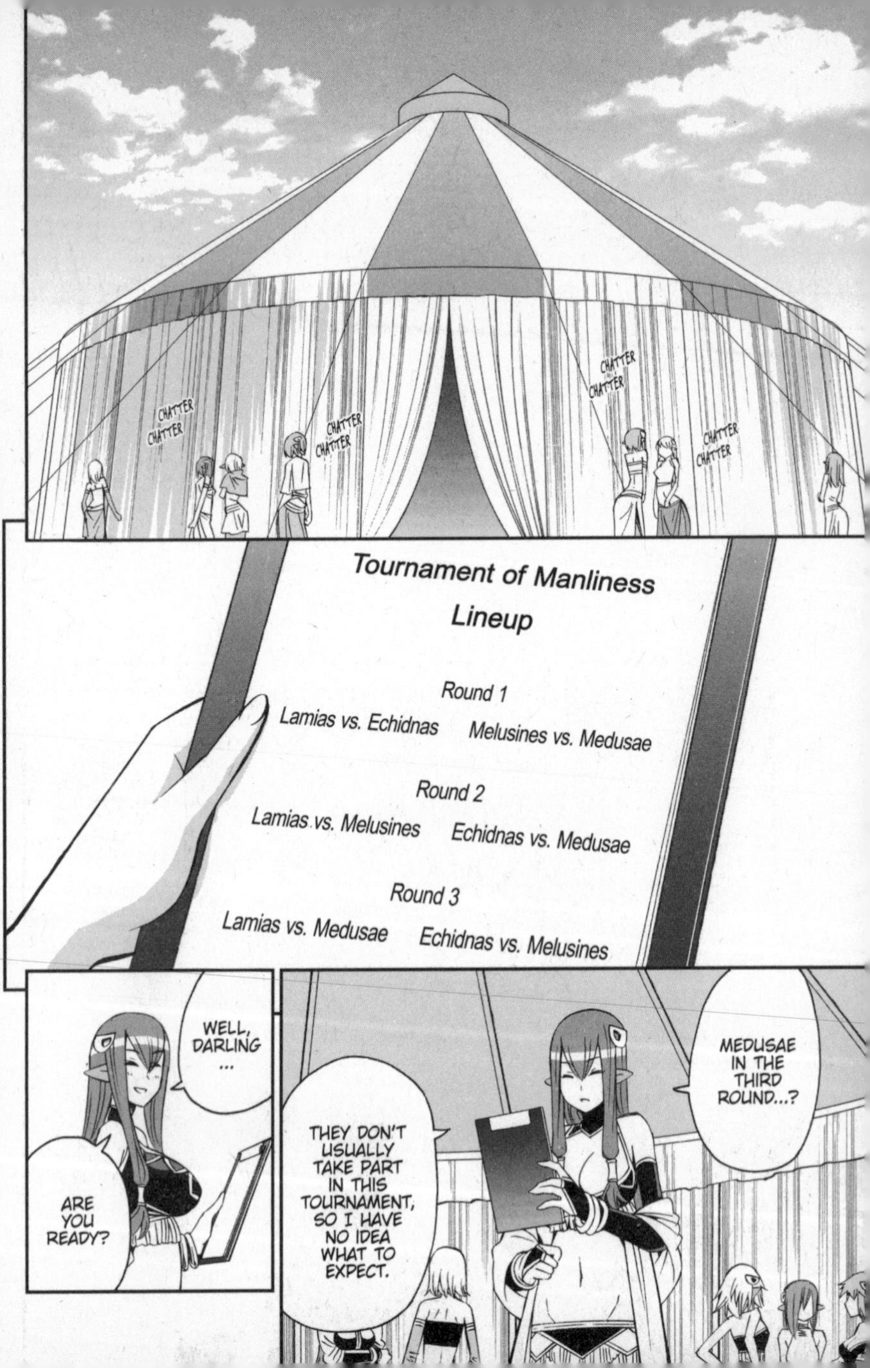
CHATTER CHATTER
CHATTER CHATTER
CHATTER CHATTER
CHATTER CHATTER
Tournament of Manliness
Lineup
Round 1
Lamias vs. Echidnas Melusines vs. Medusae
Round 2
Lamias vs. Melusines Echidnas vs. Medusae
Round 3
Lamias vs. Medusae Echidnas vs. Melusines
MEDUSAE IN THE THIRD ROUND...?
THEY DON'T USUALLY TAKE PART IN THIS TOURNAMENT, SO I HAVE NO IDEA WHAT TO EXPECT.
WELL, DARLING ...
ARE YOU READY?

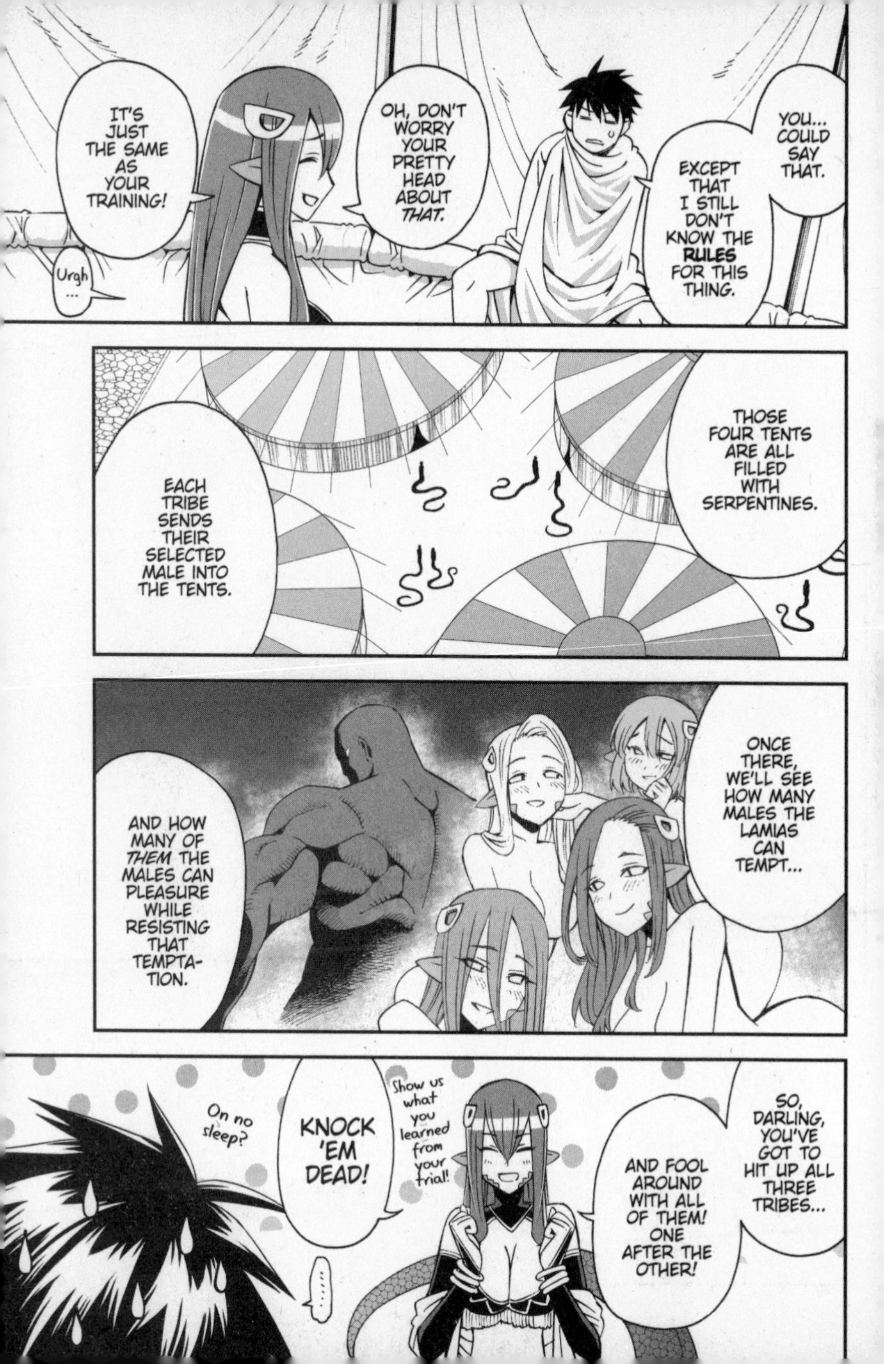
YOU... COULD SAY THAT.
EXCEPT THAT I STILL DON'T KNOW THE RULES FOR THIS THING.
OH, DON'T WORRY YOUR PRETTY HEAD ABOUT THAT.
IT'S JUST THE SAME AS YOUR TRAINING!
Urgh ...
THOSE FOUR TENTS ARE ALL FILLED WITH SERPENTINES.
EACH TRIBE SENDS THEIR SELECTED MALE INTO THE TENTS.
ONCE THERE, WE'LL SEE HOW MANY MALES THE LAMIAS CAN TEMPT...
AND HOW MANY OF THEM THE MALES CAN PLEASURE WHILE RESISTING THAT TEMPTATION.
SO, DARLING, YOU'VE GOT TO HIT UP ALL THREE TRIBES...
AND FOOL AROUND WITH ALL OF THEM! ONE AFTER THE OTHER!
Show us what you learned from your trial!
KNOCK 'EM DEAD!
On no sleep?
......

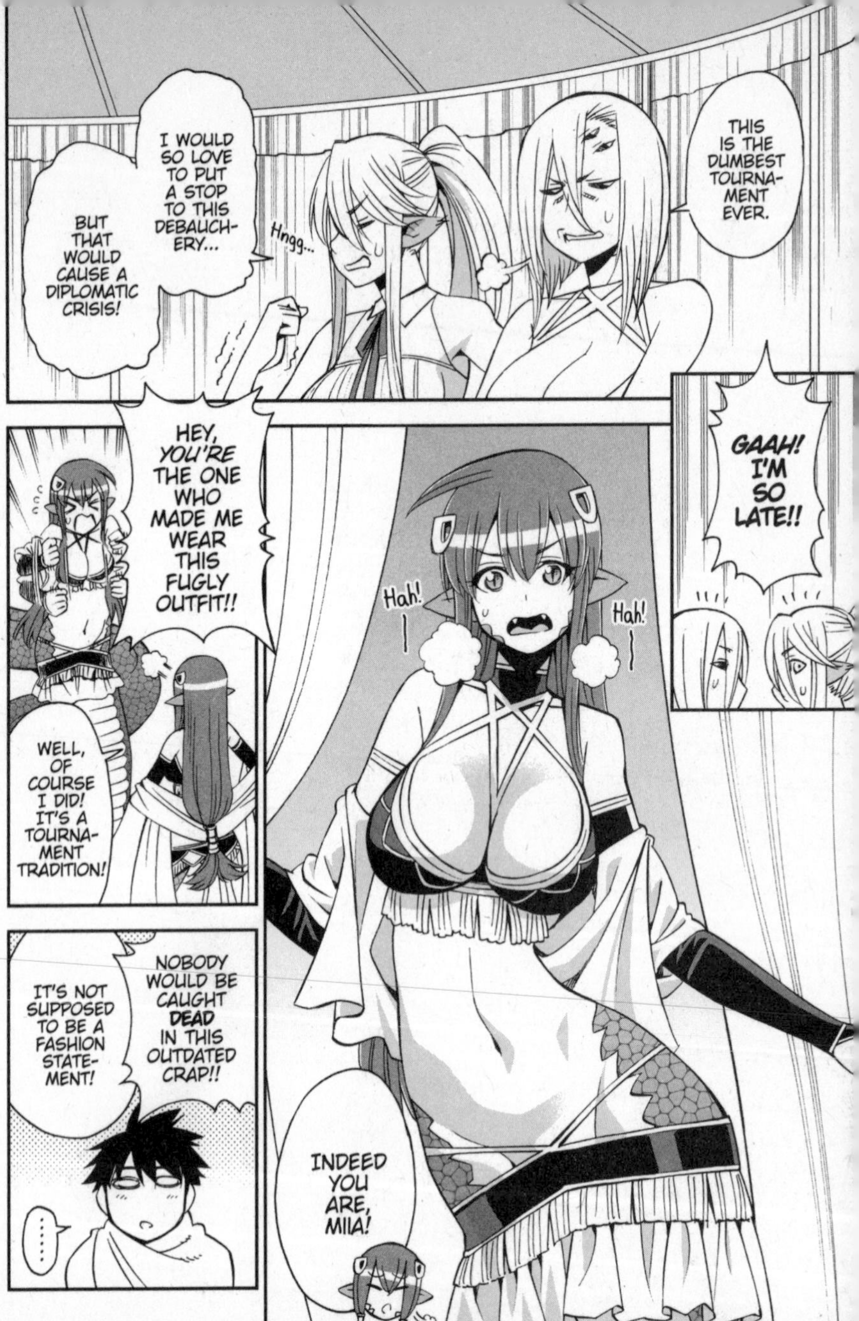
THIS IS THE DUMBEST TOURNAMENT EVER.
I WOULD SO LOVE TO PUT A STOP TO THIS DEBAUCHERY...
Hngg...
BUT THAT WOULD CAUSE A DIPLOMATIC CRISIS!
GAAH! I'M SO LATE!!
Hah!
Hah!
INDEED YOU ARE, MIIA!
HEY, YOU'RE THE ONE WHO MADE ME WEAR THIS FUGLY OUTFIT!!
WELL, OF COURSE I DID! IT'S A TOURNAMENT TRADITION!
NOBODY WOULD BE CAUGHT DEAD IN THIS OUTDATED CRAP!!
IT'S NOT SUPPOSED TO BE A FASHION STATEMENT!
......

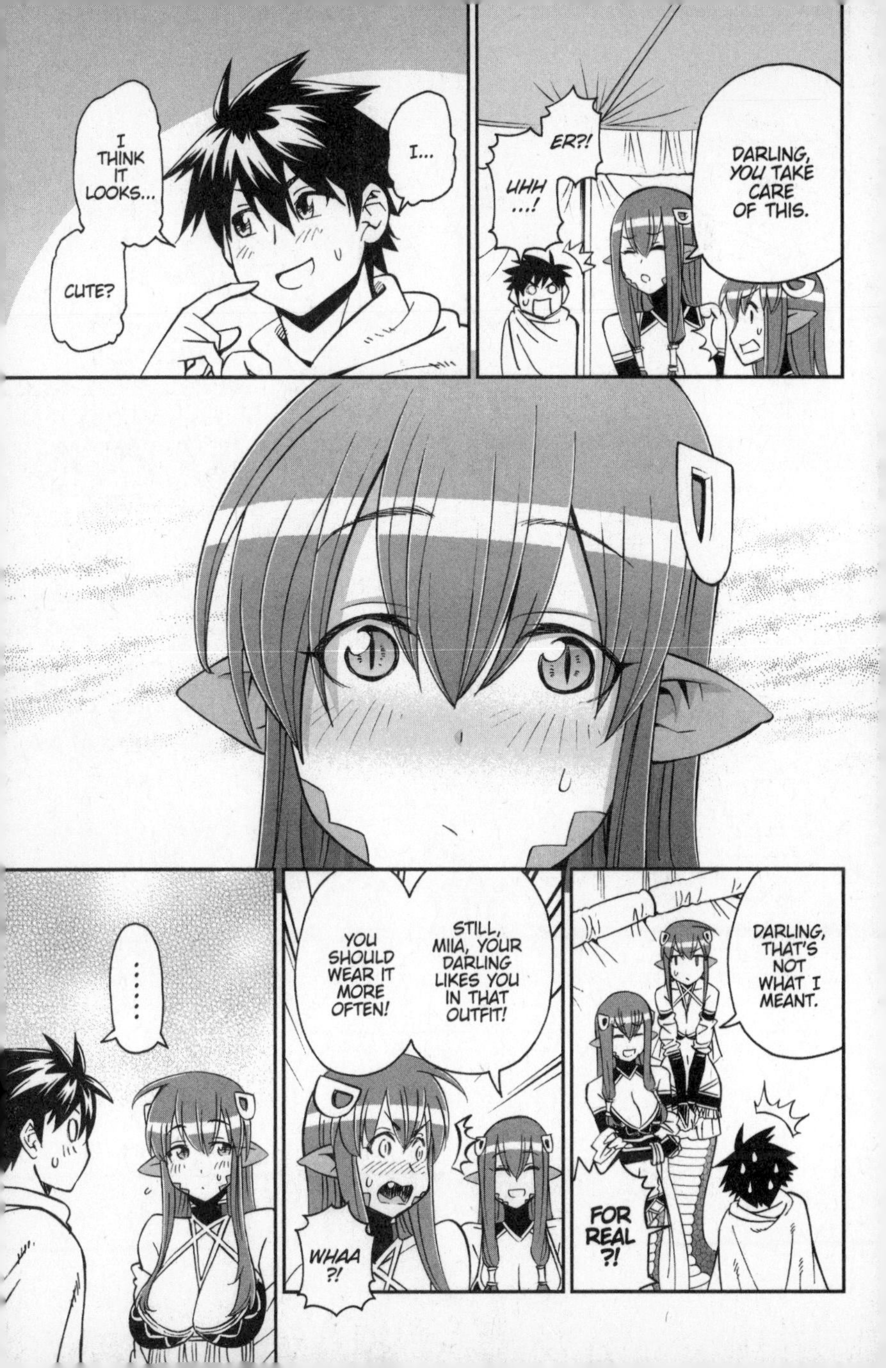
DARLING, YOU TAKE CARE OF THIS.
ER?!
UHH ...!
I...
I THINK IT LOOKS...
CUTE?
DARLING, THAT'S NOT WHAT I MEANT.
FOR REAL ?!
STILL, MIIA, YOUR DARLING LIKES YOU IN THAT OUTFIT!
YOU SHOULD WEAR IT MORE OFTEN!
WHAA ?!
......

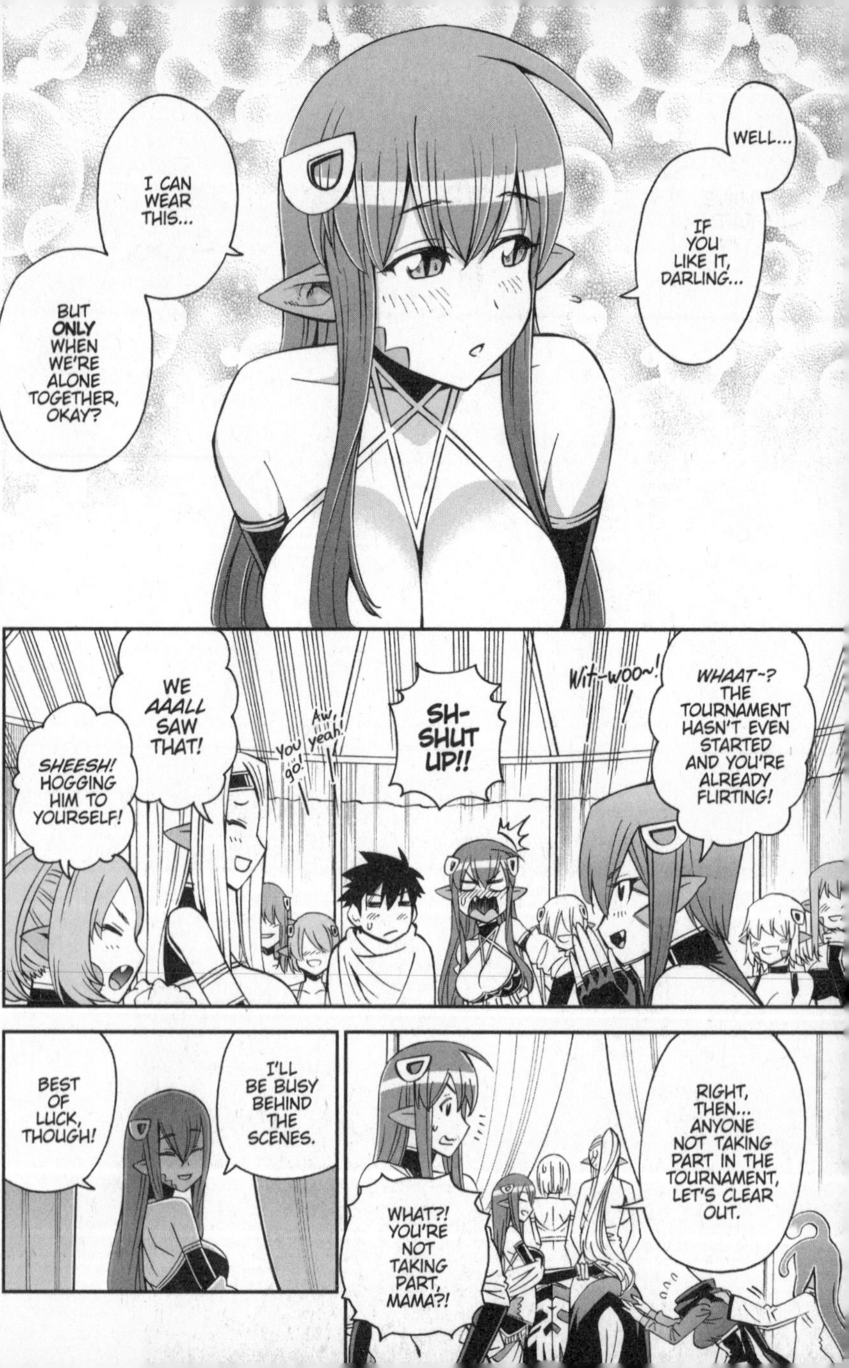
WELL...
IF YOU LIKE IT, DARLING...
I CAN WEAR THIS...
BUT **ONLY** WHEN WE'RE ALONE TOGETHER, OKAY?
WHAAT~? THE TOURNAMENT HASN'T EVEN STARTED AND YOU'RE ALREADY FLIRTING!
Wit-woo~!
SH-SHUT UP!!
Aw, yeah!
You go!
WE *AAALL* SAW THAT!
SHEESH! HOGGING HIM TO YOURSELF!
RIGHT, THEN... ANYONE NOT TAKING PART IN THE TOURNAMENT, LET'S CLEAR OUT.
WHAT?! YOU'RE NOT TAKING PART, MAMA?!
I'LL BE BUSY BEHIND THE SCENES.
BEST OF LUCK, THOUGH!

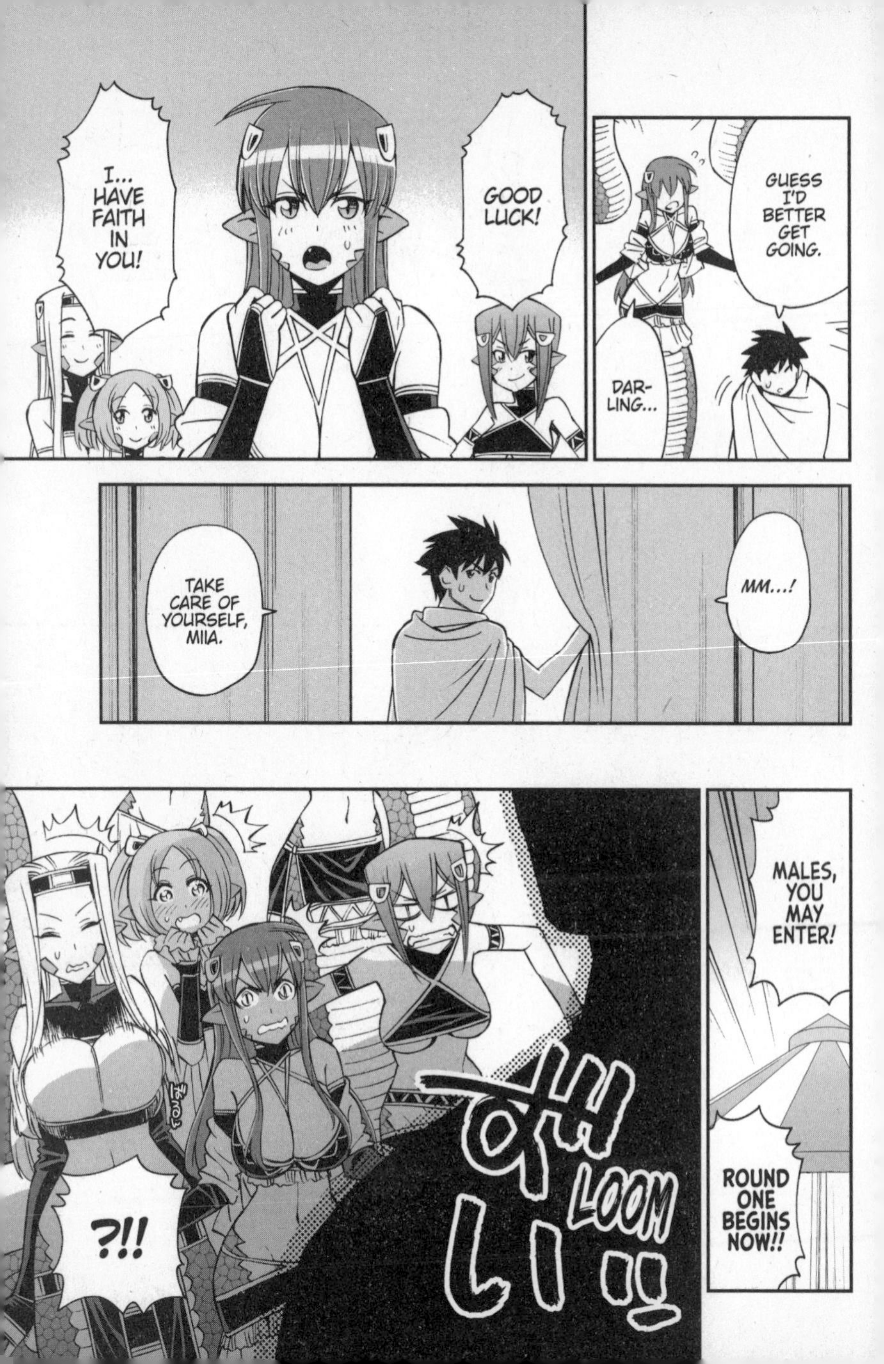
GUESS I'D BETTER GET GOING.
DARLING...
GOOD LUCK!
I... HAVE FAITH IN YOU!
MM...!
TAKE CARE OF YOURSELF, MIIA.
MALES, YOU MAY ENTER!
ROUND ONE BEGINS NOW!!
LOOM
?!!

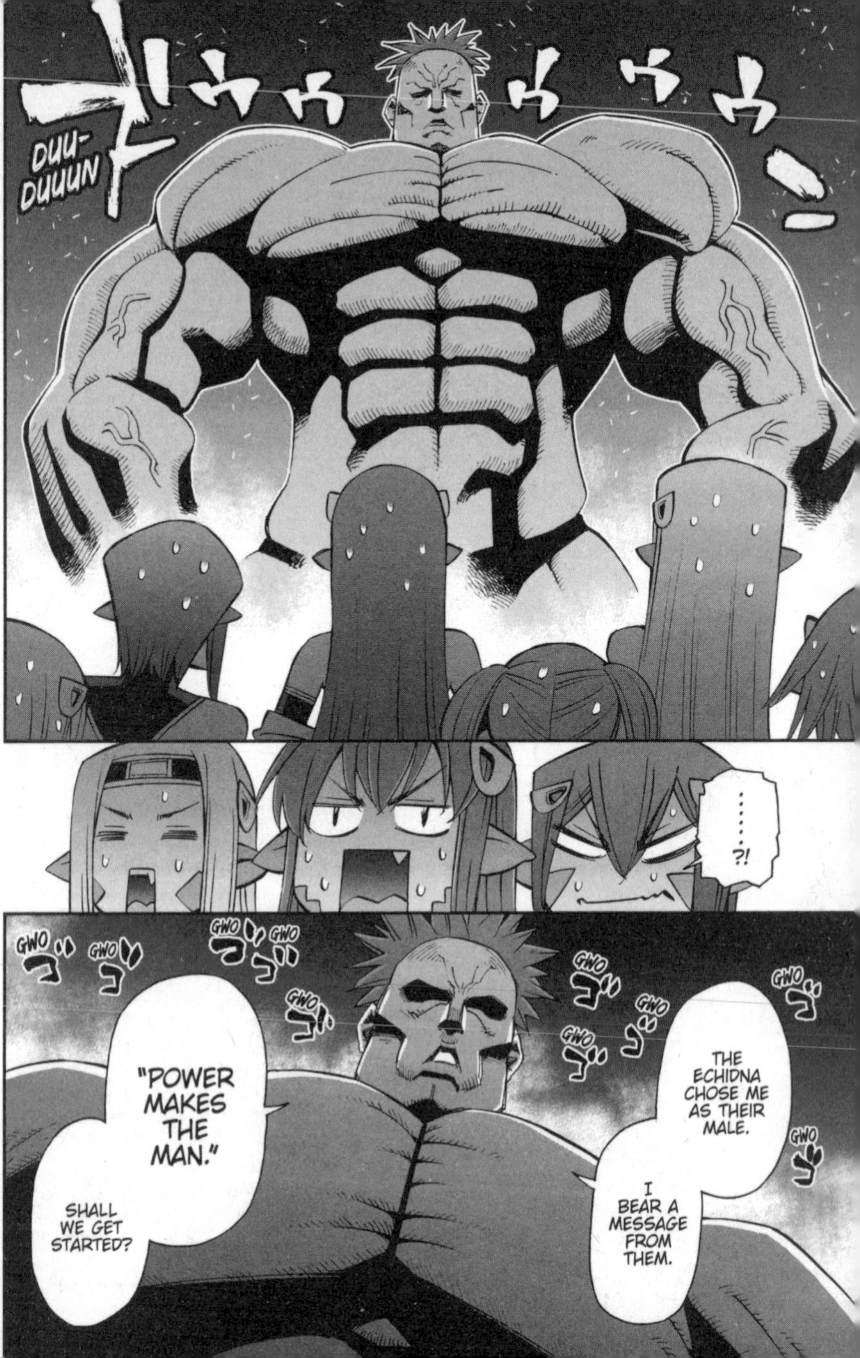
DUU-DUUUN
......?!
GWO
GWO
GWO
GWO
GWO
GWO
GWO
GWO
GWO
GWO
THE ECHIDNA CHOSE ME AS THEIR MALE.
I BEAR A MESSAGE FROM THEM.
"POWER MAKES THE MAN."
SHALL WE GET STARTED?

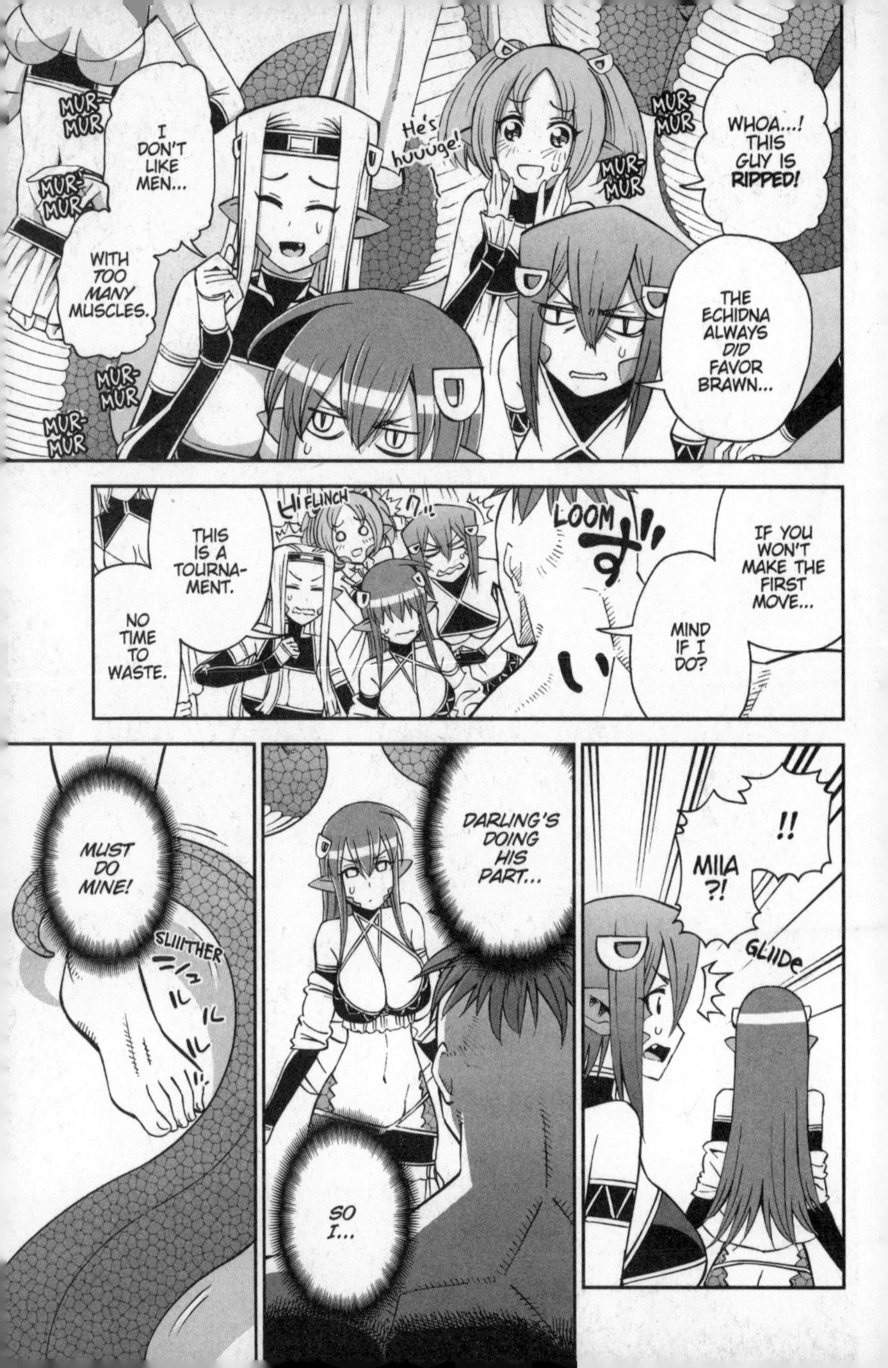
WHOA...! THIS GUY IS RIPPED!
MUR-MUR
MUR-MUR
THE ECHIDNA ALWAYS DID FAVOR BRAWN...
He's huuuge!
I DON'T LIKE MEN...
WITH TOO MANY MUSCLES.
MUR-MUR
MUR-MUR
MUR-MUR
MUR-MUR
IF YOU WON'T MAKE THE FIRST MOVE...
MIND IF I DO?
LOOM
FLINCH
THIS IS A TOURNAMENT.
NO TIME TO WASTE.
!!
MIIA?!
GLIIDE
DARLING'S DOING HIS PART...
SO I...
MUST DO MINE!
SLIIITHER

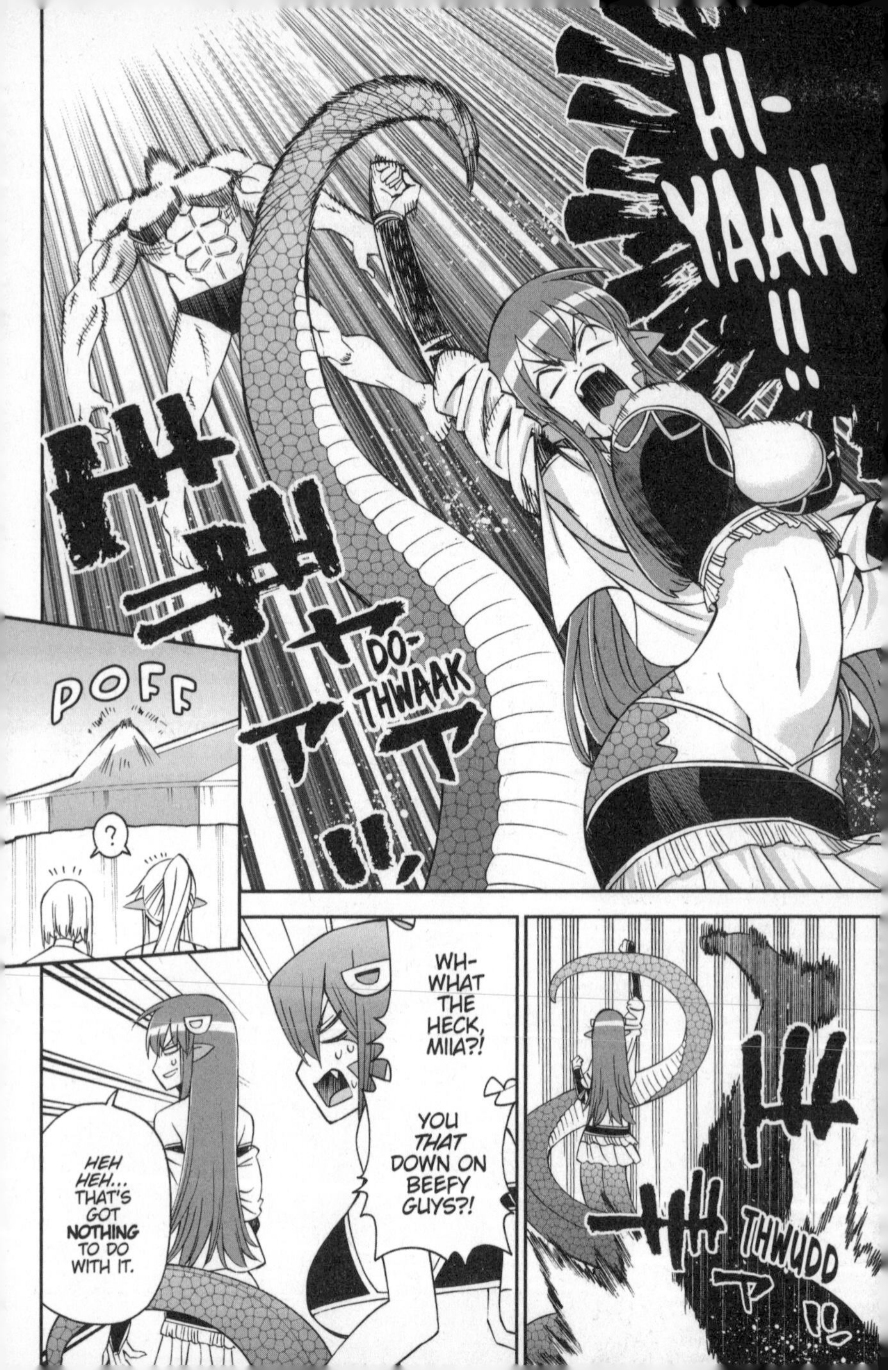
HI-YAAH!!
DO-THWAAK!!
POFF
?
THWUDD!!
WH-WHAT THE HECK, MIIA?!
YOU *THAT* DOWN ON BEEFY GUYS?!
HEH HEH... THAT'S GOT **NOTHING** TO DO WITH IT.

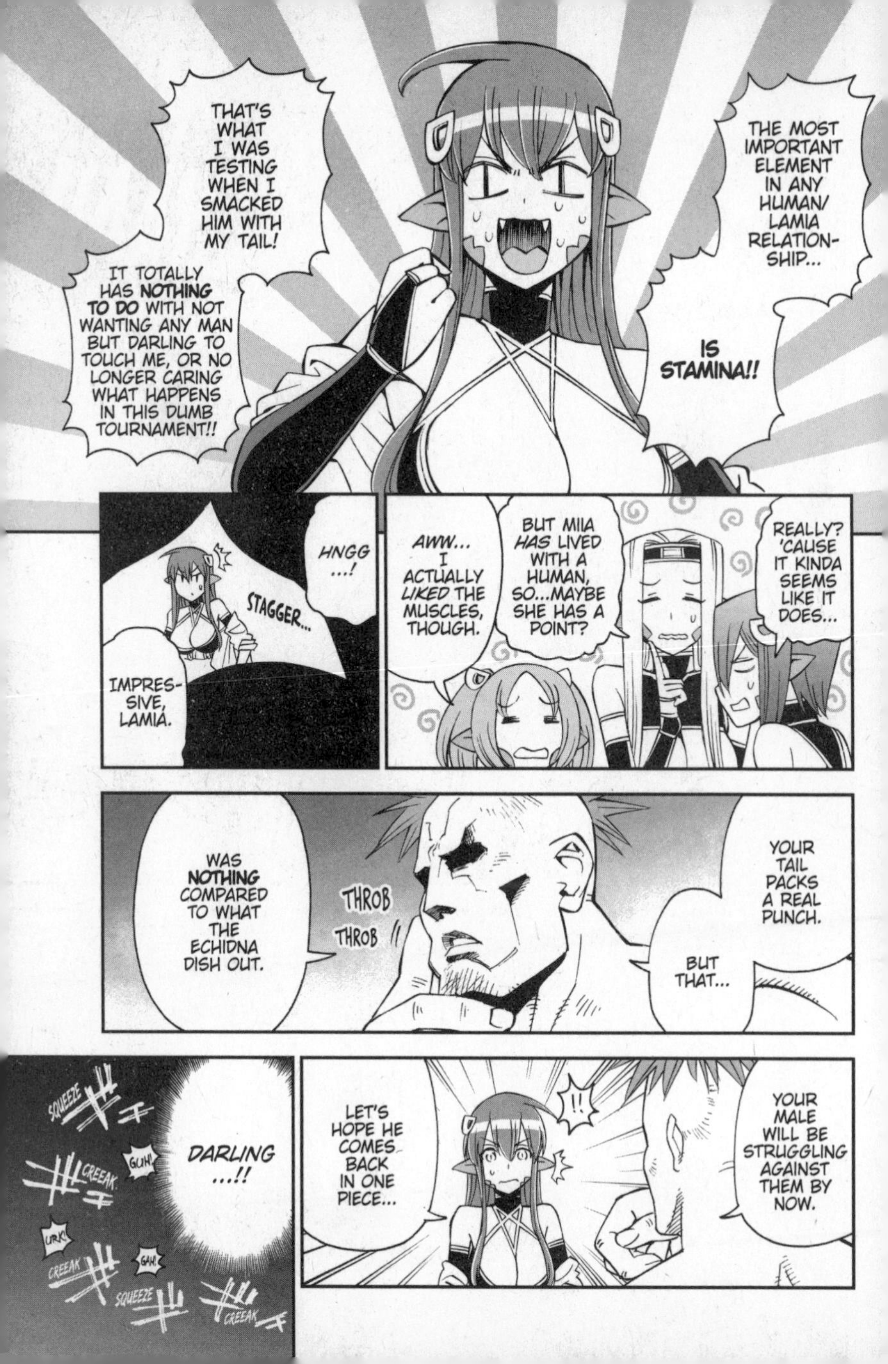
THE MOST IMPORTANT ELEMENT IN ANY HUMAN/ LAMIA RELATIONSHIP...
IS STAMINA!!
THAT'S WHAT I WAS TESTING WHEN I SMACKED HIM WITH MY TAIL!
IT TOTALLY HAS **NOTHING TO DO** WITH NOT WANTING ANY MAN BUT DARLING TO TOUCH ME, OR NO LONGER CARING WHAT HAPPENS IN THIS DUMB TOURNAMENT!!
REALLY? 'CAUSE IT KINDA SEEMS LIKE IT DOES...
BUT MIIA *HAS* LIVED WITH A HUMAN, SO...MAYBE SHE HAS A POINT?
AWW... I ACTUALLY *LIKED* THE MUSCLES, THOUGH.
HNGG ...!
STAGGER...
IMPRESSIVE, LAMIA.
YOUR TAIL PACKS A REAL PUNCH.
BUT THAT...
THROB
THROB
WAS **NOTHING** COMPARED TO WHAT THE ECHIDNA DISH OUT.
YOUR MALE WILL BE STRUGGLING AGAINST THEM BY NOW.
!!
LET'S HOPE HE COMES BACK IN ONE PIECE...
DARLING ...!!
SQUEEZE
GUH!
CREEAK
URK!
GAH!
CREEAK
SQUEEZE
CREEAK

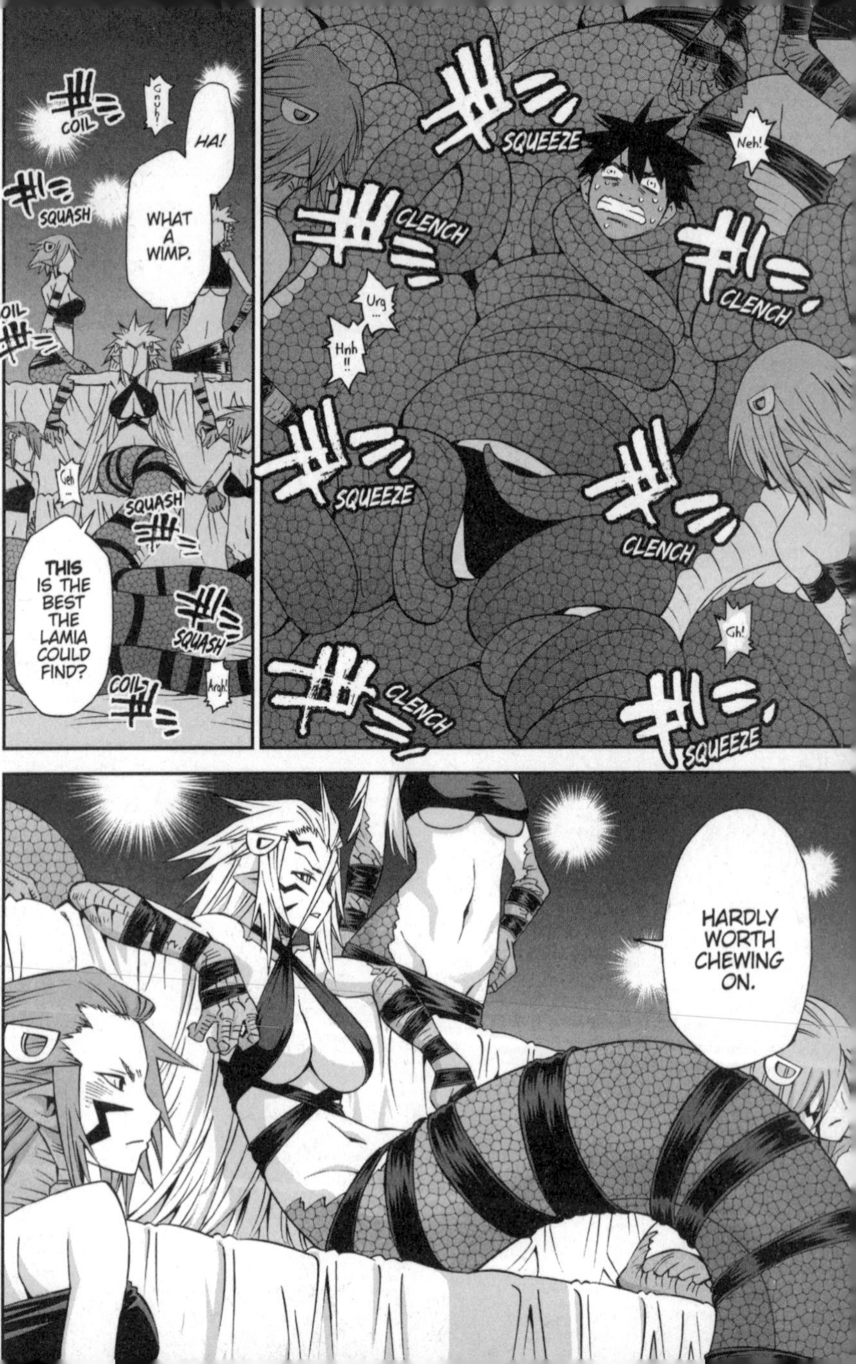
Neh!
SQUEEZE
CLENCH
CLENCH
Urg ...
Hnh !!
CLENCH
SQUEEZE
Gh!
SQUEEZE
CLENCH
Gnuh!
HA!
WHAT A WIMP.
COIL
SQUASH
COIL
Geh ...
SQUASH
THIS IS THE BEST THE LAMIA COULD FIND?
SQUASH
Argh!
COIL
HARDLY WORTH CHEWING ON.

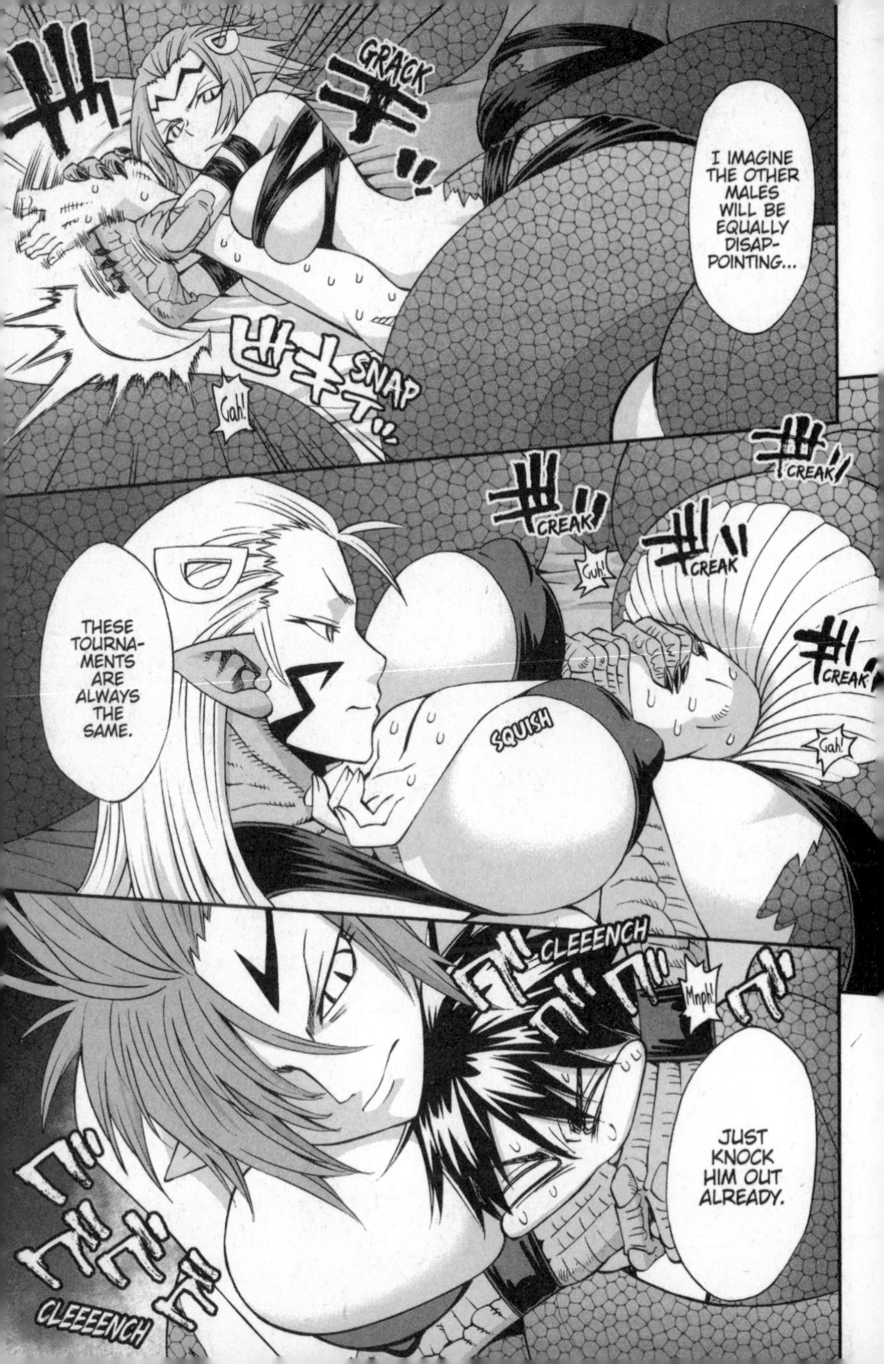
GRACK
I IMAGINE THE OTHER MALES WILL BE EQUALLY DISAP-POINTING...
SNAP
Gah!
CREAK
CREAK
CREAK
Guh!
CREAK
Gah!
SQUISH
THESE TOURNA-MENTS ARE ALWAYS THE SAME.
CLEEENCH
Mnph!
JUST KNOCK HIM OUT ALREADY.
CLEEEENCH

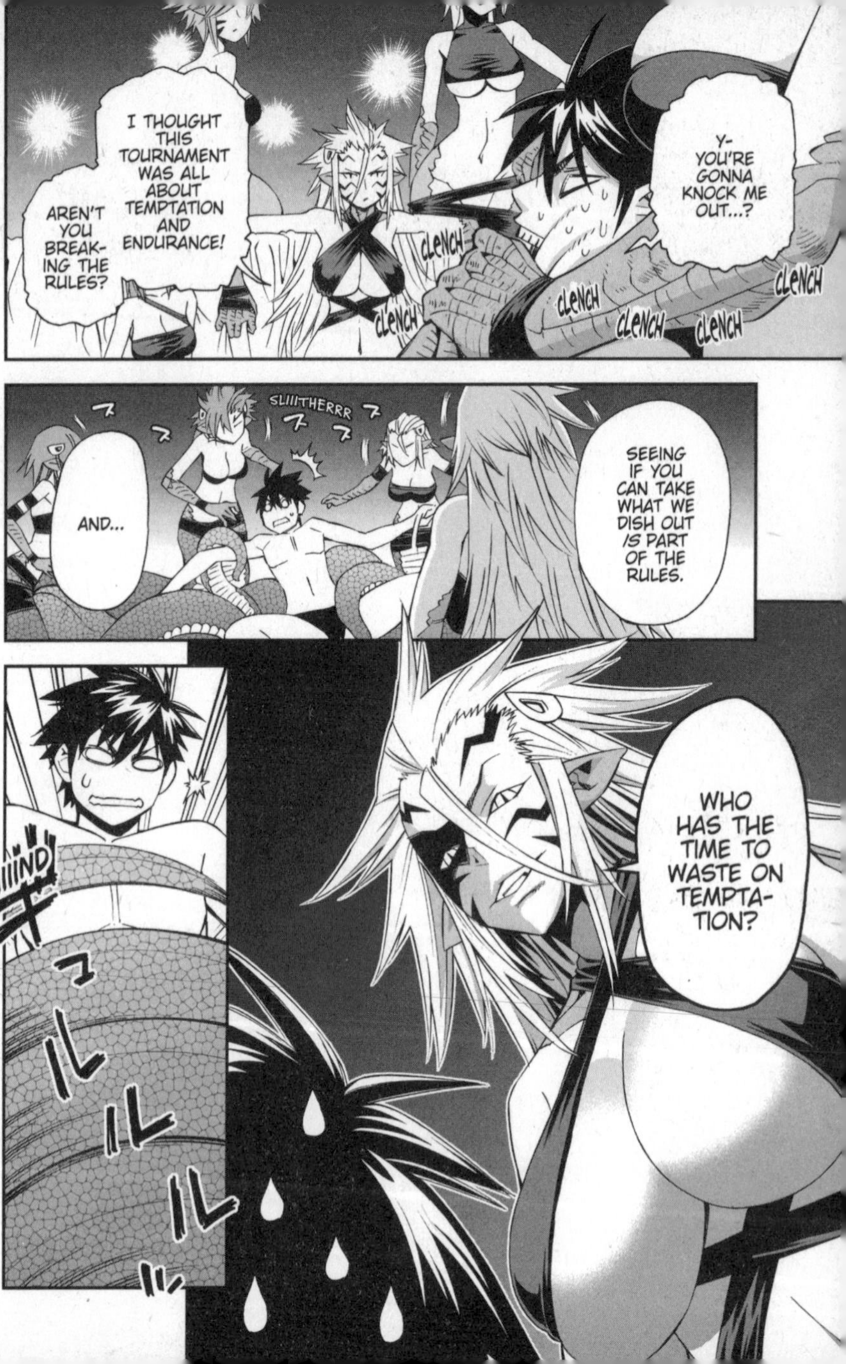
Y- YOU'RE GONNA KNOCK ME OUT...?
CLENCH
CLENCH
CLENCH
CLENCH
CLENCH
CLENCH
I THOUGHT THIS TOURNAMENT WAS ALL ABOUT TEMPTATION AND ENDURANCE!
AREN'T YOU BREAKING THE RULES?
SEEING IF YOU CAN TAKE WHAT WE DISH OUT IS PART OF THE RULES.
SLIIITHERRR
AND...
WHO HAS THE TIME TO WASTE ON TEMPTATION?
WIIIIIIND

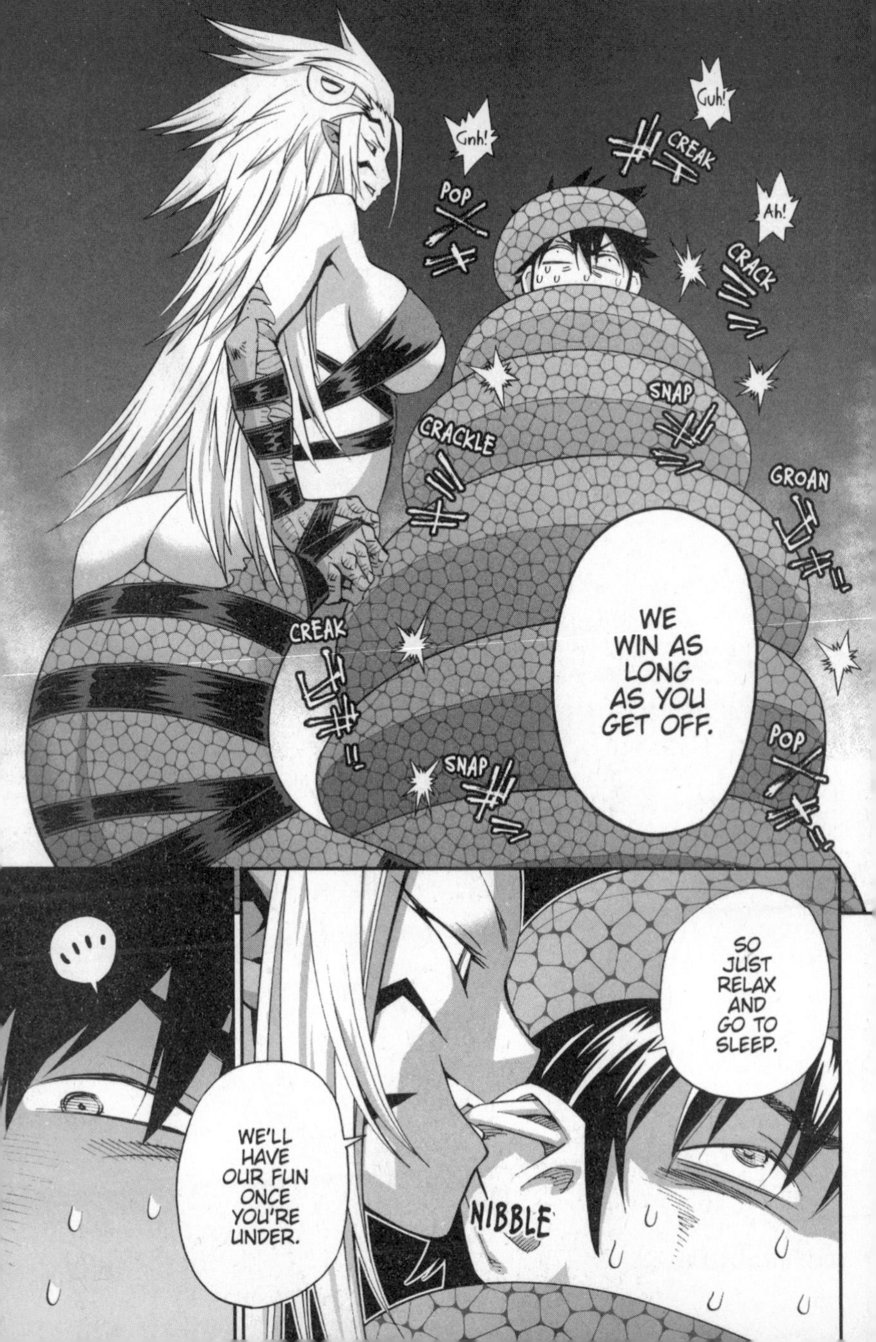
Guh!
CREAK
Ah!
CRACK
Gnh!
POP
SNAP
CRACKLE
GROAN
WE WIN AS LONG AS YOU GET OFF.
POP
CREAK
SNAP
SO JUST RELAX AND GO TO SLEEP.
WE'LL HAVE OUR FUN ONCE YOU'RE UNDER.
NIBBLE
...

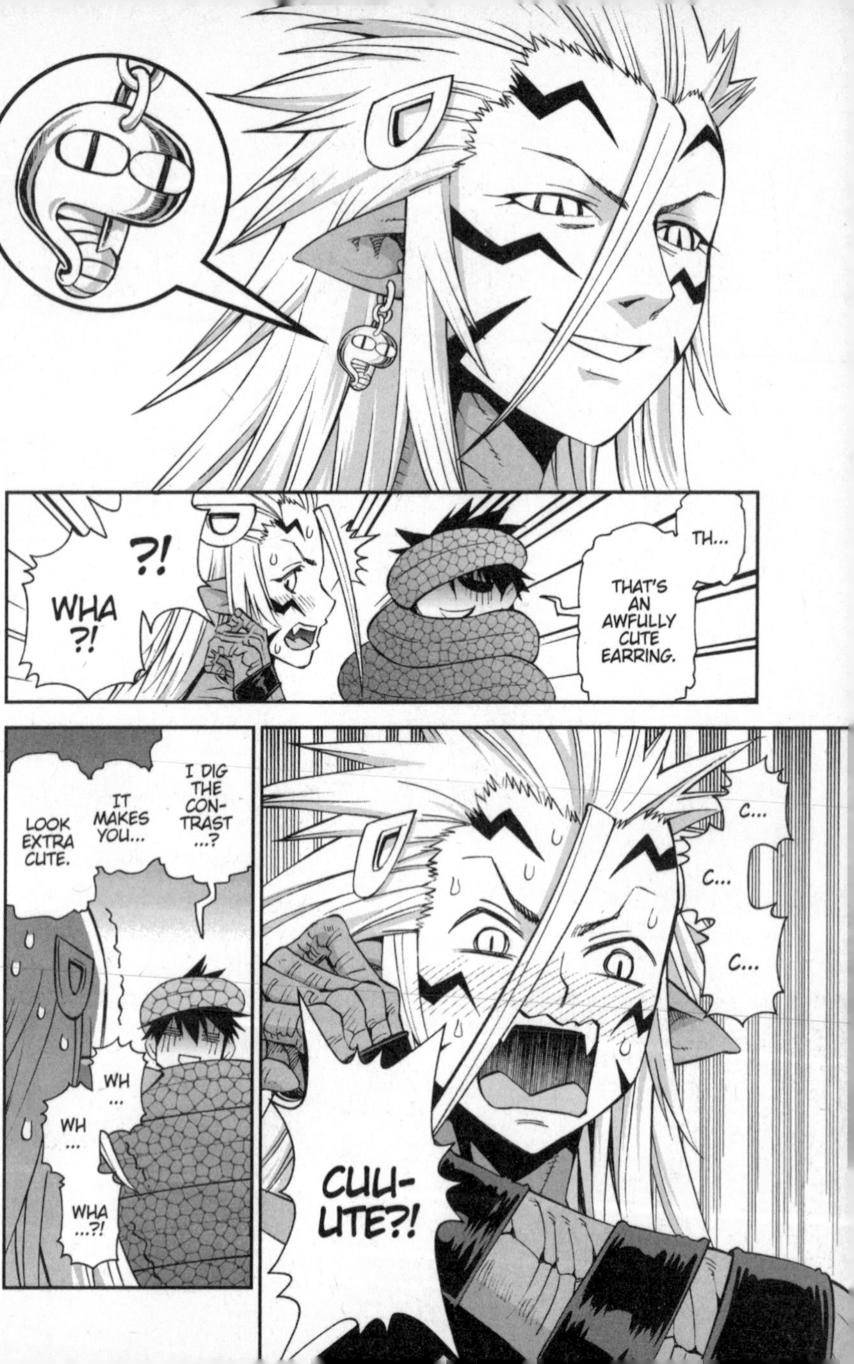

TH...
THAT'S AN AWFULLY CUTE EARRING.
?!
WHA?!
C...
C...
C...
CUU-UTE?!
I DIG THE CON-TRAST...?
IT MAKES YOU...
LOOK EXTRA CUTE.
WH...
WH...
WHA...?!

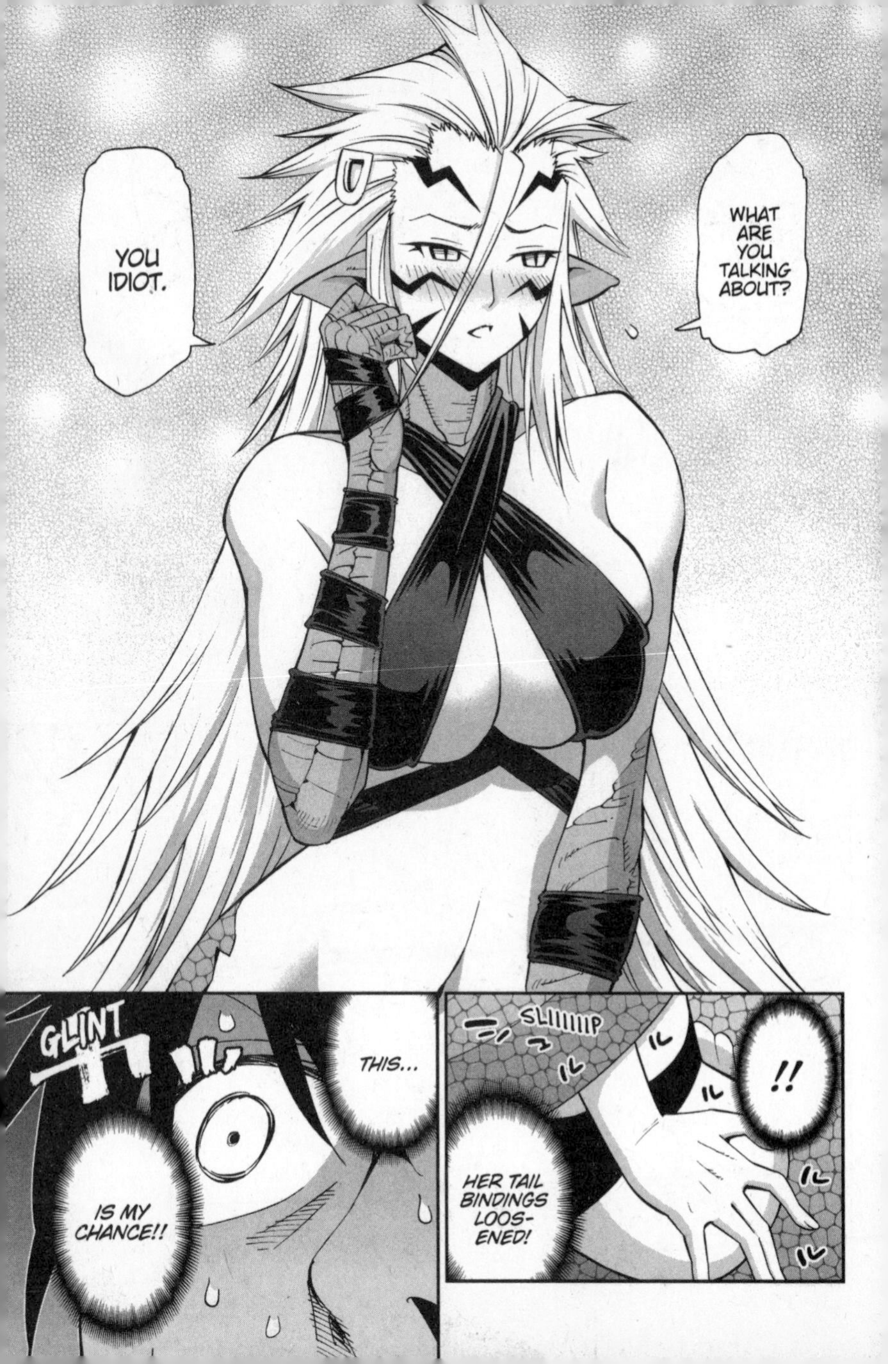
WHAT ARE YOU TALKING ABOUT?
YOU IDIOT.
SLIIIIIIP
!!
HER TAIL BINDINGS LOOS-ENED!
GLINT
THIS...
IS MY CHANCE!!

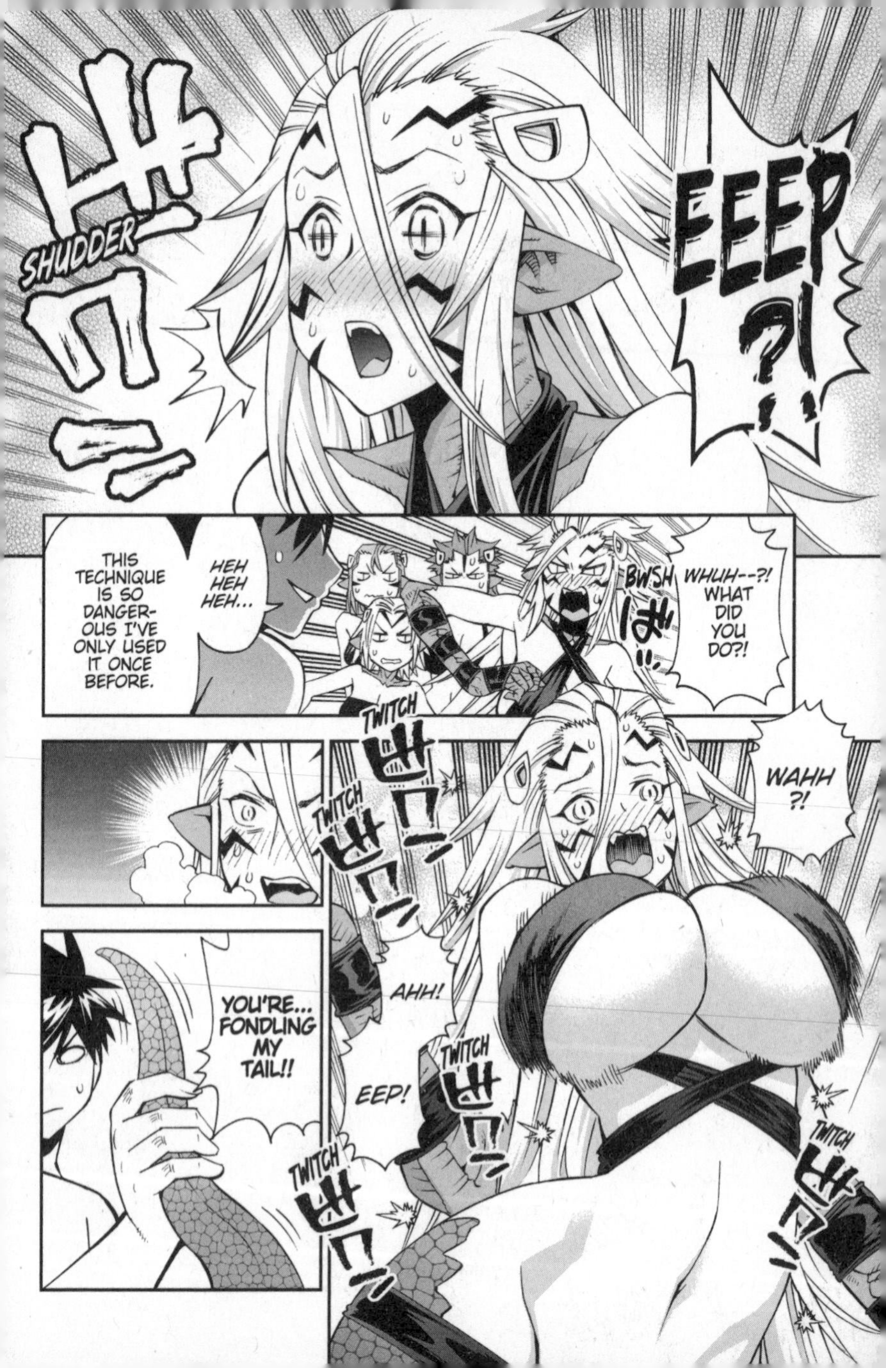
EEEP?!!
SHUDDER
WHUH--?! WHAT DID YOU DO?!
BWSH
HEH HEH HEH...
THIS TECHNIQUE IS SO DANGER-OUS I'VE ONLY USED IT ONCE BEFORE.
WAHH ?!
TWITCH
TWITCH
TWITCH
AHH!
TWITCH
EEP!
TWITCH
YOU'RE... FONDLING MY TAIL!!

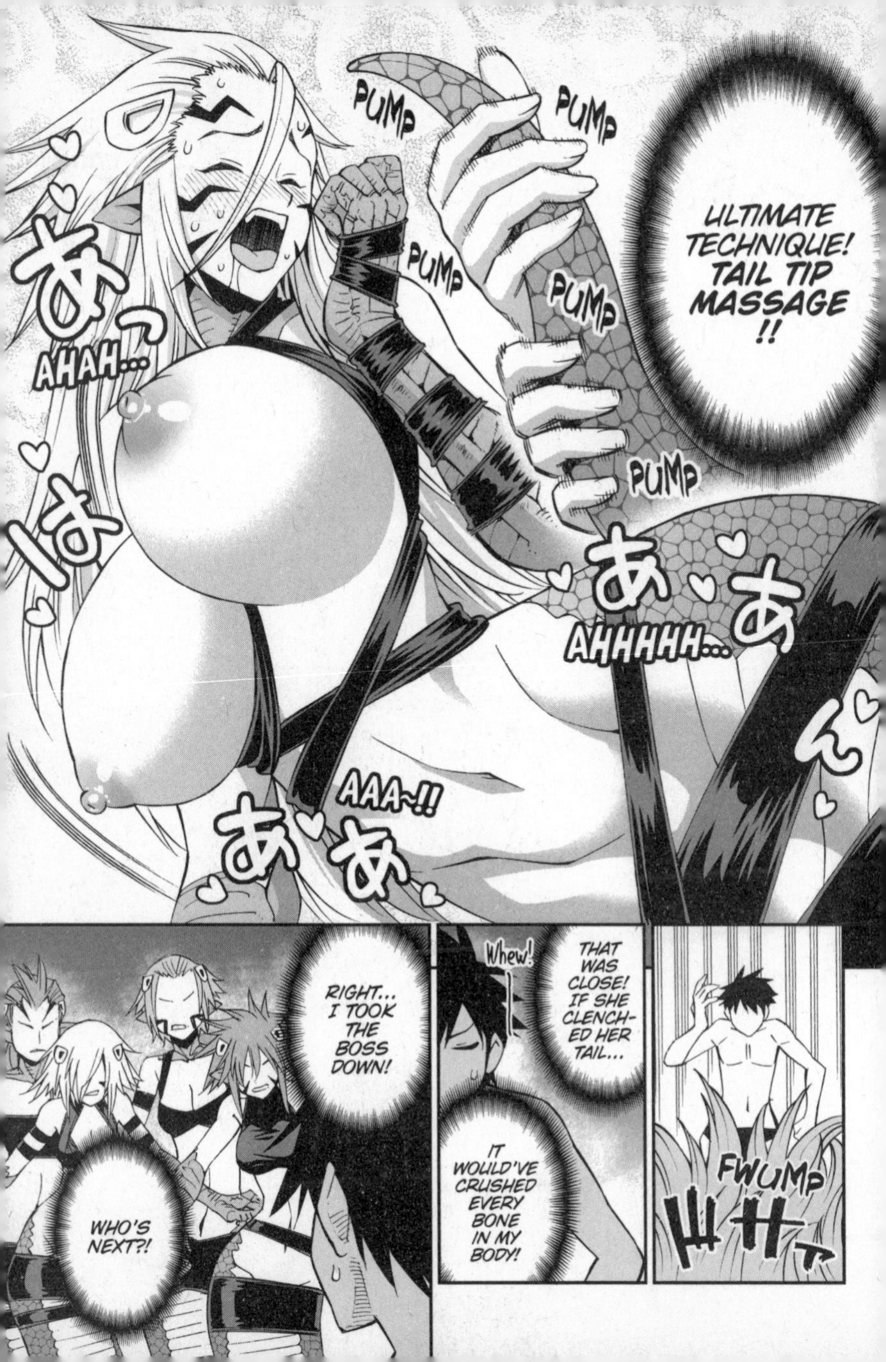
ULTIMATE TECHNIQUE! TAIL TIP MASSAGE !!
PUMP
PUMP
PUMP
PUMP
PUMP
AHAH...
AHHHHH...
AAA~!!
FWUMP
THAT WAS CLOSE! IF SHE CLENCHED HER TAIL...
Whew!
IT WOULD'VE CRUSHED EVERY BONE IN MY BODY!
RIGHT... I TOOK THE BOSS DOWN!
WHO'S NEXT?!

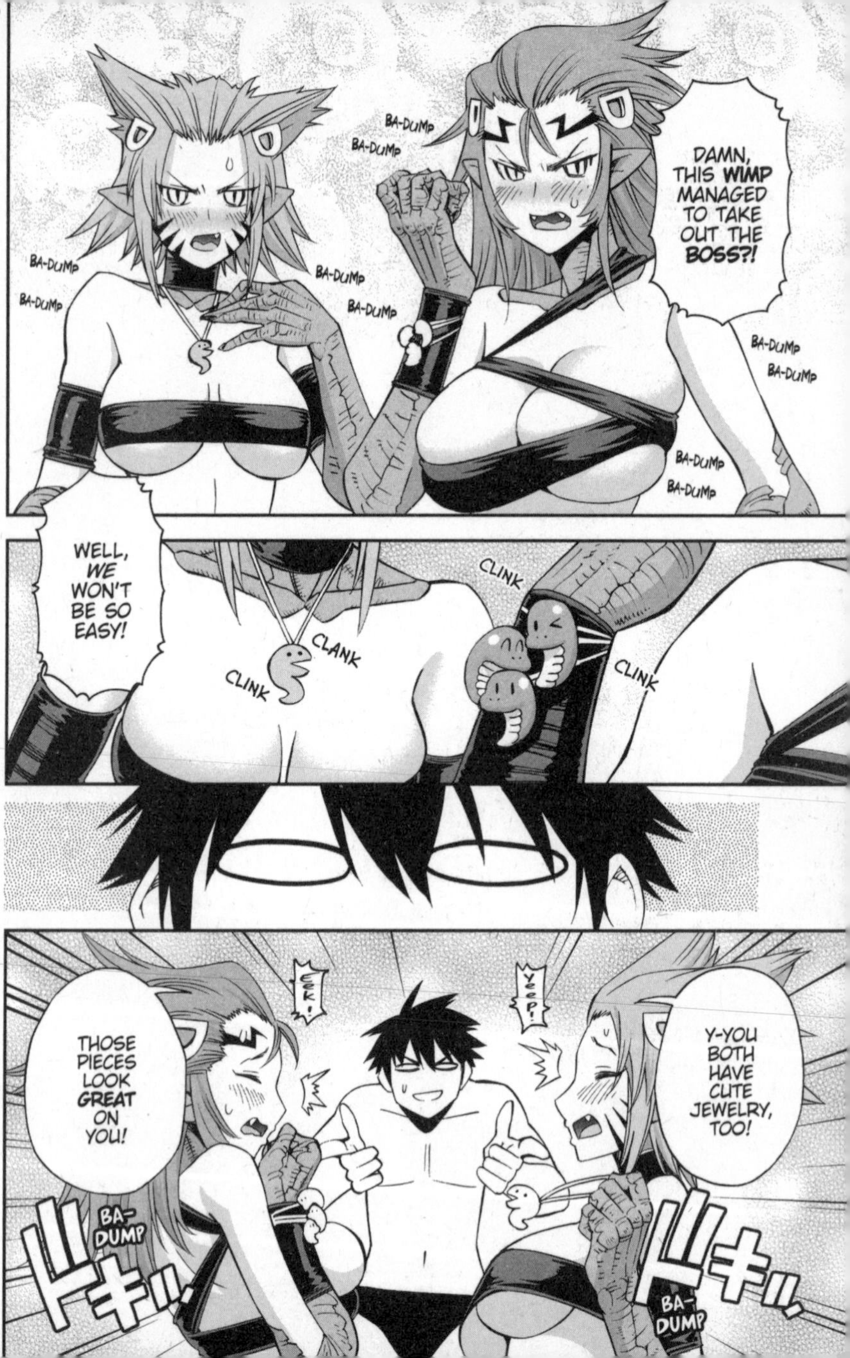

DAMN, THIS WIMP MANAGED TO TAKE OUT THE BOSS?!
BA-DUMP
BA-DUMP
BA-DUMP
BA-DUMP
BA-DUMP
BA-DUMP
BA-DUMP
BA-DUMP
BA-DUMP
BA-DUMP
CLINK
CLINK
WELL, WE WON'T BE SO EASY!
CLANK
CLINK
Yeep!
Y-YOU BOTH HAVE CUTE JEWELRY, TOO!
Eek!
THOSE PIECES LOOK GREAT ON YOU!
ドキッ、
BA-DUMP
ドキッ、
BA-DUMP

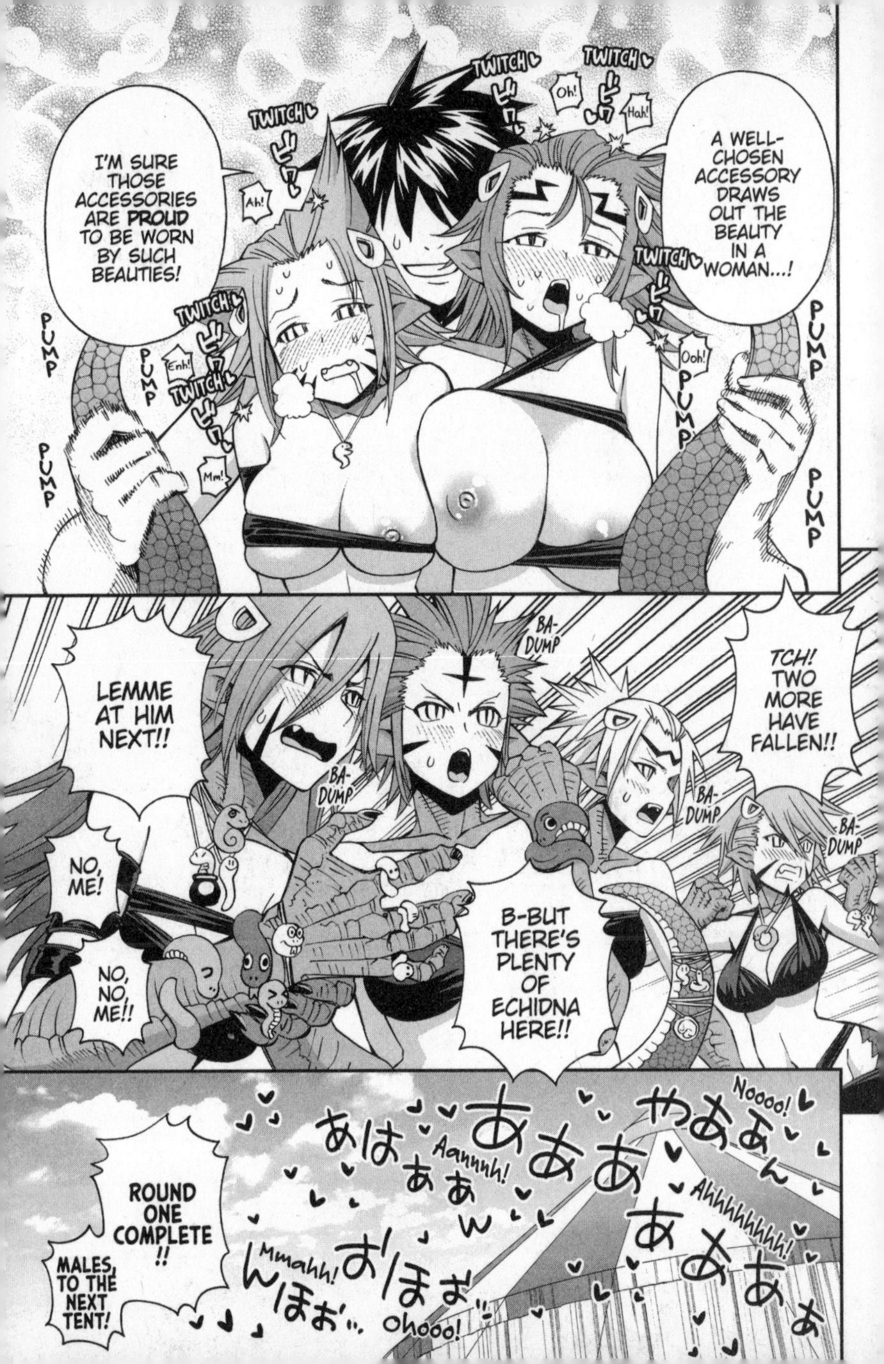
TWITCH
Oh!
Hah!
A WELL-CHOSEN ACCESSORY DRAWS OUT THE BEAUTY IN A WOMAN...!
TWITCH
Ooh!
PUMP
PUMP
PUMP
TWITCH
TWITCH
Ah!
I'M SURE THOSE ACCESSORIES ARE **PROUD** TO BE WORN BY SUCH BEAUTIES!
TWITCH
Enh!
TWITCH
Mm!
PUMP
PUMP
PUMP
TCH! TWO MORE HAVE FALLEN!!
BA-DUMP
BA-DUMP
BA-DUMP
B-BUT THERE'S PLENTY OF ECHIDNA HERE!!
BA-DUMP
LEMME AT HIM NEXT!!
BA-DUMP
NO, ME!
NO, NO, ME!!
Noooo!
Ahhhhhhhh!
Aannnh!
Mmahh!
Ohooo!
ROUND ONE COMPLETE!!
MALES, TO THE NEXT TENT!

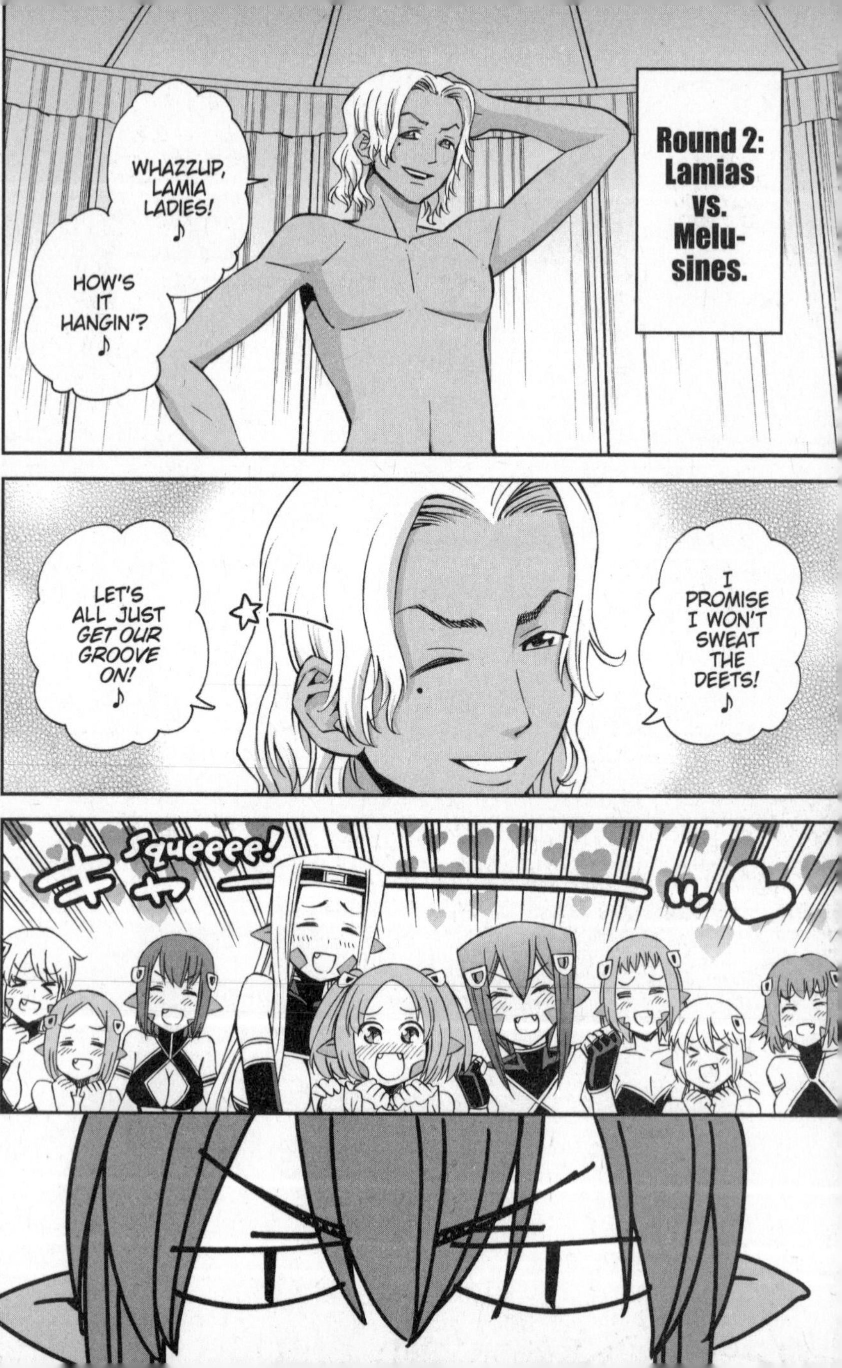
Round 2: Lamias vs. Melu- sines.
WHAZZUP, LAMIA LADIES! ♪
HOW'S IT HANGIN'? ♪
I PROMISE I WON'T SWEAT THE DEETS! ♪
LET'S ALL JUST GET OUR GROOVE ON! ♪
キャー
Squeeeee!

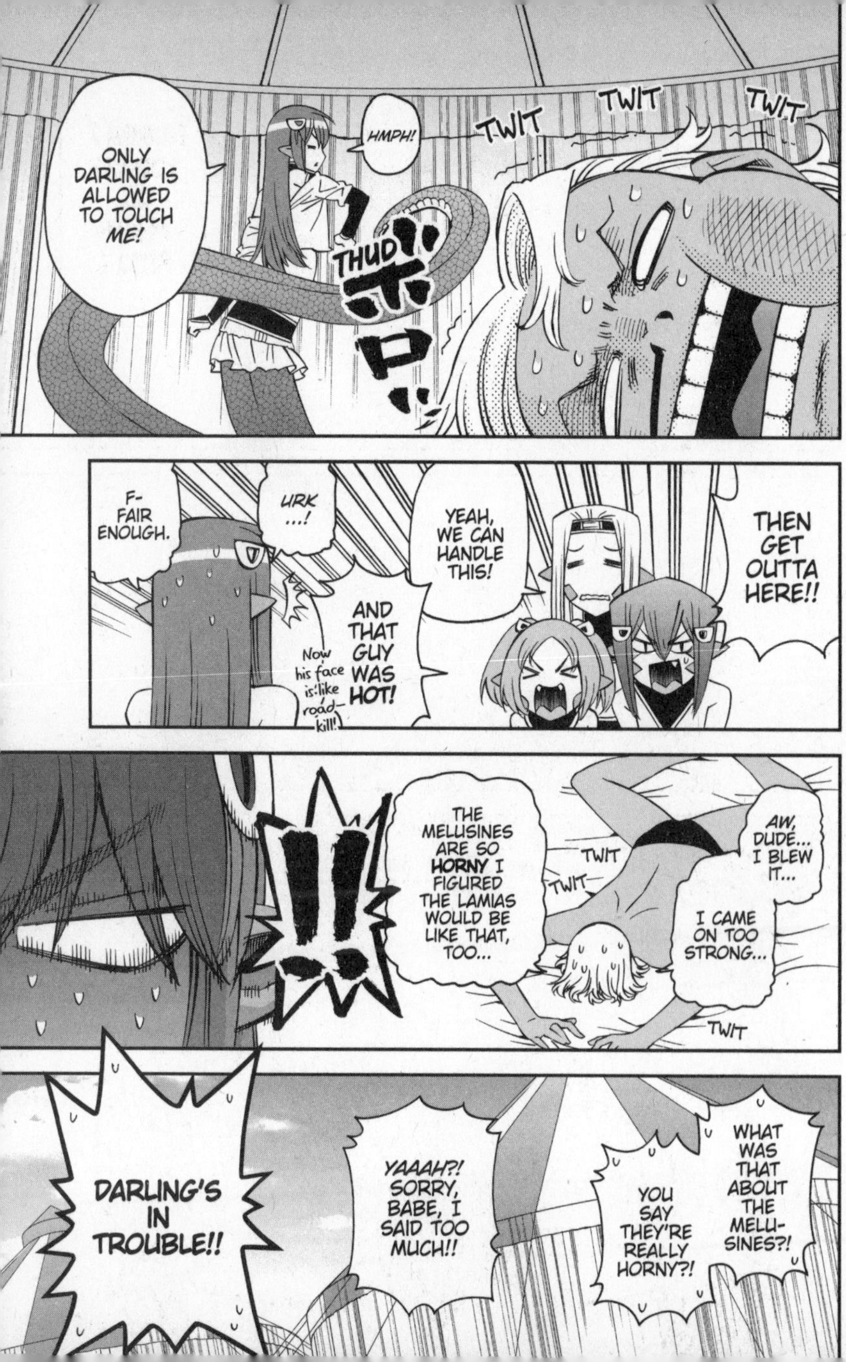
TWIT
TWIT
TWIT
HMPH!
ONLY DARLING IS ALLOWED TO TOUCH ME!
THUD
THEN GET OUTTA HERE!!
YEAH, WE CAN HANDLE THIS!
AND THAT GUY WAS HOT!
Now his face is like road-kill!
URK ...!
F-FAIR ENOUGH.
AW, DUDE... I BLEW IT...
I CAME ON TOO STRONG...
TWIT
TWIT
THE MELUSINES ARE SO **HORNY** I FIGURED THE LAMIAS WOULD BE LIKE THAT, TOO...
TWIT
!!
WHAT WAS THAT ABOUT THE MELU-SINES?!
YOU SAY THEY'RE REALLY HORNY?!
YAAAH?! SORRY, BABE, I SAID TOO MUCH!!
DARLING'S IN TROUBLE!!

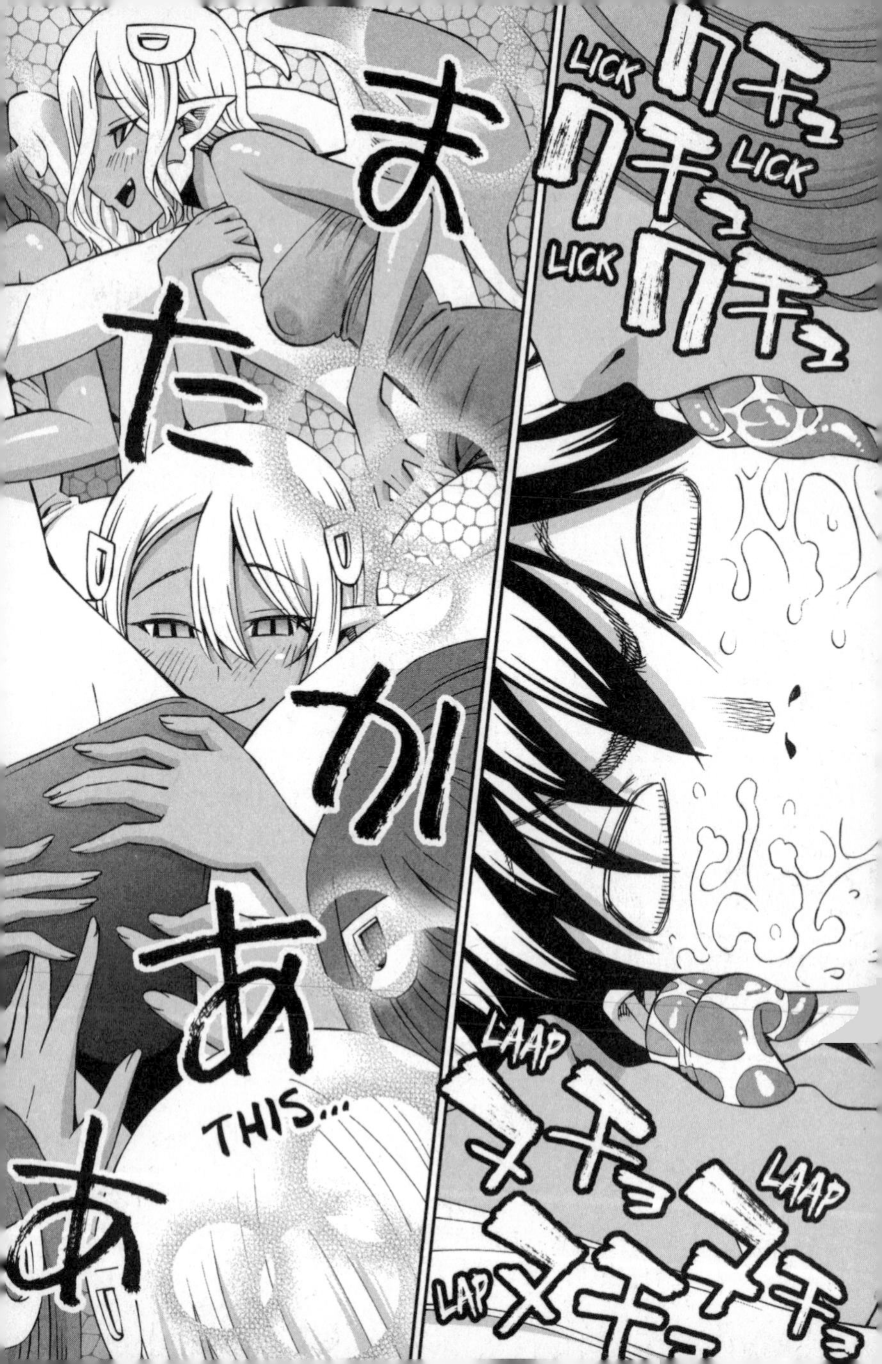
LICK
クチュ
LICK
クチュ
LICK
クチュ
LAAP
ヌチョ
LAAP
ヌチョ
LAP
ヌチュ
またかああ
THIS...

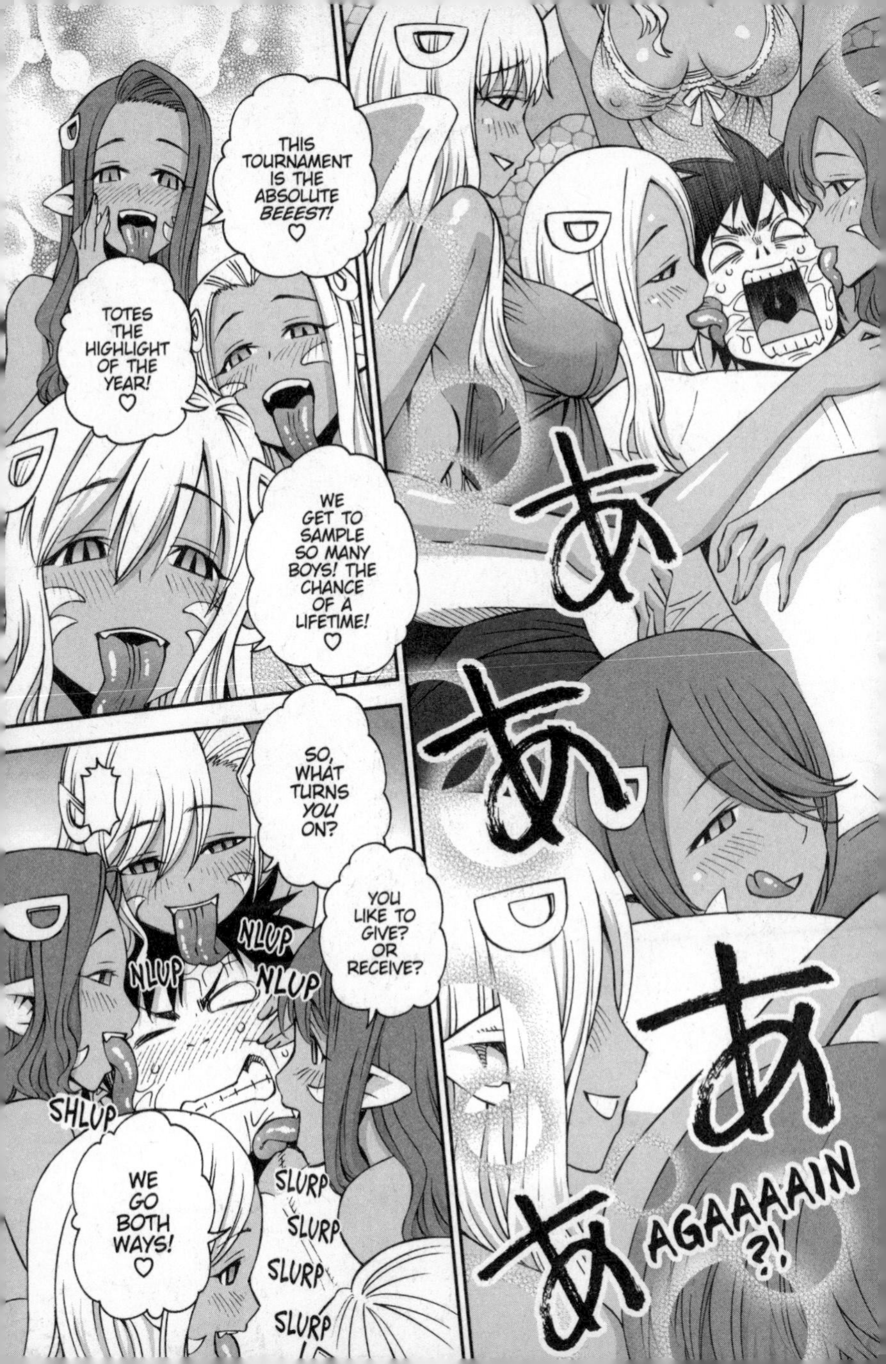

あ
あ
あ
あ
AGAAAAIN ?!
THIS TOURNAMENT IS THE ABSOLUTE BEEEST! ♡
TOTES THE HIGHLIGHT OF THE YEAR! ♡
WE GET TO SAMPLE SO MANY BOYS! THE CHANCE OF A LIFETIME! ♡
SO, WHAT TURNS YOU ON?
YOU LIKE TO GIVE? OR RECEIVE?
NLUP
NLUP
NLUP
SHLUP
WE GO BOTH WAYS! ♡
SLURP
SLURP
SLURP
SLURP

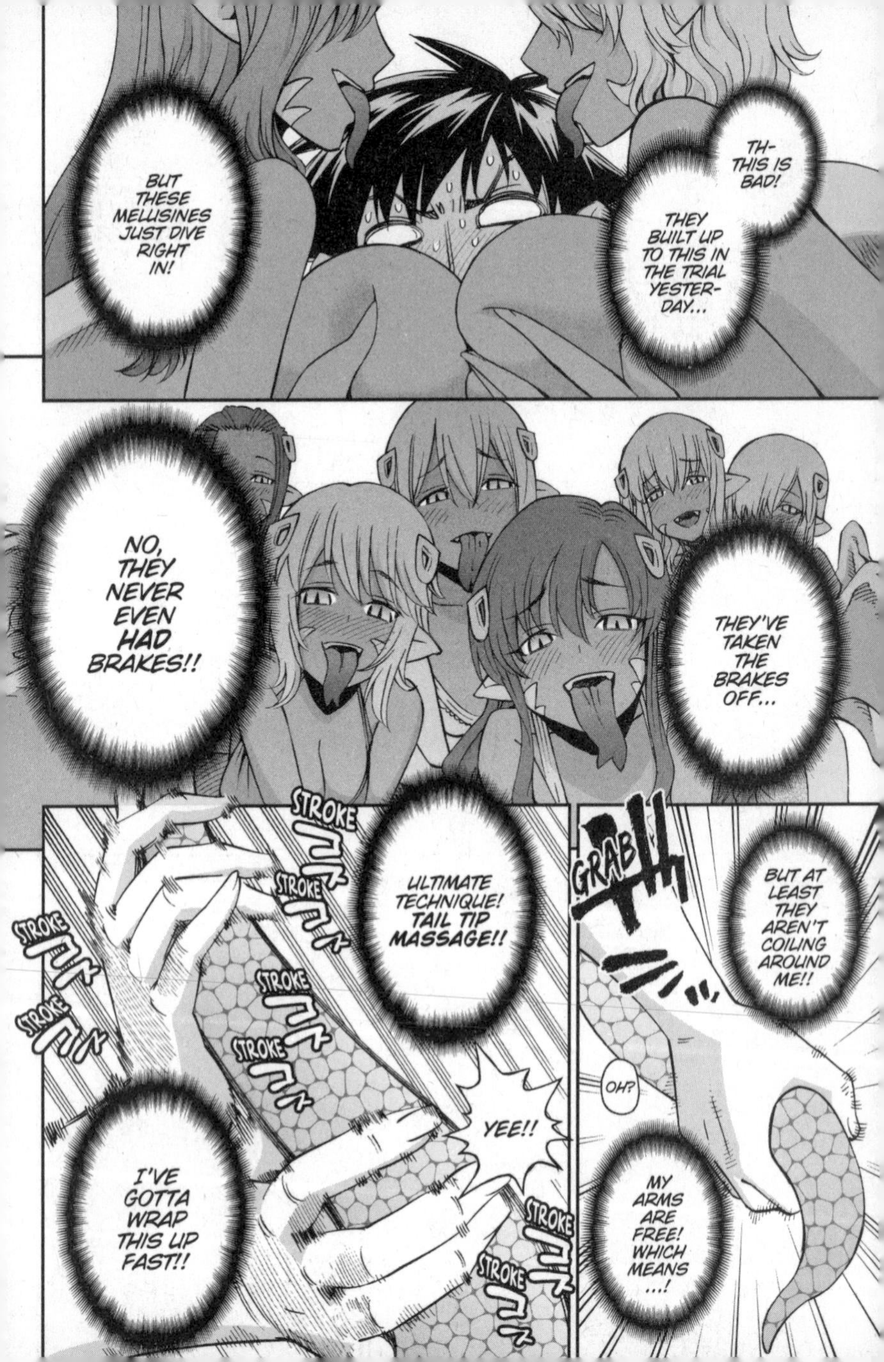
TH- THIS IS BAD!
THEY BUILT UP TO THIS IN THE TRIAL YESTER-DAY...
BUT THESE MELUSINES JUST DIVE RIGHT IN!
THEY'VE TAKEN THE BRAKES OFF...
NO, THEY NEVER EVEN HAD BRAKES!!
GRAB
BUT AT LEAST THEY AREN'T COILING AROUND ME!!
OH?
MY ARMS ARE FREE! WHICH MEANS ...!
STROKE
ULTIMATE TECHNIQUE! TAIL TIP MASSAGE!!
STROKE
STROKE
STROKE
STROKE
YEE!!
STROKE
STROKE
STROKE
I'VE GOTTA WRAP THIS UP FAST!!

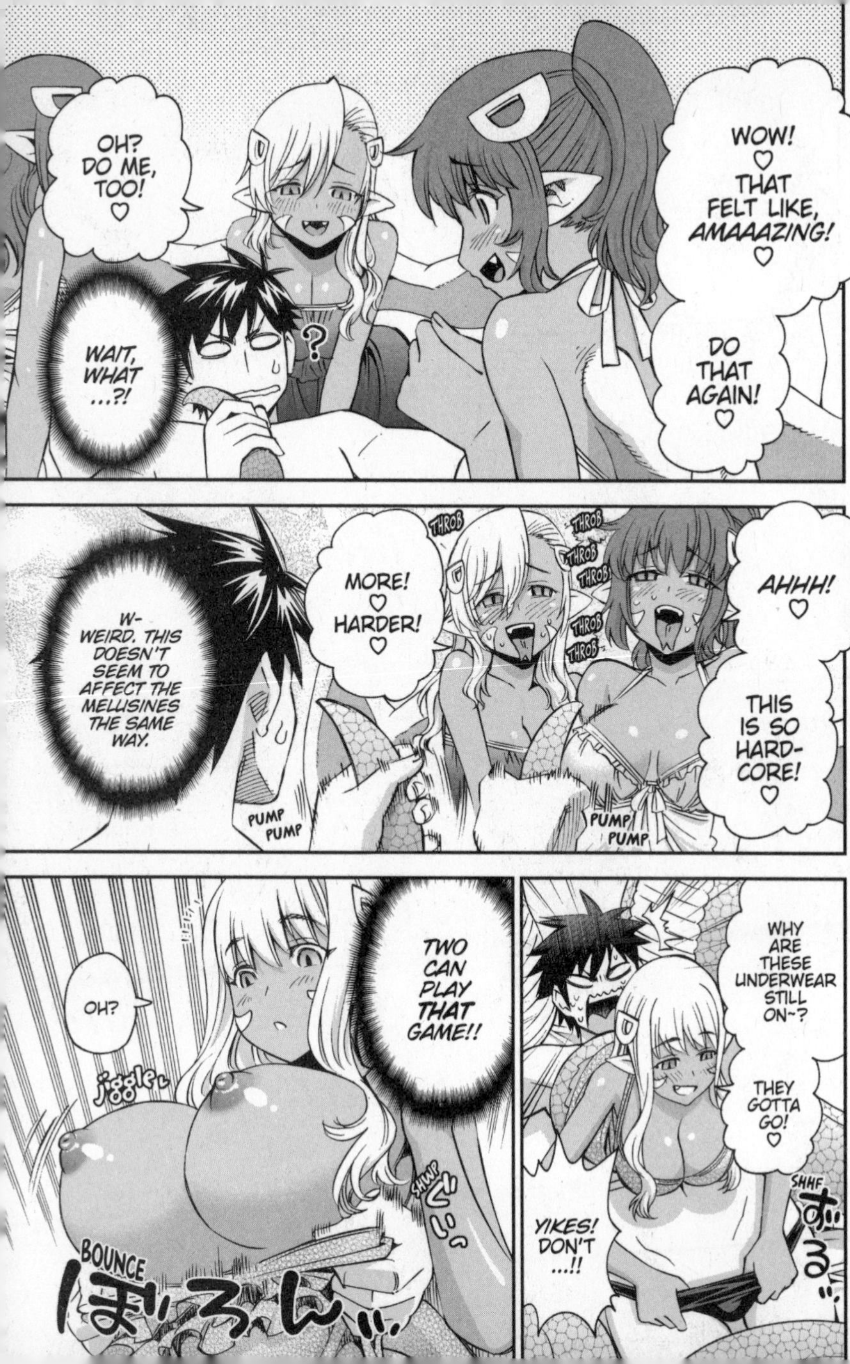
WOW! ♡ THAT FELT LIKE, AMAAAZING! ♡
DO THAT AGAIN! ♡
OH? DO ME, TOO! ♡
?
WAIT, WHAT ...?!
AHHH! ♡
THIS IS SO HARD-CORE! ♡
THROB THROB THROB THROB THROB
MORE! ♡ HARDER! ♡
W-WEIRD. THIS DOESN'T SEEM TO AFFECT THE MELUSINES THE SAME WAY.
PUMP PUMP
PUMP PUMP
WHY ARE THESE UNDERWEAR STILL ON~?
THEY GOTTA GO! ♡
SHHF
YIKES! DON'T ...!!
TWO CAN PLAY THAT GAME!!
OH?
jiggle
SHWP
BOUNCE

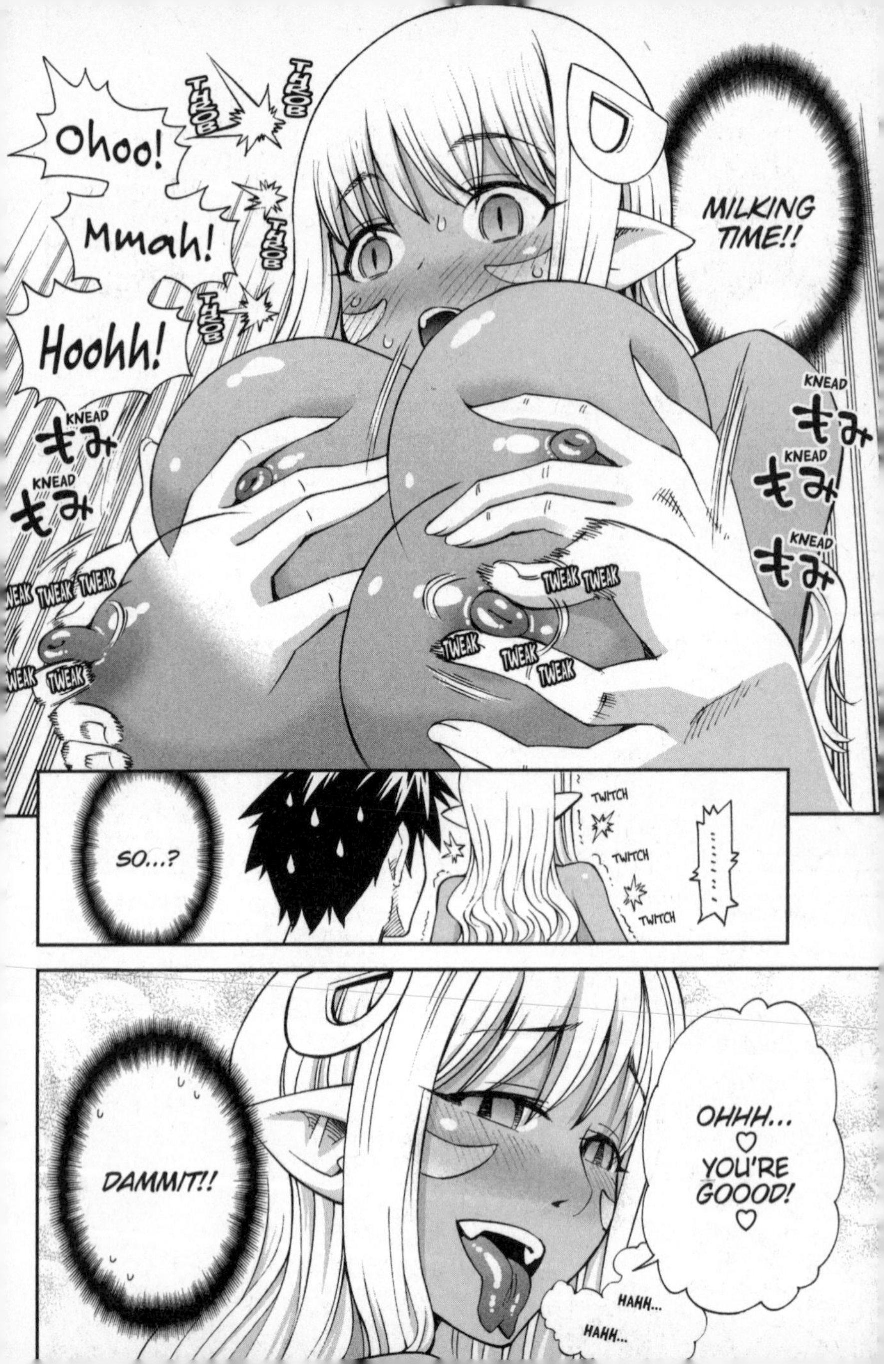
MILKING TIME!!
KNEAD もみ
KNEAD もみ
KNEAD もみ
THROB
THROB
Ohoo!
THROB
Mmmah!
THROB
Hoohh!
KNEAD もみ
KNEAD もみ
TWEAK TWEAK
TWEAK TWEAK TWEAK
TWEAK TWEAK TWEAK
TWEAK TWEAK
......
TWITCH
TWITCH
TWITCH
SO...?
OHHH... ♡ YOU'RE GOOOD! ♡
HAHH...
HAHH...
DAMMIT!!

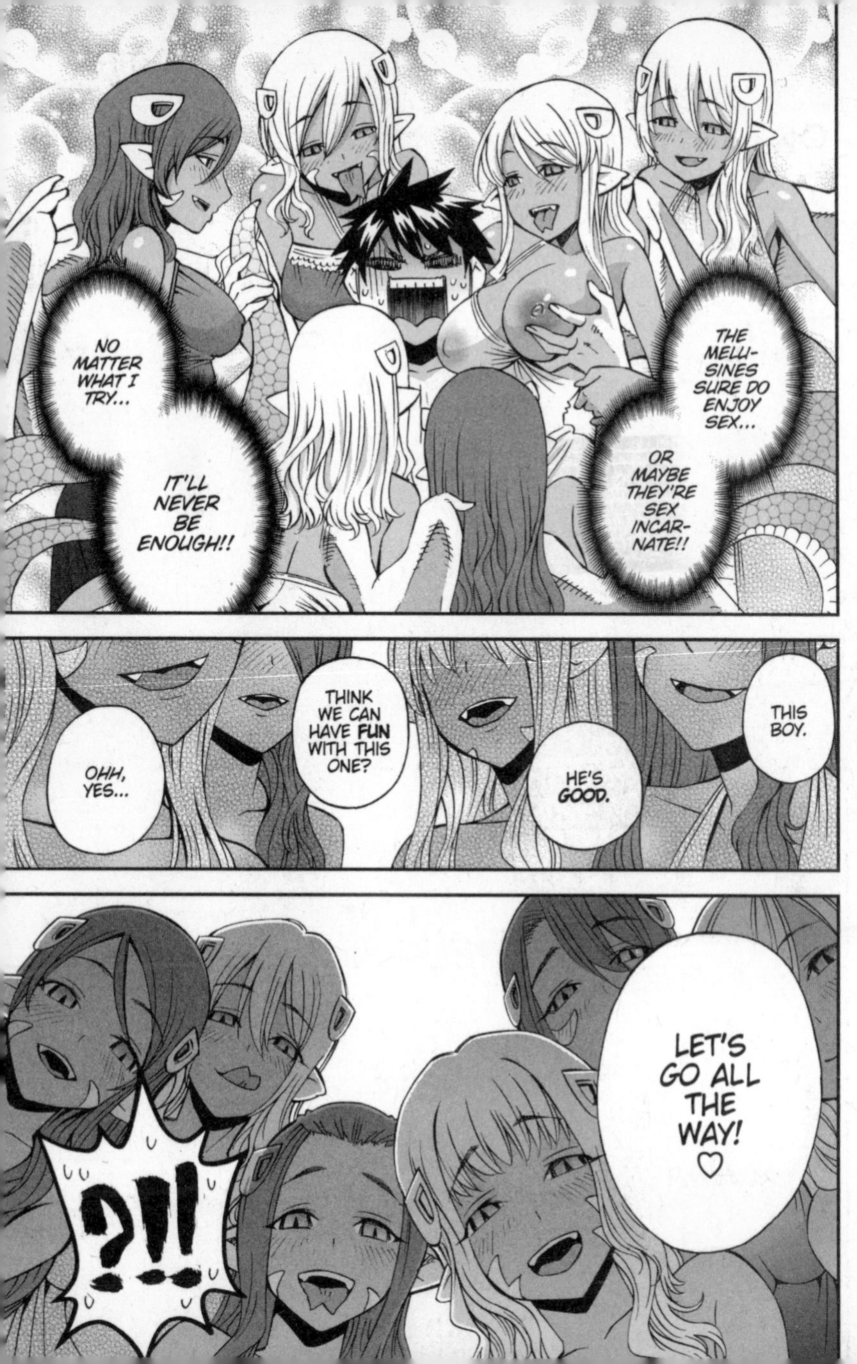
THE MELLUSINES SURE DO ENJOY SEX...
OR MAYBE THEY'RE SEX INCARNATE!!
NO MATTER WHAT I TRY...
IT'LL NEVER BE ENOUGH!!
THIS BOY.
HE'S **GOOD.**
THINK WE CAN HAVE **FUN** WITH THIS ONE?
OHH, YES...
LET'S GO ALL THE WAY! ♡
?!!

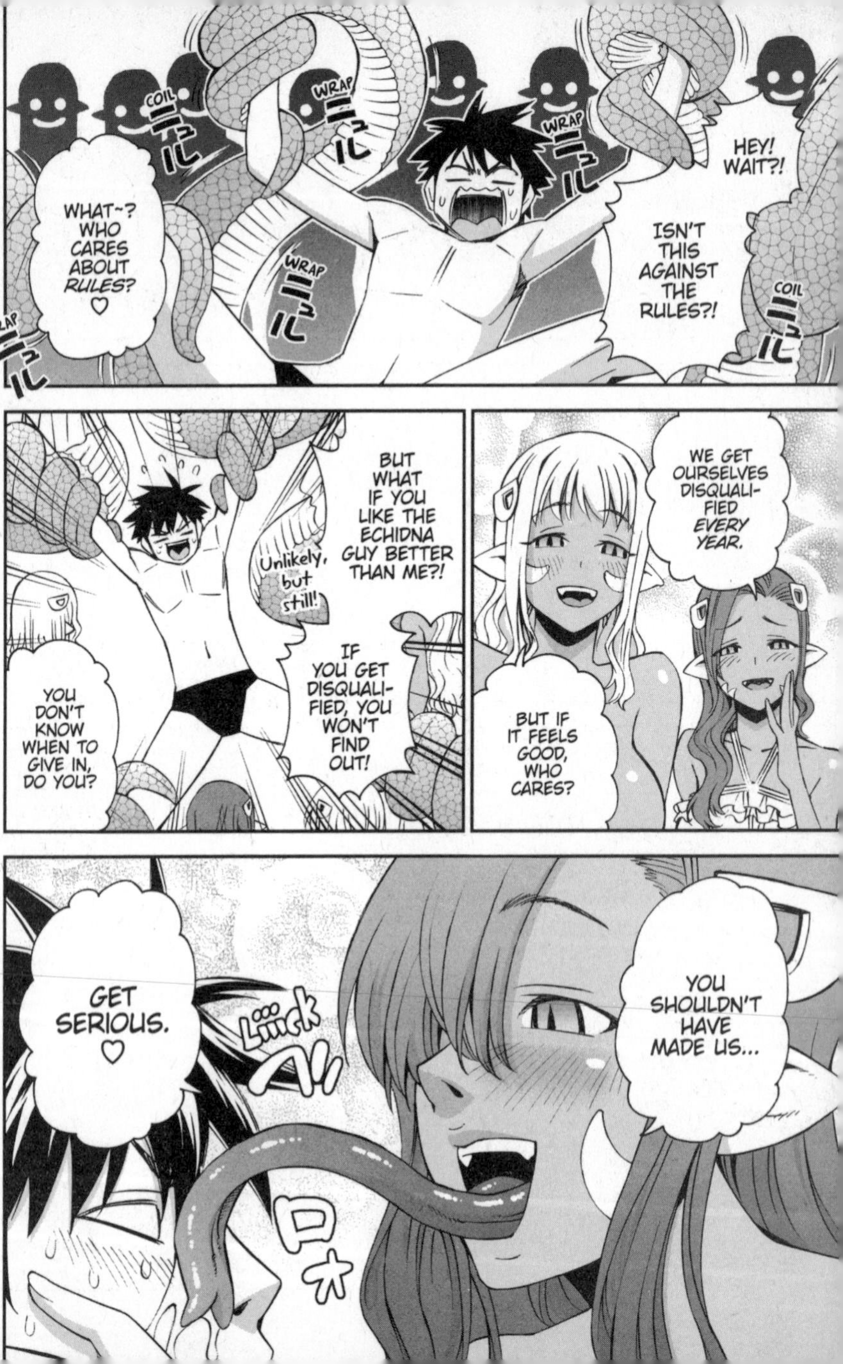
HEY! WAIT?!
ISN'T THIS AGAINST THE RULES?!
COIL ニュル
WRAP ニュル
WRAP ニュル
WRAP ニュル
COIL ニュル
WHAT~? WHO CARES ABOUT RULES? ♡
WRAP ニュル
WE GET OURSELVES DISQUALIFIED EVERY YEAR.
BUT IF IT FEELS GOOD, WHO CARES?
BUT WHAT IF YOU LIKE THE ECHIDNA GUY BETTER THAN ME?!
Unlikely, but still!
IF YOU GET DISQUALIFIED, YOU WON'T FIND OUT!
YOU DON'T KNOW WHEN TO GIVE IN, DO YOU?
YOU SHOULDN'T HAVE MADE US...
Liiick
GET SERIOUS. ♡

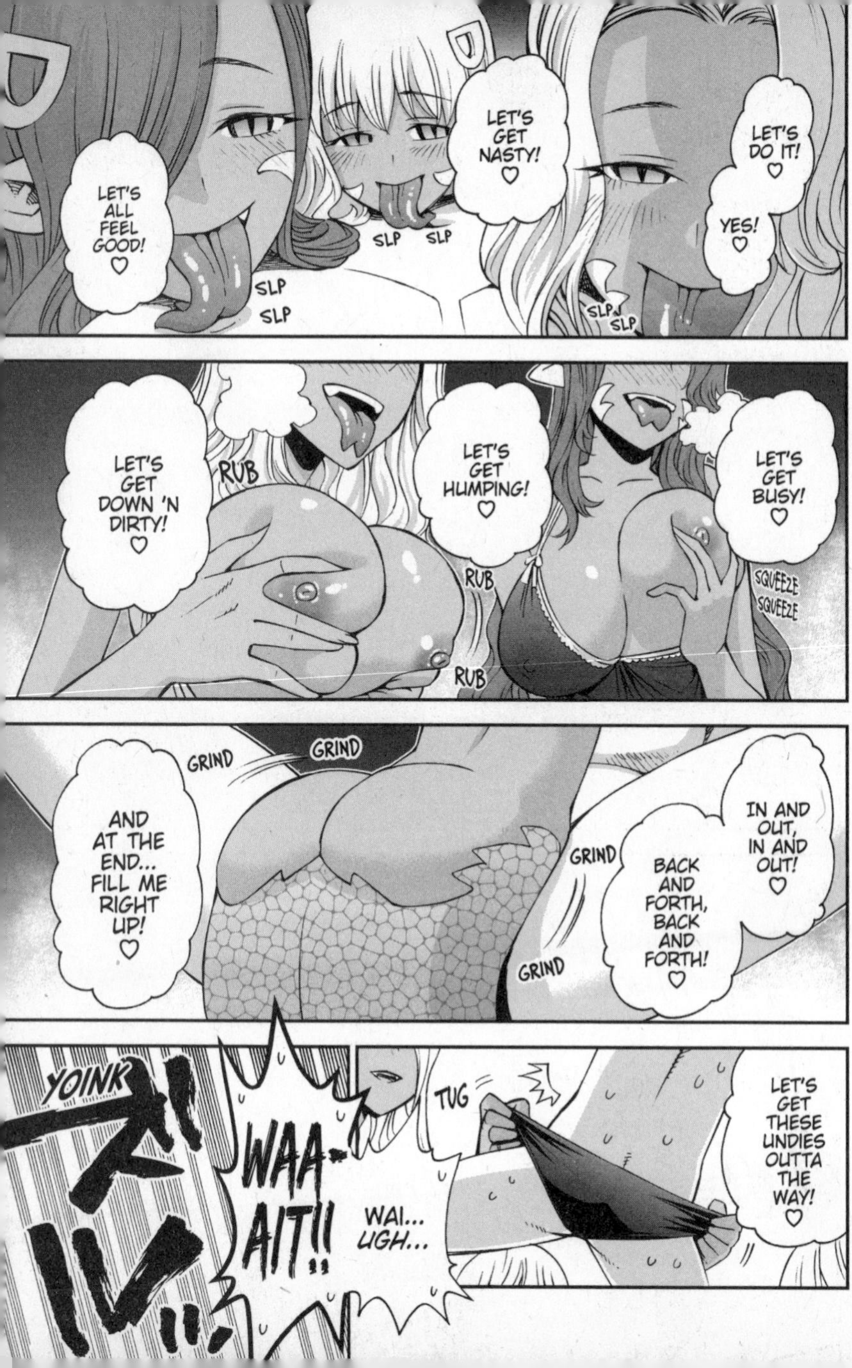
LET'S DO IT! ♡
YES! ♡
SLP SLP
LET'S GET NASTY! ♡
SLP SLP
LET'S ALL FEEL GOOD! ♡
SLP SLP
LET'S GET BUSY! ♡
SQUEEZE SQUEEZE
LET'S GET HUMPING! ♡
RUB
RUB
LET'S GET DOWN 'N DIRTY! ♡
RUB
IN AND OUT, IN AND OUT! ♡
BACK AND FORTH, BACK AND FORTH! ♡
GRIND
GRIND
GRIND
GRIND
AND AT THE END... FILL ME RIGHT UP! ♡
LET'S GET THESE UNDIES OUTTA THE WAY! ♡
TUG
WAI... UGH...
WAA-AIT!!
YOINK

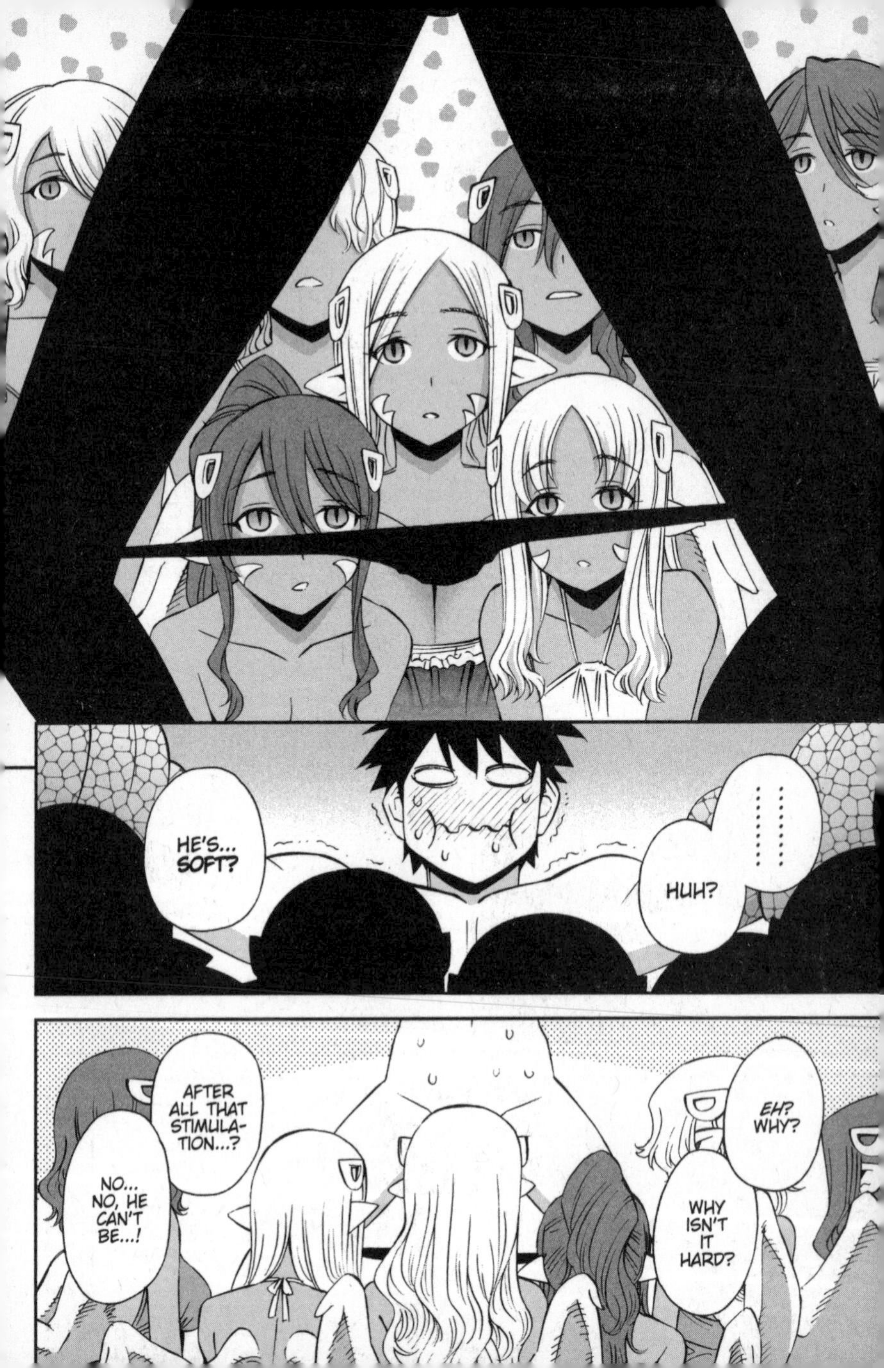
......
HUH?
HE'S... SOFT?
EH? WHY?
WHY ISN'T IT HARD?
AFTER ALL THAT STIMULATION...?
NO... NO, HE CAN'T BE...!

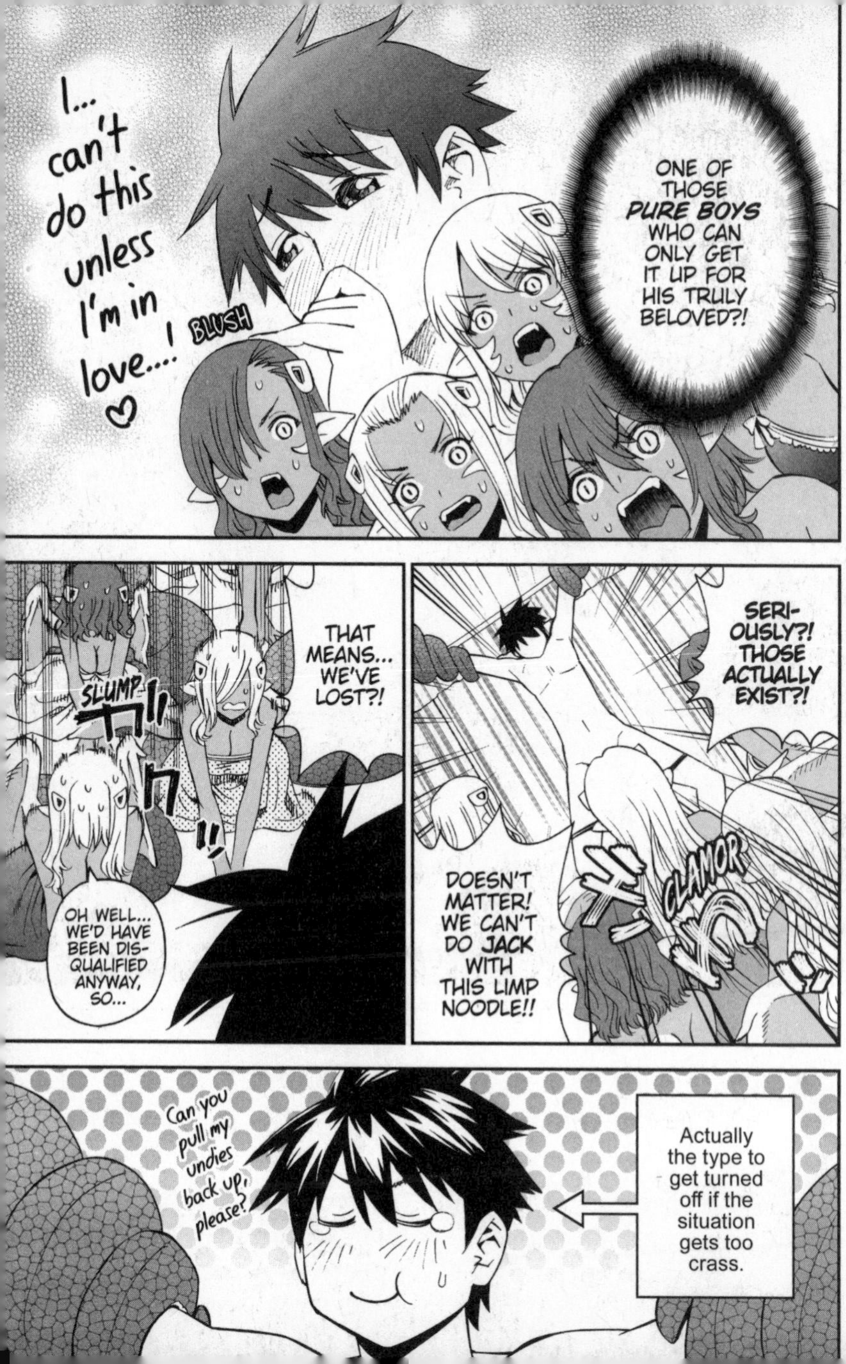
I... can't do this unless I'm in love...! ♡
BLUSH
ONE OF THOSE PURE BOYS WHO CAN ONLY GET IT UP FOR HIS TRULY BELOVED?!
SERI-OUSLY?! THOSE ACTUALLY EXIST?!
DOESN'T MATTER! WE CAN'T DO JACK WITH THIS LIMP NOODLE!!
CLAMOR
THAT MEANS... WE'VE LOST?!
SLUMP
OH WELL... WE'D HAVE BEEN DIS-QUALIFIED ANYWAY, SO...
Can you pull my undies back up, please?
Actually the type to get turned off if the situation gets too crass.

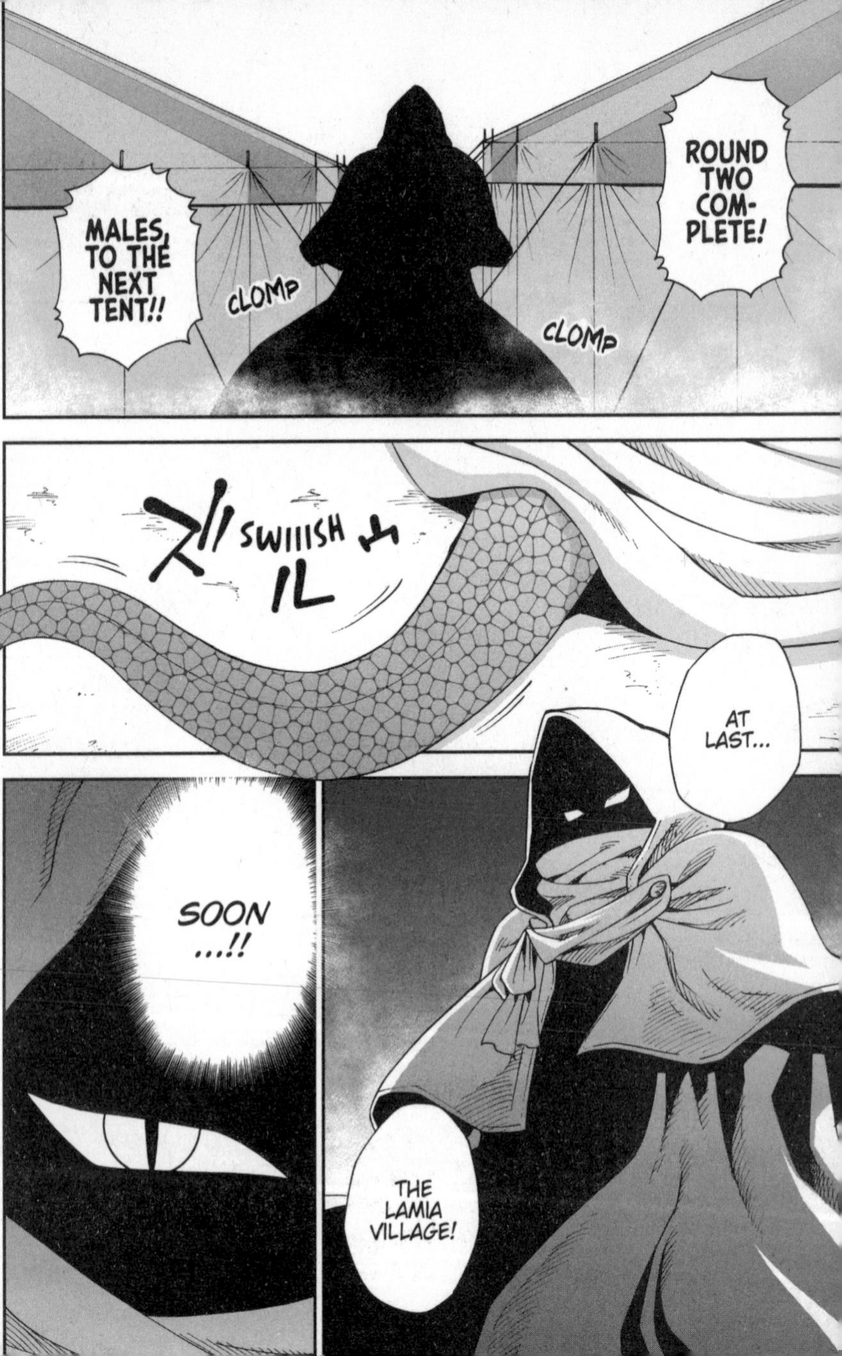
ROUND TWO COM-PLETE!
CLOMP
CLOMP
MALES, TO THE NEXT TENT!!
SWIIISH
AT LAST...
THE LAMIA VILLAGE!
SOON ...!!

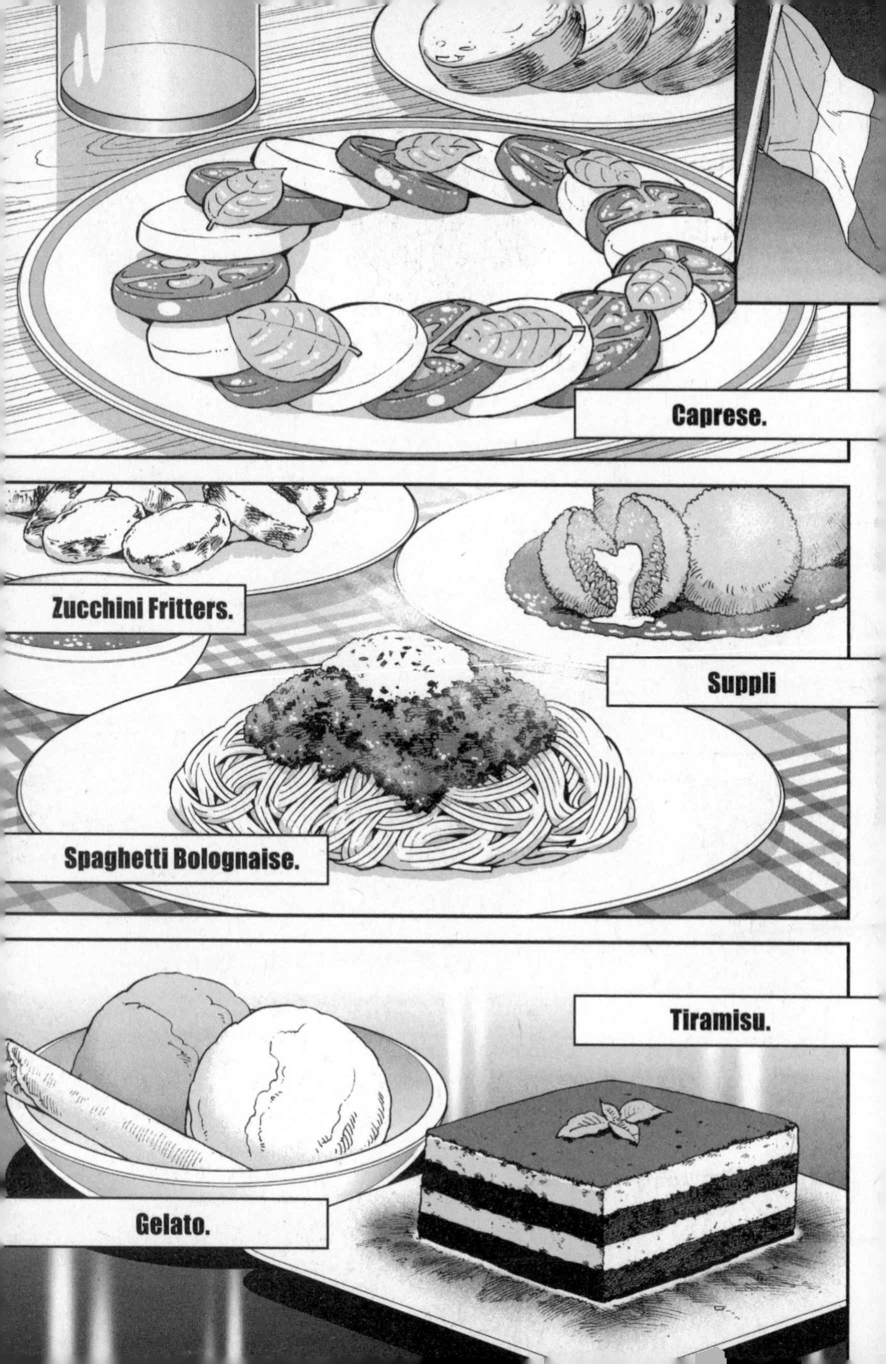

Caprese.
Zucchini Fritters.
Suppli
Spaghetti Bolognaise.
Tiramisu.
Gelato.

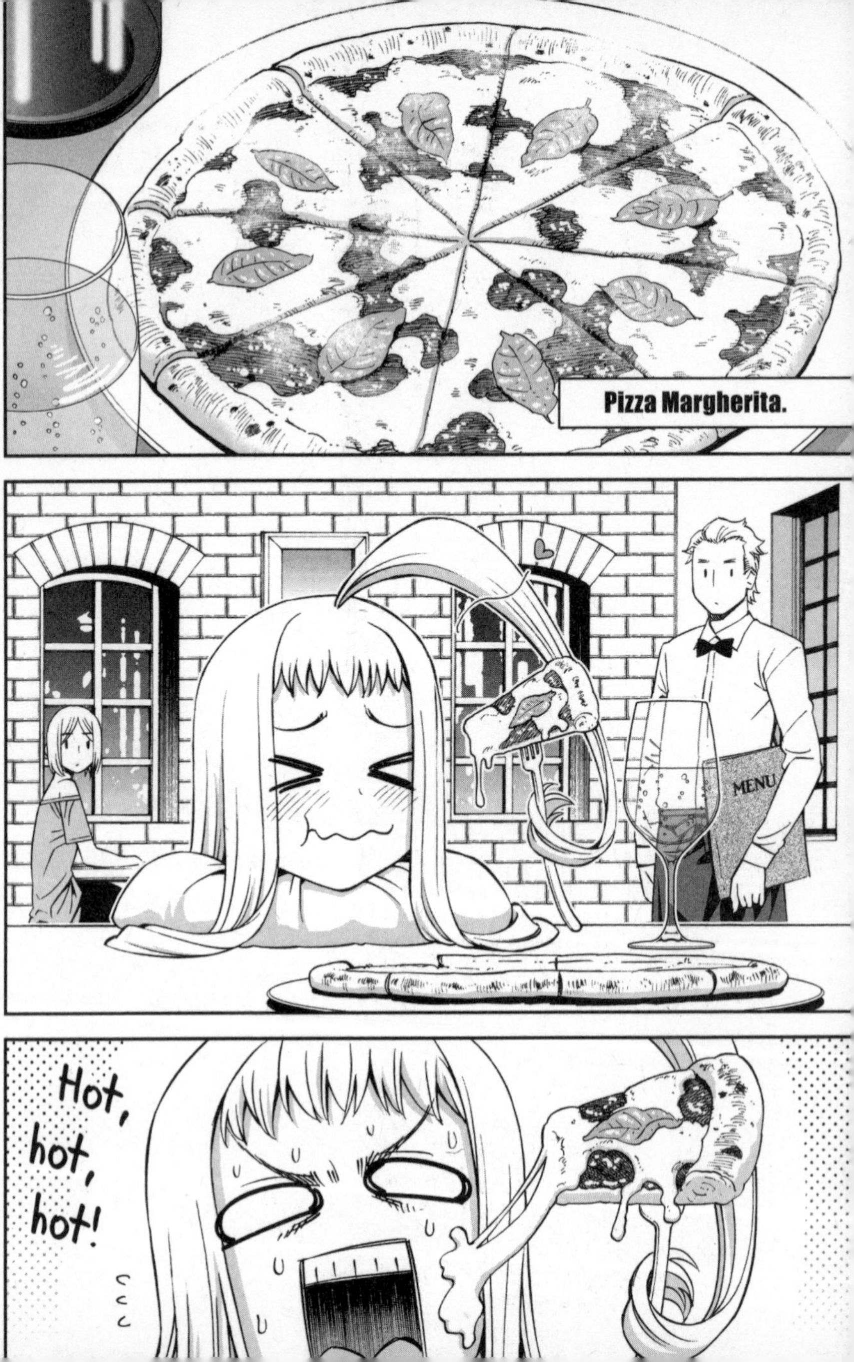
Pizza Margherita.
MENU
Hot, hot, hot!

Monster Musume

Everyday Life with Monster Girls

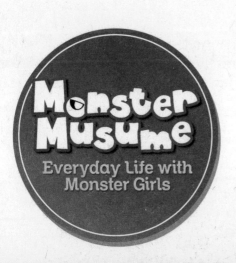

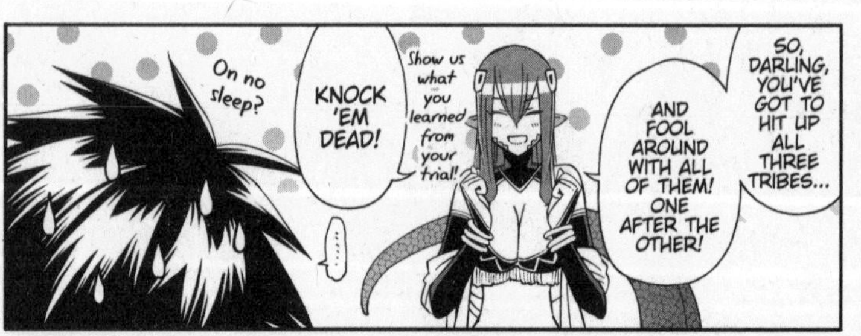
SO, DARLING, YOU'VE GOT TO HIT UP ALL THREE TRIBES...
AND FOOL AROUND WITH ALL OF THEM! ONE AFTER THE OTHER!
Show us what you learned from your trial!
KNOCK 'EM DEAD!
On no sleep?
......

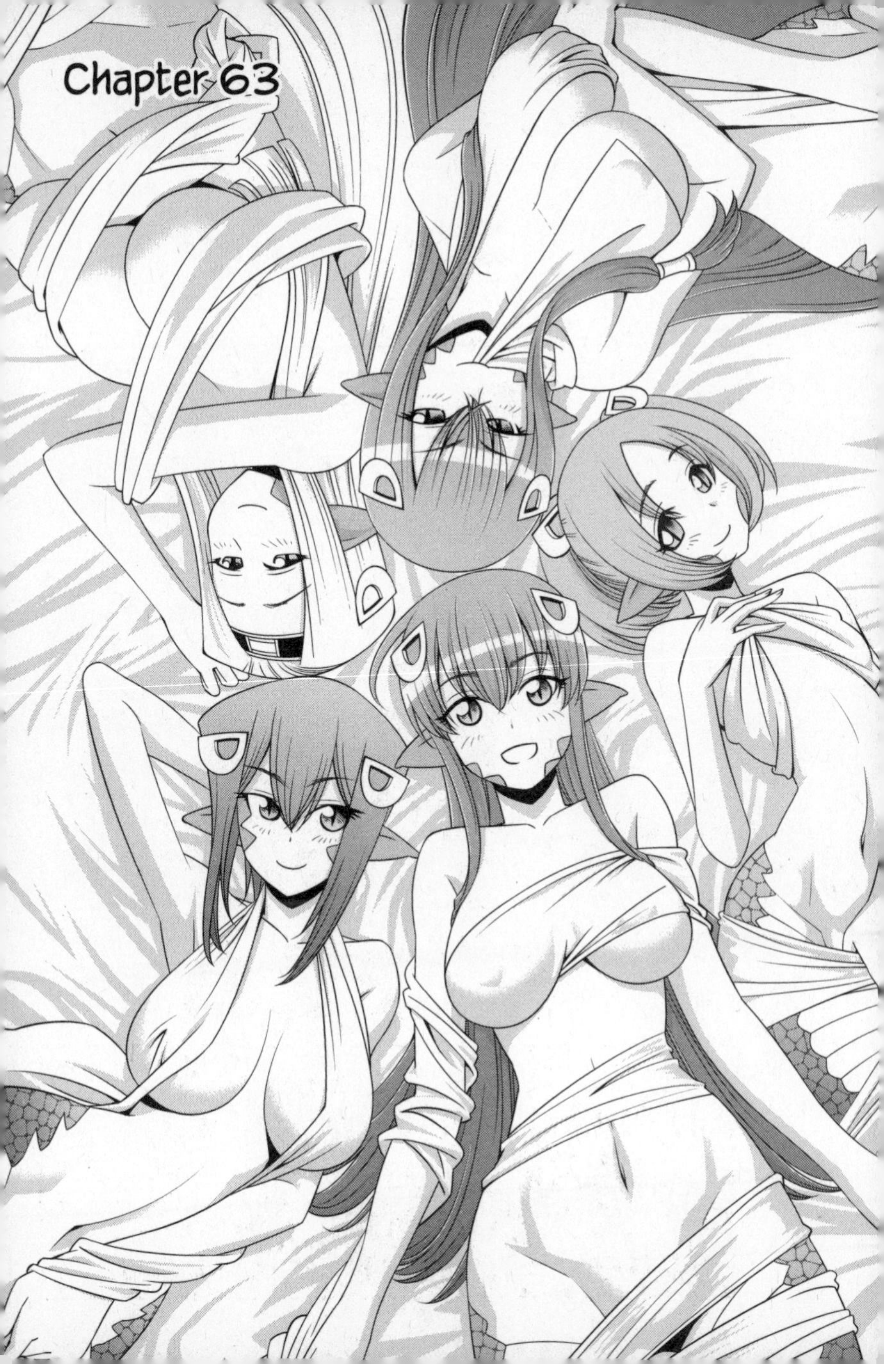
Chapter 63

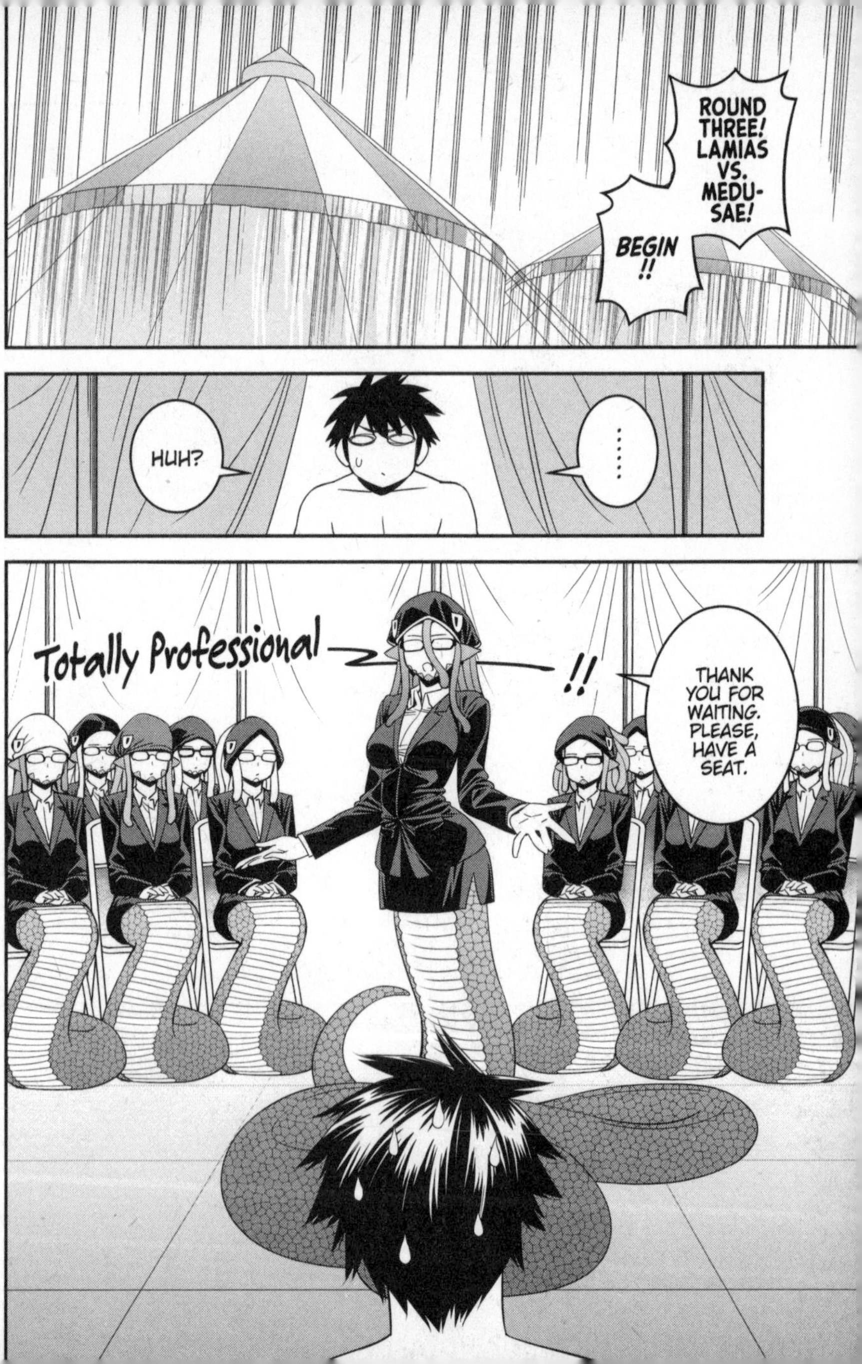
ROUND THREE! LAMIAS VS. MEDU-SAE!
BEGIN !!
......
HUH?
THANK YOU FOR WAITING. PLEASE, HAVE A SEAT.
!!
Totally Professional

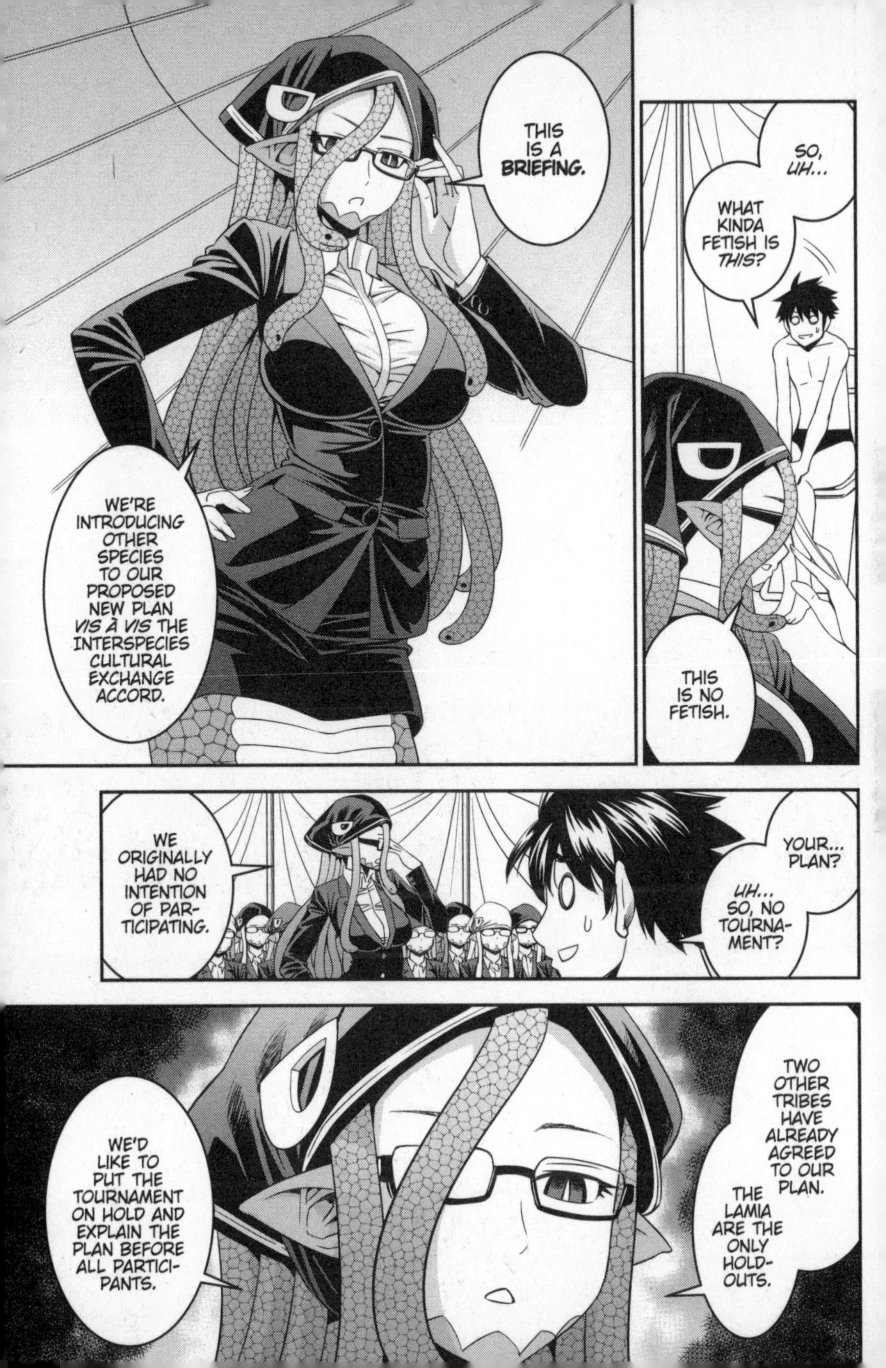
SO, UH... WHAT KINDA FETISH IS *THIS?*
THIS IS NO FETISH.
THIS IS A BRIEFING.
WE'RE INTRODUCING OTHER SPECIES TO OUR PROPOSED NEW PLAN *VIS À VIS* THE INTERSPECIES CULTURAL EXCHANGE ACCORD.
YOUR... PLAN?
UH... SO, NO TOURNAMENT?
WE ORIGINALLY HAD NO INTENTION OF PARTICIPATING.
TWO OTHER TRIBES HAVE ALREADY AGREED TO OUR PLAN.
THE LAMIA ARE THE ONLY HOLD-OUTS.
WE'D LIKE TO PUT THE TOURNAMENT ON HOLD AND EXPLAIN THE PLAN BEFORE ALL PARTICIPANTS.

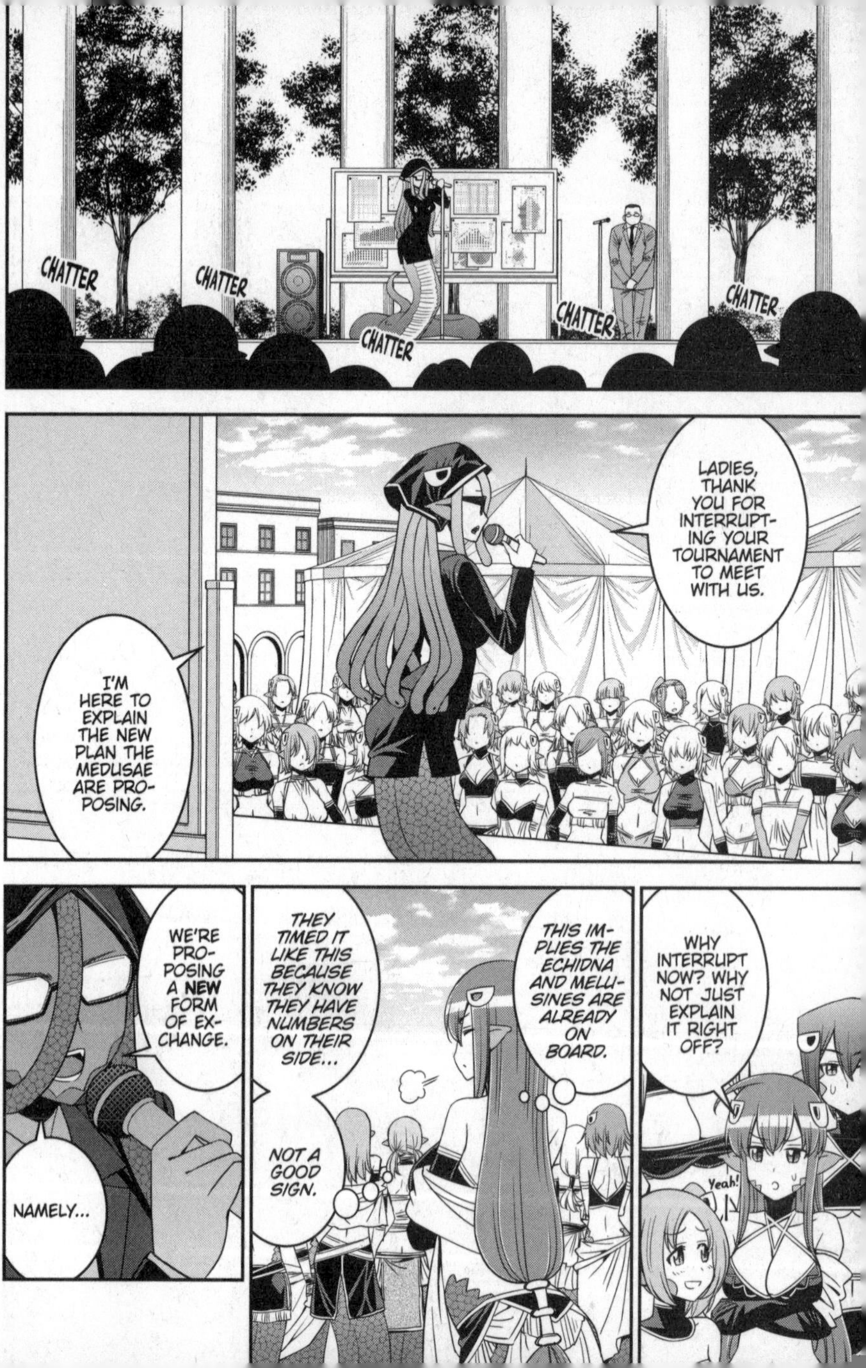
CHATTER
CHATTER
CHATTER
CHATTER
CHATTER
LADIES, THANK YOU FOR INTERRUPTING YOUR TOURNAMENT TO MEET WITH US.
I'M HERE TO EXPLAIN THE NEW PLAN THE MEDUSAE ARE PROPOSING.
WHY INTERRUPT NOW? WHY NOT JUST EXPLAIN IT RIGHT OFF?
Yeah!
THIS IMPLIES THE ECHIDNA AND MELLUSINES ARE ALREADY ON BOARD.
THEY TIMED IT LIKE THIS BECAUSE THEY KNOW THEY HAVE NUMBERS ON THEIR SIDE...
NOT A GOOD SIGN.
WE'RE PROPOSING A **NEW** FORM OF EXCHANGE.
NAMELY...

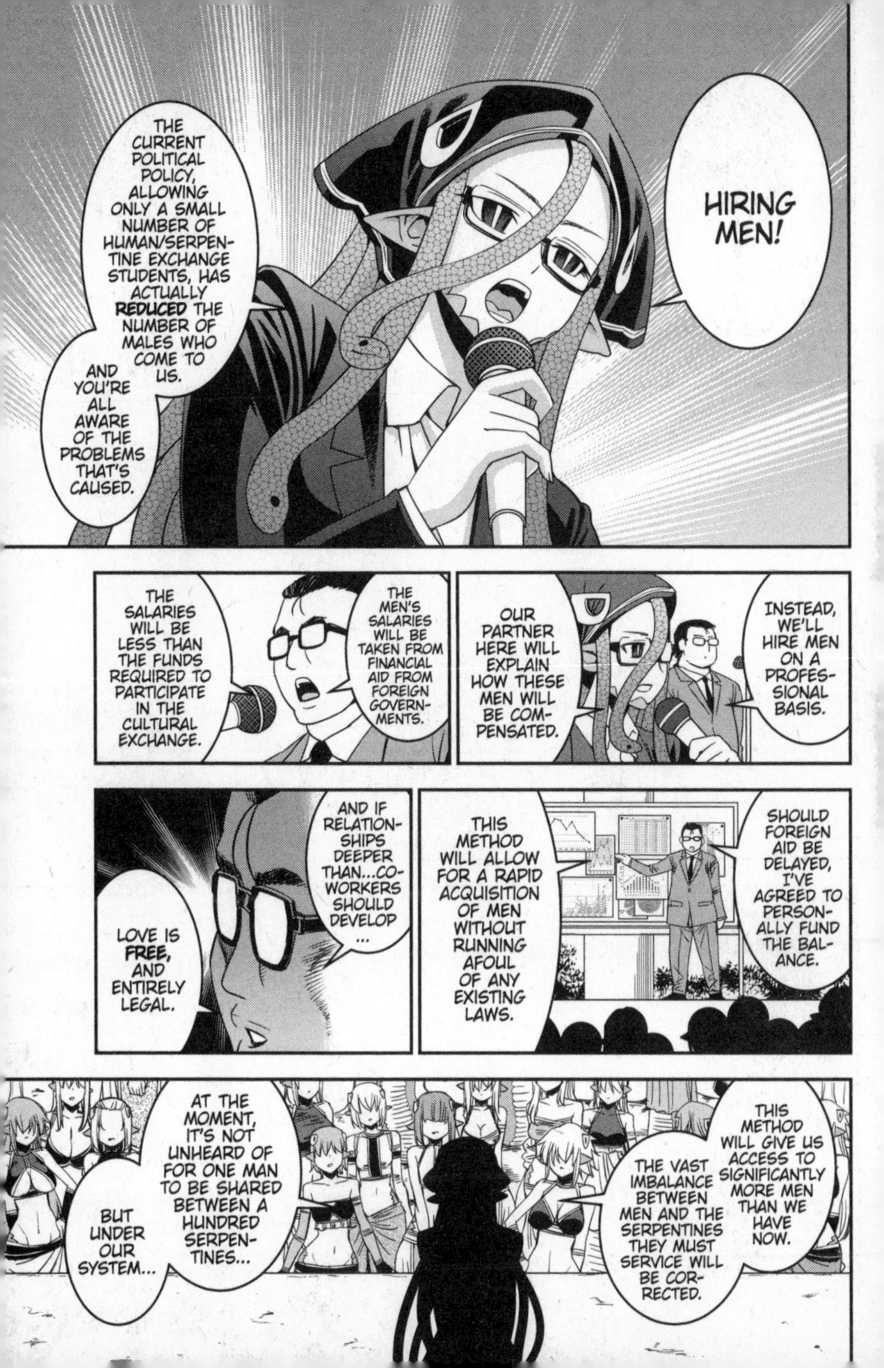
HIRING MEN!
THE CURRENT POLITICAL POLICY, ALLOWING ONLY A SMALL NUMBER OF HUMAN/SERPENTINE EXCHANGE STUDENTS, HAS ACTUALLY **REDUCED** THE NUMBER OF MALES WHO COME TO US.
AND YOU'RE ALL AWARE OF THE PROBLEMS THAT'S CAUSED.
INSTEAD, WE'LL HIRE MEN ON A PROFESSIONAL BASIS.
OUR PARTNER HERE WILL EXPLAIN HOW THESE MEN WILL BE COMPENSATED.
THE MEN'S SALARIES WILL BE TAKEN FROM FINANCIAL AID FROM FOREIGN GOVERNMENTS.
THE SALARIES WILL BE LESS THAN THE FUNDS REQUIRED TO PARTICIPATE IN THE CULTURAL EXCHANGE.
SHOULD FOREIGN AID BE DELAYED, I'VE AGREED TO PERSONALLY FUND THE BALANCE.
THIS METHOD WILL ALLOW FOR A RAPID ACQUISITION OF MEN WITHOUT RUNNING AFOUL OF ANY EXISTING LAWS.
AND IF RELATIONSHIPS DEEPER THAN...CO-WORKERS SHOULD DEVELOP ...
LOVE IS **FREE,** AND ENTIRELY LEGAL.
THIS METHOD WILL GIVE US ACCESS TO SIGNIFICANTLY MORE MEN THAN WE HAVE NOW.
THE VAST IMBALANCE BETWEEN MEN AND THE SERPENTINES THEY MUST SERVICE WILL BE CORRECTED.
AT THE MOMENT, IT'S NOT UNHEARD OF FOR ONE MAN TO BE SHARED BETWEEN A HUNDRED SERPENTINES...
BUT UNDER OUR SYSTEM...

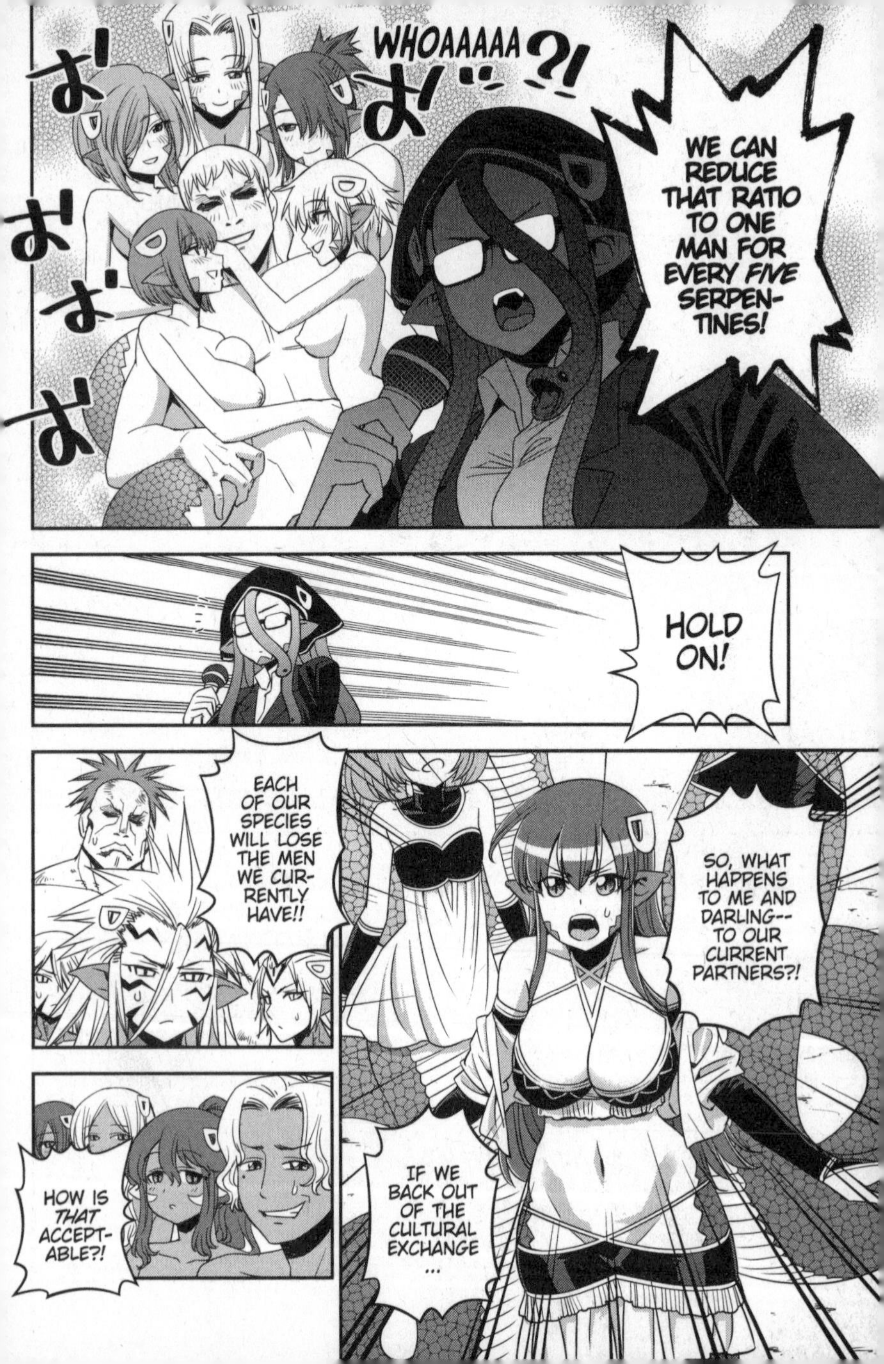
WE CAN REDUCE THAT RATIO TO ONE MAN FOR EVERY *FIVE* SERPENTINES!
WHOAAAAA ?!
HOLD ON!
SO, WHAT HAPPENS TO ME AND DARLING-- TO OUR CURRENT PARTNERS?!
IF WE BACK OUT OF THE CULTURAL EXCHANGE ...
EACH OF OUR SPECIES WILL LOSE THE MEN WE CURRENTLY HAVE!!
HOW IS *THAT* ACCEPTABLE?!

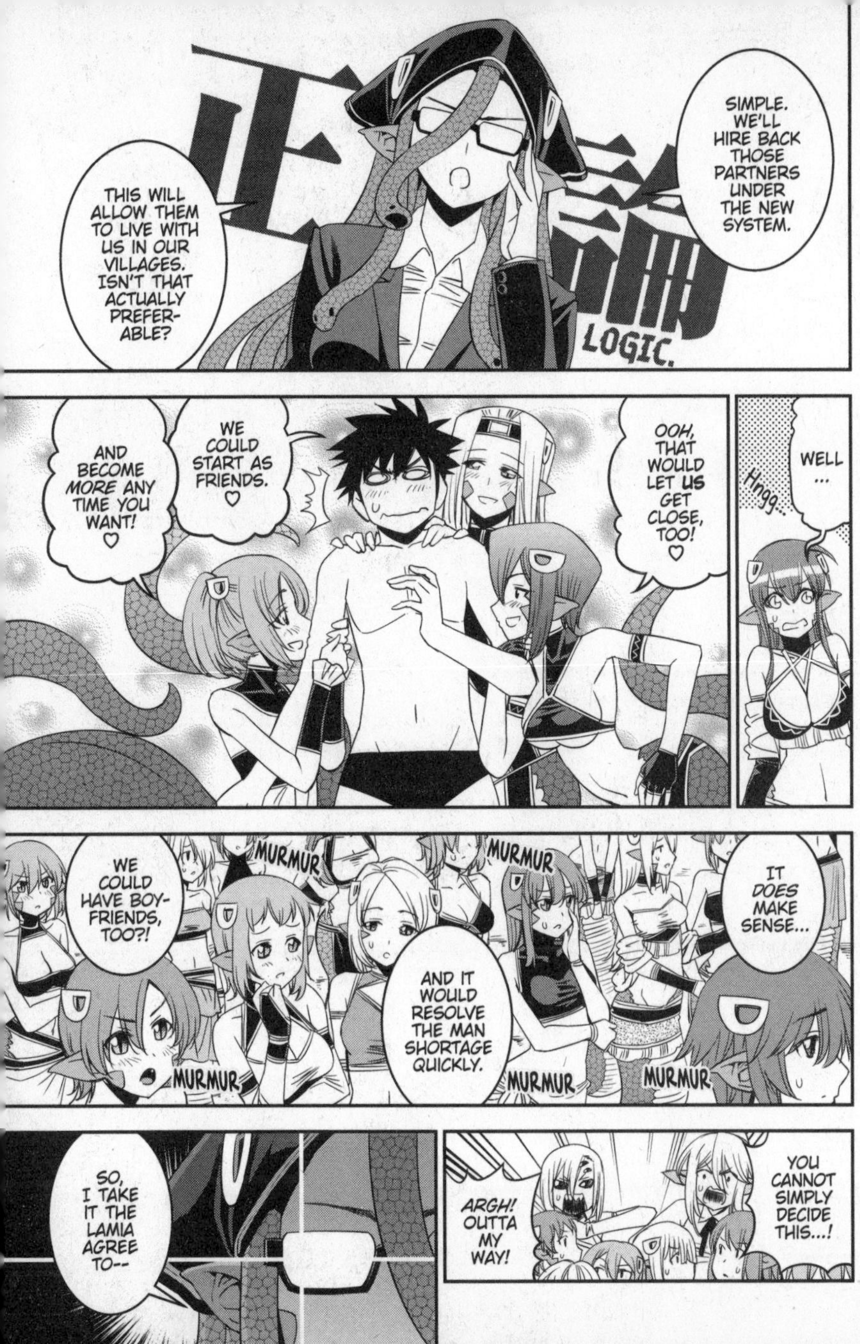
SIMPLE. WE'LL HIRE BACK THOSE PARTNERS UNDER THE NEW SYSTEM.
THIS WILL ALLOW THEM TO LIVE WITH US IN OUR VILLAGES. ISN'T THAT ACTUALLY PREFER-ABLE?
LOGIC.
WELL ...
Hngg...
OOH, THAT WOULD LET US GET CLOSE, TOO! ♡
WE COULD START AS FRIENDS. ♡
AND BECOME MORE ANY TIME YOU WANT! ♡
IT DOES MAKE SENSE...
MURMUR
MURMUR
AND IT WOULD RESOLVE THE MAN SHORTAGE QUICKLY.
WE COULD HAVE BOY-FRIENDS, TOO?!
MURMUR
MURMUR
MURMUR
YOU CANNOT SIMPLY DECIDE THIS...!
ARGH! OUTTA MY WAY!
SO, I TAKE IT THE LAMIA AGREE TO--

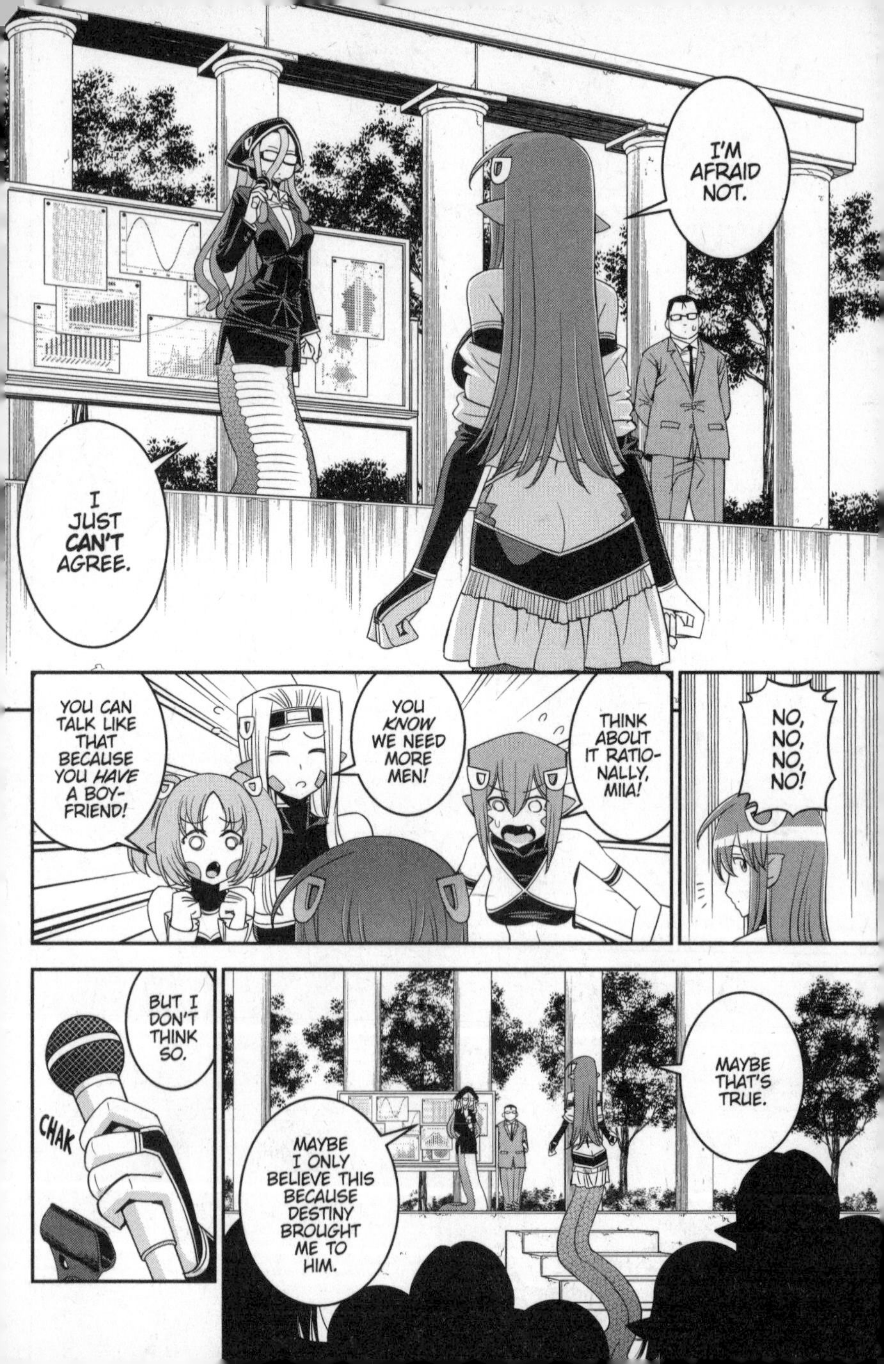
I'M AFRAID NOT.
I JUST CAN'T AGREE.
NO, NO, NO, NO!
THINK ABOUT IT RATIONALLY, MIIA!
YOU *KNOW* WE NEED MORE MEN!
YOU CAN TALK LIKE THAT BECAUSE YOU *HAVE* A BOYFRIEND!
MAYBE THAT'S TRUE.
MAYBE I ONLY BELIEVE THIS BECAUSE DESTINY BROUGHT ME TO HIM.
BUT I DON'T THINK SO.
CHAK

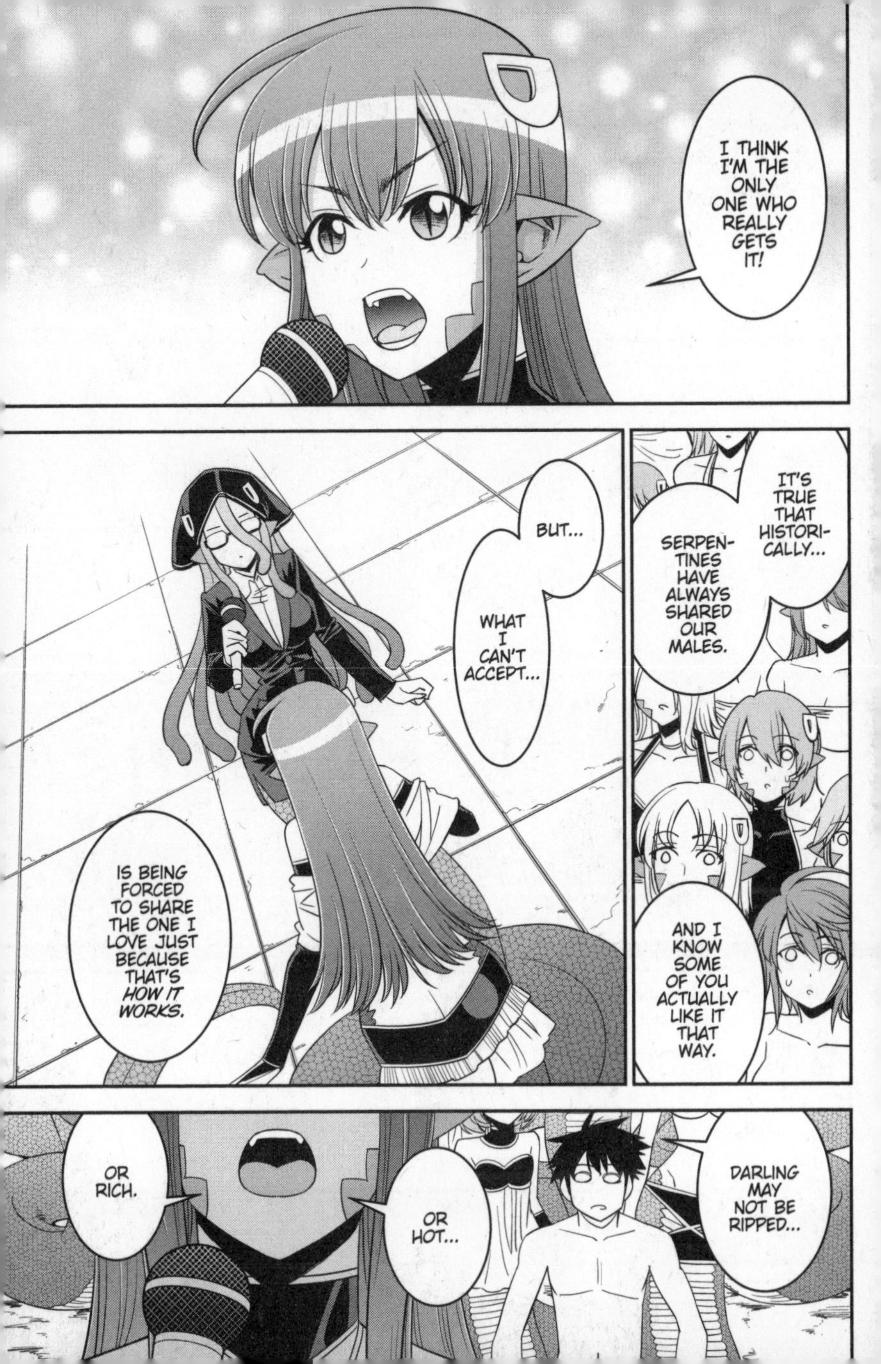
I THINK I'M THE ONLY ONE WHO REALLY GETS IT!
IT'S TRUE THAT HISTORICALLY...
SERPENTINES HAVE ALWAYS SHARED OUR MALES.
AND I KNOW SOME OF YOU ACTUALLY LIKE IT THAT WAY.
BUT...
WHAT I CAN'T ACCEPT...
IS BEING FORCED TO SHARE THE ONE I LOVE JUST BECAUSE THAT'S *HOW IT* WORKS.
DARLING MAY NOT BE RIPPED...
OR HOT...
OR RICH.

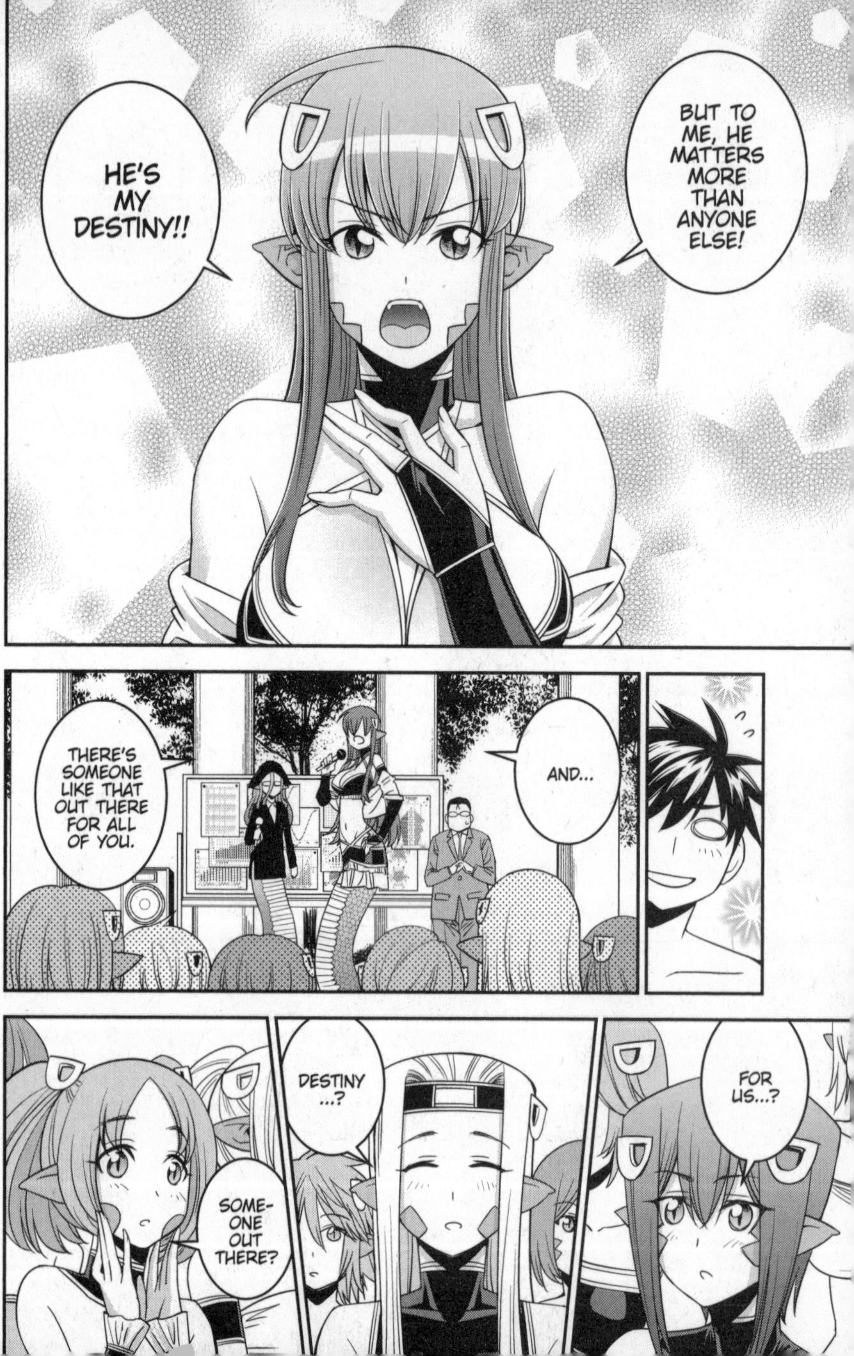
BUT TO ME, HE MATTERS MORE THAN ANYONE ELSE!
HE'S MY DESTINY!!
AND...
THERE'S SOMEONE LIKE THAT OUT THERE FOR ALL OF YOU.
FOR US...?
DESTINY ...?
SOME-ONE OUT THERE?

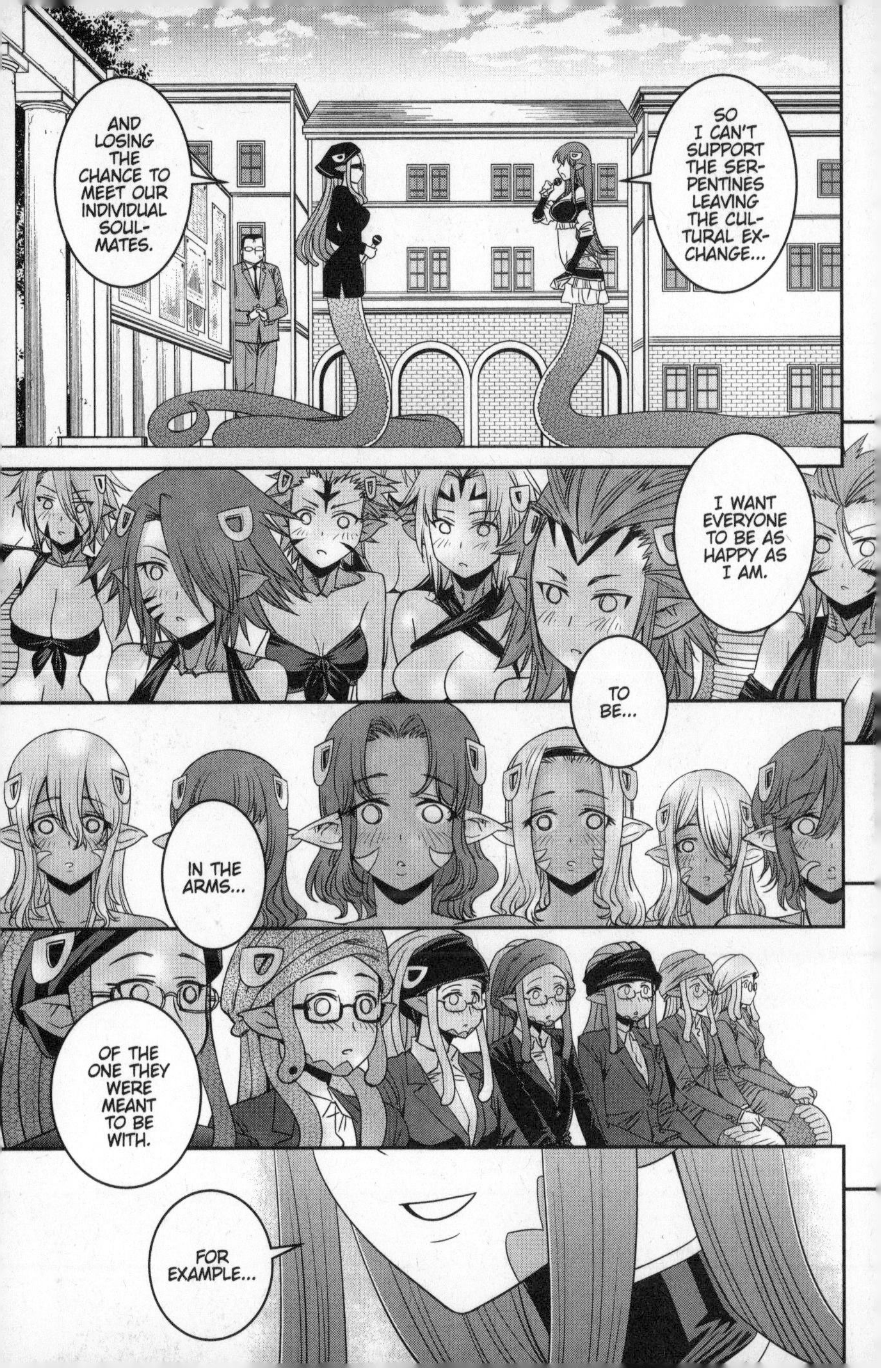
SO I CAN'T SUPPORT THE SERPENTINES LEAVING THE CULTURAL EXCHANGE...
AND LOSING THE CHANCE TO MEET OUR INDIVIDUAL SOULMATES.
I WANT EVERYONE TO BE AS HAPPY AS I AM.
TO BE...
IN THE ARMS...
OF THE ONE THEY WERE MEANT TO BE WITH.
FOR EXAMPLE...

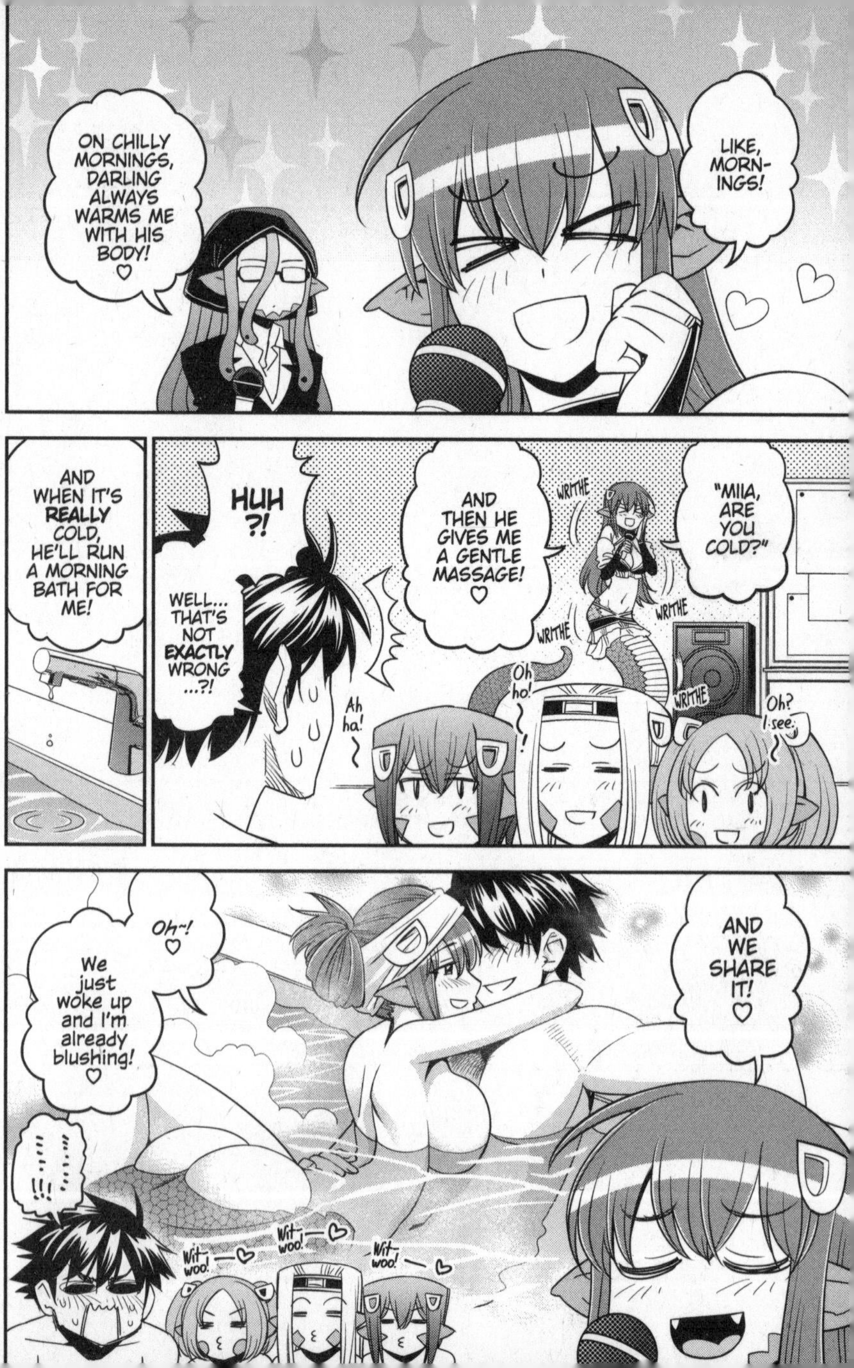
LIKE, MORN-INGS!
ON CHILLY MORNINGS, DARLING ALWAYS WARMS ME WITH HIS BODY! ♡
"MIIA, ARE YOU COLD?"
WRITHE
AND THEN HE GIVES ME A GENTLE MASSAGE! ♡
WRITHE
WRITHE
WRITHE
Oh? I see.~
Oh ho!~!
Ah ha!~
HUH?!
WELL... THAT'S NOT EXACTLY WRONG...?!
AND WHEN IT'S REALLY COLD, HE'LL RUN A MORNING BATH FOR ME!
AND WE SHARE IT! ♡
Oh~! ♡
We just woke up and I'm already blushing! ♡
......!!!
Wit-woo! ♡
Wit-woo! ♡
Wit-woo! ♡

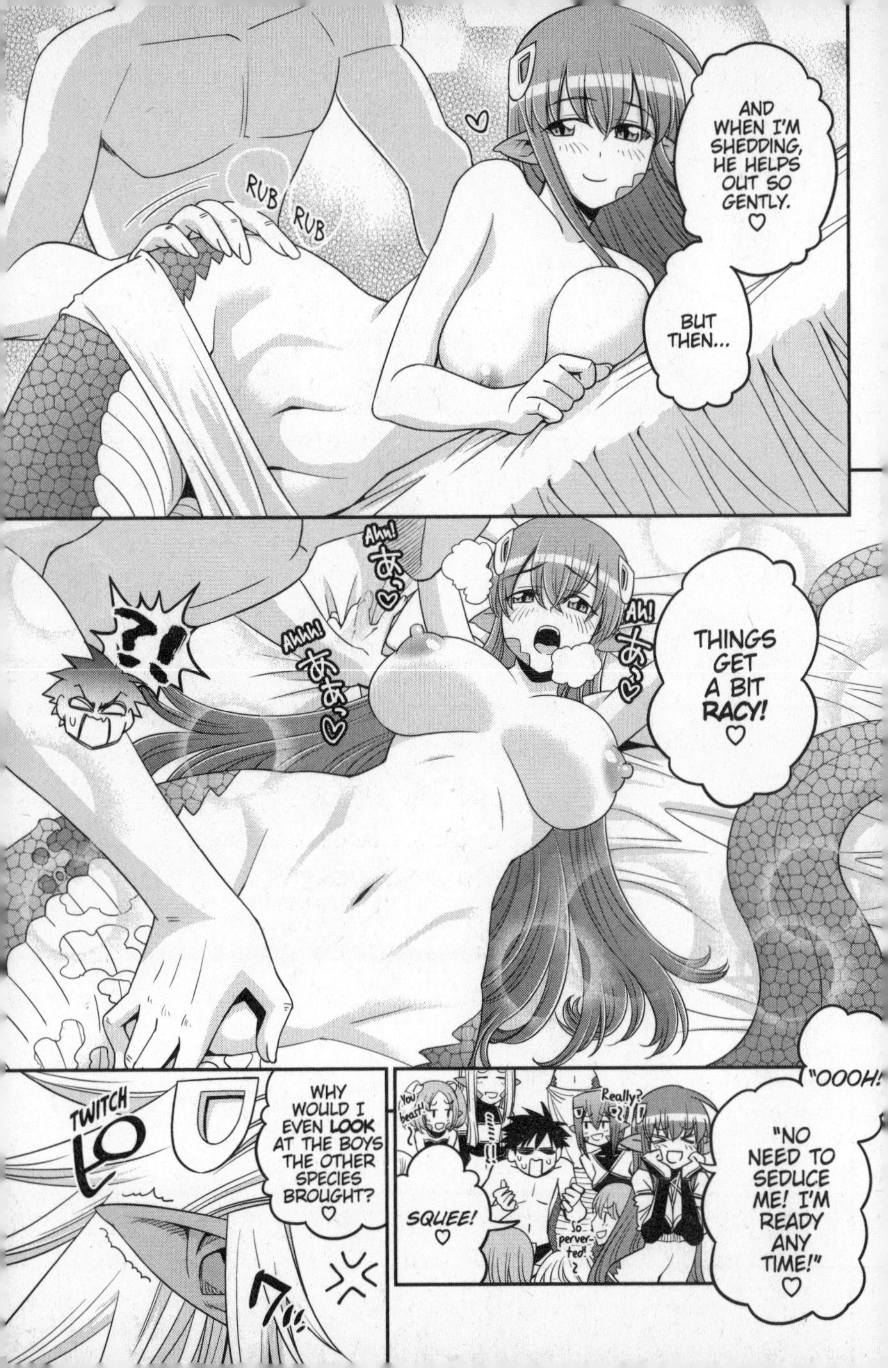

AND WHEN I'M SHEDDING, HE HELPS OUT SO GENTLY. ♡
BUT THEN...
RUB RUB
THINGS GET A BIT RACY! ♡
Ah! あっ♡
Ahh! あっ♡
Ahhh! あぁっ♡
?!
"OOOH!
"NO NEED TO SEDUCE ME! I'M READY ANY TIME!" ♡
Really?
You beast!
SQUEE! ♡
So perverted!
WHY WOULD I EVEN LOOK AT THE BOYS THE OTHER SPECIES BROUGHT? ♡
TWITCH

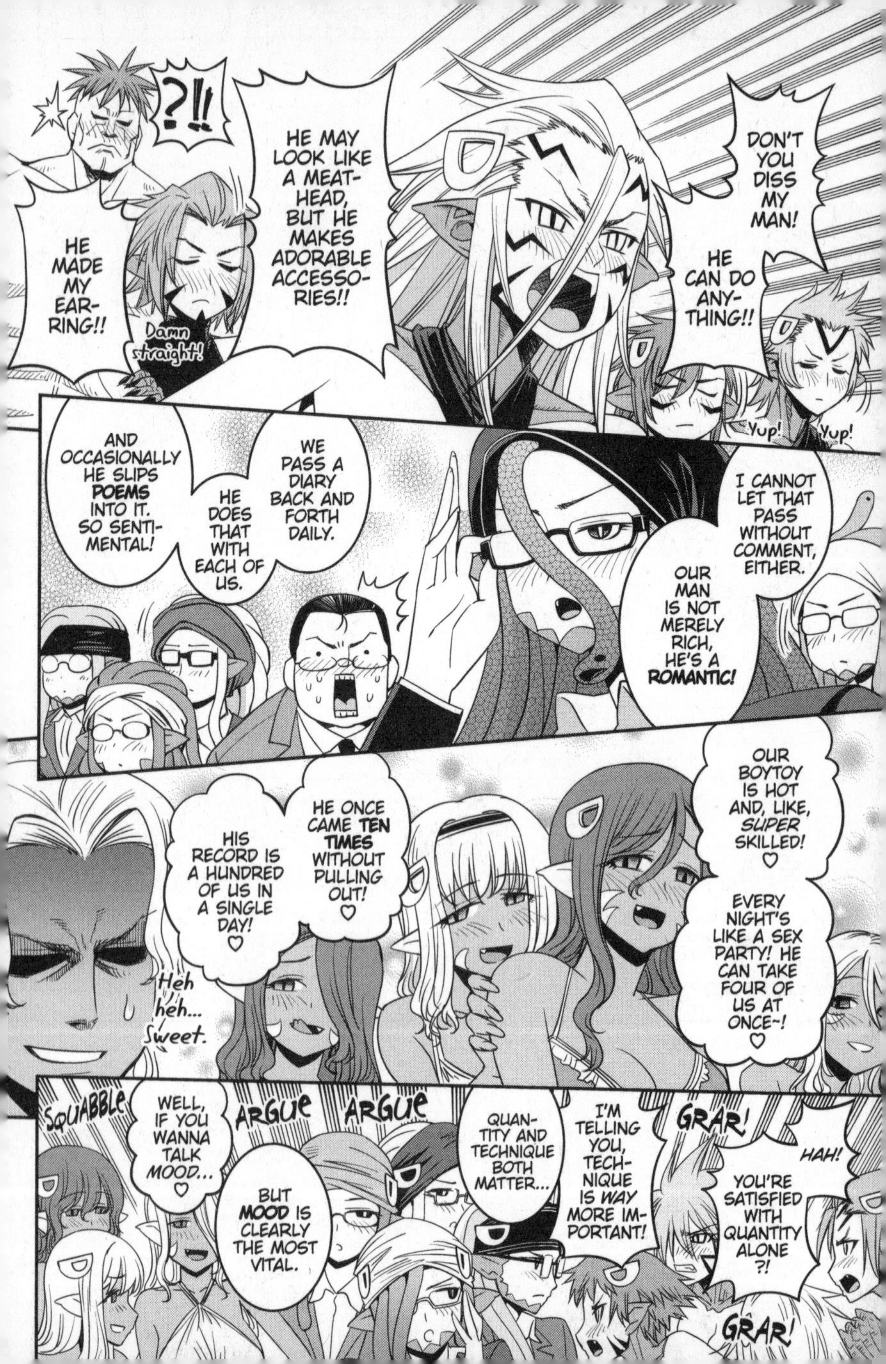
DON'T YOU DISS MY MAN!
HE CAN DO ANYTHING!!
Yup!
Yup!
HE MAY LOOK LIKE A MEATHEAD, BUT HE MAKES ADORABLE ACCESSORIES!!
?!!
HE MADE MY EARRING!!
Damn straight!
I CANNOT LET THAT PASS WITHOUT COMMENT, EITHER.
OUR MAN IS NOT MERELY RICH, HE'S A **ROMANTIC!**
WE PASS A DIARY BACK AND FORTH DAILY.
HE DOES THAT WITH EACH OF US.
AND OCCASIONALLY HE SLIPS **POEMS** INTO IT. SO SENTIMENTAL!
OUR BOYTOY IS HOT AND, LIKE, *SUPER* SKILLED! ♡
EVERY NIGHT'S LIKE A SEX PARTY! HE CAN TAKE FOUR OF US AT ONCE~! ♡
HE ONCE CAME **TEN TIMES** WITHOUT PULLING OUT! ♡
HIS RECORD IS A HUNDRED OF US IN A SINGLE DAY! ♡
Heh heh... Sweet.
GRAR!
HAH!
YOU'RE SATISFIED WITH QUANTITY ALONE?!
I'M TELLING YOU, TECHNIQUE IS *WAY* MORE IMPORTANT!
QUANTITY AND TECHNIQUE BOTH MATTER...
BUT **MOOD** IS CLEARLY THE MOST VITAL.
ARGUE ARGUE
WELL, IF YOU WANNA TALK *MOOD*... ♡
SQUABBLE
GRAR!

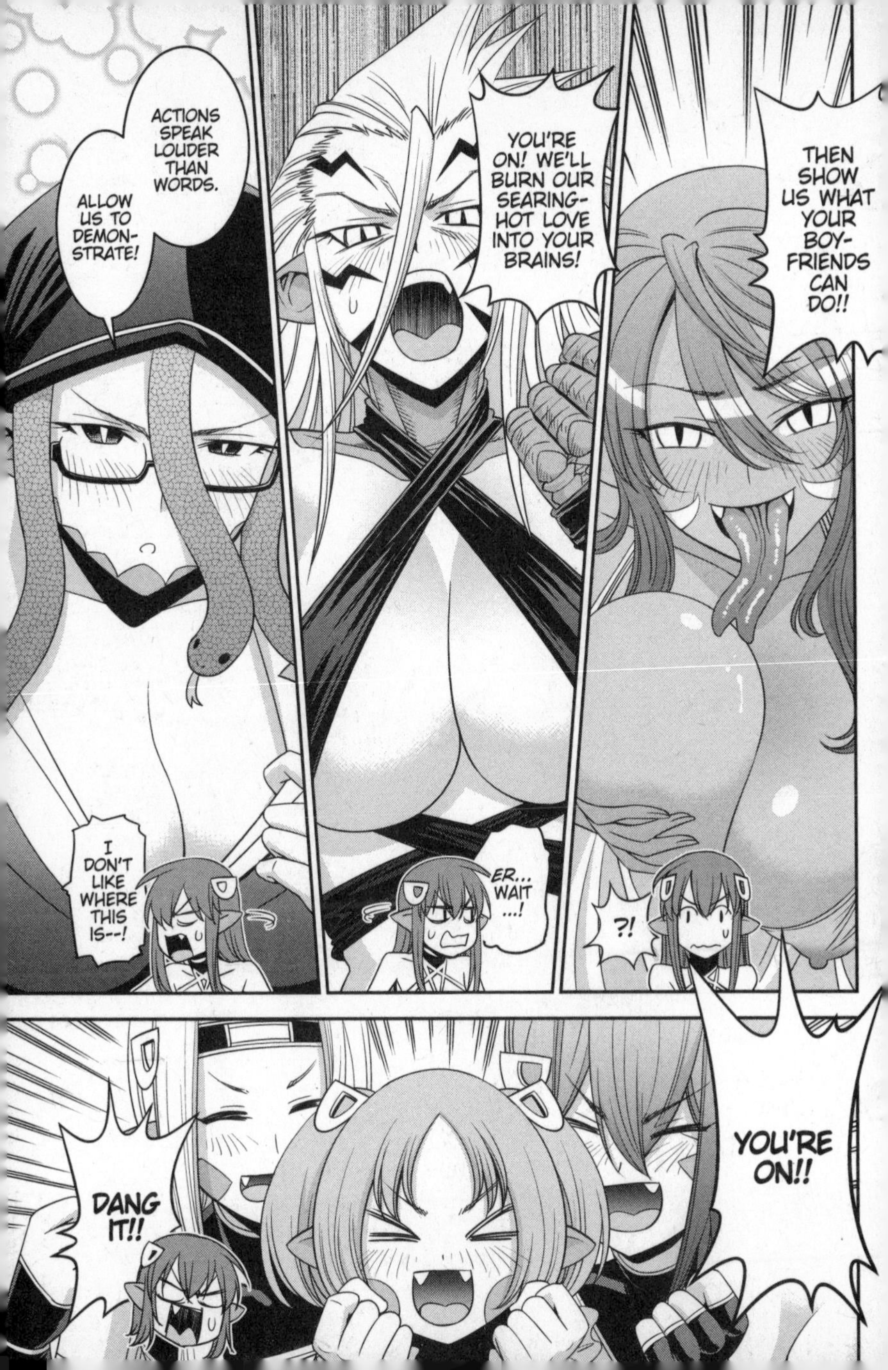
THEN SHOW US WHAT YOUR BOY-FRIENDS CAN DO!!
?!
YOU'RE ON! WE'LL BURN OUR SEARING-HOT LOVE INTO YOUR BRAINS!
ER... WAIT ...!
ACTIONS SPEAK LOUDER THAN WORDS.
ALLOW US TO DEMON-STRATE!
I DON'T LIKE WHERE THIS IS--!
YOU'RE ON!!
DANG IT!!

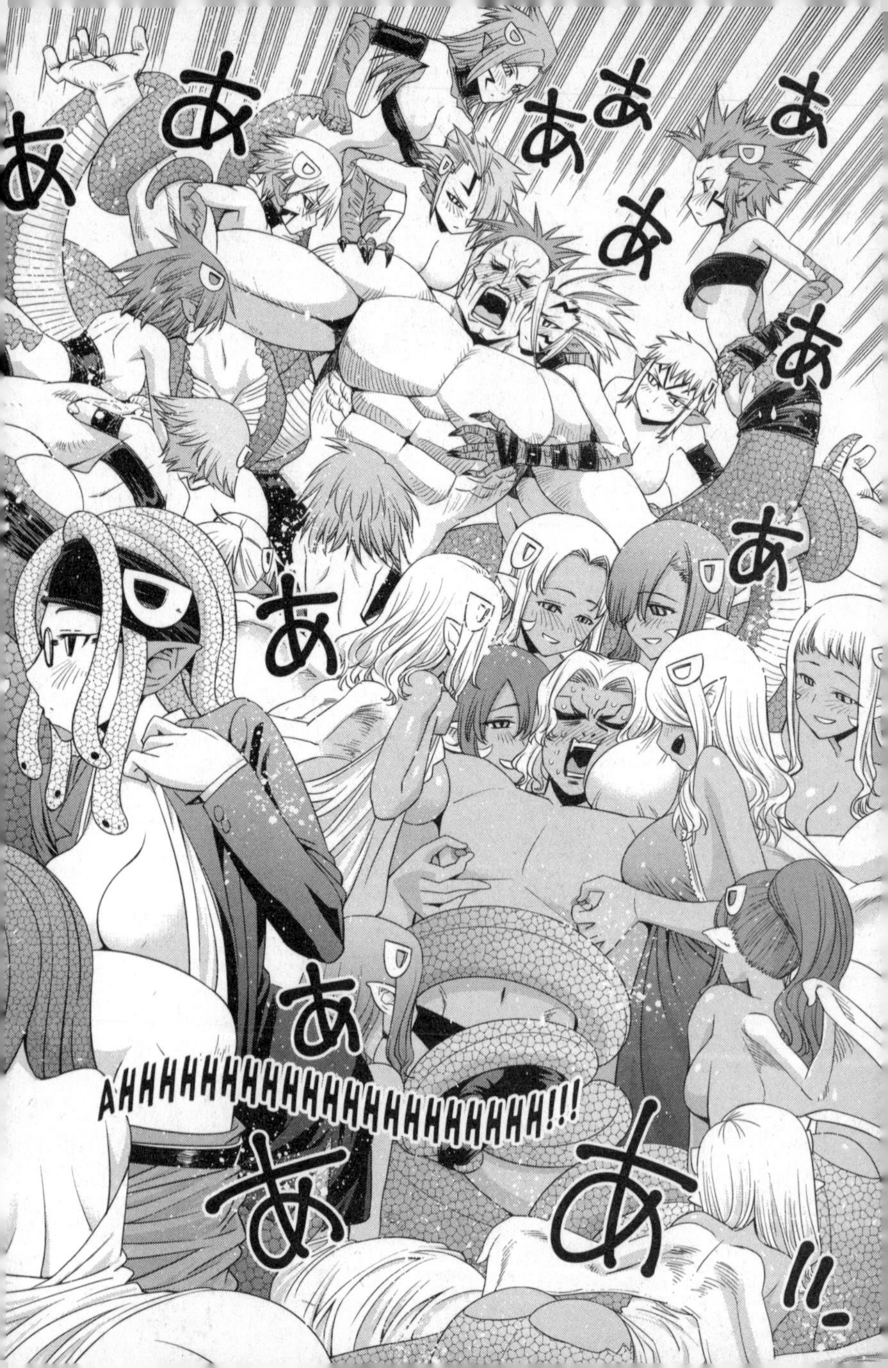
ああああああああああああ!!
AHHHHHHHHHHHHHHHHHHHHHH!!!

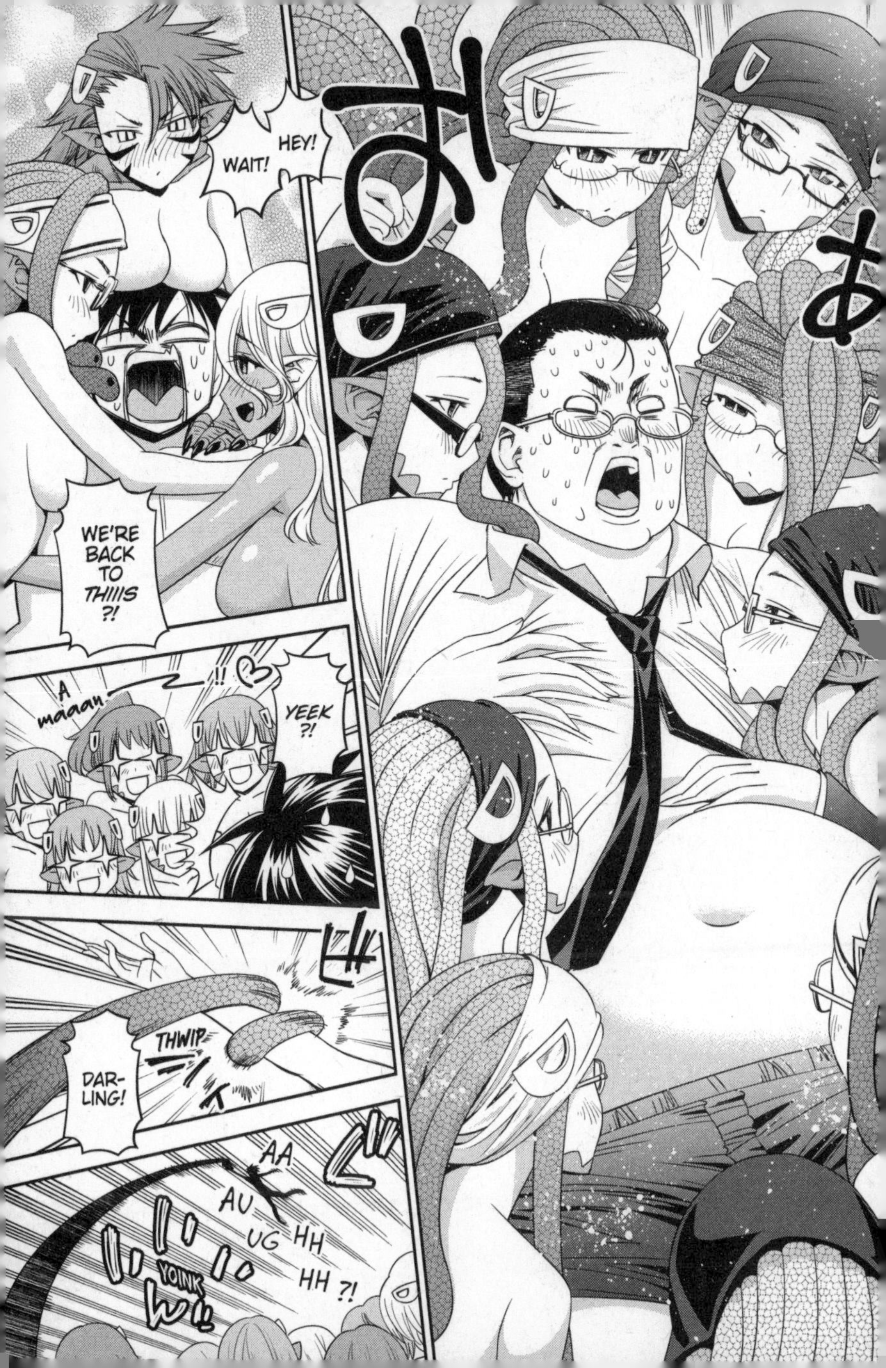

お
あ
HEY!
WAIT!
WE'RE BACK TO THIIIS ?!
YEEK ?!
A maaan!! ♡
THWIP
DAR-LING!
AA AU UG HH HH ?!
YOINK

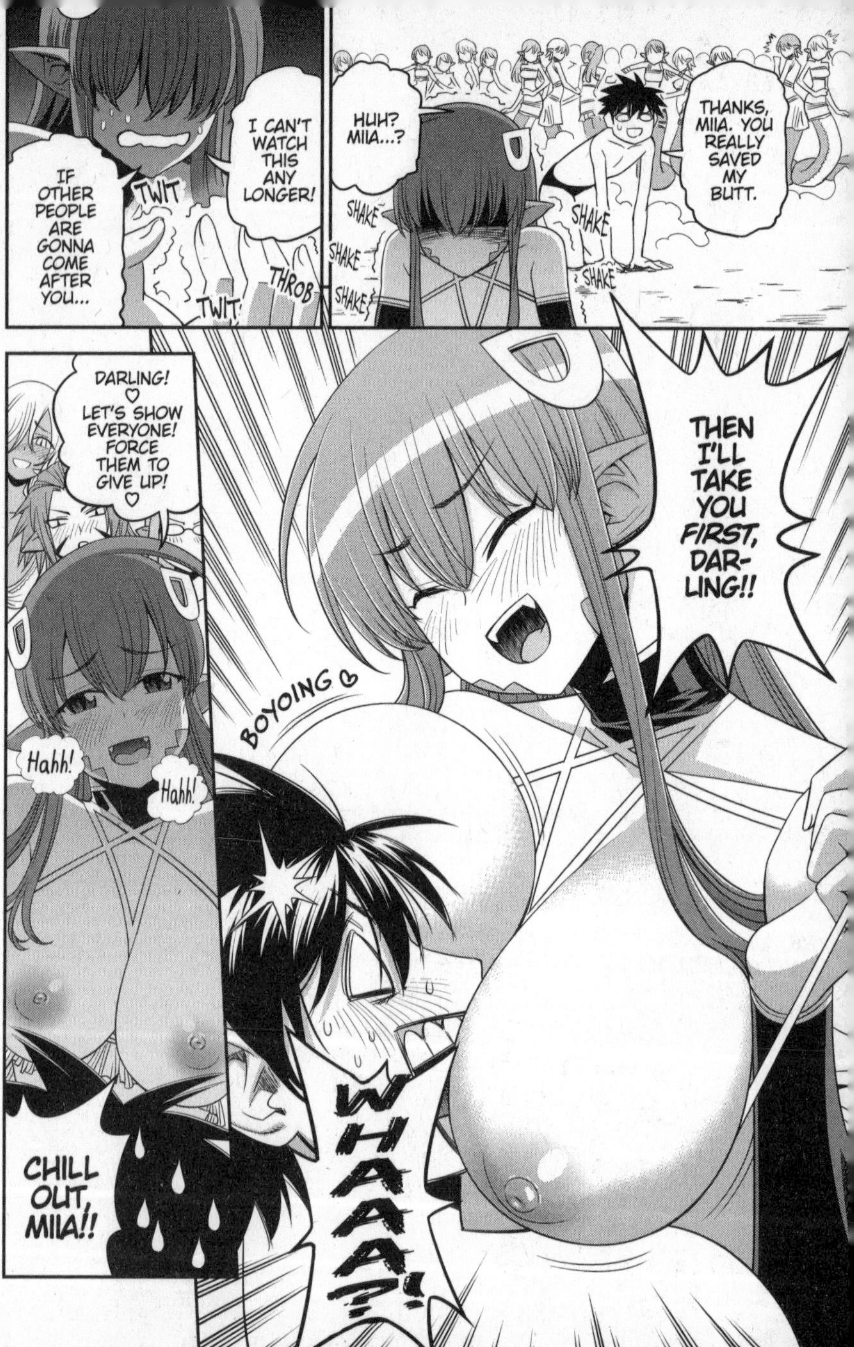
THANKS, MIIA. YOU REALLY SAVED MY BUTT.
SHAKE
SHAKE
HUH? MIIA...?
SHAKE
SHAKE
SHAKE
I CAN'T WATCH THIS ANY LONGER!
THROB
TWIT
IF OTHER PEOPLE ARE GONNA COME AFTER YOU...
TWIT
THEN I'LL TAKE YOU FIRST, DAR- LING!!
BOYOING ♡
WHAAA!?
DARLING! ♡ LET'S SHOW EVERYONE! FORCE THEM TO GIVE UP! ♡
Hahh!
Hahh!
CHILL OUT, MIIA!!

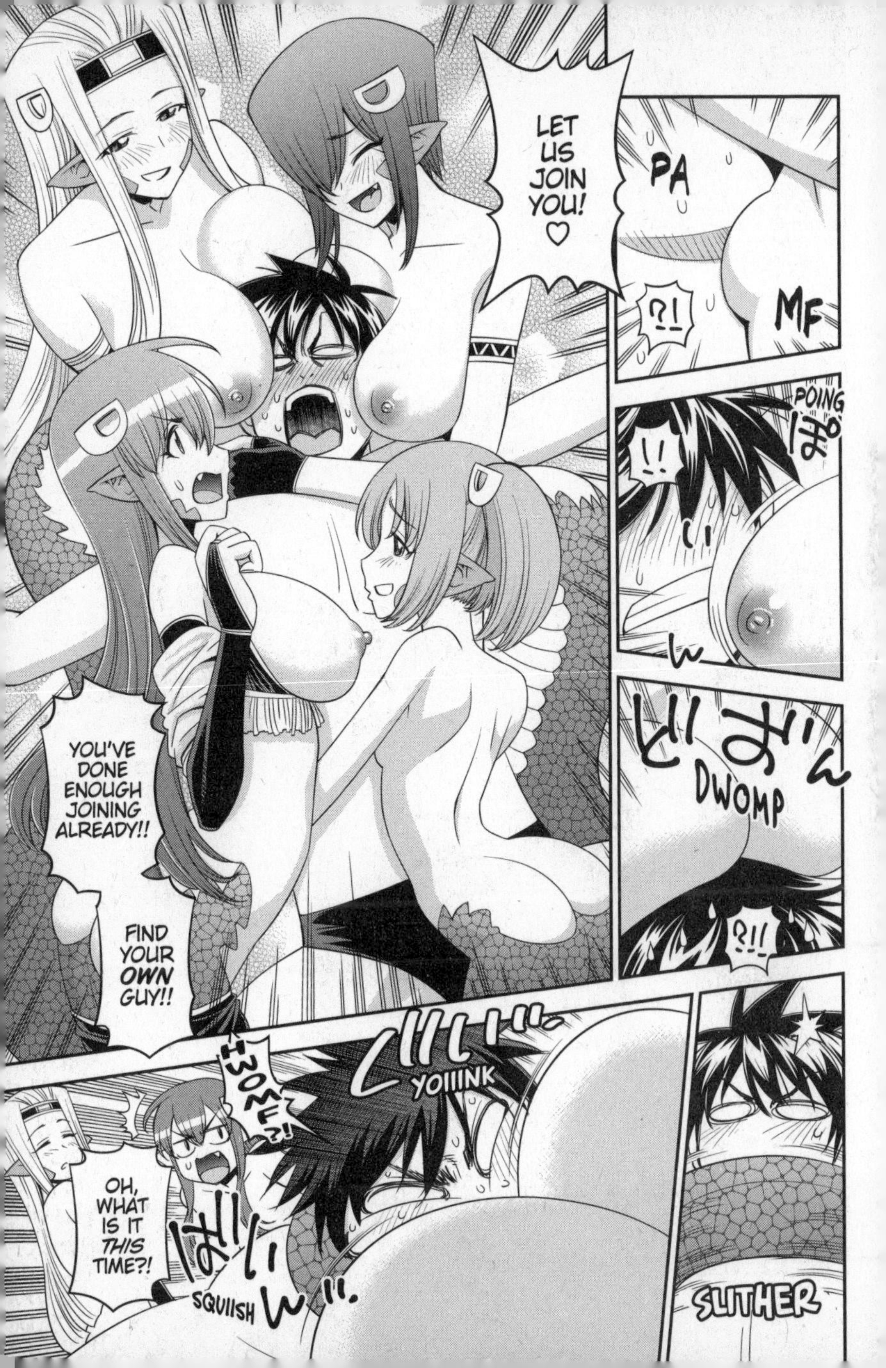
PA
MF
?!
POING
ぽ
!!
DWOMP
?!!
LET US JOIN YOU! ♡
YOU'VE DONE ENOUGH JOINING ALREADY!!
FIND YOUR *OWN* GUY!!
SLITHER
YOIIINK
WOMF?!
OH, WHAT IS IT *THIS* TIME?!
SQUIISH

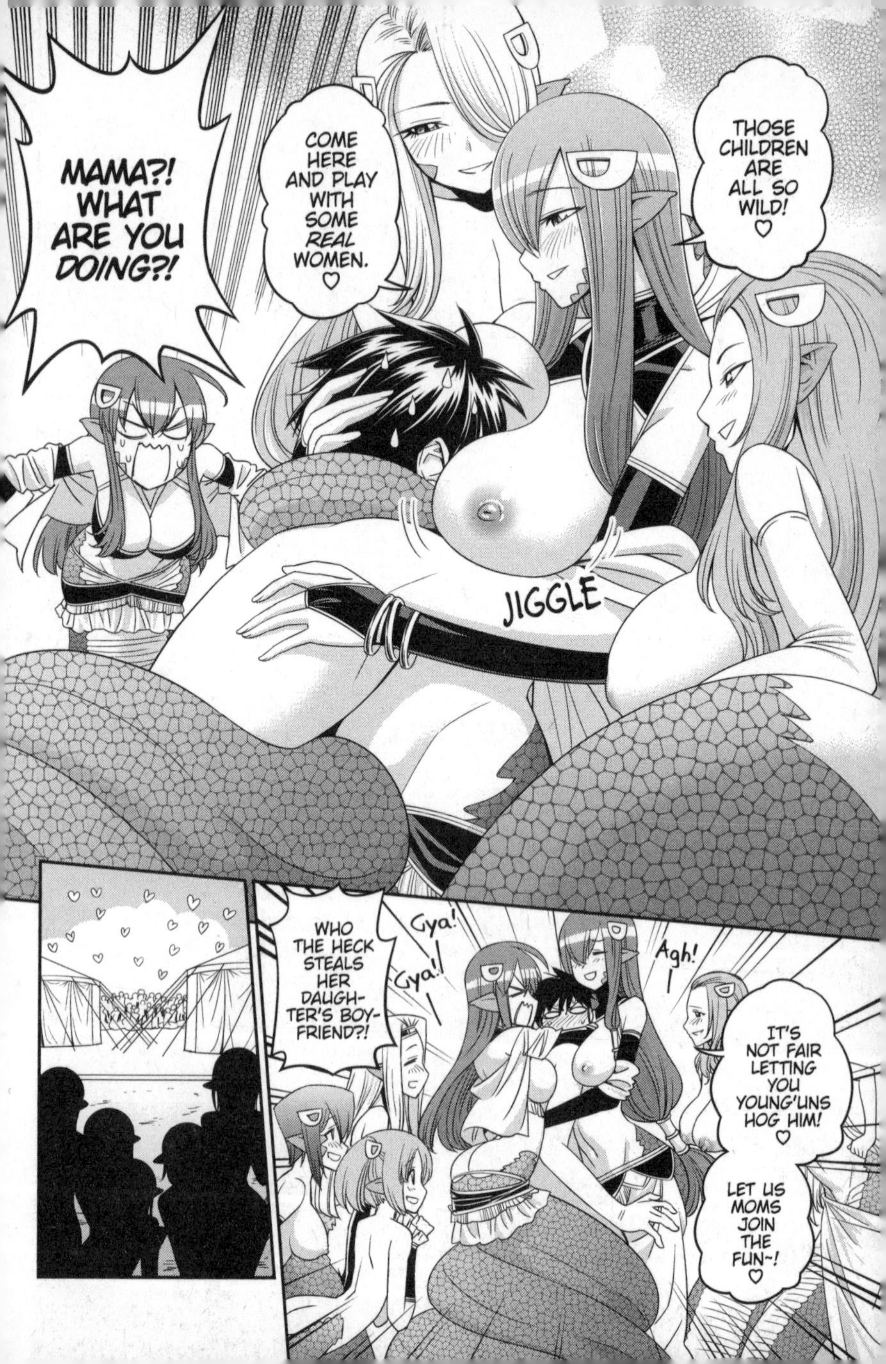
THOSE CHILDREN ARE ALL SO WILD! ♡
COME HERE AND PLAY WITH SOME *REAL* WOMEN. ♡
MAMA?! WHAT ARE YOU *DOING*?!
JIGGLE
IT'S NOT FAIR LETTING YOU YOUNG'UNS HOG HIM! ♡
Agh!
LET US MOMS JOIN THE FUN~! ♡
Gya!
WHO THE HECK STEALS HER DAUGHTER'S BOYFRIEND?!
Gya!

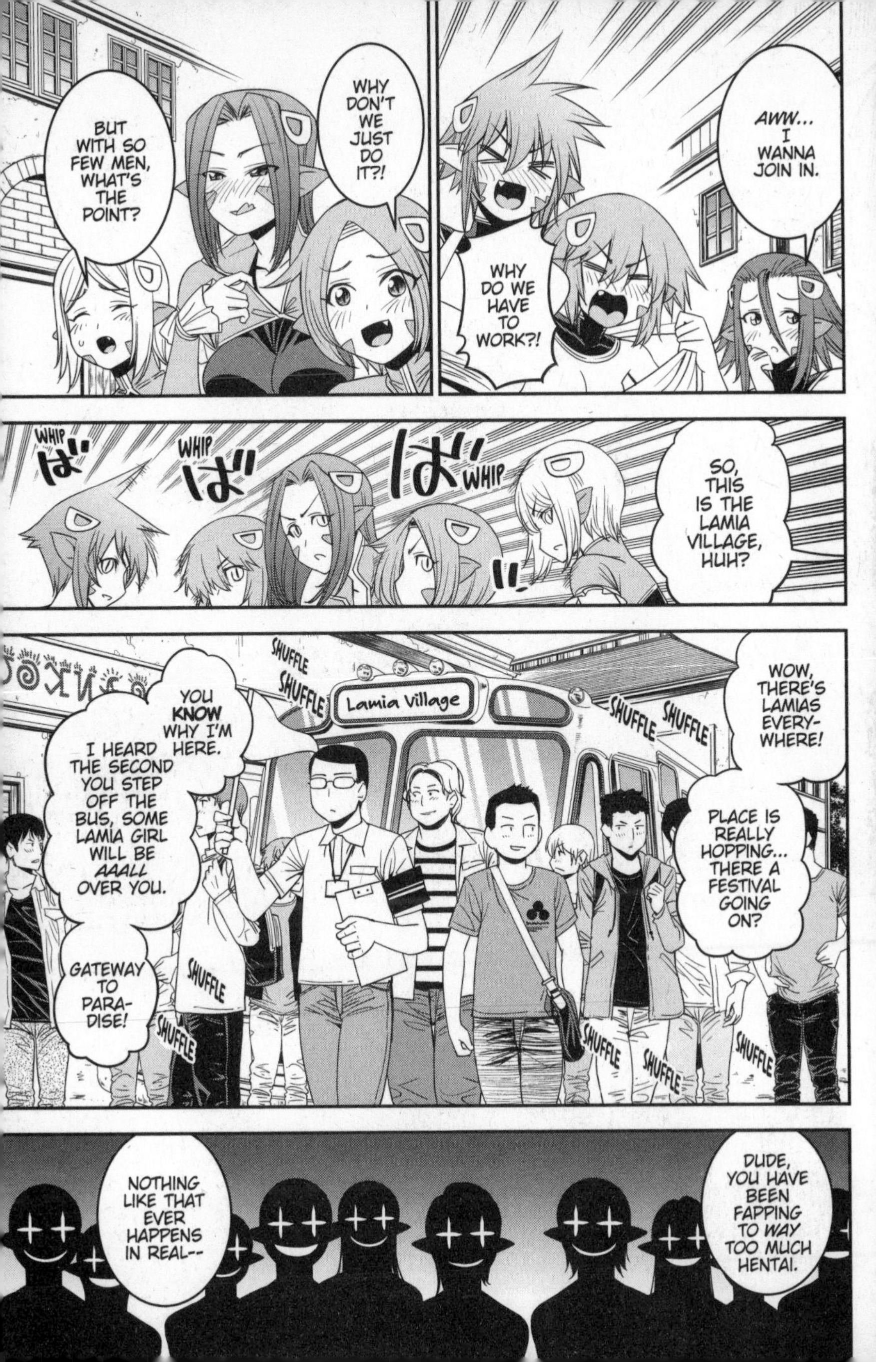
AWW... I WANNA JOIN IN.
WHY DO WE HAVE TO WORK?!
WHY DON'T WE JUST DO IT?!
BUT WITH SO FEW MEN, WHAT'S THE POINT?
SO, THIS IS THE LAMIA VILLAGE, HUH?
WHIP
ば
WHIP
ば
WHIP
ば
WOW, THERE'S LAMIAS EVERY-WHERE!
SHUFFLE
SHUFFLE
PLACE IS REALLY HOPPING... THERE A FESTIVAL GOING ON?
Lamia Village
SHUFFLE
SHUFFLE
YOU **KNOW** WHY I'M HERE.
I HEARD THE SECOND YOU STEP OFF THE BUS, SOME LAMIA GIRL WILL BE *AAALL* OVER YOU.
GATEWAY TO PARA-DISE!
SHUFFLE
SHUFFLE
SHUFFLE
SHUFFLE
SHUFFLE
DUDE, YOU HAVE BEEN FAPPING TO *WAY* TOO MUCH HENTAI.
NOTHING LIKE THAT EVER HAPPENS IN REAL--

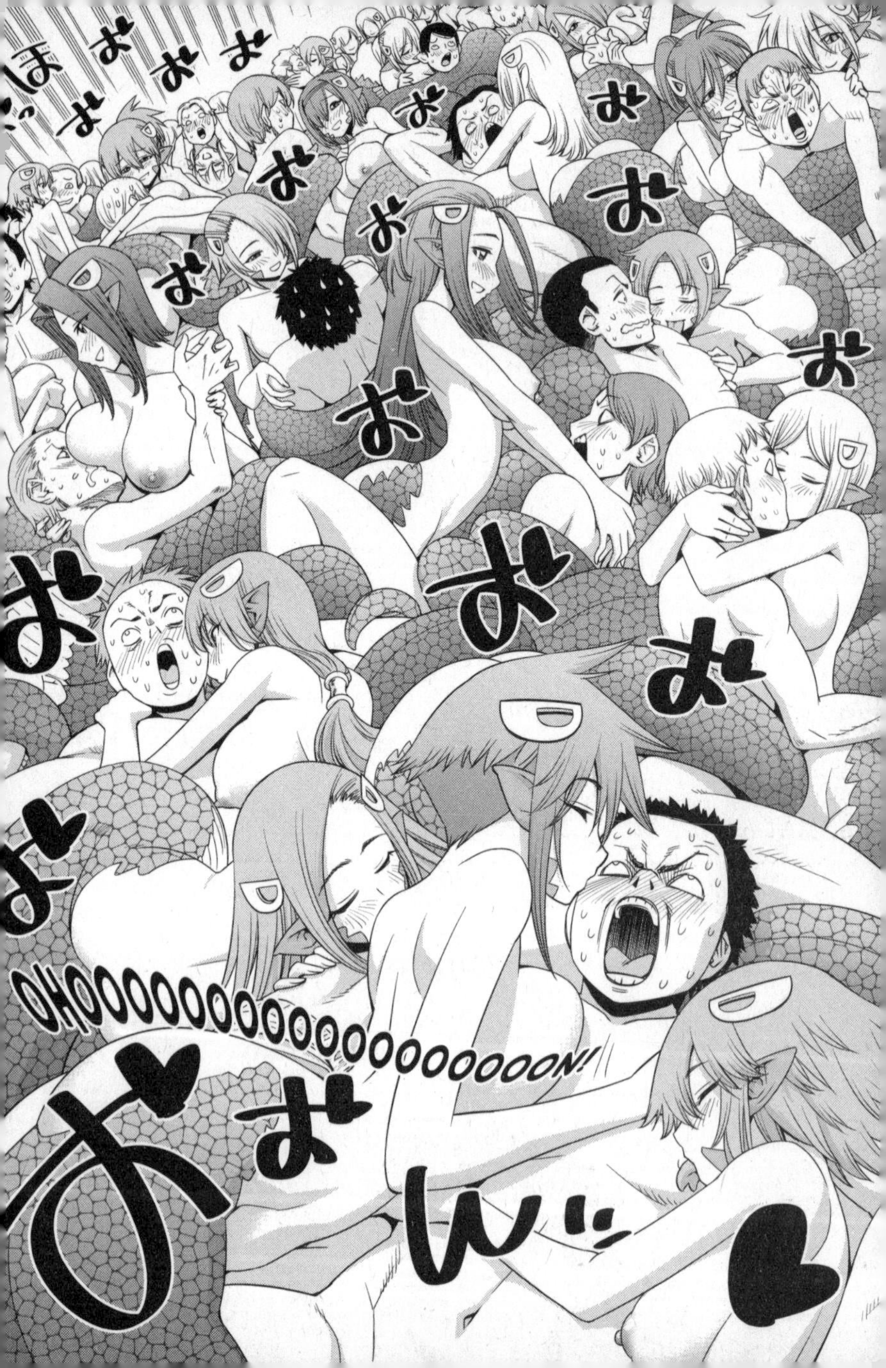

OHOOOOOOOOOOOOOOOOOOON!

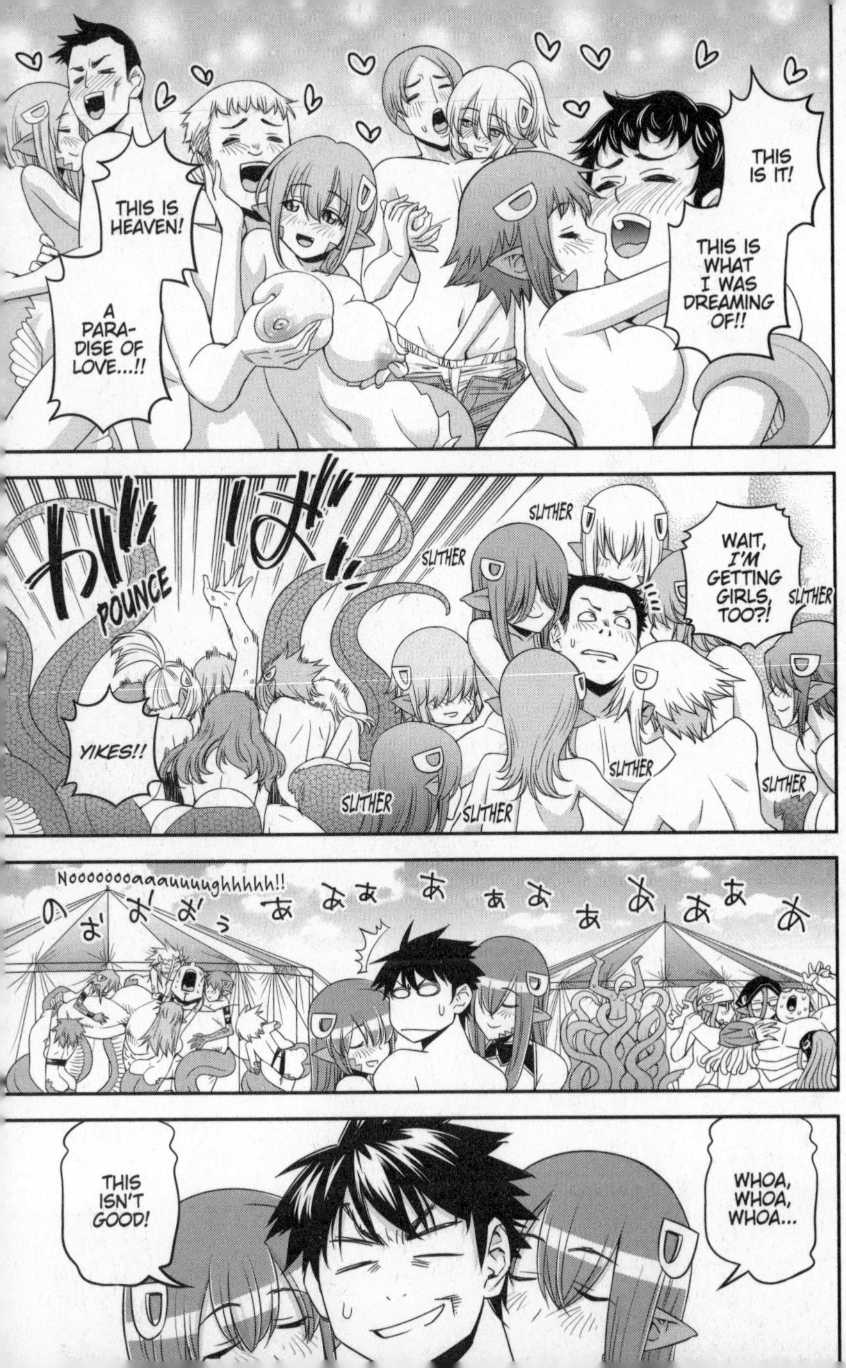
THIS IS IT!
THIS IS WHAT I WAS DREAMING OF!!
THIS IS HEAVEN!
A PARA-DISE OF LOVE...!!
SLITHER
WAIT, I'M GETTING GIRLS, TOO?!
SLITHER
SLITHER
POUNCE
YIKES!!
SLITHER
SLITHER
SLITHER
SLITHER
Nooooooaaauuuughhhhh!!
WHOA, WHOA, WHOA...
THIS ISN'T GOOD!

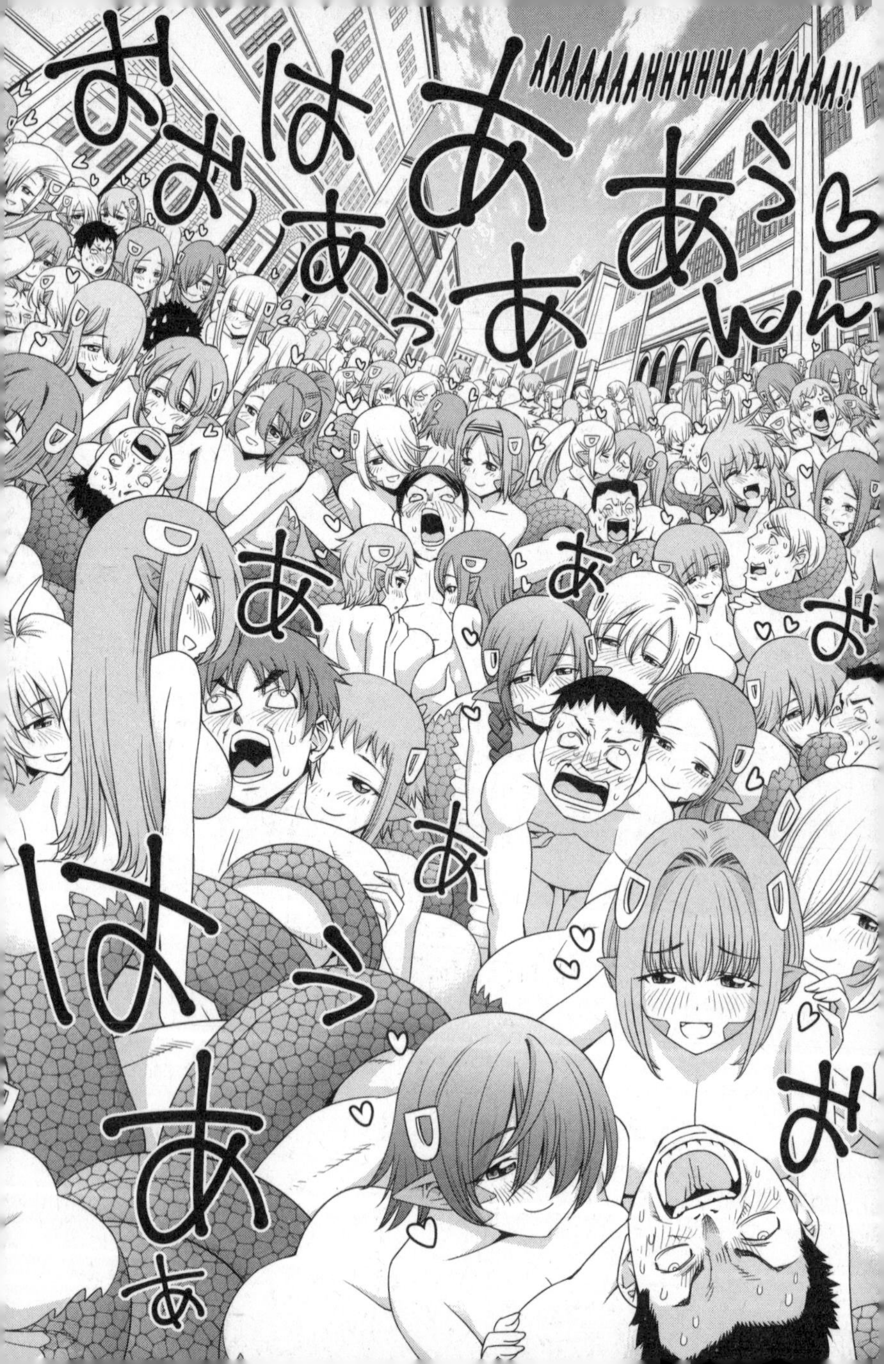
AAAAAAAHHHHHHAAAAAAAA!!

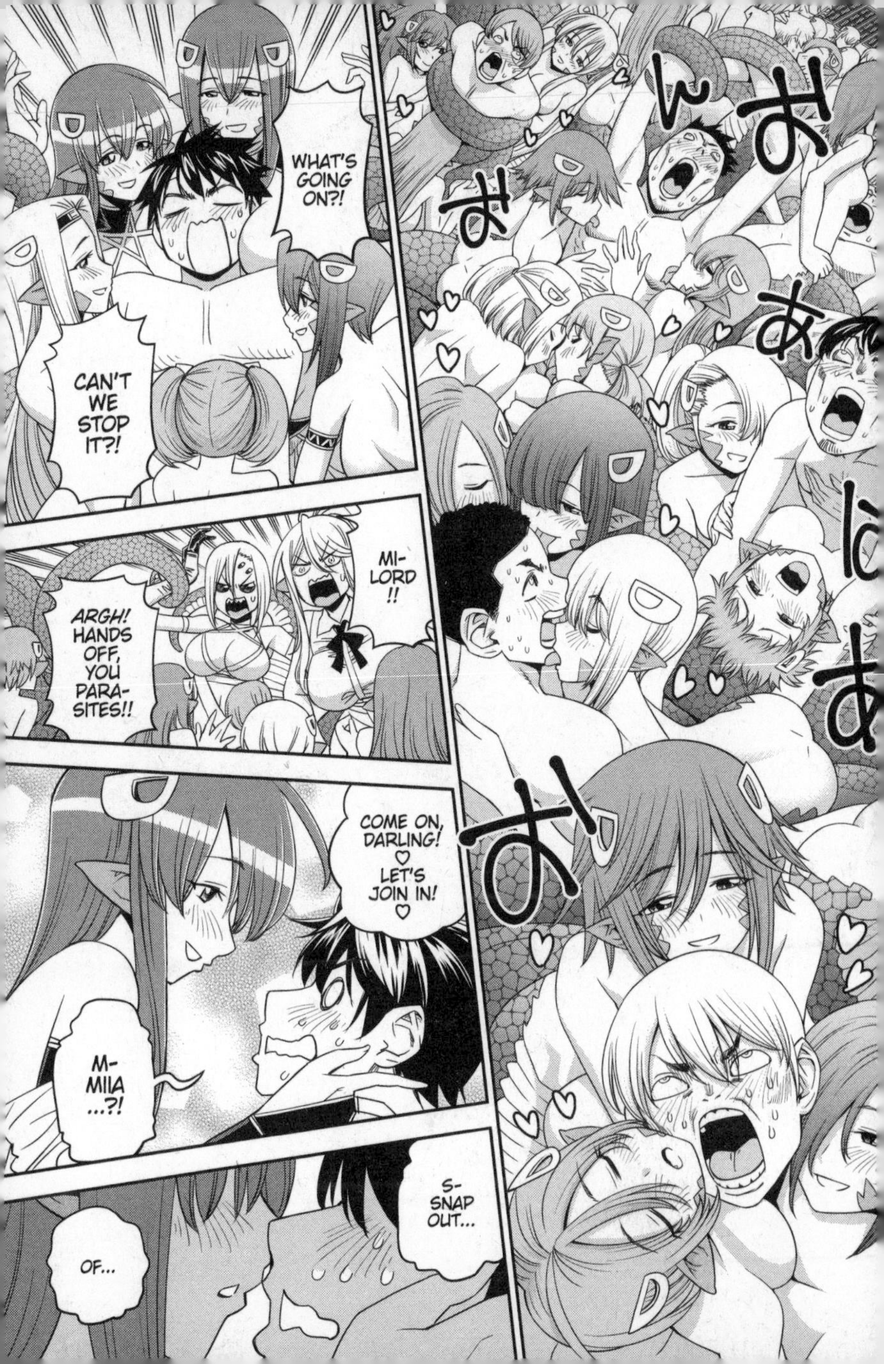
WHAT'S GOING ON?!
CAN'T WE STOP IT?!
MI-LORD!!
ARGH! HANDS OFF, YOU PARASITES!!
COME ON, DARLING! ♡ LET'S JOIN IN! ♡
M-MIIA...?!
S-SNAP OUT...
OF...

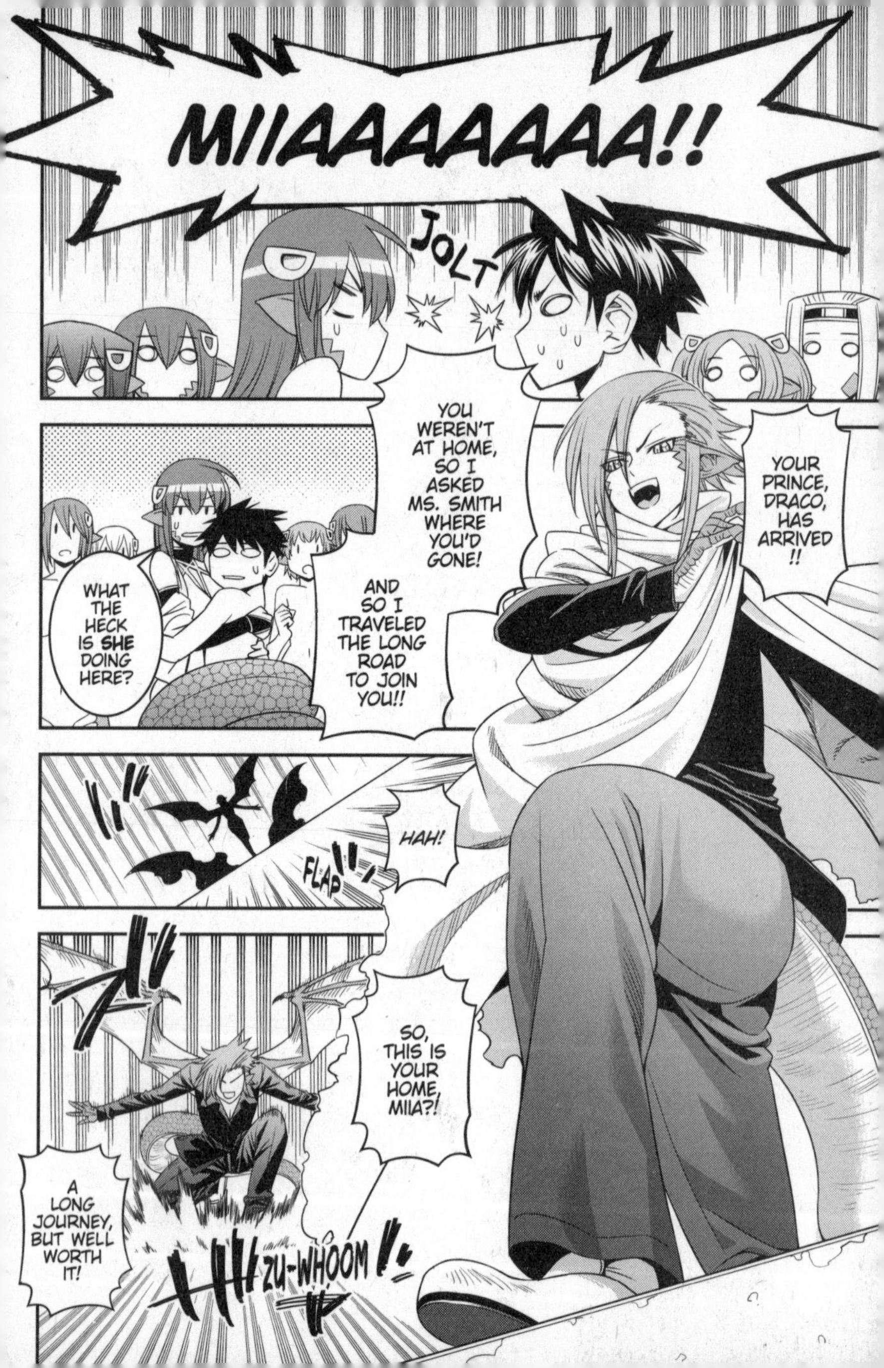
MIIAAAAAAAA!!
JOLT
YOUR PRINCE, DRACO, HAS ARRIVED!!
YOU WEREN'T AT HOME, SO I ASKED MS. SMITH WHERE YOU'D GONE!
AND SO I TRAVELED THE LONG ROAD TO JOIN YOU!!
WHAT THE HECK IS **SHE** DOING HERE?
HAH!
FLAP
SO, THIS IS YOUR HOME, MIIA?!
A LONG JOURNEY, BUT WELL WORTH IT!
ZU-WHOOM

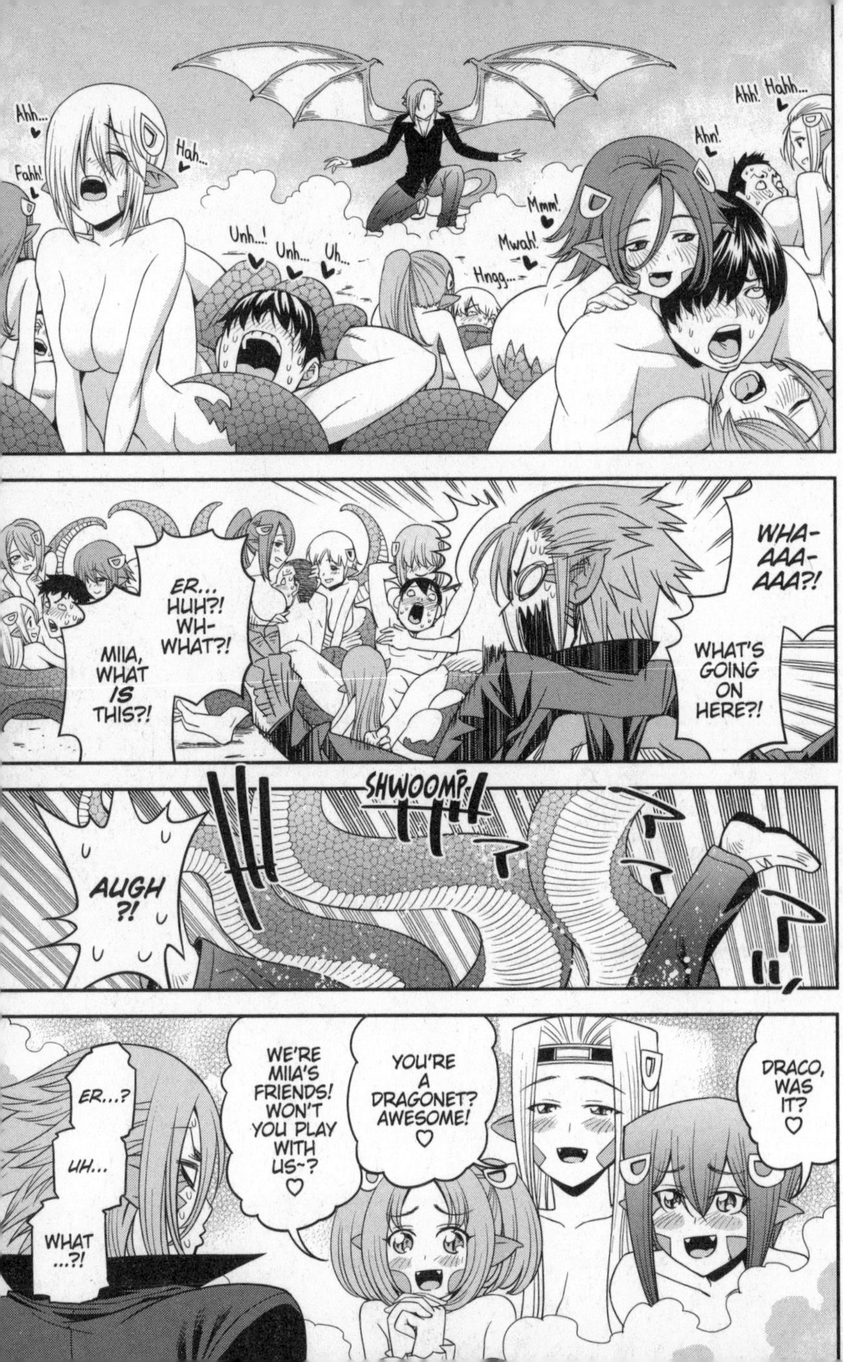
Ahh! Hahh...
Ahn!
Mmm!
Mwah!
Hngg...
Uh...
Unh...
Unh...!
Hah...
Ahh...
Fahh!
WHA-AAA-AAA?!
WHAT'S GOING ON HERE?!
ER... HUH?! WH-WHAT?!
MIIA, WHAT *IS* THIS?!
SHWOOMP
AUGH?!
DRACO, WAS IT? ♡
YOU'RE A DRAGONET? AWESOME! ♡
WE'RE MIIA'S FRIENDS! WON'T YOU PLAY WITH US~? ♡
ER...?
UH...
WHAT...?!

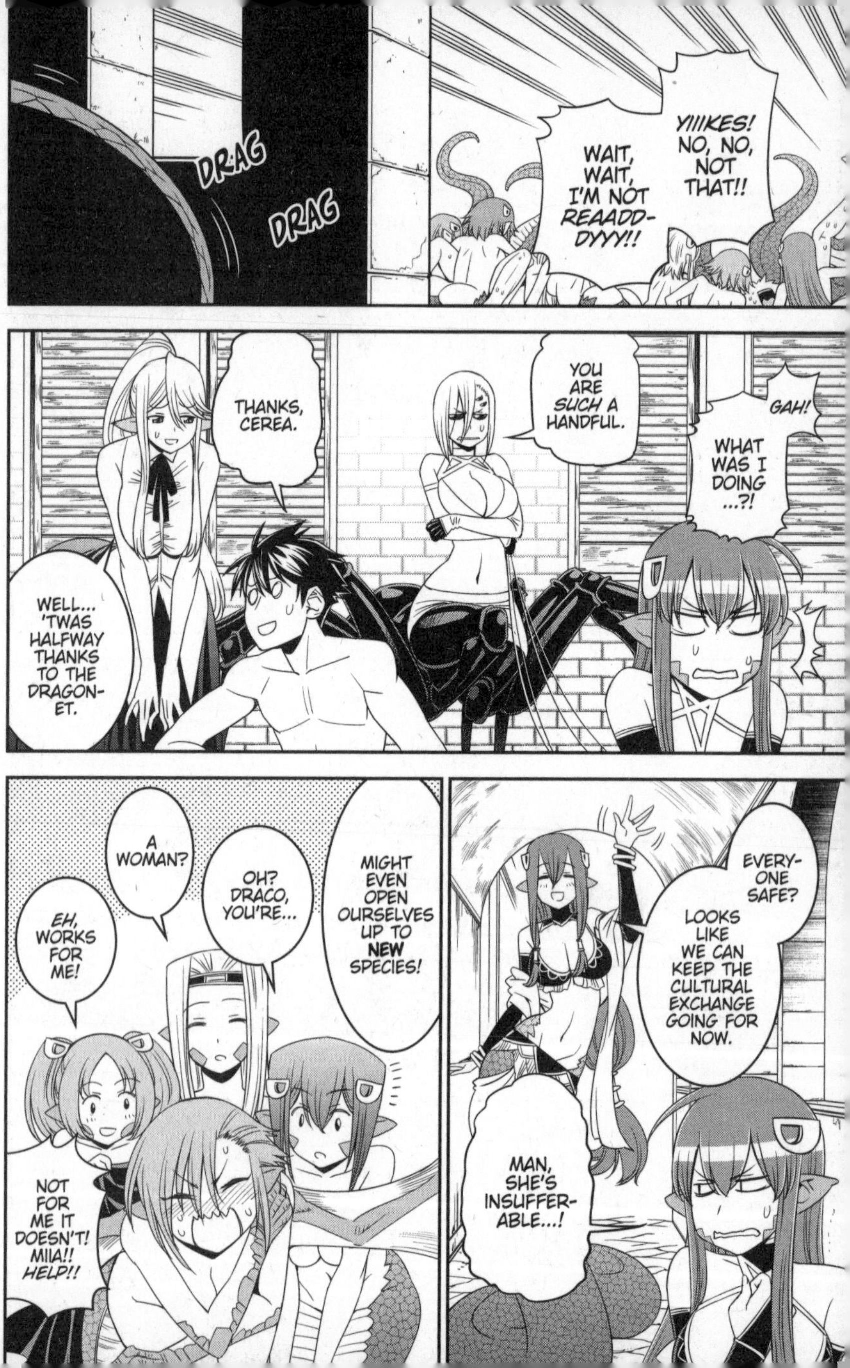
YIIIKES! NO, NO, NOT THAT!!
WAIT, WAIT, I'M NOT REAADD-DYYY!!
DRAG
DRAG
GAH!
WHAT WAS I DOING ...?!
YOU ARE SUCH A HANDFUL.
THANKS, CEREA.
WELL... 'TWAS HALFWAY THANKS TO THE DRAGON-ET.
EVERY-ONE SAFE? LOOKS LIKE WE CAN KEEP THE CULTURAL EXCHANGE GOING FOR NOW.
MAN, SHE'S INSUFFER-ABLE...!
MIGHT EVEN OPEN OURSELVES UP TO NEW SPECIES!
OH? DRACO, YOU'RE...
A WOMAN?
EH, WORKS FOR ME!
NOT FOR ME IT DOESN'T! MIIA!! HELP!!

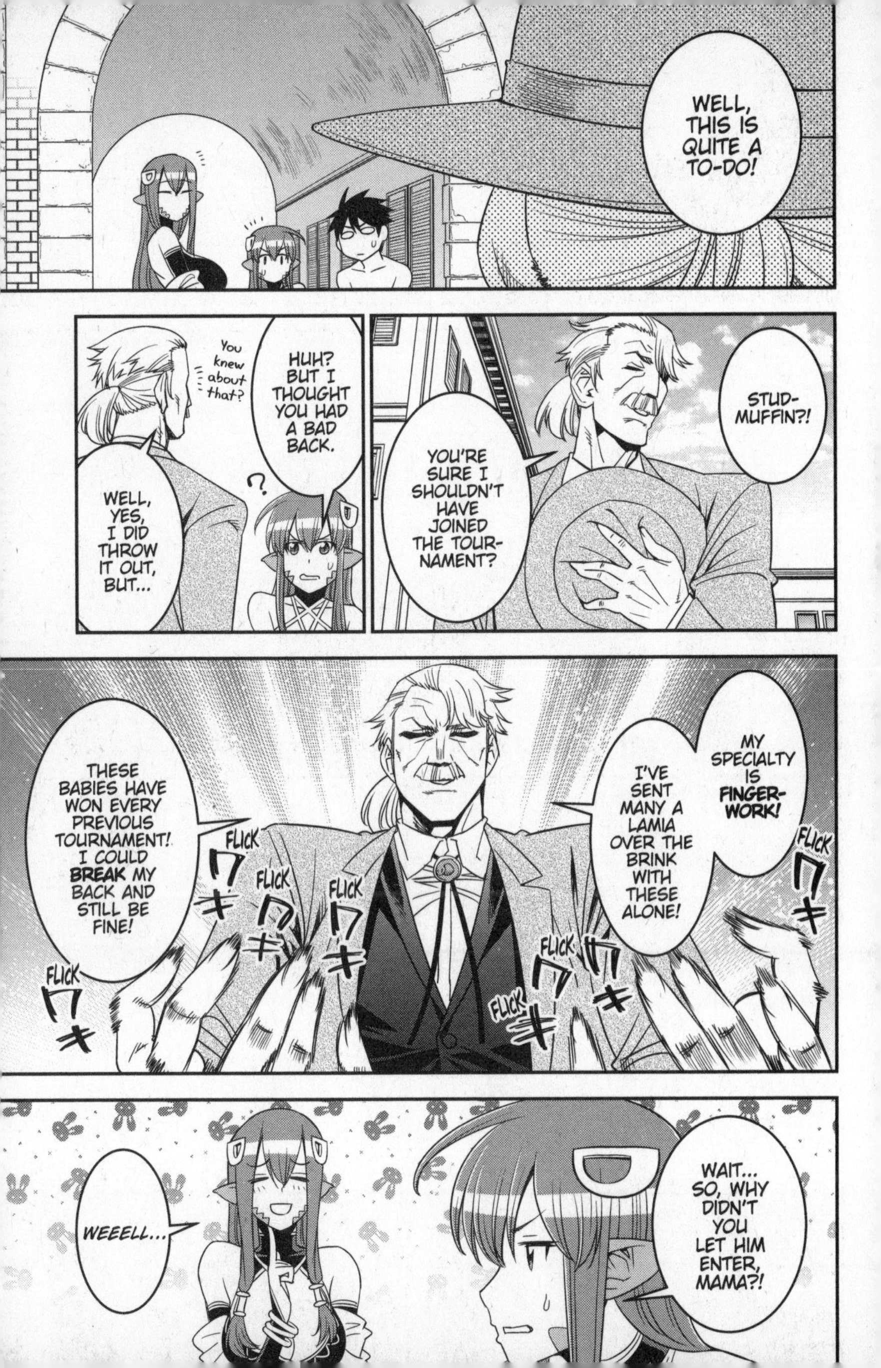
WELL, THIS IS QUITE A TO-DO!
STUD-MUFFIN?!
YOU'RE SURE I SHOULDN'T HAVE JOINED THE TOUR-NAMENT?
HUH? BUT I THOUGHT YOU HAD A BAD BACK.
You knew about that?
WELL, YES, I DID THROW IT OUT, BUT...
MY SPECIALTY IS **FINGER-WORK!**
I'VE SENT MANY A LAMIA OVER THE BRINK WITH THESE ALONE!
FLICK ワキ
FLICK ワキ
FLICK ワキ
FLICK ワキ
FLICK ワキ
FLICK ワキ
THESE BABIES HAVE WON EVERY PREVIOUS TOURNAMENT! I COULD **BREAK** MY BACK AND STILL BE FINE!
FLICK ワキ
WAIT... SO, WHY DIDN'T YOU LET HIM ENTER, MAMA?!
WEEELL...

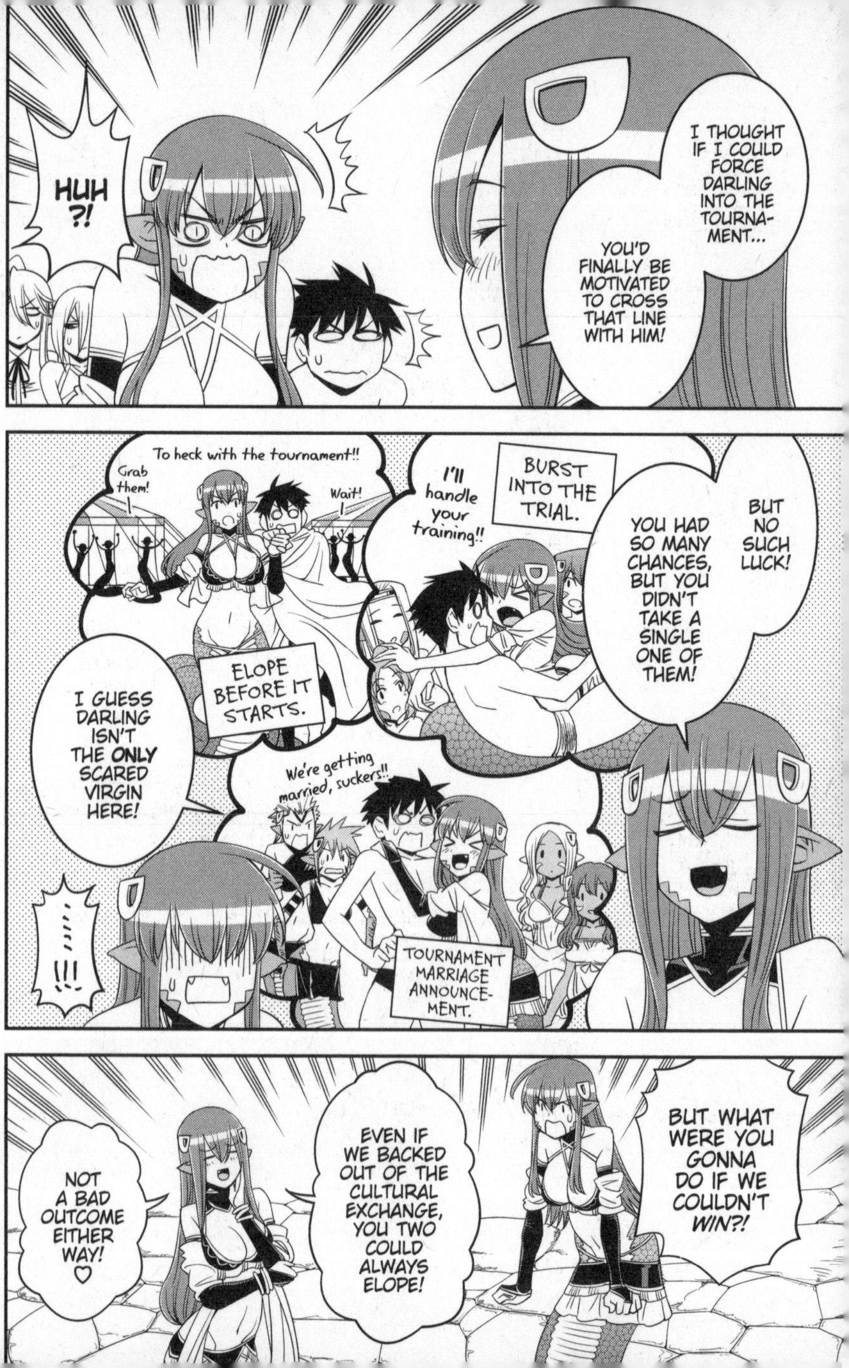
I THOUGHT IF I COULD FORCE DARLING INTO THE TOURNAMENT...
YOU'D FINALLY BE MOTIVATED TO CROSS THAT LINE WITH HIM!
HUH ?!
BUT NO SUCH LUCK!
YOU HAD SO MANY CHANCES, BUT YOU DIDN'T TAKE A SINGLE ONE OF THEM!
BURST INTO THE TRIAL.
I'll handle your training!!
To heck with the tournament!!
Grab them!
Wait!
ELOPE BEFORE IT STARTS.
We're getting married, suckers!!
TOURNAMENT MARRIAGE ANNOUNCEMENT.
I GUESS DARLING ISN'T THE ONLY SCARED VIRGIN HERE!
......!!!
BUT WHAT WERE YOU GONNA DO IF WE COULDN'T *WIN*?!
EVEN IF WE BACKED OUT OF THE CULTURAL EXCHANGE, YOU TWO COULD ALWAYS ELOPE!
NOT A BAD OUTCOME EITHER WAY! ♡

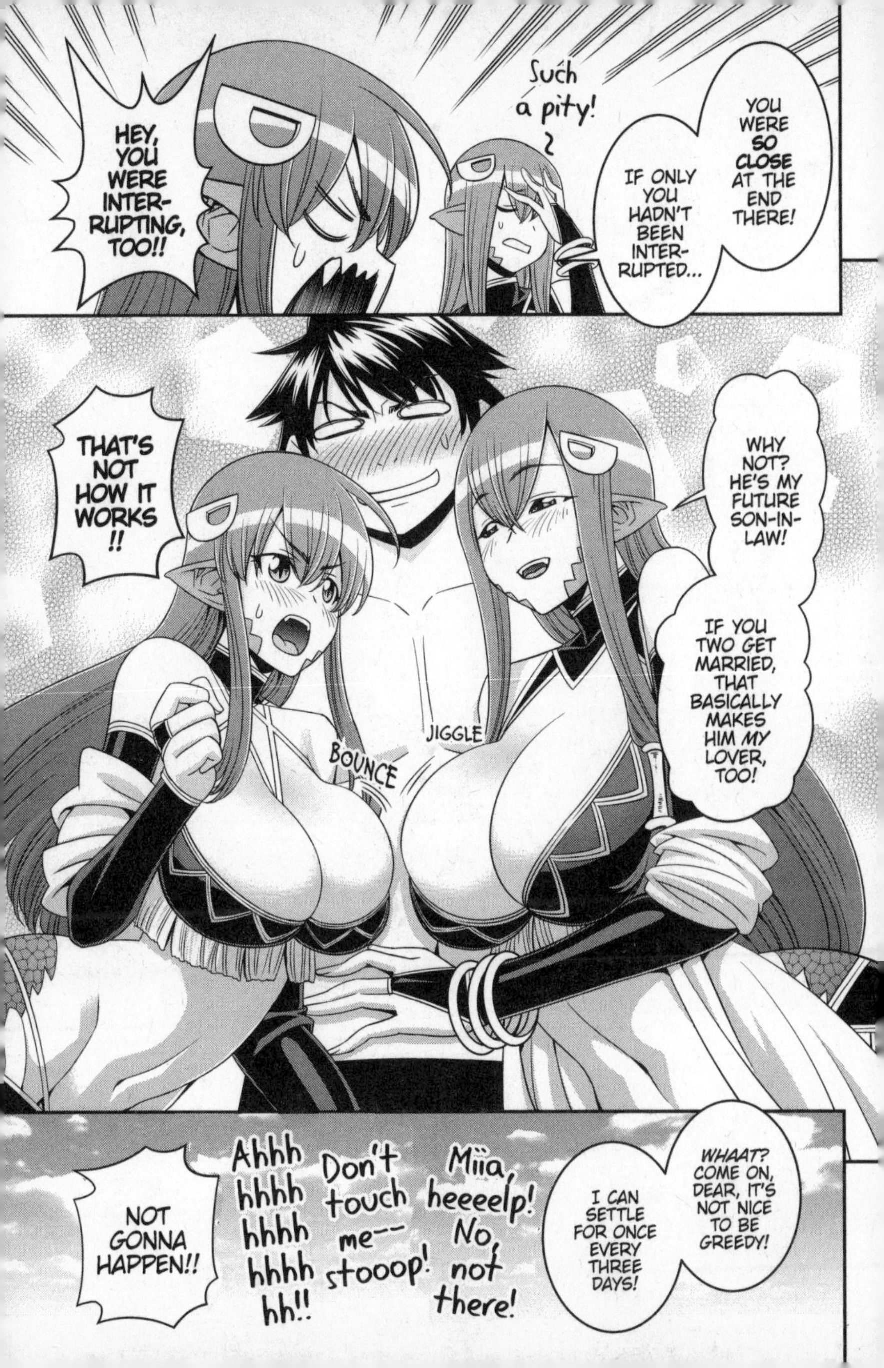
YOU WERE SO CLOSE AT THE END THERE!
IF ONLY YOU HADN'T BEEN INTER-RUPTED...
Such a pity!
HEY, YOU WERE INTER-RUPTING, TOO!!
WHY NOT? HE'S MY FUTURE SON-IN-LAW!
IF YOU TWO GET MARRIED, THAT BASICALLY MAKES HIM *MY* LOVER, TOO!
JIGGLE
BOUNCE
THAT'S NOT HOW IT WORKS!!
WHAAT? COME ON, DEAR, IT'S NOT NICE TO BE GREEDY!
I CAN SETTLE FOR ONCE EVERY THREE DAYS!
Miia, heeeelp! No, not there!
Don't touch me-- stooop!
Ahhhhhhhhhhhhhhhhhh!!
NOT GONNA HAPPEN!!

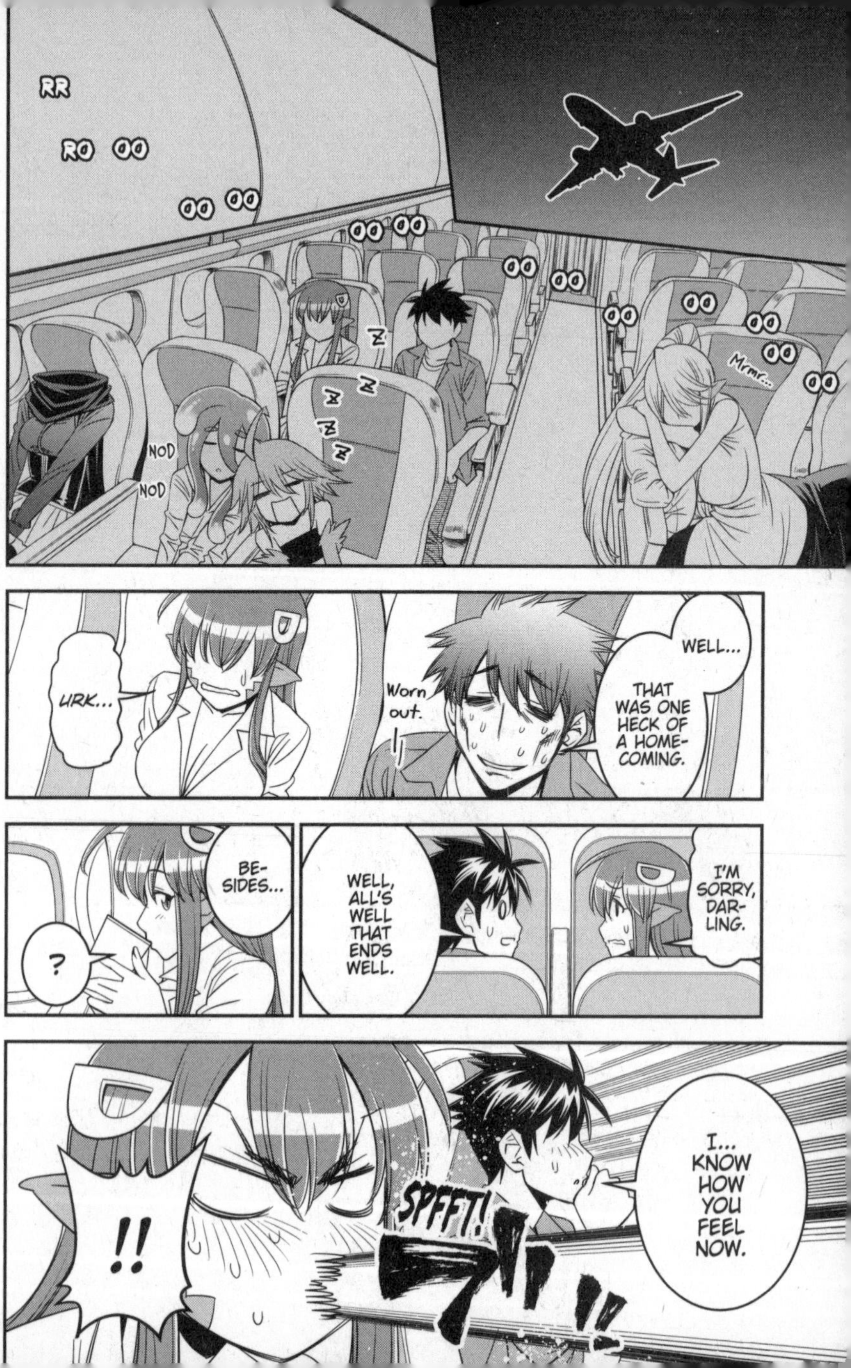
RR
RO OO
OO OO
OO OO
OO
OO
OO
OO
OO
OO
Mrmr...
OO
Z
Z
Z
Z
Z
NOD
NOD
WELL...
THAT WAS ONE HECK OF A HOME-COMING.
Worn out.
URK...
I'M SORRY, DARLING.
WELL, ALL'S WELL THAT ENDS WELL.
BE-SIDES...
?
I... KNOW HOW YOU FEEL NOW.
SPFFT!
!!

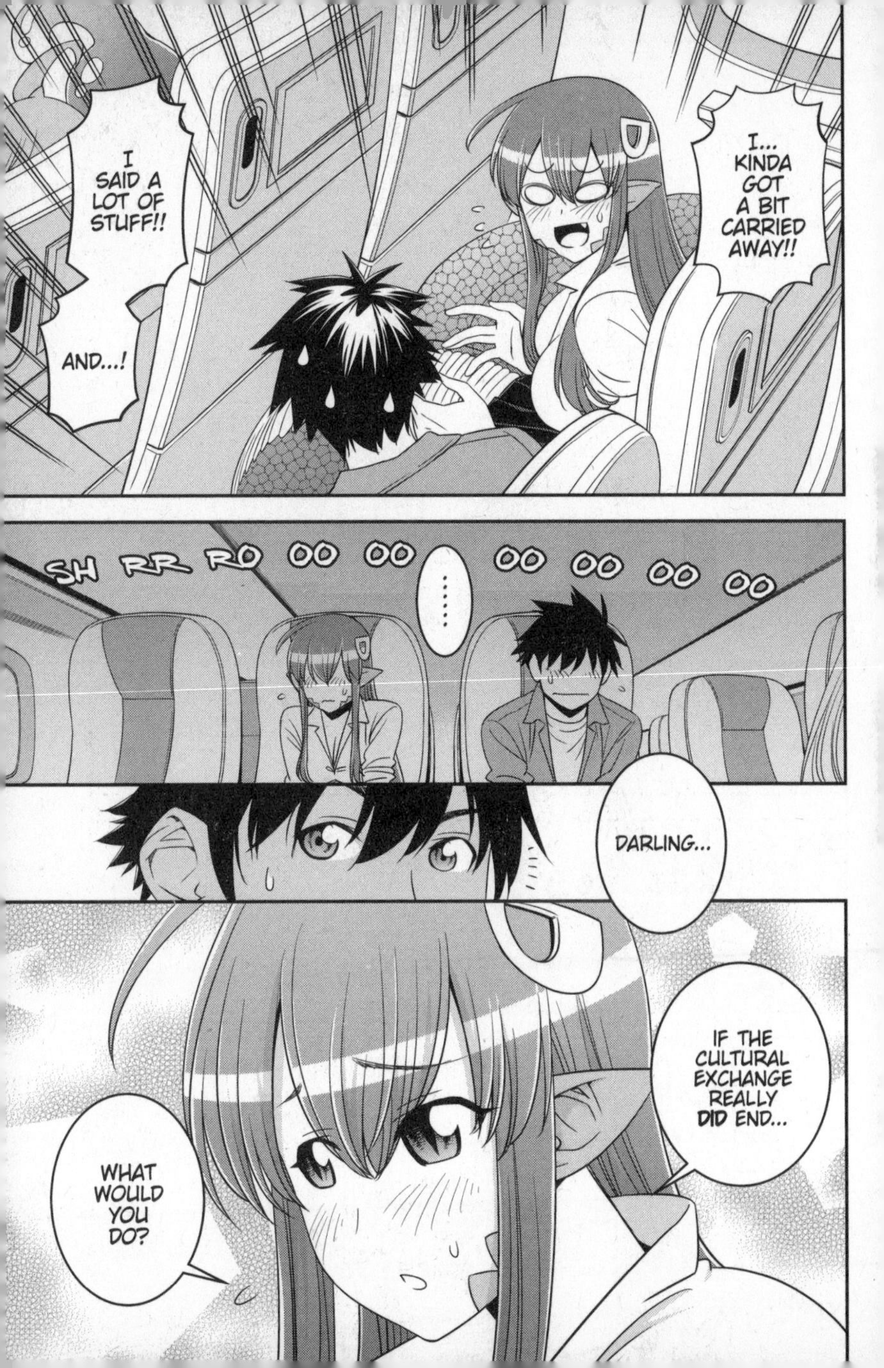
I... KINDA GOT A BIT CARRIED AWAY!!
I SAID A LOT OF STUFF!!
AND...!
SH RR RO OO OO OO OO OO OO
......
DARLING...
IF THE CULTURAL EXCHANGE REALLY DID END...
WHAT WOULD YOU DO?

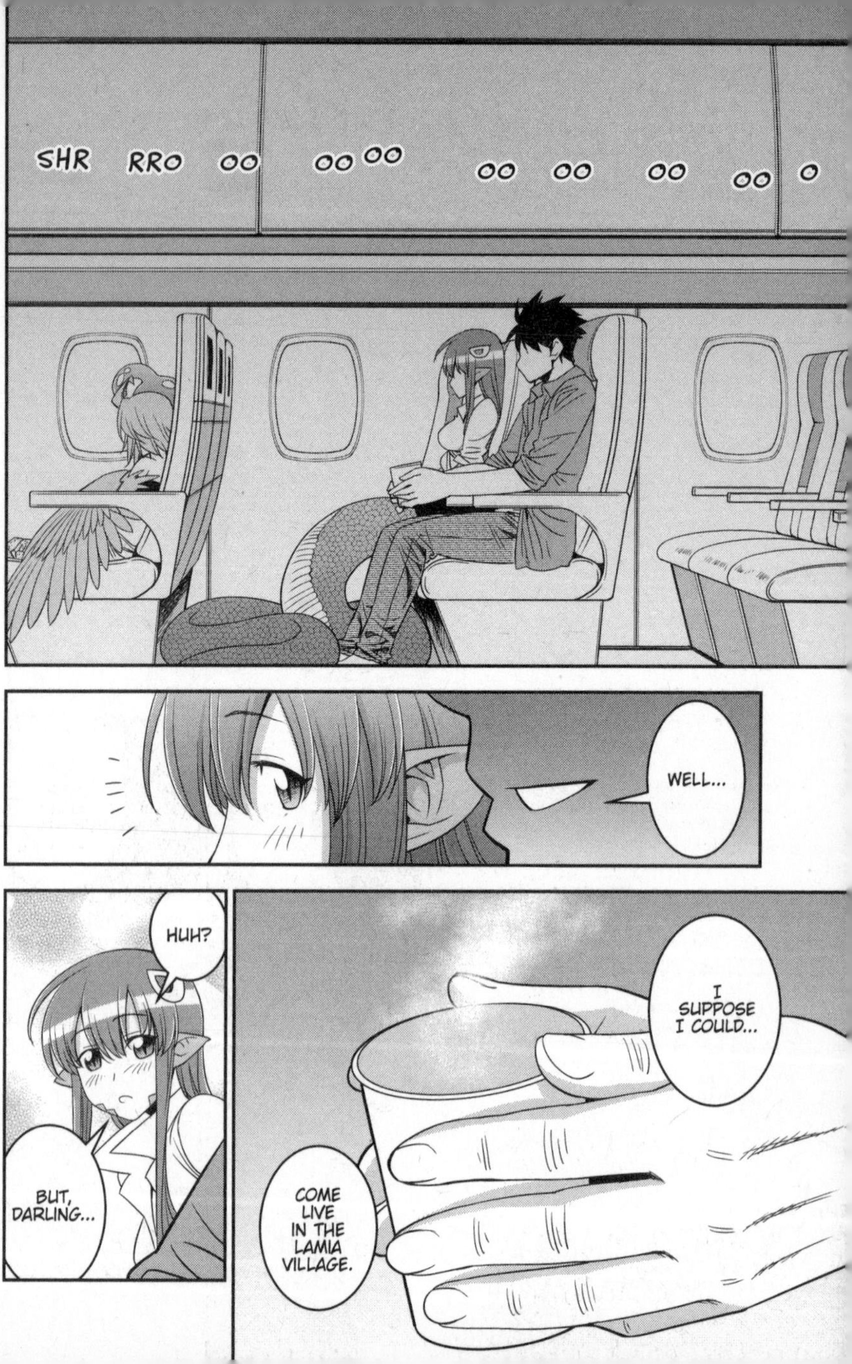
SHR RRO OO OO OO OO OO OO OO O
WELL...
I SUPPOSE I COULD...
COME LIVE IN THE LAMIA VILLAGE.
HUH?
BUT, DARLING...

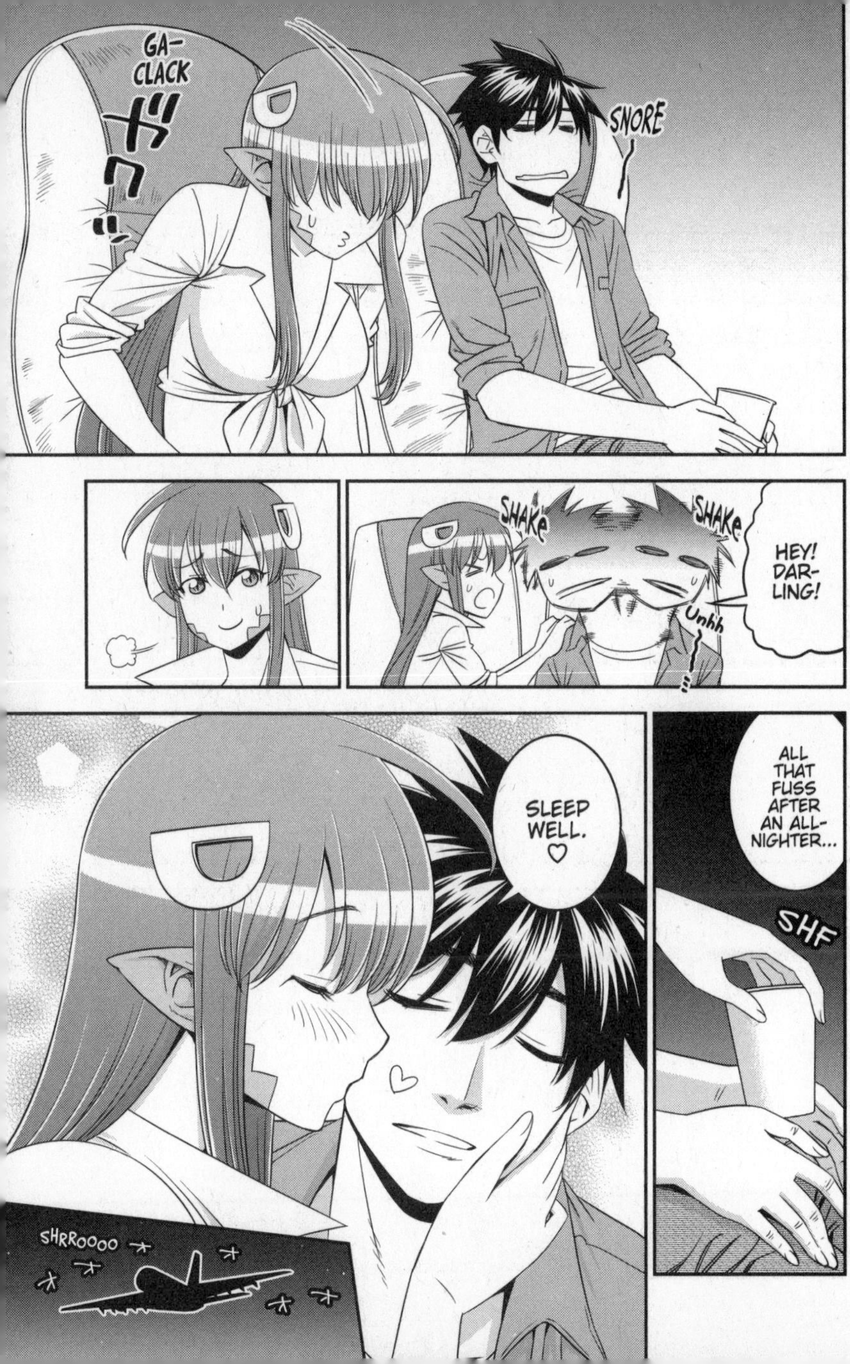
SNORE
GA-CLACK
SHAKE SHAKE
HEY! DAR-LING!
Unhh
ALL THAT FUSS AFTER AN ALL-NIGHTER...
SHF
SLEEP WELL. ♡
SHRROOOO

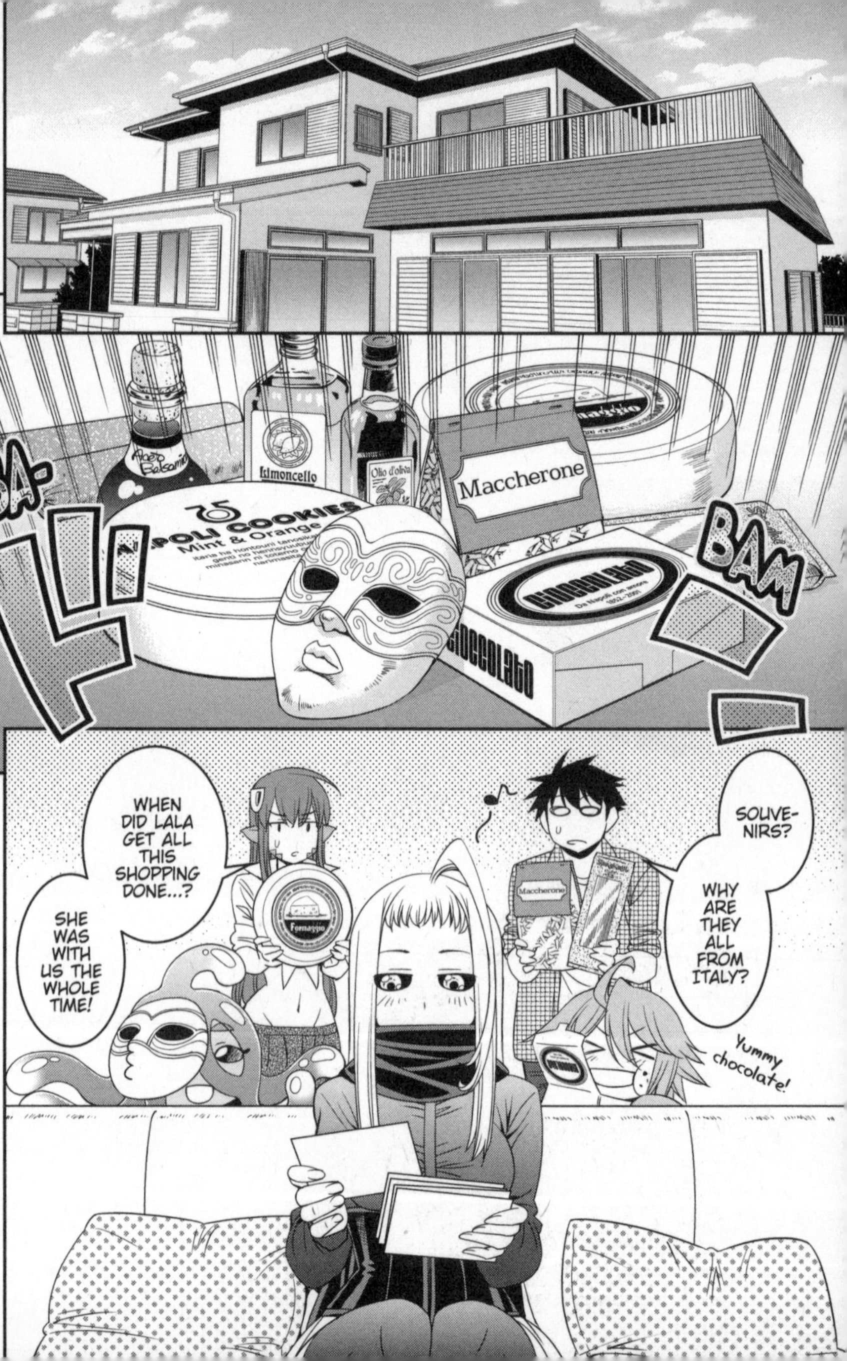
BA-
BAM
Limoncello
Olio d'oliva
Maccherone
Mint & Orange
CIOCCOLATO
SOUVE-NIRS?
WHY ARE THEY ALL FROM ITALY?
WHEN DID LALA GET ALL THIS SHOPPING DONE...?
SHE WAS WITH US THE WHOLE TIME!
Maccherone
Yummy chocolate!

Monster Musume

Everyday Life with Monster Girls

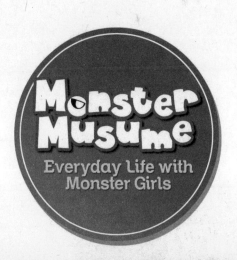

ECHIDNA/MELUSINE/MEDUSAE SERPENTINE SUBSPECIES SECRETS

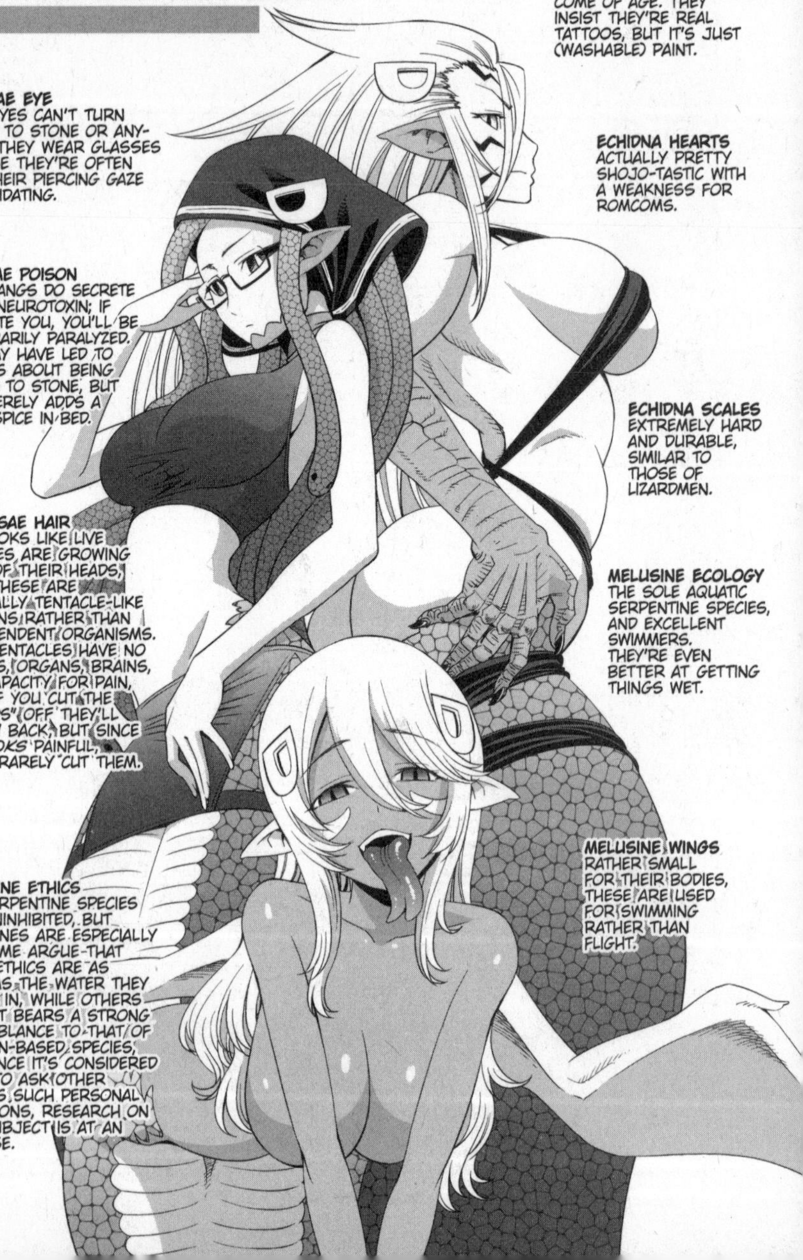

MEDUSAE EYE
THEIR EYES CAN'T TURN PEOPLE TO STONE OR ANYTHING. THEY WEAR GLASSES BECAUSE THEY'RE OFTEN TOLD THEIR PIERCING GAZE IS INTIMIDATING.

MEDUSAE POISON
THEIR FANGS DO SECRETE A MILD NEUROTOXIN; IF THEY BITE YOU, YOU'LL BE TEMPORARILY PARALYZED. THIS MAY HAVE LED TO LEGENDS ABOUT BEING TURNED TO STONE, BUT NOW MERELY ADDS A LITTLE SPICE IN BED.

MEDUSAE HAIR
IT LOOKS LIKE LIVE SNAKES ARE GROWING OUT OF THEIR HEADS, BUT THESE ARE ACTUALLY TENTACLE-LIKE ORGANS RATHER THAN INDEPENDENT ORGANISMS. THE TENTACLES HAVE NO BONES, ORGANS, BRAINS, OR CAPACITY FOR PAIN, AND IF YOU CUT THE "HEADS" OFF THEY'LL GROW BACK, BUT SINCE IT *LOOKS* PAINFUL, THEY RARELY CUT THEM.

MELUSINE ETHICS
ALL SERPENTINE SPECIES ARE UNINHIBITED, BUT MELUSINES ARE ESPECIALLY SO. SOME ARGUE THAT THEIR ETHICS ARE AS FLUID AS THE WATER THEY RESIDE IN, WHILE OTHERS CLAIM IT BEARS A STRONG RESEMBLANCE TO THAT OF DRAGON-BASED SPECIES, BUT SINCE IT'S CONSIDERED RUDE TO ASK OTHER SPECIES SUCH PERSONAL QUESTIONS, RESEARCH ON THE SUBJECT IS AT AN IMPASSE.

ECHIDNA TATTOOS
GIVEN WHEN ECHIDNA COME OF AGE. THEY INSIST THEY'RE REAL TATTOOS, BUT IT'S JUST (WASHABLE) PAINT.

ECHIDNA HEARTS
ACTUALLY PRETTY SHOJO-TASTIC WITH A WEAKNESS FOR ROMCOMS.

ECHIDNA SCALES
EXTREMELY HARD AND DURABLE, SIMILAR TO THOSE OF LIZARDMEN.

MELUSINE ECOLOGY
THE SOLE AQUATIC SERPENTINE SPECIES, AND EXCELLENT SWIMMERS. THEY'RE EVEN BETTER AT GETTING THINGS WET.

MELUSINE WINGS
RATHER SMALL FOR THEIR BODIES, THESE ARE USED FOR SWIMMING RATHER THAN FLIGHT.

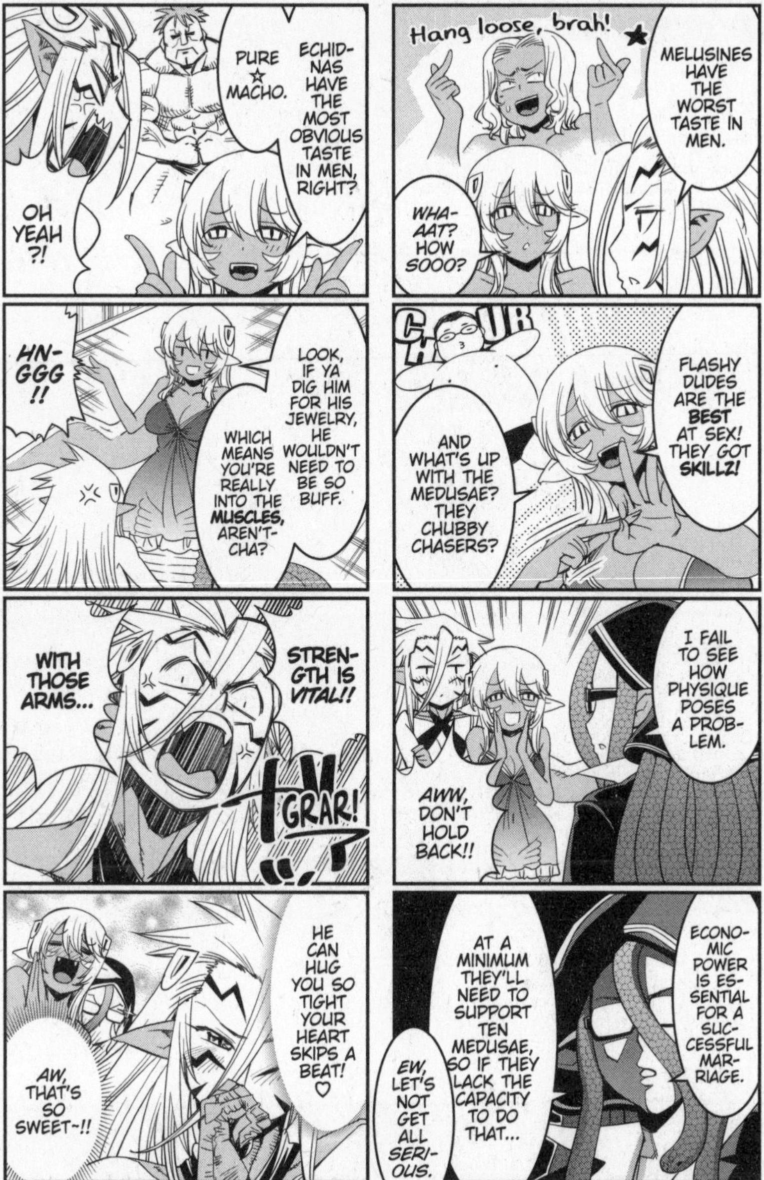
MELUSINES HAVE THE WORST TASTE IN MEN.
Hang loose, brah!
WHA-AAT? HOW SOOO?
ECHIDNAS HAVE THE MOST OBVIOUS TASTE IN MEN, RIGHT?
PURE ☆ MACHO.
OH YEAH ?!
FLASHY DUDES ARE THE **BEST** AT SEX! THEY GOT **SKILLZ!**
CHUB
AND WHAT'S UP WITH THE MEDUSAE? THEY CHUBBY CHASERS?
LOOK, IF YA DIG HIM FOR HIS JEWELRY, HE WOULDN'T NEED TO BE SO BUFF.
WHICH MEANS YOU'RE REALLY INTO THE **MUSCLES,** AREN'T-CHA?
HN-GGG!!
I FAIL TO SEE HOW PHYSIQUE POSES A PROBLEM.
AWW, DON'T HOLD BACK!!
STRENGTH IS *VITAL!!*
GRAR!
WITH THOSE ARMS...
ECONOMIC POWER IS ESSENTIAL FOR A SUCCESSFUL MARRIAGE.
AT A MINIMUM THEY'LL NEED TO SUPPORT TEN MEDUSAE, SO IF THEY LACK THE CAPACITY TO DO THAT...
EW, LET'S NOT GET ALL SERIOUS.
HE CAN HUG YOU SO TIGHT YOUR HEART SKIPS A BEAT! ♡
AW, THAT'S SO SWEET~!!

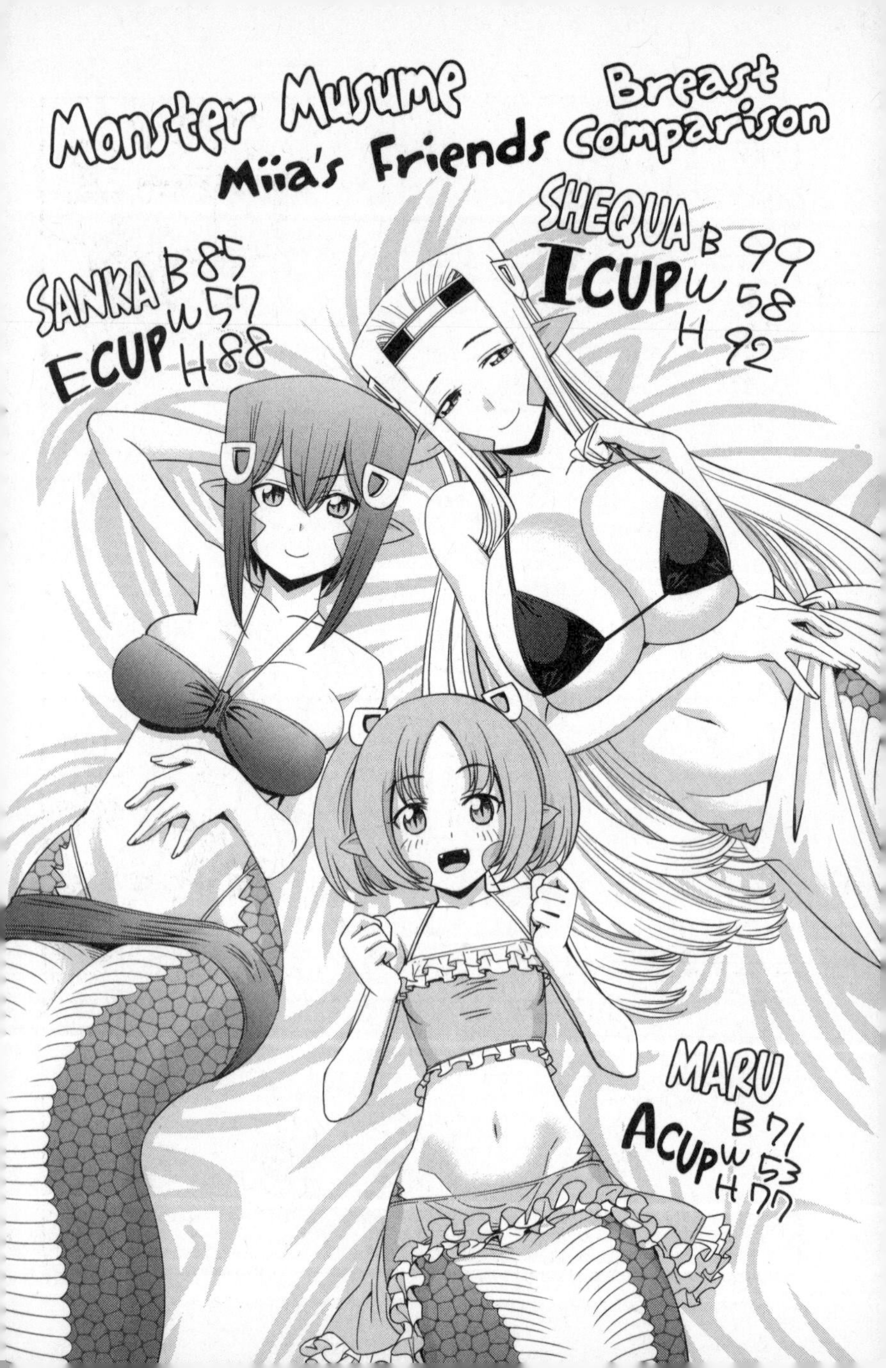
Monster Musume
Breast Comparison
Miia's Friends
SHEQUA I CUP B 99 W 58 H 92
SANKA E CUP B 85 W 57 H 88
MARU A CUP B 71 W 53 H 77

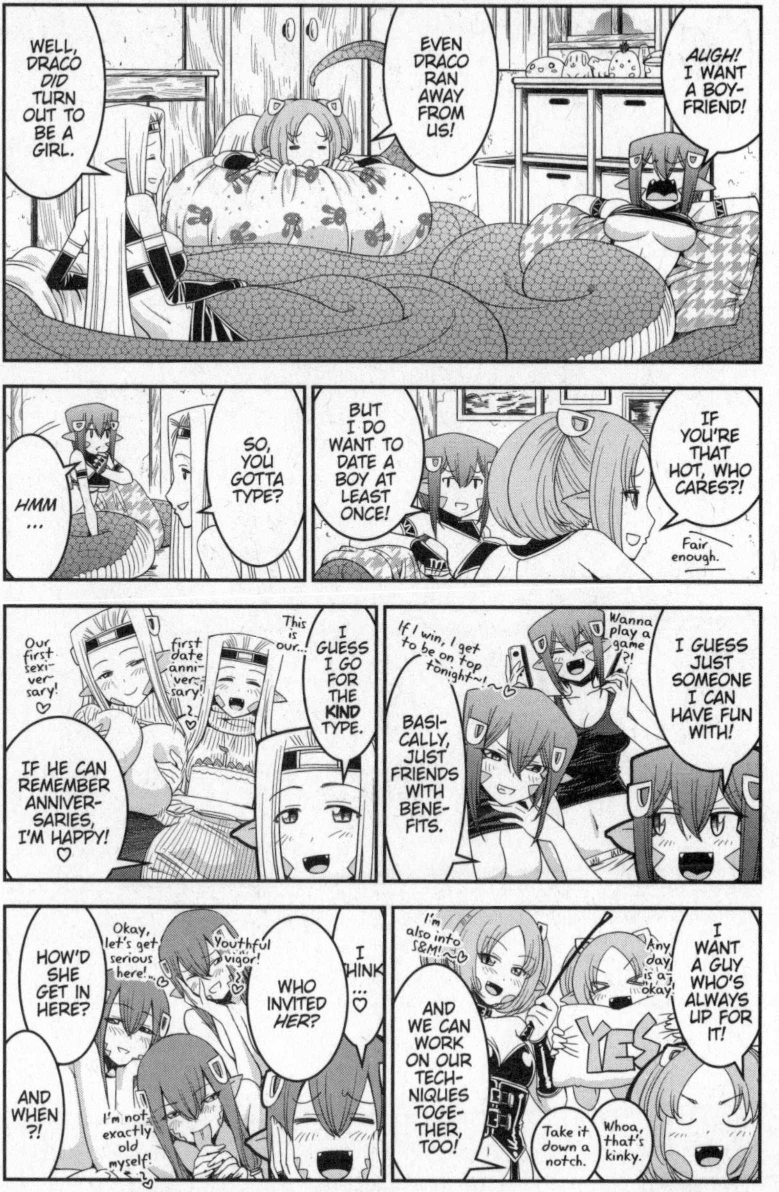
AUGH! I WANT A BOYFRIEND!
EVEN DRACO RAN AWAY FROM US!
WELL, DRACO DID TURN OUT TO BE A GIRL.
IF YOU'RE THAT HOT, WHO CARES?!
Fair enough.
BUT I DO WANT TO DATE A BOY AT LEAST ONCE!
SO, YOU GOTTA TYPE?
HMM ...
I GUESS JUST SOMEONE I CAN HAVE FUN WITH!
Wanna play a game?!
If I win, I get to be on top tonight~!♡
BASICALLY, JUST FRIENDS WITH BENEFITS.
I GUESS I GO FOR THE KIND TYPE.
This is our...
first date anniversary!♡
Our first sexiversary!♡
IF HE CAN REMEMBER ANNIVERSARIES, I'M HAPPY!♡
I WANT A GUY WHO'S ALWAYS UP FOR IT!
Any day is a-okay!
YES
I'm also into S&M!~♡
AND WE CAN WORK ON OUR TECHNIQUES TOGETHER, TOO!
Whoa, that's kinky.
Take it down a notch.
I THINK... ♡
Youthful vigor!♡
WHO INVITED HER?
Okay, let's get serious here!...♡
HOW'D SHE GET IN HERE?
AND WHEN?!
I'm not exactly old myself!♡

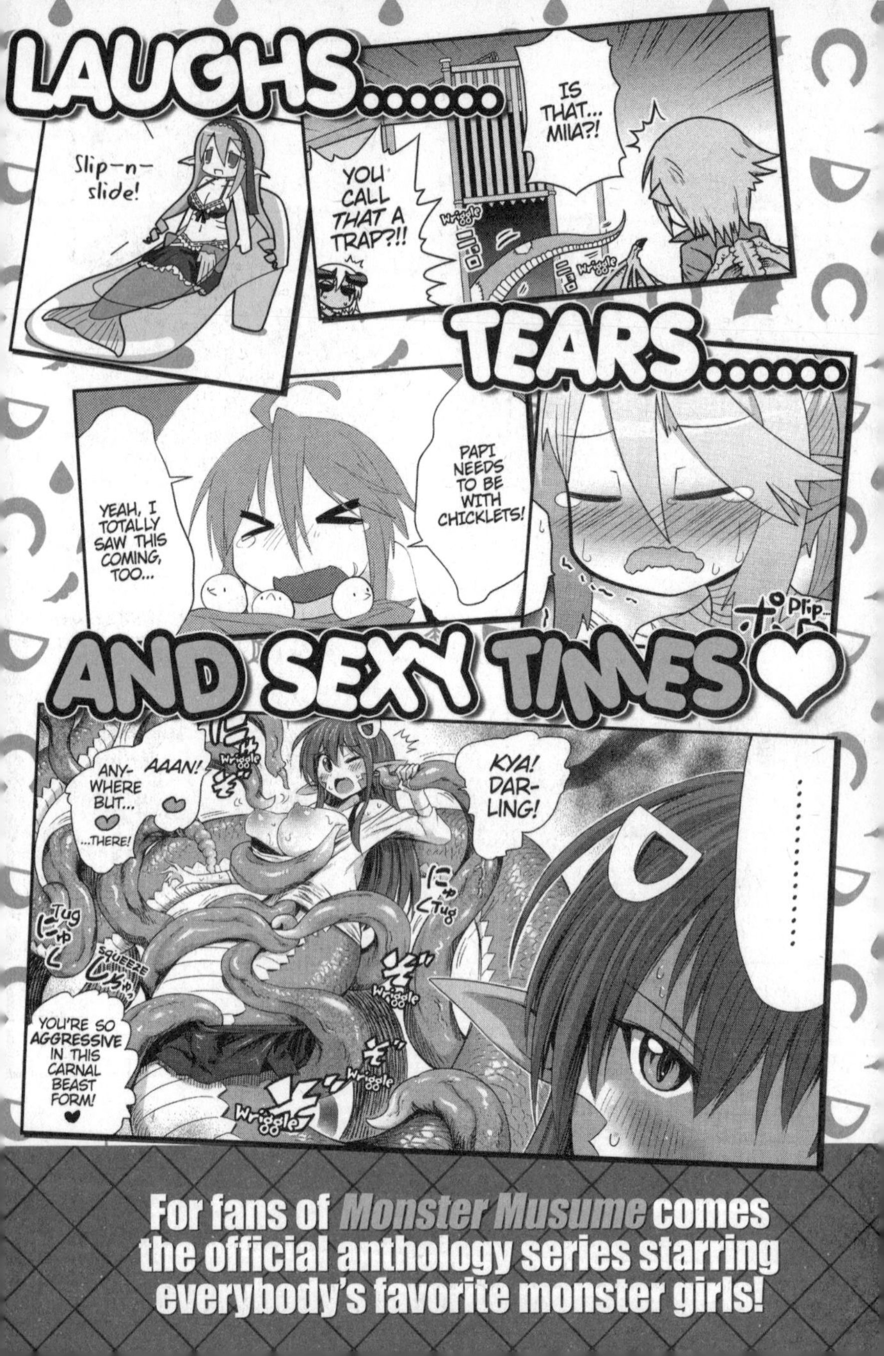

LAUGHS......
IS THAT... MIIA?!
YOU CALL THAT A TRAP?!!
Wriggle
Wriggle
Slip-n-slide!
TEARS......
Plip...
PAPI NEEDS TO BE WITH CHICKLETS!
YEAH, I TOTALLY SAW THIS COMING, TOO...
AND SEXY TIMES ♥
......
KYA! DARLING!
Tug
Wriggle
AAAN!
ANYWHERE BUT... ♥ ...THERE!
Wriggle
Wriggle
Wriggle
Tug
Squeeze
YOU'RE SO AGGRESSIVE IN THIS CARNAL BEAST FORM! ♥

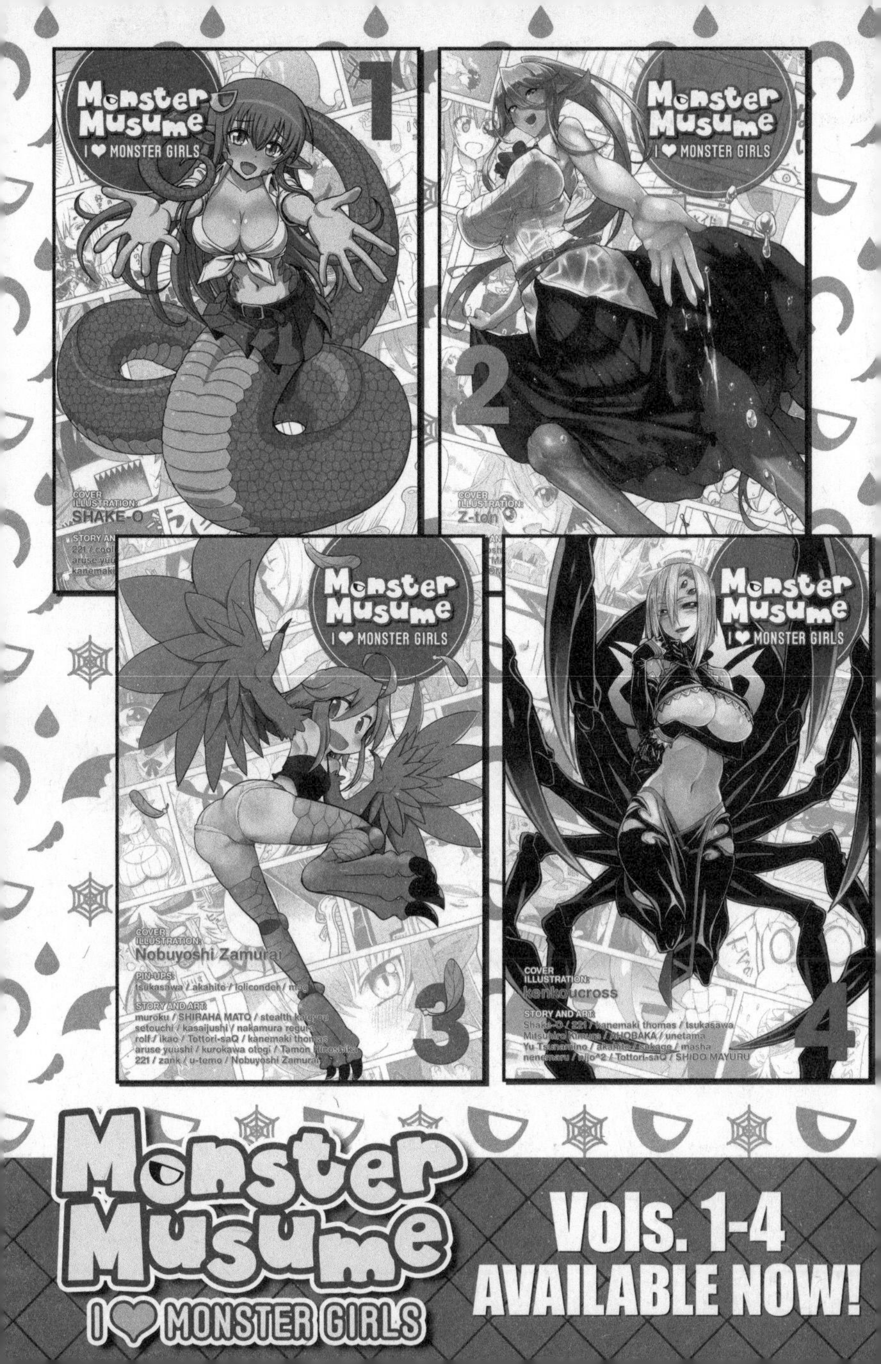

Monster Musume
I ♥ MONSTER GIRLS
1
COVER ILLUSTRATION:
SHAKE-O
Monster Musume
I ♥ MONSTER GIRLS
2
COVER ILLUSTRATION:
Z-ton
Monster Musume
I ♥ MONSTER GIRLS
COVER ILLUSTRATION:
Nobuyoshi Zamurai
PIN-UPS:
tsukasawa / akahito / loliconder / mog
STORY AND ART:
muroku / SHIRAHA MATO / stealth kaigyou
setouchi / kasaijushi / nakamura regura
rolf / ikao / Tottori-saQ / kanemaki thomas
aruse yuushi / kurokawa otogi / Tamon Hiroshika
221 / zank / u-temo / Nobuyoshi Zamurai
3
Monster Musume
I ♥ MONSTER GIRLS
COVER ILLUSTRATION:
kenkoucross
STORY AND ART:
Shake-O / 221 / kanemaki thomas / tsukasawa
Mitsuhiro Kimura / AHOBAKA / unetama
Yu Tsunamino / akahito / sukage / masha
nenemaru / nijo^2 / Tottori-saQ / SHIDO MAYURU
4
Monster Musume
I ♥ MONSTER GIRLS
Vols. 1-4
AVAILABLE NOW!

Monster Musume

Everyday Life with Monster Girls

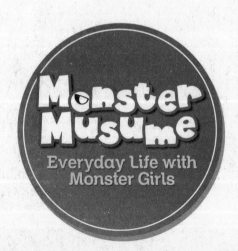

SEVEN SEAS ENTERTAINMENT PRESENTS

Monster Musume

story and art by OKAYADO

VOLUME 15

TRANSLATION
Andrew Cunningham

LETTERING AND RETOUCH
Meaghan Tucker

COVER DESIGN
Nicky Lim
Courtney Williams (Logo)

PROOFREADER
Janet Houck
Dawn Davis

EDITOR AND ADAPTATION
Shanti Whitesides

PRODUCTION MANAGER
Lissa Pattillo

MANAGING EDITOR
Julie Davis

EDITOR-IN-CHIEF
Adam Arnold

PUBLISHER
Jason DeAngelis

MONSTER MUSUME NO IRU NICHIJO VOLUME 15
© OKAYADO 2019
Originally published in Japan in 2019 by TOKUMA SHOTEN PUBLISHING
CO., LTD., Tokyo. English translation rights arranged with TOKUMA SHOTEN
PUBLISHING CO., LTD., Tokyo, through TOHAN CORPORATION, Tokyo.

Seven Seas press and purchase enquiries can be sent to Marketing Manager
Lianne Sentar at press@gomanga.com. Information regarding the distribution
and purchase of digital editions is available from Digital Manager CK Russell
at digital@gomanga.com.

Seven Seas and the Seven Seas logo are trademarks of
Seven Seas Entertainment. All rights reserved.

ISBN: 978-1-626929-63-0

Printed in Canada

First Printing: December 2019

10 9 8 7 6 5 4 3 2 1

FOLLOW US ONLINE: *www.sevenseasentertainment.com*

READING DIRECTIONS

This book reads from *right to left*, Japanese style.
If this is your first time reading manga, you start
reading from the top right panel on each page and
take it from there. If you get lost, just follow the
numbered diagram here. It may seem backwards at
first, but you'll get the hang of it! Have fun!!

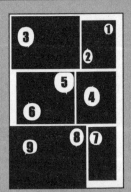